D1107486

FEDERAL FINANCE IN PEACE AND WAR

BOOKS BY G. FINDLAY SHIRRAS

INDIAN FINANCE AND BANKING

THE SCIENCE OF PUBLIC FINANCE (2 vols.)

THE BURDEN OF BRITISH TAXATION (with Dr. L. Rostas)
(National Institute of Economic and Social Research)

AN ENQUIRY INTO FEDERAL FINANCE
(National Institute of Economic and Social Research)

and other publications

FEDERAL FINANCE IN PEACE AND WAR

With special reference to the United States of America and the British Commonwealth

BY

G. FINDLAY SHIRRAS

DEAN OF THE FACULTY OF ECONOMICS AND COMMERCE,
UNIVERSITY COLLEGE, EXETER

LONDON
MACMILLAN & CO. LTD
1944

PRINTED IN GREAT BRITAIN
BY R. & R. CLARK, LIMITED, EDINBURGH

CONTENTS

United States (contd.)

Canada

Australia

Australia (contd.)

South Africa

India

List of United States Tables (contd.)

List of Canadian Tables

List of Australian Tables

List of Australian Tables (contd.)

List of South African Tables

List of South African Tables (contd.)

List of Indian Tables

INTRODUCTION

" Federal Finance in Peace and War " is an Enquiry complementary to that made into the burden of taxation,[1] and has been undertaken in consultation with the National Institute of Economic and Social Research, without whose assistance it could never have been instituted. It has involved a somewhat minute study of the Budgets and other Financial Statements of the United States of America, Canada, Australia, South Africa and India. These countries were selected because they possess fundamental constitutional likenesses and continuity of history, which make the treatment of their systems of public finance a suitable single field of study. It was decided to restrict the Enquiry for two reasons. In the first place, it was not possible to cover all Federations in the world, such as Switzerland, Germany, Russia, Mexico, Brazil and the Argentine, and, secondly, a description of the temporary structures of totalitarian countries, such as Germany, would be largely dependent upon political analysis. Municipal as well as Provincial or State finance has been examined as it is intimately connected with the Central or Federal Government's finance. The years chosen for examination include the pre-rearmament year 1937–38 and a recent war year, usually 1941–42. The effects of the greatest depression of the machine age, that of 1929–32, have been so widespread as to affect to a very remarkable degree the tax structures, and on this account crisis finance could not be omitted.

It is well known that a Budget covers only part of a nation's economic and financial activity and, therefore, in the early stages of the Enquiry it was realised that a study of the National Income technique of Public Finance had to be considered. This meant that attention had to be given to the National Income, Public Expenditures and Public Debt, apart altogether from a study of the tax structures of the countries and of the units in the Federations. It has been rightly pointed out that a Budget is not a balance-sheet in which all assets and liabilities of the concern are given, but is similar to a Profit and Loss account of a business enterprise, only the changes are over a twelvemonth. The Budget itself is no longer regarded as the national balance-sheet but only a part of it. In short, we have to take into consideration the quantitative estimate

[1] G. Findlay Shirras and L. Rostas, *The Burden of British Taxation.* The National Institute of Economic and Social Research Studies No. 2, Cambridge University Press, 1942, also American Edition, The Macmillan Company, New York, Jan. 1943.

of the whole economic activity of the country and not merely the cross-section of it with which the Government is concerned. When unemployment is at its worst an expansion, and not a contraction, of public expenditure to meet the decline in tax revenue is essential. It is only within recent years that in official circles it has been realised that unemployment could be avoided by a policy of regular and large Government expenditure.[1] Deficits are not, as Gladstonian finance always regarded them, thoroughly bad in themselves and to be avoided; they are even desirable for the stabilisation of economic life. Nothing has been so revolutionary in public finance in recent years as this idea of the inclusion of items hitherto undreamt of in the philosophy of budgetary finance. Since 1941 annual tax proposals have been based on an examination of the nation's total income and expenditure as set out in the White Paper on "The Analysis of the Sources of War Finance and an Estimate of the National Income and Expenditure". From this the so-called "Inflationary gap" can be measured. We have to consider not merely the domestic expenditure and revenue of the Government but overseas resources, extra-Budgetary receipts, sums available for investment as depreciation in war-time cannot be made good, and, most important of all, new savings obtained through the National Savings movement and similar movements for investment. Similarly, there is the "Deflationary gap" in budgeting for full employment. The difference between the potential savings of the community, the savings if the national resources had been fully used in production, and the actual loan expenditure on capital construction by private firms, individuals and local authorities other than the Central Government, has to be made good by the Government's supplementing this regularly to the extent of the difference. It has also been realised that tax policy as well as expenditure has a part to play in economic stability. May not taxation play its part as a factor helping inflation or deflation, expansion or contraction? May not a planned system of taxes be flexible enough to be used to increase or decrease saving or investment? In the downward swing of the trade cycle, tax policy may remove maladjustments by a relatively light tax burden upon spending and a relatively high tax burden on surplus savings. A tax policy might aim at reducing liquidity preference, *e.g.* in regard to undistributed profits to prevent relapse and at another to prevent excessive

[1] Accepted by the British Government in 1944, *vide* White Paper on Employment policy (Cmd. 6527), "The Government accept as one of their primary aims and responsibilities the maintenance of a high and stable level of employment after the war."

expansion by curtailing excessive profits. In both cases stability would be assisted. Even if purchasing power is being restored by Government expenditures, a taxation policy is complementary and worthy of examination, as a tax system often has many taxes the effect of which is the curtailment, during a depression, of consumers' purchasing power. In other words, the effects of a taxation policy must be considered as well as a policy of public expenditures. Financial equilibrium is not merely equilibrium of Budgetary revenue and expenditure but equilibrium of the country's annual income and expenditure, an equality between spendable income and available resources. This may indicate in the future, at all events in the countries of chief industrial importance, the very countries which tend to save too much, the presentation of a Capital Budget quite apart from a Revenue Budget. For this and other reasons in this Enquiry a study of National Income, Public Expenditures and Public Debt has been linked up with an analysis of tax structures.

The report is divided into three parts. The first deals with the Scope and Method of the Enquiry and the Public Finance and National Economy of the oldest of the Federations, the United States, and a similar analysis of the Federations comprising the British Commonwealth — Canada, Australia, South Africa and India. The tables in Part I are Summary tables and are set out in the table of Contents. Part II consists of the general principles underlying the study of Part I with special reference to intergovernmental financial relations, not merely as applied to conflicts between Federal and State Governments, between State and Local Governments and Federal and Local Governments or between States of the Federation or between Nations, but also to financial relations in regard to specific taxes and specific functions. It deals also with the solutions for these conflicts. Part III contains statistical tables other than the Summary tables in Part I. An Index has been prepared for facility of reference.

I desire to place on record my deep sense of appreciation to the Governments which have not only provided official data but explanations regarding financial relations. My second duty is to thank the High Commissioners of Canada, Australia, South Africa and India ; the Dominions Office ; the American Embassy in London ; the American Treasury Committee, over which Professor Luther Gulick was Chairman ; the Rt. Hon. Viscount Bennett, P.C., K.C., LL.D., formerly Minister of Finance and, from 1930 to 1935, Prime Minister of Canada and member of the Council of University College, Exeter ; Dr. S. A. Cudmore, Dominions

Statistician, Canada ; Professor Haig of Columbia University, New York ; Miss Mabel L. Walker, Director of the Tax Institute of the University of Pennsylvania ; and many other non-official experts. Mr. Henry Clay and Mr. Geoffrey Crowther have acted as the Sub-Committee of the Institute connected with the Enquiry, and their judgment on various points has been of great value. Mrs. F. Stone, Secretary of the National Institute of Economics and Research, has always been most ready to serve the interests of the Enquiry, and her ability and tact have been greatly appreciated. Dr. G. Rusche and, especially, my Research student, Mr. J. R. L. Schneider, B.Sc., have assisted with the heavy statistical work, and Miss Joan Ambrose and Mrs. W. M. Timms have performed the secretarial work of the Enquiry with energy and success. Mrs. E. J. Condon greatly assisted with the proofs and with the Index.

G. FINDLAY SHIRRAS

15th January 1944

PART I

CHAPTER I

THE SCOPE OF THE ENQUIRY

In the Introduction the limitation of the scope of the Enquiry has been discussed. The selection of the years was intended to cover the pre-re-armament period and the war period as well as the crisis of 1929–32 which has had so lasting an effect on Federal Finance. The pre-rearmament year of 1937–38 was taken as a most typical pre-rearmament year.

In the last decade all Federal systems of government have been subjected to much strain, and the questions underlying Federal Finance have received a new emphasis. This has been especially true in the United States and in the Federal States of the British Commonwealth. The Federal State, as is known, rests on the assumption that sovereignty in a single State can be divided among several Governments which act independently of one another. There are always, however, two distinct and conflicting forces at work. In the first place, there is the unifying influence brought about by common interests and common aims which can best be promoted by union. On the other hand, there is the desire of the States or Provinces and Local Authorities to preserve a large measure of their independence. A Federal State or Union is in fact a marriage of convenience. Interdependence reduces independence, and in recent years there has been a continuous drive towards centralisation. It is here that the Federal dilemma lies. On the one hand, with the great increase of transport and communications and the growth of large-scale organisation there has been considerable integration in the Federal State, as was well shown in the greatest depression of the machine age, the depression of 1929–32. There has been a great development of Government intervention in economic and social matters. In short, there is the move towards centralisation, but, on the other hand, if the units do not resist this tendency towards centralisation, the Federal system may be seriously weakened at its foundations. With the rising costs of government, new activities are demanded and higher standards are required for old ones. This can be seen in the large increases in expenditures on development as well as on the social services in all the countries studied. All Governments, including Federal Governments, are increasing considerably their grip on the economic life. Governments to-day are taking a much larger share of the national income than ever before. In the United States, for example, Federal, State and Local taxes were the equivalent of 4 per cent of the national income in 1850, 10 per cent in 1900, between 20 and 25 per cent in the years immediately preceding the war, 28 per cent in 1940–41, and in 1941–42 at least one-third of the national income excluding the social security taxes. The total expenditures, National, State and Local, as given in Table VI, Chapter III, show that the total expenditure as a percentage of the national income is not less than 41 per cent in 1942 as compared with 27 per cent in 1941. The Finance Minister of Canada has stated that the expenditures of the Dominion Government, including the assistance given to the United Kingdom but excluding all Provincial and Municipal expenditures, amounted in 1942 to nearly 50 per cent of the national income. Before the war it was estimated that Federal, Provincial and Municipal authorities spent from 25 to 30 per cent of the national income, and this included heavy expenditures for unemployment and agricultural relief.

In periods of national emergency, State and Local Government Budgets are eclipsed by Federal Budgets, but in normal periods between war and depressions, State and Local expenditures have exceeded Federal expenditures. Thus, in the United States, although Federal revenues and expenditures have greatly expanded in the last ten years, it is only since the current fiscal year that Federal taxes have exceeded aggregate State and Local taxes. In Canada in 1937 Dominion taxation amounted to $464 millions while Provincial and Municipal revenues were respectively $244 millions and $309 millions.

We discuss elsewhere the problem of competition and co-operation among taxing authorities in Federal States, but it will be sufficient if we state here that this urge towards centralisation is characteristic of the unification of the national economy and of the enormous growth in Government spending. The taxation of surplus income through progressive taxes is admirably suited for centralisation or Federal collection, and this is one of several reasons why, when Governments absorb a large fraction of the national income in taxation, the taxation system itself assumes great economic importance.

With the passing of the Social Security Act of 1935 in the United States, the Federal Government increased its financial power considerably. In 1930 the grants to the States were less than $150 millions covering eleven State activities. Emergency grants in connexion with the depression and the Social Security plan of the New Deal brought the total to about $800 millions in 1939, and the aided activities increased to twenty-one. About 14 per cent of the total revenues of the State Government now comes from Federal grants. Indeed, as will be seen later, there is springing up, in consequence of the dominance of Federal Government in recent years, a new Federalism — a co-operative Federalism replacing the old Federalism in which the Federal or National Government and the units went their separate ways without regard to what the others were doing. Thus in one year, 1937, over one hundred statutes were passed by forty States to aid the United States Federal Housing Administration alone.[1] The scale of Government action, in short, is now such that it affects to a very large degree the working of the national economy of a country, and tends everywhere to increase rather than to diminish. The competition between Federal, State and Local Governments for revenues is growing, and there is a decided tendency for the Federal authority to use its wider taxation powers to control the layers of government below it. There is a good deal of overlapping as we shall see. In the United States, for example, more than 90 per cent of combined Federal and State tax yields come from common tax bases. Only customs duties are denied to the States and only the property tax and motor vehicle duties are not available to the Federal Government. The multiplicity of tax authorities has been much in evidence in recent years. The number in the United States is usually estimated at 175,000.

Another interesting feature of Federalism is the changing nature of the tax systems of Federal and State Governments which is in contrast to the negligible changes in local taxes. Customs duties and taxes on liquor and tobacco were, at the beginning of the present century, the main sources of Federal revenue in the United States; to-day they produce only one-fourth of the Federal tax revenues. At the present time State Governments are obtaining 75 per cent of their taxes from sources that were negligible or non-existent at the beginning of the century. Local Governments, on the other hand, still obtain a great proportion of their revenue from the taxation on property.[2]

Events such as have been referred to in the above paragraphs have produced considerable discussion in recent years. A Royal Commission on Dominion-Provincial Relations was appointed in Canada in August 1937, and its Report in three volumes was submitted in March 1940 and published in March 1941.[3]

This monumental Report will long be a *locus classicus* on Federal

[1] V. O. Key, "State Legislation Facilitative of Federal Action", *Annals of the American Academy of Political and Social Science,* Jan. 1940. Cf. J. A. Corry, "The Federal Dilemma", *Canadian Journal of Economics and Political Science,* May 1941.

[2] *Tax Relations among Governmental Units,* Tax Policy League, New York, 1938; Mabel Newcomer, *Taxation and Fiscal Policy,* New York, Columbia Press, 1940.

[3] Ottawa, 1940. Vol. i, *Canada: 1867–1939*; vol. ii, *Recommendations*; vol. iii, *Documentation.* The Report was accompanied by research studies prepared for the Royal Commission including Comparative Statistics of Public Finance, British North American Federation, the Economic Background of Dominion-Provincial Relations, National Income, Labour Legislation and Social Services. See Appendix I.

Finance. The Commission was appointed because of general dissatisfaction in respect of Dominion-Provincial Relations, a dissatisfaction which reached an acute stage during the depression of 1929–32. Provincial and Local Governments were unable to deal with unemployment and agricultural distress, and the resulting financial difficulties in regard to administrative responsibility meant a serious strain on national unity. By an amendment to the British North America Act, the Dominion was able to introduce, as from 1st July 1941, a nation-wide scheme of unemployment insurance much the same as that existing in the United Kingdom. As will be seen in Chapter IV on Canada, the Dominion Government decided to accept the Commission's proposals to take over the whole burden of relief for the employable unemployed and their dependants, and so relieve the Provinces and, therefore, also the Municipalities. The Dominion Government also agreed to take over, as recommended by the Commission, the whole burden of Provincial net debt. In return for this, as recommended by the Commission, the Dominion Government was to have the exclusive right to tax personal incomes and corporations and to levy succession duties. National adjustment grants which were to be made to the Provinces were calculated to enable them to maintain an average Canadian standard of essential services with an average level of taxation.

Similar discussions had been going on in the United States prior to the appointment of a Committee by the American Treasury. The Chairman of the Board of Governors of the Federal Reserve system, for example, addressed the National Tax Association at the University of Minnesota in October 1941.[1] In this address the Chairman of the Board, Mr. Eccles, outlined some of the difficulties which were facing the United States to-day in some of the broader aspects of taxation. He pointed out that, except during major wars, the State and Local Governments of the United States had only been much more important from the revenue point of view than the Federal Government, and it was only in the fiscal year 1941–42 that Federal taxes exceeded aggregate State and Local taxes. Mr. Eccles stressed the importance of safeguarding against the danger of a relapse into what he called " the intolerable conditions of the early 30's ", by a " long run plan for public investment, adapted to the differing needs and conditions of the different geographical areas of the United States ". He outlined a scheme for productive public investment which should be non-competitive with private enterprise and dealt with social security, old-age pensions and unemployment benefits. In his

[1] Address by Marriner S. Eccles, Chairman of the Board of Governors of the Federal Reserve System, at a meeting of the National Tax Association at the University of Minnesota. *Federal Reserve Bulletin*, Nov. 1941.

view he believed that if progressive taxes were to be the major element of the national tax structure, it would not be possible to continue the present system of having the Federal Government and the States levying taxes on individual and corporate incomes and transfers at death. Uniformity and equity could be attained, in his view, by making the total levied on income and on inheritance a matter for Federal control, and State revenues must tend more and more to consist of taxes shared with the Federal Government which already amount to 14 per cent of State revenues. He added: "We should continue to follow the broad policy that has grown out of these activities of leaving responsibility for initiative as to the type of activity to be undertaken in the hands of State and Local Government, to leave, wherever possible, the detailed administration in their hands and to provide for Federal supervision only to the extent necessary to ensure that funds are wisely, prudently and honestly used".

In view of these remarks from so high an official, it was no surprise that Professor Luther Gulick was asked by the Treasury to conduct an Enquiry into the tax system of the United States with special reference to intergovernmental financial relations. It is not, however, only in the United States and Canada that in recent years the problem of intergovernmental financial relations has become acute, but also in other Federations which we have studied. In Australia there have been since 1934 the Reports of the Commonwealth Grants Commission, dealing with special subventions to the States of South Australia, Western Australia and Tasmania, in which the taxable capacity of these Provinces is shown to be less than in the more industrially advanced Provinces of Victoria and New South Wales. During 1941 the Commonwealth Government attempted to induce the States to accept a plan by which it would become the only authority in Australia to levy income tax, the Commonwealth Government providing for the States out of the proceeds of its uniform taxation. The difficulty arises from the fact that the Federal Government is hampered because the amounts levied in State income tax are in some cases very high. The taxpayer in Queensland, for example, has to pay to the State Treasurer more than twice as much as a taxpayer earning the same income in Victoria. All the State Premiers, except the Premier of South Australia, opposed the proposal of the Commonwealth Government at the Loan Council of Canberra at the end of June 1941. The difficulties can well be seen by the statement of the Premier of Victoria, who protested that it was proposed to penalise Victoria for her long record of prudent finance to relieve the extravagant States and, if the State vacated the income tax field, there would be a large increase in Federal taxation on low and medium size incomes in Victoria to bring the total taxation to that of Queensland and New South Wales. A Committee, consisting of

Professor R. C. Mills of Sydney University, the Right Honourable J. H. Scullin, Prime Minister of Australia 1929–31, and Mr. Spooner, subsequently appointed to consider a scheme of uniform income taxation for the Commonwealth, presented a Report recommending that the Commonwealth alone during the war and for one year afterwards should be the sole income taxing authority, and that a scheme of uniform taxation should take place from 1st July 1942, compensation being paid to the States for loss of revenue. The Report was discussed at a Conference of Premiers of the States on 22nd April 1942. As explained in the chapter on Australia (Chapter V, section II) a Constitutional Convention at Canberra approved a Bill in December 1942 transferring from the States to the Commonwealth fourteen specific powers for purposes of post-war reconstruction for five years after the cessation of hostilities. These new powers will be in operation only when the bill has been passed by all the States. Considerable opposition was offered to the passage of the bill in South Australia, West Australia and Tasmania on the ground that the powers proposed to be transferred were not sufficiently clearly defined.

In 1933 in the Union of South Africa a Provincial Finance Commission was appointed, with Mr. J. de V. Roos as chairman. This Commission reported towards the end of 1934, and, as a result of the Report, an Act was passed and a consultative Committee, consisting of the Administrators and the Executive Committee of the four Provinces, was established. This Committee is presided over by the Minister of the Interior, and meets when necessary to discuss matters common to the four Provinces. Under this Act an increased annual subsidy was paid to Natal. Subsequent to the appointment of this Commission a fact-finding Committee was set up to deal with financial relations.

In India, too, a long series of investigations have been made over fourteen years by a Royal Commission, several Committees and Round Table Conferences, and in 1936 by Sir Otto Niemeyer, now an official of the Bank of England. The Government of India Act of 1935 came into force so far as Provincial autonomy was concerned on 1st April 1937. The part of the Act dealing with Federal government, however, has not been brought into operation and never will be in the form of the 1935 Act, for reasons stated in Chapter VII. The British Cabinet offer of March 1942, of complete self-government in India, has put the whole matter of the Constitution, and therefore of financial relations, again in the melting-pot.

CHAPTER II

THE METHOD OF THE ENQUIRY

For purposes of analysis it has been necessary to classify tax systems, public expenditures and public debts and to lay down some basic principles which are widely accepted to enable us to arrive at the standards which go to make a sound system. As far as practicable an attempt has been made to evaluate the burden of taxation and to test its fairness, not merely between individuals and between taxes but also between regions in a Federation. It is sometimes forgotten how complex Federal systems are. In New York State, for example, there are approximately 150 taxes, 100 of which are Federal, 38 State and 7 Local. The exact number, of course, depends on the difference of base and of rate. There is, too, a glaring inequity of taxation in some Federations. If, for example, we take the taxes in one Province as a percentage of the total income of the area or of the surplus income, *i.e.* the total income less the cost of subsistence of the population in the area, we often find that the burden of taxation varies considerably between States or Provinces and that it is highest in those States or Provinces where the relative taxable capacity is low. It is on this account to-day that Governments aim at providing directly or indirectly normal social or developmental services, and in the carrying-out of this recourse is had to the progressive taxes, income taxes and succession duties, which, in order that they should be uniform throughout the Federation, should be entrusted to the Federal Government. Every unit should supply an adequate minimum of the social services and developmental expenditure. If it does not, it endangers the Federation. Among the new problems affecting the financial relations of the Federal Government and the units, not least is the permanent provision for the relief of unemployment. This is one of a number of problems that have arisen from the relative effects on Federal and State or Provincial finance of the great depression and of the financial policy undertaken in each Federation to solve it. In spite of the integration that has taken place in recent years, there is always present on the part of the less prosperous Provinces the suspicion that their interests are disregarded by the Federal Government and the richer units. This endangers national unity. Nothing, in fact, has received so much attention in recent years as the necessity of maintaining economic balance in federal systems. In Australia the State of Western Australia has considered withdrawing from the Commonwealth, as within the Federation where free trade prevails it cannot compete, it is alleged, with the industrially advanced States of Victoria and New South Wales.[1] The interests of the Prairie Provinces and the Maritime Provinces of Canada have received special attention in the recommendations of the Royal Commission on Dominion-Provincial Relations. In the United States the accumulated wealth of the Eastern States contrasts with the younger States which were gradually opened up to settlement. The former have found the latter an outlet for investment and a market for their industrial products. The Chairman of the Board of Governors of the Federal Reserve System emphasised this when he said that " The maintenance of economic balance in the country as a whole requires that citizens of debtor areas have enough money income both to maintain interest, amortisation and other payments on their obligations to investors in the creditor areas and to maintain at a high level their purchases of the output of the factories of the creditor areas. They must maintain their standing both as good credit risks and as good customers. This healthy state of national economic balance is continually being upset by forces that are entirely outside the control of the States or of the individual business man and the individual worker. The result is recurrent periods of breakdown and distress, bankruptcy in debtor areas, idle factories in creditor areas and widespread unemployment and hardship in the country as a whole. There is no essential difference between this situation and that resulting from international debts. Both are, in essence, exchange problems. By tariffs, quotas, exchange restrictions, or even by resort to more punitive steps of a military or economic nature, including expropriation, nations attempt to redress the situation. The Federal Government alone can remedy this condition among the States — and taxation is one of the most effective means. Through that medium funds which the creditor areas drain out of debtor areas through interest, dividends and rents, as well as payments on debt, can be kept flowing back to sustain employment, to keep mines and factories in the debtor areas in operation and continuing to yield returns to the creditor areas." In no other way can the debtor areas, in his view, continue to yield returns to the creditor areas. He advocates a progressive tax system bearing heavily upon savings concentrated in creditor areas and lightly upon the great mass of families of the low income groups.[2]

Before examining the characteristics of a fair and efficient Federal tax

[1] Cf. the Government Report on " The Case of the People of Western Australia in support of their desire to withdraw from the Commonwealth of Australia ". Perth, Government Printer, 1934.

[2] Address to the National Tax Association, 14th Oct. 1941. *Federal Reserve Bulletin*, Nov. 1941.

system, it is desirable to make the meaning of one or two terms clear. In the first place, what is a tax? A tax is a compulsory contribution to public authorities for public purposes. It has been held that there is an absence of a direct *quid pro quo* between the taxpayer and the public authority. In recent years with the development of social security legislation there have been payments out of which the citizen cannot contract. It is preferable to classify such payments as taxes even if the proceeds are kept in a separate fund. Under the United States Social Security Act, 1935, these are termed "pay-roll" taxes earmarked for old-age and unemployment benefits. The Federal old-age benefit tax is 2 per cent of the pay-roll, one-half being added to the employer's costs and one-half being deducted from the worker's wage. The unemployment benefit tax is a combined Federal and State levy of 3 per cent of pay-rolls; in some States it is slightly higher and it is one of the most prolific of all Federal and State taxes. Indeed the Government has in recent years actually been borrowing from this source for other purposes. Licences, fees, conscience money and prices have also been included in the tax structures. Licences, such as licences for motors, usually more than cover the cost of service and are rightly regarded as a productive tax. Fees which are for governmental services and prices for services of a public utility should also be included. The net profits of public utilities and gifts to Government, which are often deferred payments as in the case of conscience money, are also included. Fines and the revenue from education and other services are usually deducted from expenditure and the net figure of expenditure shown.

The expressions "progressive taxes", "regressive taxes" and "degressive taxes" also require definition. Progressive taxes are taxes which take a larger percentage of a high income than of a low income, and in discussions on tax justice are regarded as the ideal taxes. We have moved a considerable distance away from the English Classical Economists who held that progressive taxation would arrest the expansion of industry because the rate of progression would increase until no motive remained to the individual to expand industry. Was it not J. S. Mill who held "to tax the larger incomes at a higher percentage than the smaller is to lay a tax on industry and economy"? There is no real basis for this fear when the progressive principle is not allowed to increase to the point at which it might imperil the accumulation of capital and industry. Mill preferred a proportionate tax, a tax taking the same percentage of all incomes. But with the rediscovery of progressive taxation in the present century and with the increased demands of the State for means to pay for the social services, especially education, unemployment relief and public health, a tax system without a good "dose" of progression is held to be unsatisfactory from the viewpoint of tax justice. Although Adam Smith, 167 years ago, said that taxpayers should contribute " as nearly as possible in proportion to their respective abilities, that is, in proportion to the revenue which they respectively enjoy under the protection of the State ", he stated what is often forgotten in the same book (Book V) of *The Wealth of Nations*, that " it is not very unreasonable that the rich should contribute to the public expense, not only in proportion to their revenue, but something more than in that proportion ".[1] Taxes should be raised with the equality of sacrifice in view, and with progressive taxes well represented in the tax structure the system is held to be far more satisfactory than would otherwise have been the case. Least aggregate sacrifice to the citizens of a country is then possible, the main progressive taxes being the personal income tax and succession duties. The less the aggregate sacrifice, the better the tax system. In ordinary times, Governments in taxing aim at the maximum aggregate welfare. They aim at raising the standard of living as high as possible. In war-time they compress it in order that man-power and materials may be diverted to the winning of the war which, from the long-term point of view, may also be regarded as the maximum aggregate welfare. The least aggregate sacrifice means the taxing of those incomes which have the lowest marginal utility but not in a way to check the accumulation of wealth or to impede industry. While this is the sovereign principle of taxation it requires in practice to be limited.

The development of the marginal theory of value has affected the theory of taxation and it is clear that the hurt or sacrifice involved in taking a unit from a large income is not so great as taking the same unit from a small income. Whether or not we challenge the diminishing utility basis of progressive taxation, we all recognise that progressive taxation is a great engine for social improvement. In progressive taxation it is not infrequently noticed that large incomes are taxed at a higher rate than smaller ones, but not in a degree which involves so great a sacrifice as in the lower incomes. Such taxes are degressive.

It is one of the cardinal principles of tax justice that taxes should be direct rather than indirect. At first this classification was considered for the tax structure of those Federal countries analysed in the following chapters, especially as the distinction between direct and indirect taxes is well known and has even been enshrined in some of the Federal Constitutions themselves. This, however, has been the cause, as in Canada,[2] of much contention between the Centre and the units as regards taxing

[1] *The Wealth of Nations*, Book V, ed. Cannan, vol. ii, p. 327.

[2] *Vide* chap. ix (The Constitution To-day), Book I, of the Report of the Royal Commission on Dominion-Provincial Relations.

powers. Mr. Gladstone, it will be remembered, spoke of direct and indirect taxation as two attractive sisters introduced into the gay world of London, each with an ample fortune and both having the same parentage — Necessity and Invention — differing only as sisters may differ, where one is of lighter and another of darker complexion, or where there is some variety of manner, the one being more free and open and the other somewhat more shy, retiring and insinuating. "I cannot", he added, "conceive any reason why there should be any unfriendly rivalry between the admirers of these two damsels; and I frankly own, whether it be due to a lax sense of moral obligation or not, that as a Chancellor of the Exchequer, if not as a Member of this House, I have always thought it not only allowable but even an act of duty to pay my addresses to them both. I am, therefore, as between direct and indirect taxation perfectly impartial."[1]

But what is a direct tax? J. S. Mill, whom lawyers in this connexion have usually quoted, defined a direct tax as "demanded from the very persons who, it is intended or desired, should pay it", and an indirect tax as one "demanded from one person in the expectation and intention that he shall indemnify himself at the expense of another".[2] The intention is doubtless that of the legislator, but the intention of the legislator does not always fit in with the actual facts. In the British income tax under Schedule A the tax on the landlord's income from the ownership of land and buildings is collected by statute from the occupier of the land or buildings although it is legally imposed on the landlord. The tax is deducted by the occupier from the rental due to the landlord, any contract not to deduct it being legally void. According to Mill's definition this tax would be indirect, but it is really direct. The fact that the distinction between direct and indirect taxes is so closely related to the problem of incidence has led some writers to overlook the difficulty of precise definition as we can only partially succeed in making the burden of both groups of taxes fall where we desire. The burden may be transferred to other persons when it is intended to remain where it is at first imposed, and when it is intended to be transferred the transfer may be tardy or partial. In short, the intention of the legislator is not a sufficient criterion for the distinction between direct and indirect taxes. Some would regard direct taxes as those which are not shifted at all and those which are shifted legally, and indirect taxes as those which are shifted quickly through commercial competition among consumers. On the Continent direct taxes are those for which the taxpayer's names are entered on a register giving the basis of assessment and the amount due. In this case the division between direct

[1] Financial Statement, 1861. Hansard, vol. clxii, p. 584.
[2] *Principles*, Book V, chap. iii, para. 1.

and indirect taxes rests on the mode of collection and not with the incidence of the tax. Another classification is to regard all taxes which are levied immediately on the property and income of persons and those which are paid by the consumers to the State direct as direct taxes, and to regard all other taxes as indirect. A classification, therefore, of a revenue system into (1) tax revenue, (*a*) direct taxes and (*b*) indirect taxes ; and (2) non-tax revenue, (*a*) Government or public undertakings, (*b*) social services and (*c*) other sources, would be possible. No simple classification is possible without the danger of serious omissions and inaccurate inferences. Careful definition and interpretation are required in the study of each Federation, and provided this caveat is remembered this classification is not unsatisfactory. Its weak point is that it does not avoid, according to the League of Nations, the classical nomenclature of direct and indirect taxation, and thus a " terminology which might induce the reader to believe that it was employed in the particular manner customary in his own country when such, in fact, may not be the case ".

We prefer, however, to keep to the classical nomenclature of direct and indirect taxation after stating the pitfalls in the use of the term. For reasons explained below, one of the main groups adopted in the classification of the tax structures of the countries concerned is mainly " direct ". A direct tax, as we have seen, is one which falls where it is intended to fall, and an indirect tax one whose final impact does not necessarily fall where it is considered that it should fall. The burden of indirect taxation is concealed. The Government which levies the tax escapes the criticism of the burden.

On what basis, then, should we judge a tax system ? If tax justice is to be the touchstone it should possess the characteristics of equality, certainty, convenience of payment and economy in collection. The principle of equality is indeed a standard to which every sound tax system must conform. Adam Smith states that " The subjects of every state ought to contribute towards the support of the government, as nearly as possible, in proportion to their respective abilities ; that is, in proportion to the revenue which they respectively enjoy under the protection of the state ", and when he writes as above that " it is not very unreasonable that the rich should contribute to the public expense, not only in proportion to their revenue, but something more than in that proportion ", he was more than a century ahead of his time. The meaning of equality has varied at different times in the history of financial doctrine, but it cannot be denied to-day that it underlies the accepted test — the ability to pay. If carefully analysed, it indicates progressive taxation. Equal taxes do not impose equal burdens, and in the measurement of ability we look not to the attitude which the taxpayer has, but rather to that which he ought to have, *i.e.* we look to the attitude of society in regard to the sacrifice rather than to that of the taxpayer. We know that for the generality of people the test of ability is the size of income, and the taxable capacity of the individual rises more in proportion to the income, the higher the income. As a result, the progressive income tax is regarded as the fairest of taxes. It rises with the size of income, it allows to some degree for personal needs through abatements and allowance, *e.g.* on account of the size of the family or the personal exemption. It is true that the tax is intricate, but this is due to the attempt to secure tax justice at the cost of simplicity. All things considered, it is the tax that most nearly conforms to the standard of tax-paying ability. Death duties are also acceptable from the standpoint of ability to pay, whether the burden is on the deceased or on the successor. The excess profits tax if developed with care may also be regarded as the best method of recapturing war or monopoly profits that have escaped other controls. The canon of convenience, much stressed by American writers, is like the canon of economy, applicable in the long run to taxes as a whole. Productiveness is a very important factor and is often regarded as the main characteristic of a good tax. Among other characteristics of a good revenue system are elasticity, flexibility, simplicity and diversity. In recent years considerable emphasis has been laid on the taxation of surplus rather than on costs of production, and a good tax system should be one in which the taxation of surplus, *i.e.* of income in excess of that necessary for subsistence, is more important than taxation falling on costs, as, for example, taxes on consumption which are highly regressive. Taxes on costs include taxes on businesses without reference to their net incomes, and consumption taxes are those which affect the cost of living, wages and, ultimately, all costs of production. In times of depression there is a tendency to increase taxes on costs and thereby to weaken competitive power abroad and to increase the difficulties of adjustment at home. Taxes, in short, which lead to an increase in production costs restrict the national income as a general rule. They eliminate firms or even industries by destroying the margin of profit which has kept them in existence. The struggling or marginal firms, owing to the falling-off of consumption consequent on taxes on their costs of production, find they cannot make profits and tend to disappear. Investment, too, will be affected. "The result of the tendency of marginal firms to disappear and of the tendency of potential investors to refrain from engaging in new enterprises is that both labour and capital resources will be thrown out of employment and that the national income will be correspondingly diminished. Out of this diminished national income a larger revenue than before will have to be raised, as the unemployed will have to be maintained at the public cost. If, in order to raise the larger revenue, new taxes are imposed which bear on costs, the vicious circle will be completed." [1]

Before we leave the problem of an equitable or fair tax system under a Federal Constitution it is necessary to emphasise its importance not merely from the point of view of particular taxes but as between different regions. This is seen by comparing the total taxes, Central, Provincial or State, and Local, paid in each unit. This may be expressed as a percentage of the total income of the area concerned or of the total income less the cost of subsistence. If progressive taxes are levied by the Central Government, for example personal income taxes and succession duties, and adjustment grants paid to the Provinces or States in accordance with their needs, it may be possible to avoid the territorial inequalities and to provide normal educational and other social and also developmental services without recourse to heavy taxation and to types of taxation which in the long run would nullify the purpose of such adjustment grants.

For the reasons stated in the previous paragraphs, we have decided to classify the tax systems in Chapters III to VII (inclusive) on a uniform basis in an endeavour to bring out the characteristics of a good revenue system. We have grouped the taxes into four groups : in the first group are the main progressive taxes — the personal income tax and succession duties. The taxes in this group are direct. In the second group are to be found the taxes on property. Property taxes in all Federations are an important source of revenue, especially for Local Authorities. The incidence of property taxes is somewhat complicated. It is not possible to classify these taxes as direct or indirect, or as progressive or regressive without considerable explanation. On the whole, we are of opinion that the best method is to show property taxes as a group by themselves. As this group includes taxes on buildings as well as on land, there are in it taxes on consumption in addition to taxes on scarcity values. There is, in fact, no clear-cut division of property taxes, but it is the best possible for purposes of comparison. The third group consists of taxes on business which are sometimes levied on surplus and sometimes on costs. Where these are on net income, they are on surplus and fall on the shareholders ; where they are fixed taxes, they are on consumption, although under certain conditions and for short periods they may be absorbed by the producers. Group four contains taxes on commodities. These are taxes on costs and are normally paid by consumers. The classification of taxes can never be perfect for all purposes. Sometimes a progressive tax may contain elements of regression, and consumption taxes elements of progression. The classification adopted, however, is on balance the one

[1] Report of the Royal Commission on Dominion-Provincial Relations (in Canada), Book II, chap. viii, p. 151.

which brings out most satisfactorily the characteristics of the revenue systems of the selected countries.

Public expenditures are closely related to public revenues and the methods followed in regard to the spending of the proceeds of taxes has much to do with their effect on the national income. We have accordingly classified these expenditures to bring out the character and costs of government. No classification is always satisfactory, because it depends to a great extent on the object which we have in view. We shall consider the nature and relation of Central or Federal, State or Provincial, and Local expenditures to each other. The two main classes of public expenditures may be divided into primary and secondary. Primary expenditures include all expenditure which Governments are obliged to undertake above everything else, *e.g.* on defence, law and order, general administration and the payment of debts. Secondary expenditures include social expenditure, developmental expenditure or public undertakings and miscellaneous expenditure. In recent years, especially since the great depression of 1929–32, social security expenditure has been of considerable importance, particularly as affecting the financial relations of the Federal, State or Provincial and Local Authorities. Not only is the expenditure on the social services of great importance from the distributive viewpoint but it is advantageous from the standpoint of industrial efficiency as well as from that of social justice and general good. Under developmental expenditures are included expenditures of a quasi-commercial or quasi-industrial nature such as those on railways, roads, canals, irrigation and other public works, posts and telegraphs, and subsidies for agricultural and industrial research. In effect, developmental expenditures tend to promote economic development. Lastly, there are subsidies and other grants and contributions, most of which represent transfers between different layers of government. This classification makes possible an analysis of the increasing cost of government and shows the direction from which it is taking place.

In recent years the borrowing policy of Governments in a Federation has become of great importance as showing the close interrelation of borrowing with regard to the social services, especially education and unemployment relief, developmental expenditures such as those on railways and roads, general financial and monetary policy and the control of the foreign exchanges. The importance of borrowing policy shows the desirability, if not the necessity, of a uniform policy between the Federal Government and units. Municipal indebtedness also is linked up with Provincial indebtedness, although to a much lesser extent. In Australia and in India, for example, the Federal Government has concatenated the borrowing of the units as well as its own borrowings, and the Dominion Government in

Canada has proposed to the State Governments the assumption of Provincial debts. This proposal would strengthen Canadian credit by removing the danger of Provincial default. It would remove the burden of debt from the people who dwell in the areas incapable of bearing it, and it would ensure a considerable saving when refunding becomes necessary.[1]

After an analysis of the tax structures and public expenditures of the five Federations studied it will be necessary to examine very briefly the general problem of intergovernmental financial relations with special reference to the conflicts between the Federal Government and the States or Provinces and between the latter and the Local Authorities. There are also the conflicts between Federal and Local Authorities, between States and States and between Federal Government and countries abroad. As long as there are Federations there will be irreconcilable conflicts, and the most that can be hoped for is a series of beautiful compromises. There are, it should be remembered, various overlapping taxing authorities and communities are burdened with several layers of government. This means competition for revenues between Federal and State and between State and Local Governments. In recent years there is a tendency for the higher layer of government to use its taxing powers to control the lower layers. " Although there is a more or less traditional assignment of functions ", says Seligman,[2] " to the various agencies local, state and federal, the shifting basis of economic life is gradually bringing about some alteration. This change is especially noticeable as between State and Local Governments. Recent decades have witnessed a decided drift towards centralisation, partly for administrative, partly for economic reasons." Among the problems arising are the realignment of governmental functions consequent on the changes just referred to. There are also the devices of separation, co-operation, of sharing or the division of yield, of supplements or additions, of grants and of the ingenious plan of credits which in the United States has been used with success for succession or estate and pay-roll taxes by the Federal Government. The sphere of intergovernmental financial relations also extends, first, to specific taxes and, secondly, to specific functions such as expenditures on the social services and on development.

[1] Cf. Dominion-Provincial Conference, 14th and 15th Jan. 1941. Ottawa Government Printer.

[2] " The Co-ordination of Public Revenues ", *Economic Essays in Honour of Gustav Cassel*, p. 573. London, Allen & Unwin, 1933.

CHAPTER III

THE PUBLIC FINANCE AND NATIONAL ECONOMY OF THE UNITED STATES

FEDERAL finance in the United States cannot be understood without a study of the country's national economy and of her Constitution. The country is the richest in the world, and this gives her a place of high importance in the economy of nations. Her Constitution, as Gladstone well described it in the *North American Review* in 1879, is " the most wonderful work ever struck off at a given time by the brain and purpose of man ". This does not mean that the Fathers of the Constitution had achieved finality. The master spirit of the Philadelphia Convention, Alexander Hamilton, set his reliance not upon the document, but upon the " general genius of the Government ", for, as he said, " particular provisions, though not altogether useless, have far less virtue and efficacy than are commonly ascribed to them ". Thomas Jefferson, the third President of the United States, also held this view when he said that the Constitution should be " handed on, with periodical repairs, from generation to generation ". The revolutionary changes that have taken place in the field of American public finance, Federal, State and Local, in the present century can be understood only after an examination of these two great factors. It is proposed to examine each of them in turn.

I. THE NATIONAL ECONOMY

The United States is the richest and strongest of the countries of the world. In size it is greater than the whole of Europe (excluding the U.S.S.R.), although it has but one-third of Europe's population. It is just over 3 million square miles in area and has a population of 132 millions. The United States of Brazil has a larger area (3·3 million square miles) but it has a population of only 43·3 millions. Canada has an area of 3·7 million square miles and is therefore larger than the United States, but it has a population of only 10·4 millions. The United States has 7 per cent of the world's population, but her production of primary and secondary industry is unparalleled. In natural resources — land, forests, minerals and natural power — she once found the main basis of her economic strength ; but this is no longer so owing partly to the exploitation of her resources, but chiefly because of the very rapid advance of her manufacturing industry. Many are still apt to think of American economy in terms of the nineteenth century when agriculture was supreme, but agriculture and forestry in the twentieth century have had to give way to the remarkably high production of manufacturing industry.[1] Her mineral resources, too, are greater than those of any similar area in the world, and together with the British Commonwealth she has two-thirds of the world's mineral output. Her output, however, is small in comparison with manufactures and trade. Of eight out of the eighteen major metals she is the world's greatest producer. The character and strength of her population are of great importance. From 1820 to 1940, 38·3 millions of alien immigrants landed in the country, and before 1914 immigration sometimes reached the figure of a million a year. The war of 1914–18 led to the spectre of hyphenisation — of immigrants who, it was feared, did not become completely American citizens in outlook, and laws were passed by Congress restricting immigrants from certain countries. Quotas were first fixed on the basis of the Census of 1910, then of 1890, and, finally, on a figure which was said to represent the make-up of the population of 1790. Not only was the stream of immigration greatly curtailed but its character was changed, the "old" immigration whose predominance it was desired to preserve being mainly from North-west Europe, and Protestant. This restriction of immigration was the natural companion of high tariffs, and it was believed that with a predominantly North-west European strain assimilation of immigrants with the main population, especially in the more populous areas, would be less difficult. From the labour viewpoint trade union organisation would be far easier. In the fiscal year ended 30th June, 1940, 70,756 immigrant and 138,032 non-immigrant aliens were admitted, a total of 208,788, while 21,461 emigrant and 144,703 non-emigrant aliens departed, a total of 166,164. The net increase, therefore, for the year was 42,624. The foreign-born population of the United States to-day is 13·4 millions, of which 1·8 millions are Italians, 1·6 millions Germans, 1·3 millions Poles and 1·2 millions Russians. Norway, Sweden and the Netherlands together account for 1·1 millions. The foreign-born British population is 2·1 millions, of which 745,000 are Irish. When the size of the country and also the variety of the racial origins of the people are remembered, the unity of the people, whose common language is English, is very remarkable. There are several factors such as transportation and the press, which strengthen this unity. The American railway system is the largest in the world, and air communications are more developed than in most countries, New York, Chicago, San Francisco and other great cities being within easy reach of each other. There are nearly 1900 daily newspapers, and

[1] See Tables 18 and 19 in Part III for the distribution of the national income by industries in recent years.

40 million copies are sold daily, one newspaper for every 3·3 inhabitants. Education is also at a high level with over 26 million children in elementary public schools, 7 millions in high schools and 1·4 millions in universities. The education is such that all classes of children, rich and poor, are educated together in their early years, and in a democracy this is a unifying factor not without considerable social value.

Whereas the first characteristic of the national economy is unity over this vast continent, the second characteristic is the great differences between different areas, differences of climate, geography and, therefore, of production. This is illustrated in Chart III on p. 24. The North-eastern States differ from the Middle West States and the Middle West States from the Mountain and Great Plain States. The North-west Pacific States are also a region by themselves, as are the South-eastern States, the South-western States and California. It is difficult to delimit these groups with accuracy, and often historical accident makes even one part of a State differ from another, as, for example, Northern Ohio from Southern Ohio. These groups of States are more or less homogeneous from the economic point of view, and this has the result of cutting across State boundaries. " Sectionalism — the habit of working as one political unit — is thus imposed by a variety of forces on groups of states, and the legal units, the States, are only convenient weapons for the sections to use in the endless battle of pressure groups for the favour of the Government of the United States. It is these six or seven sections, not the forty-eight States, that are the realities underlying the American federal structure, the internal obstacles to the more perfect union promised by the preamble to the Constitution."[1] Another point which reinforces sectionalism is the locality rule by which every senator and representative must be a resident of the State he represents, and this excludes from Congress men whose party is in the minority locally. They cannot be candidates elsewhere and cannot be elected at home. The Minority, because of the constitutional proviso, accordingly looks to senators and representatives of other States. Every State regardless of its population has two senators, so that Nevada with a population of 100,000 has the same representation in the Senate (but not in the House of Representatives) as New York with 12,000,000.[2] Points of view in States not represented or ill represented in the Senate frequently find their spokesmen from Western States.

The national income is a measurement of potential economic strength

[1] D. W. Brogan, *U.S.A.: An Outline of the Country, its People and Institutions*, Oxford University Press, 1941, p. 12.

[2] This over-representation of area accounts for the importance of the " Silver " States in the Senate and explains the importance of silver in American financial policy.

which in turn depends on the interplay of the factors of production (natural resources, labour including the number and character of the population, capital and entrepreneurship or organisation) on each other. The total income is the largest in the world and before the present war was three times that of Great Britain, and equal to that of Great Britain, Germany and Russia combined. The figure for 1938 per head at factor cost was £105 ($508) as compared with £97 ($469) in Great Britain. In 1941 the corresponding figures were £186 ($749) and £133 ($534). The average *per capita* income in the United States is about one-fifth more than that in Great Britain. The American income is much more expansible and variable than that of Great Britain. For example, the United States increased its production from 23 to 29 per cent between 1939 and 1941 [1] while Great Britain increased its production by 12½ per cent between 1938 and 1941. The United States to-day has a substantial margin of increase still to be absorbed in the war effort while in Great Britain 1943 should see the ceiling reached. The Census Bureau reported that employment in the United States reached the record total of 54,300,000 during the week ended 10th July 1943, a figure which is entirely confined to civilians and excludes the armed services. In August 1943 the United States was producing about 60 per cent of the United Nations' output of munitions as compared with 17 per cent for the United Kingdom, 5 per cent for the rest of the Commonwealth and Empire (of which the greater part came from Canada) and 18 per cent for Soviet Russia and the other United Nations. So great has been the increase in production in the United States since the war effort began three years ago that in the current year ending 30th June 1944 the national income will be $150,000 millions. If the figure per occupied person is taken for 1937, the *per capita* income is £256 for the United States and £232 for Great Britain. If the fully employed worker only is taken, the value of goods and services he produced in 1937 was about £340 in the United States and £260 in Great Britain. The diagram on page 21 shows the size of average incomes in the two countries and is from *America's Economic Strength*, by C. J. Hitch.[2]

The average income per occupied person is greater in the U.S.A. than in Great Britain. If we compare wage rates, the difference is very much greater; in 1930 they were almost twice as high as in Great Britain. In 1929 the U.S.A. income per occupied person was £300, but in the depth of

[1] Cf. Mr. R. Stone's paper on "The National Income, Output and Expenditure of the U.S.A., 1929–41" (*Economic Journal*, June–Sept. 1942): cf. *Economist*, 5th Sept. 1942; "On the average of years, however, it seems probable that the average British income lies somewhere between three-quarters and seven-eighths of the American — 80 per cent might be a fair average figure to take for *prima facie* comparisons".

[2] C. J. Hitch, *America's Economic Strength*, Oxford University Press, 1941, p. 22.

the great depression it fell to £170 (in 1932), and rose to £256 in 1937.[1] The difference between the two countries in *per capita* national income, *i.e.* total national income divided by total population, is much less than as between occupied persons, because the United States, unlike this country, had in 1937 a large rural population of which the unemployed and impoverished were no small part. In that year farmers were 23 per cent of the total occupied population, but the country produced a greater agricultural output than any other country in the world. This 23 per cent received only 15 per cent of the national income, agriculture being, as

CHART I

AVERAGE INCOMES IN THE UNITED STATES AS COMPARED WITH THOSE IN GREAT BRITAIN

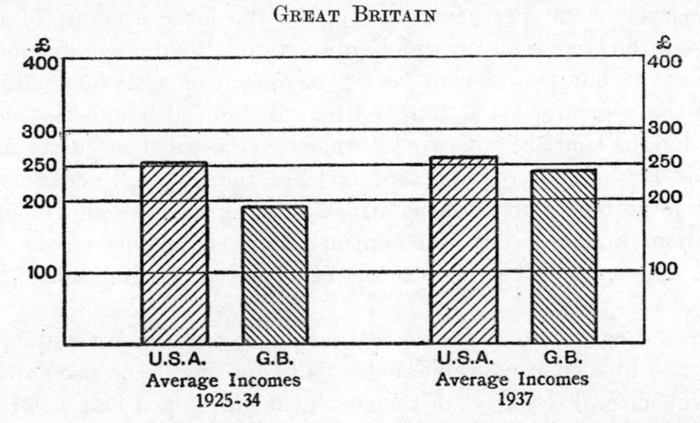

compared with services and manufacturing industry, the least gainful. In 1820 agriculture employed 70 per cent of the population and 54 per cent in 1870. Land is less fertile in proportion to the population than it was, and antiquated methods of farming still obtain : in some regions, as in the " Old South " and the western part of the Great Plains, the returns are poor. The South, with half the total farming population, produces only 30 per cent of the farm incomes as contrasted with the Middle West, where 33 per cent of the farming population lives but produces 40 per cent of the income, efficiency in agriculture in the Middle West being comparatively high. In California agricultural production is the highest in the world[2];

[1] Mr. R. Stone (*op. cit.*) gives the net national income of the U.S.A. at factor cost as follows : $87·6 billions in 1929 and $42·8 billions in 1932 ; $72·6 billions in 1937 and $99·1 billions in 1941.

[2] California's productive power is truly remarkable. Not only does the State possess a most valuable specialised agriculture, particularly fruits and vegetables, but in industry records are being broken. In 1943 in Los Angeles county alone, aeroplane production was double Germany's and four times Japan's. The shipbuilding industry in the State is greater at the moment than in the rest of the world. (Cf. *Economist*, 18th Dec. 1943, p. 810.)

the *per capita* farm income is four times the American average. In the United States as a whole agricultural output has greatly increased in the present century. The increase is estimated at 50 per cent between 1900 and 1930. On the other hand, agriculture in the United States is not as productive per man engaged in that occupation as it is in New Zealand, Australia and the Argentine, where there is a proportionately large meat production. It is more or less on a level with Danish agriculture and somewhat more productive than that of Great Britain, the Netherlands and Germany.[1] The explanation of the high American national income[2] is not to be sought in agricultural production but in the high production of manufacturing industry which employs 25 per cent of the occupied population, and in the high proportion of those engaged in distributive and other services — 50 per cent. Owing to the large amount of capital employed, the large scale on which production is conducted and the great progress in technique in recent years, the output of secondary industry is several times greater than that of Great Britain, although the numbers engaged in the United States are less than twice as great as those employed in Great Britain. Two important facts of the national economy must not be forgotten — first, the contrast between the average income by occupations and, secondly, the contrast between regions in the United States. These are well brought out in Mr. Hitch's two diagrams (Charts I and II).

The national motto, *E Pluribus Unum*, in spite of the diversities shown in the two following diagrams, holds good not merely on account of the abundant natural resources of the continent (developed long before those in South America or in the self-governing Dominions) and the high efficiency in manufacturing industry (an efficiency, especially in labour, without equal in the world) but also on account of non-economic factors. Great importance must be given to the union brought about in 1787, which is a living influence at the present time after more than a century and a half of history behind it. It is usual to describe the United States as " the greatest free trade area in the world ". Section 9 of Article I of the Constitution provides that " No tax or duty shall be laid on articles exported from any State. No preference shall be given by any regulation of commerce or revenue to the ports of one State over those of another ; nor shall vessels bound to, or from, one State, be obliged to enter, clear, or pay duties in another." The great iron ore exports, for example, in northern Minnesota are shipped from Duluth through the Great Lakes to

[1] C. J. Hitch, *op. cit.* p. 34. The estimates have been checked. In making comparisons care must be taken to compare net production figures. It is sometimes forgotten that British agriculture has to import considerable amounts of feeding stuffs which have to be allowed for in estimating net output.

[2] See Tables 18 and 19 in Part III.

the blast-furnaces of the Eastern States. Coal is sent from Pennsylvania to Duluth in the same ships. Los Angeles is able to get its supply of water from the Sierra Nevada and the Colorado River. Crude oil is pumped from one State to another where it is broken up into petrol or gasoline, kerosene and lubricating oils, and sold to the industries of the New England States. This absence of tariff barriers has led to a considerable degree of specialisation in agriculture. One region is complementary to another, and this makes for economic strength. "Without unity the North-east would be an England, the South-east a Poland, the Middle

CHART II

Average Income by Occupations in the United States in 1935

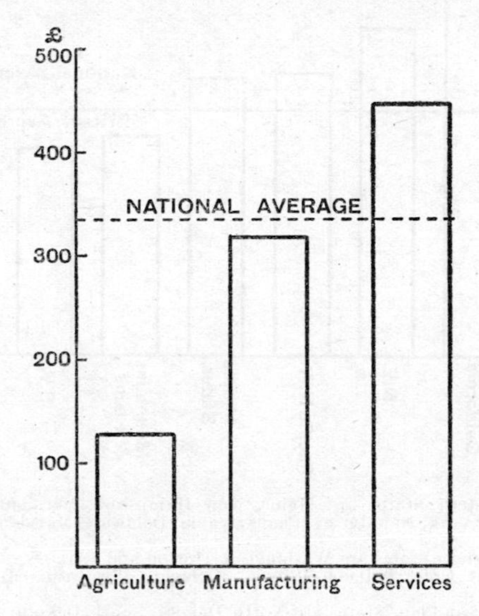

Note.—The earnings of fully employed persons are represented by the height of the columns.

West a Germany, and the Far West a Siberia. That this has not happened is due to two events which occurred at the end of the eighteenth century; one primary, the adoption of the Federal Constitution; the second subsidiary, the inclusion in that constitution of an economic clause entrusting the Federal Government with the regulation of interstate commerce, and forbidding the States to levy tariffs on it. The Federal Government's regulation has, for the most part, taken the form of active encouragement: it subsidised the early railways by grants of land, and has spent large sums in the improvement of through highways and the development of air transport. The Federal Constitution succeeded in creating the greatest area of free trade in the world, in which an extensive, if not perfect, division of labour enabled each region and each state to specialise in the production of the goods which it was best suited to make, and which made possible the utilisation of the nation's capital for the efficient manufacture of commodities on a mass production scale."[1] Especially since the great depression of the early thirties attempts have been made to circumvent the Federal Constitution in regard to internal

CHART III

AVERAGE INCOME PER OCCUPIED PERSON BY REGIONS IN 1937

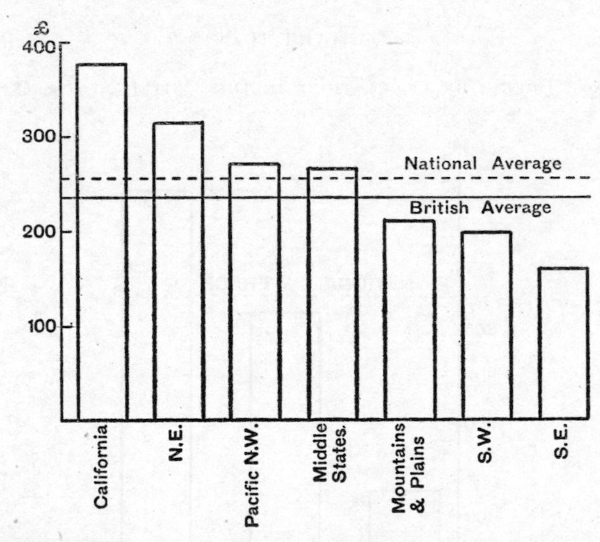

Note.—The North-eastern States are Maine, New Hampshire, Vermont, Massachusetts, Rhode Island, Connecticut, New York, New Jersey, Pennsylvania, Delaware, Maryland, (District of Columbia) and West Virginia.

The Pacific North-western States are Washington, Oregon and Idaho.

The Middle States are Ohio, Indiana, Illinois, Michigan, Wisconsin, Minnesota, Iowa and Missouri.

The Mountain and Great Plain States are North Dakota, South Dakota, Nebraska, Kansas, Montana, Wyoming, Colorado, Utah and Nevada.

The South-western States are Oklahoma, Texas, New Mexico and Arizona.

The South-eastern States are Virginia, North Carolina, South Carolina, Georgia, Florida, Kentucky, Tennessee, Alabama, Mississippi, Arkansas and Louisiana.

free trade. The inspection of agricultural products at State boundaries under the guise of preventing plant disease or of protecting a pure milk supply or of inspecting and taxing road vehicles has been a trade barrier with which the Supreme Court has been unwilling to interfere. The effect of all these measures has not been great.

A country with so pre-eminently strong a national economy as the United States must necessarily have an important place in international economy. In international trade the United States has the second place,

[1] C. J. Hitch, *op. cit.* p. 31.

the United Kingdom taking the first place. The exports of primary industry — agricultural products and raw materials — were in 1937 not quite a quarter of the total exports as compared with 75 per cent, the average in the second half of the nineteenth century. The remaining three-quarters were manufactured or semi-manufactured goods, mainly machinery of all kinds, motor cars, aircraft (especially since the war), iron and steel, raw cotton, petroleum and oil, and chemicals. Imports have also changed. Raw materials and articles of food (not produced or only produced in relatively small quantities) such as crude rubber, pulpwood and products, cane sugar, coffee, vegetable oils, raw silk, wool, tin and chemicals are now the main imports and not manufactured goods. Exports are a fraction of total production, about 5 per cent. In recent years the direction of trade has been changing ; the percentage of foreign trade with Europe has been declining in favour of Asia, South America and Africa. But in 1937 Europe (including the whole of the U.S.S.R.) still took 41 per cent of American exports, though it supplied only 27 per cent of its imports. Since the war of 1914–18 the United States has become a creditor country. But she has not behaved as a creditor country, viz. by importing more than she exports, or making loans rather than by importing gold. She has imported gold since the defaults of the thirties, which has been an expensive policy to the American Treasury and to the country as a whole. As a shipping country she holds the second place after the United Kingdom, but in railway mileage she is easily first with a mileage of 248,000 miles.[1] The general conclusion from the international viewpoint is that the United States is not, like Canada, in a vulnerable position in international trade. She depends mainly on her home market. On the other hand, her natural resources are so great and her industrial production so efficient that Europe and other continents look to her for her products, but the exports of these products are a small part of her total production.

The United States Economy in War-Time

The most arresting fact of American economy in war-time is its great reserve of productive power. This is clearly seen in the increase in national income and in the increase in production. In the calendar year 1938 American national income at factor cost, *i.e.* excluding indirect taxation and subsidies, was $66·1 billions [2]; in 1941 it was $99·1 billions, an increase of 50 per cent. (At the end of 1942 it was of the order of $125 billions.) Between 1938 and 1941 the British national income increased from £4595 millions to £6338 millions, an increase of 38 per cent. In

[1] Mileage operated by steam railways in 1939.

[2] United States billions (1000 millions) ; not the million millions as used in Great Britain.

1939–41 United States production rose between 23 and 29 per cent according to Mr. Stone's estimates in the *Economic Journal*,[1] as compared with 12½ per cent between 1938 and 1941 in Great Britain.[2] "This large increase in American output is mainly to be attributed to the comparatively low level of the employment of resources in that country even at times of 'good' trade. The level of unemployment has been high in the United States for many years, and average hours of work have been sufficiently low to allow a considerable rise in output through their increase. Thus, between 1939 and 1941 civil non-agricultural employment is estimated to have increased by some 4·3 millions, or 12 per cent, while in the latter year there were still some 4 million workers unemployed. Over the same period average weekly hours in factories increased by 2·9 hours per week, or nearly 8 per cent." [3] Another factor is the lower proportion of men called up for military service. Increased output rather than diminished consumption and disinvestment accounted for the increase in national income in the United States since the war. In short, full economic mobilisation is still distant in the United States, whereas in 1943 this has been almost achieved in Great Britain. This greater elasticity in the American National Economy is reflected in the increase in Federal expenditures, which were as follows :

TABLE I

GOVERNMENT EXPENDITURES IN THE U.S.A. IN RECENT YEARS

($ billions)

	1938–39	1940–41	1941–42
Federal . .	9·1	13·3	32·6
State and Local .	10·5	10·0	11·0
	19·6	23·3	43·6

Source.—Economist, 24th Jan. 1942, p. 106.

The United States is indeed fortunate in being able to make a gigantic war effort with so little effect on present consumption or on its future wealth, a contrast with Great Britain. In ordinary years the United States *per capita* income is from 10 to 15 per cent higher than that of Great Britain, but it is very much more variable from year to year. At the present time it is 25 per cent greater.

The *Economist* has shown in the following table [3] that in 1942–43 the Governments of the United States and of Great Britain will be spending

[1] *Economic Journal*, June–Sept. 1942, p. 169.

[2] N. Kaldor, "The 1941 White Paper on National Income and Expenditure", *Economic Journal*, June–Sept. 1942.

[3] *Economist*, 5th Sept. 1942, p. 300.

roughly the same percentage of pre-war national income in each country, but the manner in which it is paid for is very different because of the very large increase in output that is still possible in the United States. This means that the expenditure can be met by reducing consumption to the pre-war level and by reducing by half the pre-war rate of additions to capital. In Great Britain, however, the increase has to be met by a considerable decrease in consumption and by a heavy inroad on capital.

TABLE II

DISTRIBUTION OF THE NATIONAL INCOME IN REAL TERMS

(Net national income of base year = 100)

	Base Year		1940		1941		1942–43	
	U.S., 1939	U.K., 1938	U.S.	U.K.	U.S.	U.K.	U.S.	U.K.
Personal expenditure	78	77½	82½	71½	88	69	76½	64
Government expenditure	17¼	16	18¼	49	26½	61	69	67
Net investment	4¾	6½	8¾	−16½	11½	−19	2½	−17
Net national income at market prices	100	100	109½	104	126	111	148	114

The figures in the table are approximate, but they show that in the pre-war years, both in the American and British economies, there were no great differences in the distribution of expenditure between consumers' expenditures, Government expenditure and net investment. The changes in 1940, 1941 and 1942–43 are very noticeable. The *Economist*, on the assumption that the cost of the war measures the increase in Government expenditures, distributes the increase as follows, the figures being — like the totals in the table above — percentages of the net national income in the base year:

TABLE III

DISTRIBUTION OF THE INCREASE IN GOVERNMENT EXPENDITURES, 1942–43

	U.S.A.	U.K.
From increased output	48	14
From diminished consumption	1½	13½
From reduction in net investment (or from drafts on capital)	2¼	23½
	51¾	51

Economic strength, in the sense of capacity to produce goods and services, is the equivalent of a country's war potential, and the United

States possesses a military potential not far short of the whole of the continent of Europe. But for a short period the United States is vulnerable because, unlike Germany, she is not armed to the teeth. She therefore has to swing over in the shortest possible time to a planned long-period war economy, and that is what the N.D.A.C. (the National Defence Advisory Commission) is doing. This has its financial implications, especially in the sphere of Federal finance. This swing-over from peace to war has been noticeable in a special degree since the third quarter of 1941. Mr. Stone has shown that, assuming the net national income of the United States at factor cost (*i.e.* the current value of goods and services produced by the factors of production before indirect taxation) = 1, then—

TABLE IV

PROPORTION OF THE NATIONAL INCOME DEVOTED TO GOVERNMENTAL ACTIVITIES

	1938	1939	1940	1941	1941				1942	
					1st qr.	2nd qr.	3rd qr.	4th qr.	1st qr.	2nd qr.
Consumption . .	0·81	0·78	0·75	0·70	0·72	0·72	0·69	0·67	0·65	0·60
Government goods and services .	0·18	0·18	0·18	0·22	0·20	0·20	0·22	0·26	0·32	0·41
Net investment .	0·01	0·04	0·07	0·08	0·08	0·08	0·09	0·07	0·03	-0·01

Source.—Paper read to the Manchester Statistical Society, 28th Oct. 1942.

II. THE CONSTITUTION

The United States is governed in accordance with a written constitution, interpreted by the Supreme Court. The Supreme Court of nine judges interprets the Constitution in the light of what it calls "the rule of reason", and this means in effect what the majority of five thinks reasonable. It gives not merely a legal but a political or philosophical meaning to its decisions, and, be it noted, it has no hesitation in changing its opinions. The reversal of previous decisions, particularly since 1937, has been of great constitutional importance, especially from the viewpoint of financial relations. The meaning, for example, of the "due process of law" in the Fourteenth Amendment given in 1935 in *Colgate* v. *Harvey* [1] was reversed in 1940 in *Madden* v. *Kentucky* [2] when the Supreme Court found the 1935 decision "repugnant", and declared that it "must be and is overruled". The decisions in *Adkins* v. *Children's Hospital* [3] in 1923 and the *Tipaldo* case [4] in 1936 were reversed in 1937 when the Court

[1] *Colgate* v. *Harvey*, 296 U.S. 404.
[2] *Madden* v. *Kentucky*, 309 U.S. 83, 93.
[3] *Adkins* v. *Children's Hospital*, 261 U.S. 525.
[4] *Morehead* v. *New York ex. rel. Tipaldo*, 298 U.S. 587.

upheld the minimum wage law of the State of Washington[1] and repudiated the doctrine that used the due process clause to forbid minimum wage legislation generally. " The case of *Adkins* v. *Children's Hospital* ", said the majority of the Court, " should be, and is, overruled." Even before changes in the Court's personnel took place which brought the number of Roosevelt appointees to seven in a Court of nine, the due process clauses of the Fifth and Fourteenth Amendments were no longer regarded as restraints on the legislative control of economic policy. The reversal of the Supreme Court's invalidation of the Congressional Acts relating to the New Deal, such as the National Recovery Act of 1933[2] in 1935 and the first Agricultural Adjustment Act[3] in 1936, is well known, as is the upholding of the National Labor Relations Act in 1937 and the Fair Labor Standards (Wage and Hour) Act of 1938[4] in 1941. Who would have anticipated so precipitous a change from the position taken up in 1935 and 1936 in the interpretation of the Constitution ? The Supreme Court rightly stated in 1938 that " Mathematical or rigid formulas . . . are not provided by the great concepts of the Constitution, such as ' interstate commerce ', ' due process ' and ' equal protection ' ".[5]

The sections of the Constitution dealing with finance and with financial relations are these :

(1) Representatives and direct taxes shall be apportioned among the several States which may be included within this Union, according to their respective numbers. (Art. I, Sect. 2.)

(2) The Congress shall have power to lay and collect taxes, duties, imposts and excises, to pay the debts and provide for the common defence and general welfare of the United States ; but all duties, imposts and excises shall be uniform throughout the United States ;
To regulate commerce with foreign nations, and among the several States. (Art. I, Sect. 8.)

(3) No capitation or other direct tax shall be laid, unless in proportion to the census or enumeration herein before directed to be taken.
No tax or duty shall be laid on articles exported from any State. (Art. I, Sect. 9.)

(4) The powers not delegated to the United States by the Constitution, nor prohibited by it to the States, are reserved to the States respectively or to the people. (Amendment X, 1791.)

(5) No State shall make or enforce any law which shall abridge the privileges or immunities of citizens of the United States ; nor shall any State deprive any person of life, liberty, or property, without due

[1] *West Coast Hotel Co.* v. *Parrish,* 300 U.S. 379.

[2] *Schechter Poultry Corporation* v. *U.S.,* 295 U.S. 495 (1935).

[3] *United States* v. *Butler,* 297 U.S. 1 (1936).

[4] *National Labor Relations Board* v. *Jones & Laughlin Steel Corporation,* 301 U.S. 1.

[5] *Santa Cruz Fruit Packing Company* v. *National Labor Relations Board,* 303 U.S. 453, 467.

process of law; nor deny to any person within its jurisdiction the equal protection of the laws. (Amendment XIV, 1868.)

(6) The Congress shall have power to lay and collect taxes on incomes, from whatsoever source derived, without apportionment among the several States, and without regard to any census or enumeration. (Amendment XVI, 1913.)

Except for Amendments X, XIV and XVI above, the sections quoted are those drawn up in 1787 and brought into force on 30th April 1789 after ratification by eleven out of the thirteen original States. In the century and a half of its existence it has changed less than perhaps any other system of government in the world. It has, however, a very different meaning to President Roosevelt from any that could have been conceived by Alexander Hamilton. It is no mere antique symbol but a living influence upon the lives of Americans, as the history of the New Deal has shown.

In three directions it differs from the British Constitution, although both nations start from the same foundation — government by consent of the governed. In the first place it is not a Parliamentary system of government. Since the time of their first President, George Washington, the American people feel themselves represented primarily by their executive officer, the President, and by members of his Cabinet rather than by Congress. In 1868 in the clash between the Executive and the Legislature over the impeachment of President Andrew Johnson it was the Constitution and the loyalty of Americans to it that made the Executive supreme. A second difference from the British system, perhaps a unique feature of American polity, is the absence of that opposition between the Government and the industrial classes which has been traditional in Europe. The whole American social and political system is based on industrial property right, and American lawyers accordingly have held that the Fifth and Fourteenth Amendments apply to all " persons ", real or fictitious, *i.e.* the corporate persons of industry have also their rights, the Supreme Court being the custodian of all American liberties, whether of individuals or of corporations or of cities or of States. A third contrast with the British system is the idea of federation, an idea subsequently adopted by Canada, Australia and South Africa. The Centre is the trustee of federation which will always be the central thread of American constitutional development. The gradual strengthening of the Central or Federal Government, as the Amendments to the original Constitution have shown, is the most characteristic development of the Constitution to-day. In no small degree this is due to the increased complexity and the increased cost of government. The States or the people have all those powers not delegated to the Federal authority, but they have to accept the lead of the Centre even in activities in which they are nominally sovereign. As the New Deal has shown, a new federalism has sprung up which requires for its effectiveness [1] co-operation by the States in the form of legislation. Federal financial power has had powerful centralising influences in recent years, and the States have been willing partners in national action. This has been essential to ensure uniform or integrated action on common problems. In 1930 the Federal Government gave grants to States amounting to about $150 millions to assist eleven different State activities. Nine years later the total was $800 millions, and the number of assisted activities was twenty-one. Fifteen per cent of the total revenues of State Governments now comes from federal grants.[2] The Constitution links the spending power of Congress to general welfare, as in Section 8 of Article I — " The Congress shall have power to lay and collect taxes . . . to pay the debts and provide for the common defence and general welfare of the United States ". The Supreme Court in 1938 declined to permit private utilities not operating under exclusive franchises to challenge the grants and loans of the Public Works Administration to municipal and other public electrical plants,[3] and in 1939 went further and supported the Tennessee Valley Authority's contention that it was not merely within its rights in damming the bed of the river but in making contracts for the supply of power to neighbouring cities.[4] Experience shows that in a federation the Federal Government must be in most cases the leader. A policy which takes into account the interests of all does not satisfy everybody. National or Federal interests and State interests do not invariably coincide. If they did, federation would be meaningless and unnecessary. The American Constitution was and is the embodiment of the idea of Union, the idea that the States of the Union in their own interest and although unequal in size and wealth must forgo their jealousies and transfer elements of their sovereignty to a central Government. The trend of judicial interpretation by the Supreme Court is in the direction of extending the powers at the Centre. John Marshall, Chief Justice of the United States from 1801 to 1835, was the first to erect the Constitution as a superior paramount law, and invoked the concept of political nationhood as against the rights of the States. Roosevelt, like Jackson, has used the Constitution to good purpose ever since he came into office, which was at a time when the United States was feeling the

[1] Cf. *The Rise of a New Federalism*, by Jane Perry Clark. New York, 1938.

[2] Cf. J. P. Harris, *The Future of Federal Grants-in-Aid*; A. F. MacDonald, " Federal Aid to the States : 1940 Model ", *American Political Science Review*, vol. xxxiv, 1940, p. 489.

[3] *Alabama Power Company* v. *Ickes*, 302 U.S. 464 ; *Duke Power Company* v. *Greenwood County*, 302 U.S. 485.

[4] *Tennessee Electric Power Company* v. *Tennessee Valley Authority*, 306 U.S. 118.

results of the great depression more severely than any other country of the world. His aim was to cure, " under the framework and in the spirit and intent of the American Constitution ", the causes of the great depression at a time of world-wide change, creating problems " for which the masters of the old practice and theory were unprepared ". These causes were mainly the concentration of economic power in the hands of the few and the lack of investment. In spite of all that has been said and done, " We have ", he said, " not weeded out the over-privileged, and we have not effectively lifted up the under-privileged ". Social justice was a definite goal and he had no quarrel with the profit motive, which he defined as " the right to work to earn a decent livelihood for ourselves and our families ". He declared, " Americans must forswear that conception of the acquisition of wealth which through excessive profits creates undue private power over private affairs, and, to our misfortune, over public affairs as well ". That this was an accurate diagnosis of the facts was undoubtedly true. The diagram on p. 33 shows the catastrophic fall in the national income between 1929 and 1933, and the recovery from that year to 1937. There was a fall from 1937 to 1938 followed by a rise, so that at the end of 1941 the national income was larger than in 1929.

The concentration of economic power was clear from the fact that the proportion of the occupied population employed by others had risen from 50 per cent in 1870 to 80 per cent of the total occupied population in 1935. It was also seen in the unequal distribution of income and in the growth of large corporations. Three per cent of the population, according to one estimate, owned shares in 1929, and three-tenths of 1 per cent received 78 per cent of the dividends. In 1930 1 per cent of the corporations owned half the wealth of all corporations, and it was calculated that if the 200 largest grew as fast as they did in the 1920s they would have half the country's wealth by 1950. The decline in investment was due to several factors such as the slowing-down in the growth of population assisted by the decline in immigration, the completion of the railway system and similar means of investment, and the state of Europe making investment too risky.[1] President Roosevelt, therefore, set about the

[1] Cf. C. J. Hitch, *op. cit.* chap. v, " Depression and New Deal ". Also Hansen, *Fiscal Policy and Business Cycles*, London : Allen & Unwin (New York : Norton & Co), 1941. Professor Hansen distinguishes between a circular-flow economy in which consumption and net income are equal and a dynamic economy where there is a constant tendency for consumption and net income to be unequal. A dynamic economy tends to run down like a clock and requires winding up repeatedly — by fresh opportunities for investment. This is the best book yet written on full employment as it affects the United States to-day. According to Professor Hansen, the decline in investment was caused not so much by the decline in the demand for consumption goods as such as by that in the demand for residential construction. In his view, the United States ceased to have an expanding economy, partly because the growth of population and immigration have declined, and monopoly and other factors have produced a rigid price structure which prevents the growth of

solution of these problems by legislation. In order to remedy the bad effects of the first factor, he tried to make the worker more secure and more powerful in bargaining with capital. To this class of measures belong the Social Security Act, the National Recovery Act, the Wagner Act and amending Acts, the Wages and Hours Act. He also assisted farmers by

CHART IV

NET NATIONAL INCOME, 1929–41

(Income of 1929 = 100)

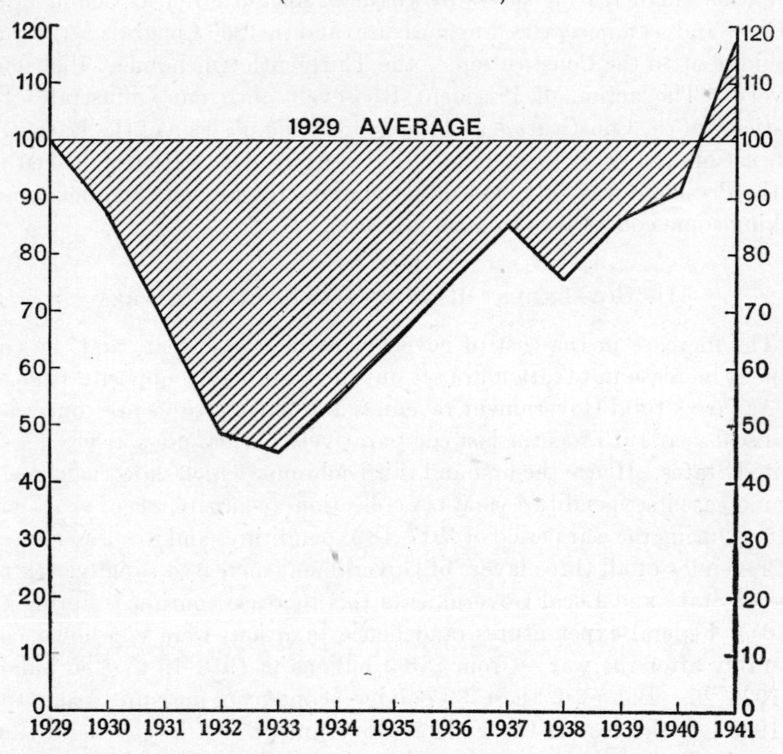

Note.—The net national income figures are those in Table I on p. 162 of Mr. Stone's article on "The National Income, Output and Expenditure of the U.S.A.", *Economic Journal*, June–Sept. 1942.

raising the prices of farm products. Legislation was passed to deal with the concentration of economic power, both industrial and financial, such as the reduction of regulated prices in certain industries in which corporations or large firms were dominant. Attempts were made to increase and stimulate investment by "pump-priming" the control of credit, and the construction of public works by the W.P.A. (Works Progress Adminis-

"intensive" private investment. On the depression and the New Deal, as well as the general background, see also Allan Nevins and Henry Steele Commager, *America: The Story of a Free People*, Oxford University Press, 1942, especially pp. 408 ff.

tration) and the P.W.A. (Public Works Administration).

The war has brought rather different financial problems. On 7th September 1942 the President, in a message to Congress, bluntly told Congress that if it did not pass the necessary legislation to prevent inflation — the fixing of prices and wages and the increase in taxation — for which the Administration asked, he would be compelled to act himself on account of his inescapable responsibility to the people of the country. He had precedent for this. Abraham Lincoln on 1st January 1863 issued a proclamation emancipating slaves by virtue of his authority as Commander-in-Chief and as a necessary war measure, and in 1865 Congress ratified an amendment to the Constitution — the Thirteenth Amendment abolishing slavery. The action of President Roosevelt once more illustrates the elasticity of the Constitution and the dominating position of the Executive in taxation and other matters in recent years.[1] The legislation asked for by the President was duly passed by Congress, though with an amendment making some concessions to farm interests.

III. Government Revenues and Expenditures

The increase in the cost of government in recent years and the consequent increase in taxation are set out in the table on opposite page.

As far as total Government revenues and expenditures are concerned, the fiscal year 1915 was the last comparatively normal pre-war year in the United States. Hence the first and third columns, which show the percentage increase in expenditures and tax collections, compare recent years with 1915. During the war period of 1917–18 expenditures and to a lesser extent tax revenues of all three layers of Government increased rapidly. In the case of State and Local Governments this increase continued during the 1920s. Federal expenditures (and hence taxation) were cut down considerably after the war — from $18·5 billions in 1918–19 to $3·5 billions in 1924–25. But even these " Coolidge economy " measures from 1923 to 1929 left the cost of the Federal Government at a level several times higher than it had been before the war, and from the middle 1920s onwards the upward trend began slowly to reassert itself. Then, in 1929 and 1930, came the great depression, and with it revolutionary changes in American public finance. National income in money terms fell by more than half (see Chart IV, p. 33). With the emergence of mass unemployment, the burden of relief fell at first on the Local Authorities. But soon these found themselves quite unable to cope with the situation. Their revenues were shrinking (in some cases there were even taxpayers' strikes),

[1] Cf. W. B. Graves, " The Future of the American States ", *American Political Science Review*, vol. xxx, 1936, p. 24, where the dominance of the Federal Government in recent years is discussed.

TABLE V

Government Expenditures and Revenues in the U.S.A.

($ billions)

	Fiscal Year ending 30th June										Percentage Increase			
	1910	1915	1920	1925	1930	1935	1938	1940	1941	1942	1938 over 1915	1938 over 1930	1942 over 1915	1942 over 1938
A. *Expenditures* :														
National . .	0·9	1·0	6·0	3·5	3·8	7·3	7·5	10·3	13·3	32·6	650	100	3160	330
State . .	0·5	0·5	0·9	1·4	2·1	2·2	3·6	4·5	4·3	4·7	620	70	840	30
Local . .	2·0	2·2	3·3	5·6	7·2	5·5	5·9	6·0	5·9	6·0	170	– 20	190	...
Total .	3·4	3·7	10·2	10·5	13·1	15·0	17·0	20·8	23·5	43·3	360	30	1070	150
B. *Revenues* :														
National . .	0·6	0·6	5·7	3·1	3·6	3·7	5·3	4·9	7·1	11·6	783	47	1830	120
State . .	0·3	0·4	0·6	1·1	1·8	2·1	3·1	3·3	3·5	3·9	675	72	870	30
Local . .	1·7	1·9	2·4	3·7	4·9	4·8	4·7	4·7	4·9	5·0	147	– 4	160	10
Total .	2·6	2·9	8·7	7·9	10·3	10·6	13·1	12·9	15·5	20·5	352	28	610	60

Note.—Various statistics are available, especially for National and State figures ; but it is very difficult to get *comparable* figures for all three layers of government. For this reason we have taken Dr. Mabel Newcomer's figures for Expenditures and interpolated those for 1938 and extrapolated those for 1910, 1941 and 1942 (with the help of some official figures in the U.S. Statistical Abstract in the cases of 1910 and 1937, and that of figures given in the *Economist* for 1941 and 1942). Revenue figures are figures of *tax yields only* (excluding social insurance contributions) as published by the Tax Institute, University of Pennsylvania (figures for 1940, 1941 and 1942 extrapolated as for Expenditures). The percentage increases given are rounded figures, except in the cases of the percentage increases in Revenues in 1938 over 1915 and over 1930.

and they had to cut down expenditures accordingly. The State and National Governments had to come to their aid, and before long the responsibility for relief was largely taken over by the higher layers of Government, especially after the coming of the New Deal in 1933. The expenditures of the National Government doubled and trebled during the 1930s. Taxation was increased, but to a much lesser extent, partly because it would have been difficult to do more during the depression, partly for a more important reason. That reason is the New Deal policy of "pump-priming", that is attempting to stimulate recovery by investment in durable goods through continued large-scale deficit financing, which was not on a sufficient scale to restore activity to the spending levels of the 1920s. It has been suggested that amounts equal to at least three times the amounts in the Budget would have been required to restore activity. This is further illustrated by Table 21 in Part III. Then came the rearmament programme and the present war, which greatly reinforced the tendency of National Government expenditures to increase out of proportion either to revenues or to State and Local expenditures. Federal Government expenditures in 1937–38 were 7½ times what they had been in 1914–15 and double those of 1929. By 1941–42 they were over 4⅓ times as great as in 1937–38, and 32½ times as great as in 1914–15, while the Budget for 1942–43 provides for an estimated expenditure of $58·9 billions (of which $52·8 billions is for defence), or nearly a sixty-fold increase over 1914–15! In August 1943 aggregate expenditure of the year which began on 1st July 1943 was estimated at $106 billions. The increase in Federal tax revenues has been somewhat less spectacular since the depression; but even so, Federal tax revenues in 1937–38 were 883 per cent of the corresponding 1914–15 revenues and 147 per cent of those of 1929–30, while those of 1941–42 are over 19 times and those budgeted for 1942–43 ($17·6 billions, including non-tax revenue) over 25 times as great as those in 1914–15. The increase during both wars has been associated with a rise in the relative importance of the income tax, though this feature was much more marked during the last war than it has been so far during this.

The proportionate increase in State expenditures and revenues between 1914–15 and 1937–38 was of a magnitude similar to that of the corresponding changes in the finances of the National Government. The percentage increase in expenditures between 1929–30 and 1937–38 was naturally somewhat less than that in Federal expenditures (70 per cent as compared with 100 per cent for Federal expenditures), but still very considerable. For, as we have seen, State Governments have participated in the movement of taking over from Local Governments and developing further such functions as relief. The system of unemployment insurance introduced by the Social Security Act of 1935 is worked by Federal and State authorities together. The increases in State revenues and expenditures since the outbreak of war have naturally been much smaller than the corresponding changes in Federal figures.

As might be expected in these circumstances, the changes in Local Government revenues and expenditures have been far smaller than has been the case with the higher layers of Government. The figures never rose to much more than $2\frac{1}{2}$ times the level of 1914–15, and there was actually a slight decline, both in expenditures and revenues, after 1930–31. No very great changes in the Local totals seem to have been caused by the present war.

It is of interest to compare the statistics of Government expenditures and revenues in Table V with those of the national income (Table VI).

This table brings out even more clearly the features already noted, such as the gradual upward trend and the impact of wars and depressions. National Government figures vary much more than either State or Local ones, both in absolute terms and in terms of the national income. In the most recent years, when national income has increased rapidly as a result of rearmament and war expenditure, the ratio of Federal expenditures to the national income has naturally risen at a rapid rate, while the similar ratios relating to the more stable State and Local expenditures have fallen. As mentioned above, some of the changes due to the depression, the New Deal and the war are further illustrated by Table 21 in Part III.

Two more points should be noted in this connexion. In the first place, the burden of taxation and the weight of expenditure are rather heavier than in most of the other Federations studied in this Enquiry. In the year 1937–38, Government revenues in the United States from taxation alone amounted to the equivalent of 19 per cent and expenditures to 24 per cent of the national income.[1] This compares with 17 per cent in South Africa (total revenues only), 13 per cent in India (for both revenues and expenditures) and 25 per cent (for both revenues and expenditures) in Australia. Since the war the contrast has become even greater, especially in the field of expenditures, where the American percentage reached 27 in 1939–40 and approximately 41 in 1941–42. The Budget estimate for 1942–43 provides for an expenditure of something like 60 per cent of the national income (all Governments), though such figures should be used with caution as merely indicating the order of magnitude of the proportion. Mr. Stone, in his paper referred to above,[2] compares percentages calculated on

[1] See G. Findlay Shirras, *Science of Public Finance*, vol. i, 3rd ed., Macmillan & Co., London. Cf. *Facing the Tax Problem*, A Survey of Taxation in the United States and a Program for the Future, The Twentieth Century Fund, New York, 1927, chap. 5 and pp. 393-4.

[2] Richard Stone, *op. cit.* pp. 157 and 158. See also Table 20 in Part III of this Enquiry.

TABLE VI

Government Expenditures and Revenues expressed in Terms of the National Income [1]

	Fiscal Year ending 30th June									
	1910	1915	1920	1925	1930	1935	1938	1940	1941	1942
National Income [2] ($ billions)	34·3	41·0	63·0	80·5	81·8	53·6	69·4	75·9	89·5	106·0
Revenues : [3]										
(*a*) $ billions :										
National	0·6	0·6	5·7	3·1	3·6	3·7	5·3	4·9	7·1	11·6
State	0·3	0·4	0·6	1·1	1·8	2·1	3·1	3·3	3·5	3·9
Local	1·7	1·9	2·4	3·7	4·9	4·8	4·7	4·7	4·9	5·0
Total	2·6	2·9	8·7	7·9	10·3	10·6	13·1	12·9	15·5	20·5
(*b*) As per cent of the National Income :										
National	2	1	9	4	4	7	8	6	8	11
State	1	1	1	1	2	4	4	4	4	4
Local	5	5	4	5	6	9	7	6	5	5
Total	8	7	14	10	12	20	19	16	17	20
Expenditures : [3]										
(*a*) $ billions :										
National	0·9	1·0	6·0	3·5	3·8	7·3	7·5	10·3	13·3	32·6
State	0·5	0·5	0·9	1·4	2·1	2·2	3·6	4·5	4·3	4·7
Local	2·0	2·2	3·3	5·6	7·2	5·5	5·9	6·0	5·9	6·0
Total	3·4	3·7	10·2	10·5	13·1	15·0	17·0	20·8	23·5	43·3
(*b*) As per cent of the National Income :										
National	3	2	10	4	5	14	11	13	15	31
State	1	1	1	2	3	4	5	6	5	4
Local	6	5	5	7	9	10	8	8	7	6
Total	10	8	16	13	17	28	24	27	27	41

[1] See also Table 20, Part III.

[2] National Income : 1930–41 : net national income at factor cost, as given by R. Stone in the *Economic Journal*, June–Sept. 1942. As Mr. Stone's figures are for calendar years, we have taken as the national income for each fiscal year the average of the figures for the two calendar years concerned. For 1910–25 and for 1942 the net national income is estimated with the help of Mr. Stone's figures and those given in Lutz, *Public Finance*.

[3] See Table V.

a somewhat different basis with those given for the United Kingdom in the Budget White Paper.[1] His percentages for expenditures are : in the United States 20 per cent in 1938 and 1939, 21 per cent in 1940 and 26 per cent in 1941. In the United Kingdom, 19 per cent in 1938, 44 per cent in 1940 and 52 per cent in 1941. The following figures represent the proportion of the national income devoted to taxation : United States, 20 per cent in 1938 and 1939, 21 per cent in 1940 and 24 per cent in 1941 : United Kingdom, 25 per cent in 1938, 29 per cent in 1940 and 37 per cent in 1941. Estimates on another different basis appeared in the *Economist* of 24th January 1942 (p. 106). According to these, total Government revenues in the United States were 22·1 per cent of the national income in 1938–39, 21·6 per cent in 1940–41 and 24·1 per cent in 1941–42. The corresponding estimate based on the Budget figures for 1942–43 is about 33½ per cent. The figures given for total Government revenues in the United Kingdom are 27·8 per cent of the national income in 1938–39, 31·2 per cent in 1940–41 and 37·3 per cent in 1941–42. Total Government expenditures (and in brackets those on defence or war) expressed as a percentage of the national income are given as follows : United States—1938–39, 29·1 (1·8) ; 1940–41, 28·4 (7·6) ; 1941–42, 45·9 (27·4) ; 1942–43 (on the basis of the Budget estimate), 66·5 (51). United Kingdom—1938–1939, 30·9 (8·7) ; 1940–41, 58·8 (42·1) ; 1941–42, 67 (45-50). For the fiscal year 1st July 1943 to 30th June 1944, $38 millions out of the total expenditure of the Federal Government (or about 36 per cent) are provided for by taxation. The total national income is estimated to reach $150 millions in the same period. Great Britain's taxation to total expenditure is 52 per cent and Canada's 47 per cent.

The second point refers to the New Deal policy of promoting recovery by " pump-priming ", by public works and by planning industry in various directions. Clearly, the figures give no conclusive proof whether recovery, or the slow pace of recovery, was due to the New Deal or to the fact that it was not carried out rigorously. What they do indicate is that in spite of the huge increase, by peace-time standards, in Federal expenditures and deficits, neither reached a very large proportion of the national income of so great a country. The percentages of Government expenditure in the table are small compared with the tremendous fall in the national income. On the supposition that the New Deal was the correct policy for combating the depression, it could not have fully succeeded unless Government activities extended to a far greater sector of the national economy than was possible within the existing constitutional and economic framework. Pessimism among business men and the decline in private building construction more than counteracted the large expenditures by Govern-

[1] Cmd. 6347, sections B and E.

ments, and therefore unemployment remained at a high level.

We turn now to a feature in which the United States differs from the other Federations studied in this Enquiry — the relative importance of Local Government in public finance. Until the depression Local expenditures exceeded Federal ones — before the war of 1914–18 they were considerably larger than Federal and State expenditures combined. The contrast, even now, is larger than the tables suggest, because a substantial proportion of State expenditures — one-third in 1936–37 — consists of grants, mostly in aid of specified activities, to Local Governments. Nevertheless, as we have seen, H. C. Adams was mistaken when, in 1898, he expected Local expenditures to increase more rapidly than State and Federal expenditures.[1] As the modern community grows and becomes more complex, there is not only a steady tendency for Government functions to expand and to multiply, but also for the higher layers of Government to assume an even greater share of the responsibility. The case of relief during the great depression has already been mentioned. We shall return to this question when considering the details of public expenditure. Meanwhile, it is necessary to analyse briefly the tax structure of the United States.

Government Revenues

Revenues from taxation only have been given, because of the difficulty of obtaining comparable data of other revenues for all three layers of Government. Detailed statistics are very scarce, especially in the case of Local finance. Fairly complete data for a considerable proportion [2] of Local Government units are collected at ten-year intervals, but the last year for which they are available is 1932. Figures for cities of 100,000 or more inhabitants are available for other years. To the total tax collections of these cities in 1937–38, amounting to $1940 millions has, therefore, been added a rough estimate [3] of $2800 millions representing all other Local Authorities. It has been assumed that the general property tax accounted for 95 per cent of all Local tax revenues, and not only of those of cities with a population of 100,000 or more. This is probably not very far from the truth.[4] Local figures for " miscellaneous taxes " contain items which, if data were available, would be classified under other heads such as business or consumption taxes. The Local totals exclude grants and shared taxes.

[1] H. C. Adams, *Science of Finance*, New York, 1898, p. 45, quoted by Dr. Mabel Newcomer, *Taxation and Fiscal Policy*, New York, Columbia University Press, 1940.

[2] Totals (though not details) relating to the year 1931–32 are available for all Local Authorities.

[3] Made by the Tax Institute, University of Pennsylvania.

[4] Dr. Mabel Newcomer (*op. cit.* p. 28) gives the proportion of Local Government tax revenue derived from the property tax as 87 per cent in 1900 and 94 per cent in 1939.

State revenues from taxation given in Table VII represent total collections by the States, whether or not shared with Local Governments, plus the State share of locally collected taxes. Separate data for individual and corporate State income taxes are not available for all States, though in some cases they are available for a few years other than 1937–38. In the latter cases the figures have been utilised to estimate roughly the

TABLE VII

THE REVENUE SYSTEM OF THE U.S.A., ALL GOVERNMENTS, 1937–38

(Tax Yields only: $ millions)

	National	State	Local [1]	Total
GROUP I. *Progressive Taxes:*				
Personal (net) income taxes	1286	224	..	1,510
Estate and gift taxes	417	145	..	562
Total	1703	369	..	2,072
GROUP II. *Taxes on Property:* [2]				
Capital Stock	139	..	..	139
General Property	..	253	4435	4,688
Total	139	253	4435	4,827
GROUP III. *Taxes on Business:*				
Corporate (net) income taxes [3]	1124	178	..	1,302
Excess profits tax	37	..	..	37
Unjust enrichment tax [4]	6	..	..	6
Undistributed profits tax	176	..	..	176
Franchise taxes [5]	1	107	..	108
Insurance company taxes	..	85	..	85
Chain store taxes	..	7	..	7
Licence taxes	..	14	..	14
Stock transfer and document registry	42	27	..	69
Tonnage	2	..	..	2
Total	1388	418	..	1,806

[1] No detailed data for all Local Authorities are available except for 1931–32. Tax revenues of cities of 100,000 or more inhabitants amounted, in 1937–38, to $1940 millions, of which $1815 millions represented the property tax. Total tax revenues of other local governments were estimated at about $2800 millions by the Tax Institute, University of Pennsylvania. It has been assumed that the proportion of total local tax revenues derived from the property tax was the same as in the case of cities of 100,000 or more inhabitants. (See also text.) The totals do not include shared taxes, grants, service charges for current services and other minor items. Details for cities of 100,000 or more inhabitants in 1936–37 are given in Table 9 in Part III.

[2] Group II includes taxation of property of various kinds, not only real estate, as it has not been possible to separate out the latter. This fact should be kept in mind when comparisons are made with other chapters of this Enquiry.

[3] This excludes (*a*) taxes on gross receipts or turnover of businesses, which have been given under General Sales Taxes, and (*b*) the Unjust Enrichment Tax, shown separately.

[4] A tax levied on net income arising from Federal excise taxes shifted to the vendee but not paid, Federal excise taxes shifted by the vendee for which he was reimbursed by the vendor, and refunds and credits of Federal excise taxes shifted to others.

[5] Licences and fees for the privilege of conducting business, except (*a*) those based on net income (included under income taxes) and (*b*) those levied specifically on public utilities (included under utility taxes).

[*Table continued overleaf*

TABLE VII—(*continued*)

	National	State	Local[1]	Total
GROUP IV. *Mainly Consumption Taxes:*				
Customs	357	..	..	357
Excise and Similar Selective Taxes:				
Liquor	568	221	..	789
Soft drinks, etc.	1	3	..	4
Tobacco	568	56	..	624
Sugar	31	..	..	31
Oleomargarine, etc.	30	1	..	31
Severance [6]	..	62	..	62
Gasoline and lubricating oils . .	235	786	..	1,021
Motor vehicles	90	381	..	471
Racing	..	11	..	11
Utilities	75	117	..	192
Sub-total	1598	1638	..	3,236
General Sales and Similar Taxes:				
Sales and use, gross receipts and gross income	53	447	..	500
Admissions and dues [7]	27	6	..	33
Subtotal	80	453	..	533
Miscellaneous	12	10	305	327
Total	2047	2101	305	4,453
GRAND TOTAL (excluding pay-roll taxes) .	5277	3141	4740	13,158
Pay-roll taxes (social insurance contributions)	743	746	..	1,489
GRAND TOTAL (including pay-roll taxes) .	6020	3887	4740	14,647

Note.—In order to get comparable figures for all Governments, the table has had to be limited to revenues from taxation. This should be borne in mind when comparisons are made with other chapters of this Enquiry. See also Table I.

For grants, etc., from the Federal Government to the States, from the States to the Local Authorities and from the latter to the States, see Table 10 in Part III.

[6] Taxes levied on natural resources at the time of production, or severance from the earth.
[7] Includes various taxes, among them admissions and licences of various amusement places.

Sources.—Tax Yields, 1940; Statistical Abstract for the United States, 1940.

proportions of the State income tax collections representing individual and corporate taxation. In this way the known totals of income tax collections of States for which details are missing have been split up, and approximate total figures for individual and corporate income tax collections obtained.

The revenue system as a whole can hardly be said to be either very progressive or very regressive. There is a tendency for it to become more progressive and it is among the more progressive of the revenue systems studied.

Tax revenues are fairly evenly divided among three divisions: (1) Groups I and III, *i.e.* Progressive Taxes (taxes on individual income and death duties, etc.) and taxes on business (mainly on corporate income and undistributed profits). These two groups together comprise a little over 29 per cent of total tax revenues. Out of this, personal and corporate income taxes together represent 21 per cent of the total. Personal income taxes represent 11 per cent, estate and gift taxes over 4 per cent, making a total for Group I (Progressive Taxes) of 16 per cent. Corporate income taxes represent 10 per cent, the Federal tax on undistributed profits 1 per cent, and other business taxes 3 per cent, making a total for Group III (Taxes on Business) of 14 per cent. (2) Group II, Taxes on Property. This division comprises 36 per cent of total tax revenues, of which 35 is general property taxation and consists almost entirely — to nearly 95 per cent — of local property taxes. Hence, even in 1937–38, the general property tax was still by far the most important tax in the United States so far as yield is concerned. It should be remembered that this is a *general* property tax which is levied not merely on real estate but on other property as well. It has not been possible to eliminate from Group II taxes levied on property other than real property. Care should therefore be taken in any comparisons between these figures and those in other chapters of this Enquiry. (3) Group IV, mainly Consumption Taxes. This division comprises 34 per cent of total tax revenues. Of all taxes placed under this head, only about 4 per cent go to Local Governments, the remainder being divided evenly between the Federal and State Governments. The most important part of the 34 per cent of total tax revenues represented by this group is the excise taxes on gasoline, etc. — 8 per cent, largely State taxes. Other excise and similar taxes are those on liquor, 6 per cent; tobacco, 5 per cent (both mainly Federal); motor vehicles, 4 per cent (mainly State); other excise taxes, 2 per cent: total excise taxes, 25 per cent. Then there are customs (a Federal tax), 3 per cent; general sales [1] and similar taxes, 4 per cent; and miscellaneous taxes, 2 per cent. Finally, social insurance contributions ("pay-roll taxes"), which have been excluded from the main part of Table VIII, comprised 10 per cent of all taxes *including* pay-roll taxes (a figure comparable in magnitude with those quoted above would be 11).

We have said that the revenue system as a whole is neither very progressive nor very regressive. But there are great differences in this respect between different Governments. The Federal revenue system is much more progressive than the others; in fact, it goes very far in that

[1] See *Facing the Tax Problem*, The Twentieth Century Fund, New York, 1937, pp. 460-63.

TABLE VIII

THE REVENUE SYSTEM OF THE U.S.A., ALL GOVERNMENTS, 1937–38
(Tax Yields only : percentage distribution)

	Percentage Share of each Government in Total Revenues				Percentage Distribution of each Government's Revenue			
	National	State	Local	Total	National	State	Local	Total
GROUP I. *Progressive Taxes :*								
Personal (net) income	85	15	..	100	24	7	..	11
Estate and gift	74	26	..	100	8	5	..	5
Total	82	18	..	100	32	12	..	16
GROUP II. *Taxes on Property :*[1]								
Capital stock	100	..	..	100	3	..	..	1
General property	..	5	95	100	..	8	94	35
Total	3	5	92	100	3	8	94	36
GROUP III. *Taxes on Business:*								
Corporate (net) income	86	14	..	100	21	6	..	10
Excess profits	100	..	..	100	1	..	..	..
Unjust enrichment	100	..	..	100	..	..	..	..
Undistributed profits	100	..	..	100	3	..	..	1
Franchise	1	99	..	100	..	3	..	1
Insurance companies	..	100	..	100	..	3	..	1
Chain stores	..	100	..	100	..	..	..	..
Licence	..	100	..	100	..	..	..	..
Stock transfer and document registry	61	39	..	100	1	1	..	1
Tonnage	100	..	..	100	..	..	..	..
Total	77	23	..	100	26	13	..	14
GROUP IV. *Mainly Consumption Taxes :*								
Customs	100	..	..	100	7	..	..	3
Excise and Similar Selective Taxes :								
Liquor	72	28	..	100	11	7	..	6
Soft drinks, etc.	27	73	..	100	..	..	..	..
Tobacco	91	9	..	100	11	2	..	5
Sugar	100	..	..	100	1	..	..	..
Oleomargarine, etc.	97	3	..	100	1	..	..	..
Severance	..	100	..	100	..	2	..	1
Gasoline and lubricants	23	77	..	100	4	25	..	8
Motor vehicles	19	81	..	100	1	12	..	4
Racing	..	100	..	100	..	..	..	..
Utilities	39	61	..	100	1	4	..	1
Sub-total	49	51	..	100	30	52	..	25
General Sales and Similar Taxes :								
Sales and use, gross receipts and gross income	11	89	..	100	1	15	..	4
Admissions and dues	82	18	..	100	1	..	..	..
Sub-total	15	85	..	100	2	15	..	4
Miscellaneous	4	3	93	100	..	..	6	2
Total	46	47	7	100	39	67	6	34
GRAND TOTAL (*excluding pay-roll taxes*)	40	24	36	100	88[2]	81[2]	100[2]	90[2]
Pay-roll taxes	50	50	..	100	12[2]	19[2]	..	10[2]
GRAND TOTAL (*including pay-roll taxes*)	41	27	32	100	100	100	100	100

[1] Group II includes taxation of property of various kinds, not only real estate, as it has not been possible to separate out the latter. This fact should be kept in mind when comparisons are made with other chapters of this Enquiry.

[2] These are percentages of the grand total *including* pay-roll taxes ($6020 millions ; $3887 millions ; $4740 millions ; $14,647 millions).

direction compared with the other Federations studied in this Enquiry. Income and estate and gift taxes of all kinds accounted for 53 per cent of all Federal tax revenues; individual income tax for 24 per cent, estate and gift taxes for 8 per cent (a total of 32 per cent for Group I — Progressive Taxes). Corporate income taxes accounted for 21 per cent, the excess profits tax[1] for 1 per cent, the tax on undistributed profits for 3 per cent and those on stock, transfer and document registry for 1 per cent (a total of 26 per cent for Group III — Taxes on Business). The only other taxes yielding a significant share of total Federal tax revenues were customs (7 per cent), and among excise and similar selective taxes those on liquor (11 per cent), tobacco (11 per cent), and gasoline and lubricating oils (4 per cent). All excise and selective taxes combined produced 30 per cent and general sales and similar taxes 2 per cent of Federal tax receipts, making (together with customs) a total of 39 per cent for Group IV — Mainly Consumption Taxes. In Group II — Taxes on Property — there was only the tax on capital stock (3 per cent).

Finally, there are the pay-roll taxes, or social insurance contributions.[2] These have only been making a significant contribution to revenues since 1936–37, and on a full scale only since 1937–38. In that year they produced 12 per cent of all Federal taxes *including* pay-roll taxes (a figure comparable in magnitude with those given above for other taxes would be 14). According to Dr. Mabel Newcomer,[3] "the pay-roll tax is the youngest member of the tax family in this country, and promises to become the largest of all the State and Federal taxes. It may, in time, overtake the local property tax if the present movement for the relief of real estate continues."

State pay-roll taxes[4] on account of unemployment insurance, introduced together with the Federal ones, amounted to $19 millions in 1935–1936, $333 millions in 1936–37, $746 millions in 1937–38, $801 millions in 1938–39 and $851 millions in 1939–40. In 1937–38 they accounted for 19 per cent of all State taxes including pay-roll taxes, and a figure comparable in magnitude with those given for other State taxes above (per cent of total State taxes *excluding* pay-roll taxes) would be 24.

Originally the Federal Government relied for its revenue mainly on customs, and the State and Local Governments on poll and property taxes. We have seen that with the expanding cost of Government and the general change in economic conditions the Federal Government has come to rely mainly on progressive taxes such as those on income, and to

[1] Cf. *Facing the Tax Problem,* The Twentieth Century Fund, New York, 1937, pp. 491-4.
[2] *Ibid.* pp. 494-500.
[3] Mabel Newcomer, *op. cit.* pp. 25 and 26.
[4] Including those in the District of Columbia.

some extent on excise taxation. A similar change has taken place in State revenues. The poll tax has dwindled into insignificance. The property tax is still the mainstay of Local Government finances, and partly for this reason the States have, with the general rise in expenditures, tended to relinquish it more and more, and to develop new sources of revenue. The general property tax now accounts only for 8 per cent of State tax revenues. Among the new State taxes those on income (of which about 7 per cent is on individual incomes) and estate and gift (5 per cent, making a total of 12 per cent for Group I) are indicative of the trend towards more progressive taxation. Other taxes on business (excluding public utilities) account for 6 per cent (a total of 13 per cent for Group III). But generally speaking, various sales and excise taxes, motor vehicle licences, etc., are far and away the most important part of the State revenue system. Group IV (Mainly Consumption Taxes) comprises no less than 67 per cent of the total. Of this, the most important items are taxes on gasoline and lubricants (25 per cent), motor vehicles (12 per cent), sales and use, gross receipts and gross income (15 per cent) and liquor (7 per cent). Actually, these figures hide the very great differences between individual States, which are illustrated by Table 14 in Part III. There is some degree of a general pattern, the principal feature of which is the reliance on consumption taxes, especially those on gasoline and motor vehicles, which marks the State revenue system as regressive. Nevertheless, the variations between States are very striking. At one end of the scale is New York, with far greater revenues (and expenditures and debt) than any other State, and, for a subordinate unit of Government, with a very progressive revenue system indeed. Various taxes on net income comprise 39·7 per cent of the total, of which 27·8 per cent of the total, or 70 per cent of income tax revenue, represents taxation of personal income. Estate taxation comprises 7·7 per cent; the property and poll taxes are entirely absent, and even gasoline represents only 15 per cent of total tax revenue. On the other hand, thirteen of the forty-eight States levy no income tax at all; Nevada has no estate or similar taxes. A few States like Nevada still rely heavily on property taxation; others, such as Georgia and Florida, derive about half their tax revenue from gasoline. Texas, Oklahoma and Louisiana receive a considerable proportion of theirs from severance taxes[1] which do not exist at all in twenty-eight States. Again, the relative yield of individual taxes sometimes changes rapidly; for instance, general sales and similar taxes were of no importance before the depression; even in 1932–33 they comprised only about 1 per cent of

[1] Taxes levied upon natural resources at the time of production, or severance from the earth. Examples are taxes on mineral resources, oil and gas, timber, and sea products.

total State tax collections. In the next year they suddenly shot up to 9·2 per cent; in 1937–38 they represented 14·4 per cent, and two years later 15·2 per cent of all State tax receipts. Taxes on liquor, which comprised 11 per cent of Federal and 7 per cent of State tax revenues in 1937–38, were, of course, practically non-existent during the Prohibition era — one of the main reasons why Prohibition was abolished at the bottom of the depression.

Finally, there is Local taxation. This has been much more constant, as a whole, than either Federal or State taxation, both in amount and, especially, in composition. As of old, the property tax is by far the most important source of Local Government revenues, and hence, in view of the relative importance of Local Authority finance, has remained, at any rate until the present war, the largest single source of revenue in the United States.

It must, however, be remembered that nearly a third (32 per cent in 1936–37) of State expenditures consists of grants to Local Authorities,[1] and that a not inconsiderable proportion (over 8 per cent in 1936–37) of total State tax collections are actually shared taxes forming part of Local Government revenues. This reduces the preponderance of property taxation in Local Government finance. Another factor working in the same direction are the receipts from public utilities, as may be seen from Table 9 in Part III. (The effect shown there, relating as it does to the 94 largest cities only, is naturally greater than for Local Governments as a whole.)

The summary figures for Local Governments hide the great diversity between different types of Local Authority, of which there are at least half a dozen. Some more details, relating to 1931–32, have been given in Tables 6 to 9 in Part III. A summary of the total figures is given in Table IX overleaf.

The importance of the property tax for all types of Local Authorities is obvious. Only "cities, towns, villages and boroughs" derived a considerable revenue ($487 millions) from public service enterprises. The importance of the school districts should be noted. It is really greater than is apparent from the above figures, as there is much overlapping between school districts and cities, towns, etc. A characteristic of Local Government in the United States is the enormous number of Local Authorities, many of them small or overlapping. In order to sum up the situation we can hardly do better than to quote Dr. Newcomer on this subject:[2]

There are approximately 175,000 taxing jurisdictions in the United States. New York alone has 12,000. Many of these jurisdictions are too small to give efficient service. This is often true of the rural school district.

[1] See Table 10 in Part III. [2] Mabel Newcomer, *op. cit.* pp. 10 and 11.

TABLE IX

LOCAL GOVERNMENT REVENUES AND EXPENDITURES, SUMMARY FIGURES, 1931–32

($ millions)

Civil Division	Revenues			Expenditures				
	Total	Tax (including property tax)	Property Tax	Total	Operation and Maintenance		Interest	Outlays [4]
					General Government	Public Service Enterprises		
Counties . . .	1314	1021	877	1412	981	..[3]	119	311
Cities, towns, villages, boroughs . .	3374	2251	2057	3594	2070	283	424	817
School districts [1] .	1515	1121	1119	1537	1250	..[3]	109	178
Townships . .	248	208	195	253	187	2	17	47
Other civil divisions [2]	194	115	112	261	60	16	63	122
Total . .	6645	4716	4360	7057	4548	301	732	1475

[1] Exclusive of schools under administration of counties, cities, towns, villages and boroughs.
[2] Includes townships of Missouri, South Carolina and Washington.
[3] Less than $500,000.
[4] Capital expenditure out of revenue.

Moreover, there has been a tendency to transfer functions from the smaller to the larger jurisdictions as improved means of communication have become available. This rarely results in the abolition of the smaller unit of government. Too many political offices are involved. Consequently, the useless shell of government remains long after its activities have been abandoned.

The New York town is a case in point. Its chief activity is the maintenance of minor rural roads. The county could do this more efficiently with economy of road machinery and a better co-ordinated system. However, a town has at least twenty officials. For New York State as a whole, this means approximately 20,000 political jobs. The emoluments of office are for the most part pathetically small, but they may represent the only cash income of the recipient. This is a power to be reckoned with.

In Illinois where counties with and without townships are to be found side by side, the per capita cost of government is appreciably lower in the counties without townships. About half the states in the country manage well enough without this subdivision. Some local government is desirable; but one, or at most two, layers of local government in addition to Federal and State governments are probably adequate. Certainly the five layers of government existing in some New York villages (county, town, village, school district and special district) are hard to justify.

To sum up, the Local Government system of taxation has changed very little during the past decades. It still relies mostly on the taxation of property, not always organised in the most economical manner. It is definitely regressive, a feature common to Local Government revenue systems.

On the other hand, the Federal and State systems of taxation have undergone revolutionary changes during the present century. In 1900 the Federal Government drew nearly all its revenues from customs and from excise taxes on liquor and tobacco. In 1937–38 these had declined to 28 per cent of Federal tax revenues and a little less than 25 per cent of total Federal revenues. Apart from the tax on gasoline, the new taxes which are now the main Federal revenue-producers are almost entirely taxes on individual and corporation income and estate and gift taxes. Thus, the Federal tax system has changed from a very regressive to a considerably progressive one.

The change in the State revenue system is also very marked, but is of a slightly different character. At the beginning of the century about half the total State revenues were derived from the property tax. By 1937–38 it had declined to 8 per cent of State tax revenues and about 6 per cent of total State revenues. Since then it has been declining still further. The new taxes which have taken its place are of two kinds. First, there are the taxes on income and succession, which have tended to make the State revenue system more progressive. But much more important than these are the various excise and similar taxes which fall mainly on consumption — gasoline, motor vehicles, liquor, general sales. In addition, there are the pay-roll taxes, comparatively new revenues for both the Federal Government and the States.

Now let us turn to the question of intergovernmental and other non-tax revenues. For the reasons already stated, it has not been possible to show the figures for these receipts in Tables VII and VIII, as has been done in the other chapters of Part I of this Enquiry.

According to the figures given in the Statistical Abstract of the United States, 1940, and summarised in Table 1 of Part III (see especially footnote 4), tax collections as given in Table VII of this chapter represented about 84·6 per cent of the total Ordinary Receipts of the National Government during 1937–38. Of the remaining 15·4 per cent, 12·1 represents social insurance contributions, 0·4 Panama Canal tolls, etc., 0·5 seigniorage, 1·1 interest and other receipts from securities, and 1·3 miscellaneous receipts. Hence nearly the whole of the revenues of the National Government are derived from taxation and social insurance contributions. This contrasts, for instance, with India, where the Central Government derives about 39 per cent of its ordinary revenue from public utilities (especially railways) and from miscellaneous sources such as interest, contributions from Indian States, and defence receipts.[1]

Revenue figures for States in 1936–37 (the latest year for which fairly full details are available), as given in the Statistical Abstract of the

[1] See Chapter VII, Table VI, pp. 202 and 203.

United States, are summarised in Table 3 of Part III. According to this, 75·9 per cent of State revenues in 1936–37 were derived from taxation. Of the remaining 24·1 per cent, 14·3 were derived from grants (13·8 grants from the Federal Government and 0·5 from Local Authorities), 4·4 from charges for current services, 1·2 from contributions from public service enterprises, 0·1 from special assessments and special charges and 4·1 from all other sources. Thus, the proportion of revenue derived from taxation is appreciably lower than in the case of the Federal Government. A figure comparable with the 84·6 per cent given for Federal tax revenues would be even lower than 75·9 per cent. The definition of a tax used by the United States Department of Commerce, like that used in the Enquiry into the Burden of British Taxation,[1] is appreciably wider than that used by the Tax Institute, University of Pennsylvania, on whose compilations Tables VII and VIII are based.[2] The figure of total State tax collections given by the Institute for 1936–37 ($2932·2 millions less $260·0 millions of local shares of shared taxes, making a tax revenue of $2672·2 millions) represents 65·3 per cent of total State revenues as given in Table 3 of Part III ($4093·2 millions). This compares with 73 per cent in the case of the Indian Provincial Governments.

The latest detailed Local Government figures, as has already been mentioned, are those for 1932, since when the totals have declined as a result of the expansion of National and State Government functions consequent on the depression and the New Deal. In 1932 total Local revenue receipts, as shown in Table 6 of Part III, amounted to $6644·0 millions. Of this, taxes comprised $4715·9 millions, or 71·0 per cent.[3] Since then the proportion may have risen. Thus, for all Governments together, the percentage of revenue derived from taxation in 1937–38 must have been in the neighbourhood of 78 per cent.

Table 10 of Part III, as well as Tables 3 (especially footnote 2), 4 and 5, illustrate the system of intergovernmental grants as it exists in the United States. Most of the figures are for 1936–37, the last year for which we have been able to obtain fairly detailed data. The system has several striking characteristics, of which the following three should be noted.

First, there is a much closer link between the revenues and expenditures

[1] *The Burden of British Taxation*, by G. Findlay Shirras and L. Rostas. National Institute of Economic and Social Research, Economic and Social Studies II, Cambridge University Press, 1942; New York, Macmillan & Co., 1943.

[2] *E.g.* the percentages in Table VIII exclude social insurance contributions, though they include under State tax collections (instead of under Local ones) the Local shares of State-collected shared taxes.

[3] Of the remaining 29·0 per cent, grants from higher layers of Government amounted to 9·3 and earnings of public service enterprises to 7·8 per cent of total Local Government revenues. The smallness of the proportion due from public utilities is a point of contrast with that of other Federations studied in this Enquiry.

of State and Local Governments than there is between either and the National Government. This shows itself mainly in two ways: a considerable proportion of State and Local tax revenues consists of taxes shared between State and Local Governments, quite apart from grants; and nearly a third (32 per cent in 1936–37) of State expenditures consists of grants to Local Authorities, as mentioned above.

This last phenomenon is closely connected with the second point, namely, the fact that most grants, even those from the Federal to State Governments, are made for specified purposes. We find, therefore, not so much a system in which the higher layers of Government subsidise the lower, *e.g.* as a result of having more progressive and more expanding sources of revenue, but rather a system in which the higher layers of Government use the administrative machinery of the lower layers to translate the allocation of their financial resources into effective services. As can be seen from Tables 5 and 10 in Part III, State aid to Local Authorities is allocated almost exclusively to the secondary functions of Government, and here again, with the notable exception of highway maintenance, mostly to the social services. Of these, education is definitely the most important in this respect, with relief (usually classified as "charities") in the second place. In 1936–37, out of all State grants to Local Authorities (or "minor civil divisions"), 99·7 per cent represented secondary functions of Government, of which 77·5 per cent was spent on social services (education 57·4 per cent, relief 19·9 per cent and public health 0·2 per cent) and 19·0 per cent on developmental expenditure (of which 18·9 per cent went to highways).

Similar features characterise Federal grants to the States, and this leads to the third point, the way in which the States have become the agents carrying out the National Government's social security legislation. (The relevant parts of the tables are the footnote to and Section E of Table 10 in Part III.) In 1936–37 grants comprised, as we have already seen, 14·3 per cent of State revenues, 0·5 per cent being grants from minor civil divisions and 13·8 per cent grants from the Federal Government. Of the latter ($564·8 millions), 56 per cent was for highways, 27 per cent for relief, 4 per cent for education, 2 per cent for public health, 2 per cent for unemployment compensation administration and 8 per cent for other purposes. But the place of the States in the system created by the New Deal is only appreciated when we remember that in 1939–40 (the last year for which it has been possible to obtain detailed figures) Federal grants to States and Territories[1] for public assistance and for administration of the unemployment compensation laws and State employment services amounted to $345·0 millions. Of this total, $61·6 millions represents

[1] The share of the Territories in these figures is very small.

unemployment compensation and $283·4 millions public assistance ($231·1 millions for old age-pensioners, $46·1 millions for dependent children and $6·2 millions for the blind). In Table X below and in Table 2 of Part III the expenditure of the National Government under the Social Security Act in 1937–38 is given as $332 millions. Apart from administrative expenses, this figure represents entirely grants to States and refunds to States of taxes collected under the Act. Reference has already been made to the growing source of revenue which the States have found in the pay-roll taxes for unemployment insurance which they, together with the Federal Government, levy. It can thus be seen that as the higher layers of Government, and especially the National Government since the New Deal, have taken over more of the responsibility for the expanding social services, the financial and administrative division between the various Governments has become less clear-cut, and co-operation in specific fields has increased.

Government Expenditures

The discussion of the American system of intergovernmental grants for social services has led us from the field of revenue into that of expenditure. This is now to be discussed in more detail. A summary picture of the situation is conveyed by Tables X and XI.

Owing to the lack of complete and comparable data for all Governments, only National Government figures for 1937–38 [1] and State and Local figures for the latest available years could be given. This means 1936–37 figures for States (taken from the Statistical Abstract of the United States, 1940) [2] and 1931–32 figures for Local Governments.[3] In the latter case, the figures summarised in the Statistical Abstract and reproduced in Table 6 in Part III of this Enquiry are taken from *Financial Statistics of State and Local Governments, 1932* (United States Department of Commerce, Bureau of the Census).[4] That volume contains details for all States and all types of Local Government so far as they are available. Unfortunately there are large gaps in the details, though the total expenditures on operation and maintenance of general departments, on operation and maintenance of public service enterprises, on interest and on outlays,[5] and hence the grand totals, are complete. We have utilised such details as are given to estimate the distribution among the various heads of the total expenditure on operation and maintenance of general departments. As the figures refer to different years (one of them before the New Deal),

[1] See also Table 2 in Part III.
[2] See also Tables 4 and 5 in Part III.
[3] See also Tables 6 and 8 in Part III.
[4] See also Table IX on page 48 above.
[5] Expenditure of a capital nature out of revenue, *e.g.* for purchase and improvement of land, erection of new buildings, extension of water-supply systems, or purchases to increase the collection of libraries.

TABLE X

PUBLIC EXPENDITURES FROM REVENUE, ALL GOVERNMENTS [1]

($ millions)

	National, 1937–38	State, 1936–37	Local, 1931–32
1. *Primary Functions :*			
Legislation, administration and justice .	500	151	512
Protection to person and property .	..[2]	106	568
Correction	..	66	..[3]
Pensions	655	..[4]	..[4]
Debt services	926	122	731
Defence	975	..[5]	..
Total, Primary Functions . .	3056	445	1811
2. *Secondary Functions :*			
(1) *Social Services :*			
Education	..[2]	830	1965
Public health	..[2]	226 [6]	355 [7]
Charities,[8] hospitals and corrections .	..	612 [9]	373
Recovery and relief . . .	2238	..	..
Social Security Act . . .	332	..	..
Old-age reserve account . .	387	..	..
Railroad retirement . . .	145	..	..
Sub-total, Social Services . .	3102	1668	2693
(2) *Developmental :*			
Post Office	47 [10]	..	..
Public buildings	61	..[4]	..[4]
Public highways	152	458	598
Shipping Board	3	..	..
River and harbour work and flood Control	165	..	..
Panama Canal	11	..	..
Tennessee Valley Authority . .	42	..	..
Rural electrification administration .	11	..	..
Reclamation projects . . .	40	..	..
Civilian Conservation Corps . .	325	..	..
Development and conservation of natural resources . . .	..	78	12
Agriculture	473	..	..
Public works, etc.[11] . . .	134	..	..
Public service enterprises . .	..	3 [12]	302
Sub-total, Developmental . .	1464	539	912
(3) *Outlays* [13]	..	712	1476
(4) *Miscellaneous*	4	99	161
Total, Secondary Functions . .	4570	3018	5245
GRAND TOTAL	7626	3463	7056

[1] Owing to the impossibility of giving comparable detailed data for 1937–38 for all Governments, National expenditures from revenue for that year have been given as in Table 2 in Part III, State cost payments of general government (*i.e.* excluding public service enterprises) for 1936–37 as in Table 4 in Part III, and Local cost payments (including public service enterprises) for 1932 — the last year for which details are available — as given in Table 16 in Part III. It should be noted that the State figures include a substantial proportion of grants to Local Authorities, the 1932 counterpart of which has not been eliminated from the Local figures ; also that many of the Local items (as distinct from the grand total) have had to be estimated on the basis of figures available for some authorities in some of the States. For further details see the footnotes to the tables referred to.

[2] A few small items are included in "Legislation, administration and justice".

[3] Given under "Charities, hospitals and corrections".

[4] Not shown as a separate item in the official statistics.

[5] Militia and armouries included under "Protection to person and property".

[6] Includes hospitals and recreation.

[7] Excludes hospitals which are included in the following item.

[8] Mainly poor relief.

[9] Charities only.

[10] Mainly postal deficiency.

[11] Includes U.S. Housing Authority ($165,000).

[12] Contribution from general Government funds only.

[13] State and Local capital expenditure out of revenue.

TABLE XI

Public Expenditures from Revenue, All Governments [1]

(Percentage distribution)

	National, 1937–38	State, 1936–37	Local, 1931–32
1. *Primary Functions :*			
Legislation, administration and justice	6·6	4·4	7·2
Protection to person and property	.. [2]	3·1	8·1
Correction	..	1·9	.. [3]
Pensions	8·6	.. [4]	.. [4]
Debt services	12·0	3·4	10·4
Defence	12·8	.. [5]	..
Total, Primary Functions	40·0	12·8	25·7
2. *Secondary Functions :*			
(1) *Social Services :*			
Education	.. [2]	24·0	27·8
Public health	.. [2]	6·5 [6]	5·0 [7]
Charities,[8] hospitals and corrections	..	17·7 [9]	5·4
Recovery and relief	29·3	..	..
Social Security Act	4·4	..	..
Old-age reserve account	5·1	..	..
Railroad retirement	1·9	..	..
Sub-total, Social Services	40·7	48·2	38·2
(2) *Developmental :*			
Post Office	0·6 [10]	..	..
Public buildings	0·8	.. [4]	.. [4]
Public highways	2·0	13·2	8·5
Shipping Board	*	..	..
River and harbour work and flood control	2·2	..	..
Panama Canal	0·1	..	..
Tennessee Valley Authority	0·6	..	..
Rural electrification administration	0·1	..	..
Reclamation projects	0·5	..	..
Civilian Conservation Corps	4·3	..	..
Development and conservation of natural resources	..	2·3	0·2
Agriculture	6·2	..	..
Public works,[11]	1·8	..	..
Public service enterprises	..	0·1 [12]	4·3
Sub-total, Developmental	19·2	15·6	13 0
(3) *Outlays* [13]	..	20·6	20·9
(4) *Miscellaneous*	0·1	2·8	2·2
Total, Secondary Functions	60·0	87·2	74·3
Grand Total	100·0	100·0	100·0

Note.—For footnotes see Table X. * Less than 0·05 per cent.

it is, of course, impossible to give details for total Government expenditures (National, State and Local combined). Since 1931–32 Local expenditures have declined a little, both in absolute terms and relatively to National and State expenditures. In 1937–38 they must have amounted to about $5900 or $6000 millions. The figures include duplication due to inter-governmental grants. The most important of these are the State grants to Local Governments (32 per cent of total State expenditures), as we have already seen.

The true significance of the figures, especially of the percentages in Table XI, is grasped only when we compare them with the system existing before the New Deal. Tables 16 and 17 in Part III show public expenditures from revenue for all Governments in 1931–32, in millions of dollars (Table 16) and percentages (Table 17). There is a slight difference in arrangement between the two sets of tables. The State figures for "Charities,[1] hospitals and corrections" in Tables 16 and 17 contain all the items named. In Tables X and XI above "Correction" (State figures only) has been given as a separate item under Primary Functions, and State expenditure on hospitals included under "Public health". As it has not been possible to split up the 1932 figures in the same way, Local figures for "Charities, hospitals and corrections" in all four tables contain all these three items. The following other points should be borne in mind. First, State expenditure on public service enterprises in Tables X and XI above only represent contributions from general Government [2] funds, whereas the corresponding figures in Tables 16 and 17 as well as the Local figures throughout represent total expenditure from revenue on public service enterprises in 1931–32. Secondly, pensions are not given separately in the State and Local statistics. This means that the figure for "Pensions" in the totals columns of Tables 16 and 17 refer to National Government expenditure only, and that State and Local expenditures on primary functions as given in all four tables are somewhat below the true figures. Thirdly, the figures for Federal expenditures in Tables 16 and 17 include trust and related accounts totalling $326·5 millions. This is the reason for the discrepancy between total Federal expenditures in 1931–32 as given in Table 16 and as given in Table 12. The latter total is the one which is comparable with that given in Table X for 1937–38.

The picture presented by the 1932 figures is one of fairly clear-cut division between the functions of the National Government and those of State and Local Governments. Apart from protection to person and property and debt services [3] (neither a very large proportion of either

[1] Mainly poor relief.
[2] *I.e.* State finances other than those relating to public service enterprises.
[3] And pensions.

State or Local expenditures), the subordinate political units were concerned almost wholly with the secondary functions of Government, such as social services and development.

The Federal Government, on the other hand, was mainly concerned with the primary functions — general administration, legislation and justice ; pensions ; debt services ; defence. Federal expenditure on the social services was very small indeed ; of the 33 per cent of Federal expenditures devoted to development 4 per cent represented the postal deficiency,[1] 16 per cent the Reconstruction Finance Corporation [2] and 12 per cent agriculture,[3] *i.e.* even in 1931–32 the depression had caused an abnormal increase in the proportion of Federal expenditures devoted to secondary functions, thus foreshadowing the New Deal.

With the coming of the latter, the picture has changed completely, as can be seen by comparing Table XI above with Table 17 in Part III. In 1929 primary functions absorbed 87 per cent of Federal expenditures. In 1932, at the bottom of the depression and just before the New Deal, they absorbed 65 per cent ; and in 1938, 40 per cent. In the last-named year, the proportion of Federal expenditures devoted to the social services (40·7 per cent) exceeded that devoted to primary functions, or that devoted to the social services by either State or Local Governments in 1931–32. The relevant proportion of State expenditures was considerably higher in 1936–37 (48·2 per cent) than in 1931–32 (37 per cent). Nevertheless, Federal expenditures on the social services in 1937–38 were proportionately higher than the corresponding State expenditures in 1936–37, if grants to subordinate Governments be excluded from both totals. In the field of developmental expenditures, the National Government figures are proportionately the highest and the Local Government ones the lowest, whether or not grants are excluded. This is not very different from 1931–32. But it has to be borne in mind that Federal figures in that year were already affected considerably by the depression. In 1928–29 the proportion of Federal expenditures devoted to development was 10 per cent. If grants are eliminated it is safe to say that the pre-depression order was the reverse of that prevailing after the depression — viz. Local Governments devoted the highest proportion of their expenditures to development and the National Government the lowest. Nevertheless, the difference in this field in none of the years concerned was as striking as that in the field of social services.

It should also be borne in mind that the figures are profoundly affected

[1] A regular feature of U.S. finance, in striking contrast to other countries which derive a net revenue, sometimes substantial, from their Post Offices.

[2] A depression measure. The year in question was the first in which there was any expenditure under this head.

[3] Swollen to 3·4 times the 1929 level as a result of the depression.

by the way in which National Government expenditure on "Recovery and Relief" is classified. Much of it would normally be regarded as developmental. Nevertheless, we have classified the whole of this expenditure as social services, because their object is not so much to develop the country as to combat depression and unemployment.

Before the depression the National Government was mainly concerned with the primary functions of government, and the State and Local Governments with the secondary functions. After the depression and the New Deal had had their effect, the National Government still devoted a much higher proportion of expenditures to primary functions than did the other Governments, but the difference was very much less marked, and another difference had appeared. The latter only becomes apparent when we analyse into their components the otherwise proportionately similar expenditures on the social services. The expenditure of the States and Local Authorities on social services is devoted to education (by far the most important head), public health (including hospitals and recreation) and poor relief. The latter is the least important of these heads in the case of Local Government expenditures, but the proportion of State expenditures devoted to it rose considerably between 1931–32 and 1936–1937.[1] The new Federal expenditure on social services is devoted almost entirely to social security measures — the recovery and relief programmes to combat depression and unemployment — and unemployment, health and pension insurance schemes. This brings home once more the essential characteristic of the depression and post-depression era in respect of Government functions. These functions expanded, and expanded mainly in the field of those social services which have not been described. As they expanded, a proportionately larger share of such expenditure was taken over by the higher layers of Government, and especially by the Federal Government.

The distribution of expenditures as presented in Tables X and XI above may be summarised briefly as follows.

National Government expenditure on primary functions in 1937–38 was 40·0 per cent of the total. Of this 12·8 per cent was on defence, 12·0 per cent on debt services (other than debt retirement), 8·6 per cent on pensions and 6·6 per cent on legislation, administration and justice (including a few small items on protection to person and property, education, etc.). Secondary functions absorbed 60·0 per cent of National Government expenditures. Of this 40·7 per cent was on social services —

[1] State expenditure on "Charities, hospitals and corrections" combined was 11·0 per cent of total State expenditures in 1931–32 and 24·9 per cent in 1936–37. Of the latter figure, 17·7 per cent of total State expenditures represents charities (poor relief). 5·3 per cent hospitals and 1·9 per cent corrections.

29·3 per cent recovery and relief, 4·4 per cent expenditure under the Social Security Act, 5·1 per cent old-age reserve account and 1·9 railroad retirement; 19·2 per cent was on development — 6·2 per cent agriculture (including Department of Agriculture), 4·3 per cent Civilian Conservation Corps, 2·2 per cent river and harbour work and flood control, 2·0 per cent public highways,[1] 1·8 per cent public works,[2] 0·8 per cent public buildings, 0·6 per cent Post Office,[3] 0·6 per cent Tennessee Valley Authority, 0·5 per cent reclamation projects, and 0·2 per cent other heads. Miscellaneous expenditure (District of Columbia, United States share) absorbed 0·1 per cent of total Federal expenditures.[4]

In 1936–37 [5] primary functions absorbed 12·8 per cent of all State expenditures (18·7 per cent of direct expenditure and 0·3 per cent of grants).[6] Of this, 4·4 per cent of the total (6·4 per cent of direct expenditure) represents general administration, legislation and justice, 3·4 per cent (5·2 per cent of direct expenditure) represents debt services, 3·1 per cent (4·3 per cent of direct expenditure and 0·3 per cent of grants) represents protection to person and property, and 1·9 per cent (2·8 per cent of direct expenditure) correction. Secondary functions absorbed 87·2 per cent of total, 81·3 per cent of direct and 99·7 per cent of grant expenditures. Of this, 48·2, 34·4 and 77·5 per cent respectively went to social services — education 24·0 (8·2, 57·4) per cent,[7] public health 6·5 (9·5, 0·2) per cent, relief 17·7 (16·6, 19·9) per cent; 15·6 per cent of total State expenditure (13·9 per cent of direct expenditure and 19·0 per cent of grants) went to development — 13·2 (10·5, 18·9) per cent on highways, 2·3 (3·3, 0·1) per cent on development and conservation of natural resources, and 0·1 (0·1, 0·0) per cent on contributions to public service enterprises.[8] Outlays [9] absorbed 20·6 per cent of total and 30·2 per cent of direct expenditure, and miscellaneous items 2·8 per cent of total, 2·8 per cent of direct and 3·2 per cent of grant expenditures.

Grants represented 32 per cent of total expenditure, 1 per cent of that on primary functions (4 per cent of that on protection to person and

[1] $152 millions. Additional expenditure, amounting to $85 millions, is included under "Recovery and Relief", making a total Federal expenditure on highways of $237 millions. A large proportion of this consists of grants to States.

[2] Mostly loans and grants to States, municipalities, etc.

[3] Mostly postal deficiency.

[4] The larger figures for 1931–32 in Tables 16 and 17 in Part III are due to the inclusion of trust and related accounts.

[5] See also Table 5 in Part III.

[6] Note, however, that pensions have not been given as a separate item under primary functions, but included under the various departments with which they are connected.

[7] 77 per cent of State expenditure on education consists of grants to minor civil divisions such as school districts.

[8] But see p. 55 above on the significance of this last figure.

[9] See note 5 above.

property), and 37 per cent of that on secondary functions. 51 per cent of all expenditures on social services (education 77 per cent, public health 1 per cent, relief 36 per cent) took the form of grants. The figures for development are 39 per cent — 46 per cent for highways and 1 per cent for development and conservation of natural resources. No grants were made for outlays, and grants for general purposes represented 35 per cent of miscellaneous expenditure.

As in the case of revenues, these figures hide substantial differences between States, into which we cannot, unfortunately, enter into more detail here. An indication of the differences is given by Table 15 in Part III, which compares interest payments in 1936–37 with total expenditures of all States, individually and by regions.

Of Local Government expenditures in 1931–32, 25·7 per cent went to primary functions — debt services 10·4 per cent, protection to person and property 8·1 per cent, and legislation, administration and justice 7·2 per cent.[1] Secondary functions absorbed 74·3 per cent; 38·2 per cent represents social services — education 27·8 per cent, public health 5·0 per cent, and charities (relief),[2] hospitals and corrections 5·4 per cent; 13·0 per cent represents development — public highways [3] 8·5 per cent, public service enterprises 4·3 per cent and development and conservation of natural resources 0·2 per cent; 20·9 per cent of total Local Government expenditures in 1931–32 represents outlays and 2·2 per cent miscellaneous items.

As in the case of revenues, there is considerable diversity between different types of Local Authorities. This is illustrated to some extent by Table IX on p. 48 above, and by Tables 6 and 8 in Part III. To take an example, the estimated expenditure of Local Authorities on education,[4] as given in Table X above, was $1965 millions in 1931–32. The (known) total expenditure of school districts [5] under this head was $1243·6 millions, or 63 per cent of all Local expenditure on education and 99·5 per cent of the total expenditure of school districts. Expenditure on public service enterprises, interest and outlays was proportionately higher for cities, towns, villages and boroughs than for other Local units. Especially is this true of expenditure on public service enterprises — 7·9 per cent as compared with 0·03 per cent in the case of counties, 0·9 per cent in that of

[1] But see p. 58, note 6 above on pensions. Moreover, expenditure on correction is included in " Charities, hospitals and corrections " given under Social Services.

[2] This item has probably declined in importance since 1931–32.

[3] Duplication is unusually large in the case of figures for highways, as these figure are an important item among the grants both from the Federal Government to the States and from the latter to Local Authorities.

[4] Schools and libraries.

[5] Exclusive of schools under the administration of counties, cities, towns, villages and boroughs.

other Local Authorities and 4·3 per cent for all Local Governments together. County expenditure on highways (16·7 per cent of total county expenditures) was nearly twice as high proportionately as that of all Local Authorities taken together (estimated at 8·5 per cent). For as we have seen, there is a multiplicity of Local Governments and a division of function between them in the United States which contrasts with the consolidation that has characterised the British system since the Local Government Acts of 1888 and 1889. Details of revenues and expenditures of cities of 100,000 or more inhabitants in 1936–37 are given in Table 9 of Part III.

Tables 11 and 12 in Part III give total revenues and expenditures of all Governments, by regions, for 1931–32 and 1936–37, as well as the percentage increases between the two years in question. Local figures for the second year are not available, and only rough estimates of the grand totals have been given. The figures show throughout a proportionately greater increase in revenues than in expenditures,[1] largely owing to the abnormal deficit position in the depression year 1931–32. In the case of State and Local Governments this applies also to the figures given in Table V above (cf. the second percentage column). In the case of the National Government it seems at first sight to be the other way round. The puzzle is solved if we remember that in Table V 1937–38 is compared with 1929–30, and in Tables 11 and 12 in Part III 1936–37 is compared with 1931–32 — a year in which the Federal Government already had a considerable deficit ($2·5 billions). The increase in revenues was most marked in the case of the National Government and, among States, in that of the North-eastern and Middle States and of California (in ascending order). This means that the predominance of the National Government and of the regions concerned has been further increased. The matter is less simple in the case of expenditures. The National Government leads again, and California among State regions, with the Middle States second. But the increase in the North-eastern States is the second lowest, the order being California, Middle, Pacific North-west, South-west, Mountain and Great Plains, North-east and South-east. There was a decline in Local Government expenditures.

IV. The Public Debt

The composition of and the changes in the public debt of the United States in recent years are shown in Tables XII and XIII below and in Tables 13 and 21 in Part III.

[1] Local expenditures actually decreased, while the change, probably an increase, in revenues was slight.

TABLE XII

THE PUBLIC DEBT OF THE UNITED STATES

($ millions)

	Debt of the National Government on 30th June—		
	1932	1938	1940
1. *Interest-bearing Debt:*			
Bonds [1]	14,250	23,602	29,920
Notes [1]	1,260	9,147	6,383
Certificates of indebtedness [1]	2,726	..	..
Treasury bills	616	1,154	1,302
Special issues to Government agencies and trust funds	309	2,676 [2]	4,775
Total interest-bearing debt	19,161	36,579	42,380
2. *Non-interest-bearing Debt:*			
Matured debt	60	141	205
Other non-interest-bearing debt [3]	266	447	386
Total non-interest-bearing debt	326	588	591
TOTAL GROSS DEBT [3, 4]	19,487	37,167	42,971
Less net balance held by the Treasurer of the United States	261	1,313	1,589
TOTAL NET DEBT [4]	19,226	35,854	41,382

[1] Excludes special issues to Government agencies and trust funds.
[2] Bonds $500·2 millions, and notes $2175·5 millions.
[3] After deducting gold reserve against United States notes.
[4] Includes matured debt on which interest has ceased.

Source.—Statistical Abstract of the United States, 1940.

The debt of the National Government reflects very closely in its changes the political and economic events of recent decades. The gross debt amounted to $1225 millions on 30th June 1916. Three years later the war had swollen it to $25,842 millions. Then began a period of steady reduction, the lowest level being reached in 1930 with a gross debt, on 30th June, of $16,185 millions. Then came the depression and the New Deal, and with them a new era of deficit-financing. By 1932 the gross debt had risen to $19,487 millions. The New Deal came, and by 1934 the debt amounted to $27,053 millions. Four years later, by 1938, another $10 millions had been added, making a total of $37,167 millions. Since then it has risen steadily as a result of rearmament and war. The

TABLE XIII

DEBT OF ALL GOVERNMENTS, 1937

A. *Federal, State and Local Debt*

	$ millions			
	Federal	State	Local	Total
Funded or fixed debt . .	21,824·4	3023·1 [1]	..[2]	..
Floating or current debt .	14,602·7 [3]	252·6 [1]	..[2]	..
Total Gross Debt . .	36,427·1 [3]	3275·7 [1]	..[2]	..
Less (i) net balance held by the Treasurer of the U.S.A. . .	1,960·4	..	..	..
(ii) State sinking fund assets . .	..	598·5 [1]	..	..
Total State net debt in respect of general Government .	..	2677·2	..	..
Plus State debt in respect of public service enterprises .	..	93·2	..	..
TOTAL NET DEBT . .	34,466·7	2770·4	14,824·1 [4]	52,061·2
Percentage distribution .	66·2	5·3	28·5	100·0

B. *Debt of Cities of 100,000 or More Inhabitants* [5]

	Net Debt [6]		Gross Debt	
	$ millions	Per cent	$ millions	Per cent
General Government . .	3904	61·0	5359	65·7
Public service enterprises .	2499	39·0	2797	34·3
TOTAL . . .	6403	100·0	8156	100·0

[1] General Government only, *i.e.* excluding public service enterprises.
[2] Not available.
[3] After deducting gold reserve against U.S. notes.
[4] Made up as follows: Municipal debt, $8934·8 millions; all other local debt, $5889·2 millions; total, $14,824·0 millions.
[5] The figures cover the Government of the city corporation proper and independent school districts, sanitary districts and other independent districts practically co-extensive with cities; they also include a percentage of the financial statistics of the county Governments in which there are cities having over 300,000 population.
[6] Net debt is funded or fixed debt less assets in general sinking funds. *Note the difference in definition as compared with "A" above.*

figures are: 1940, $42,971 millions; 1941, $48,979 millions; 1943 (Budget estimate), $110,421 millions.

Side by side with the increase in the amount of debt there have been changes in its composition. In 1932 three-quarters of it consisted of funded debt, or bonds. The following years, the first of the New Deal, saw an enormous increase in the floating debt, especially of notes (which increased from $1260 millions on 30th June 1932 to $11,381 millions on 30th June 1936). The first " pump-priming " deficits were financed very largely from this source. By 1935 the floating debt represented half the total gross debt. Then the tide began to turn. The floating debt was reduced (notes alone fell to $6203 millions on 31st December 1939), and bonds rose from $14,936 millions on 30th June 1935 to $23,602 millions in 1938 and $29,920 millions in 1940. All the above figures for bonds and notes exclude special issues to Government agencies and trust funds. The special issues were fairly stable and not large in amount until 31st December 1936, when they amounted to $632 millions. But after that date they increased quickly — to $1558 millions on 30th June 1937, $2676 millions in 1938 and $4775 millions in 1940. On 30th June 1938 they consisted of $500·2 millions of bonds and $2175·5 millions of notes. The increase in this item thus offset to some extent the decline in the market issues of notes and Treasury bills. Nevertheless, it remains true to say that whereas in the early years of the New Deal the increase in the public debt was largely an increase in the floating debt, in the later years it was mainly an increase in the funded debt.

We have seen how, in the past decade, Federal revenues and expenditures gradually overtook State and Local ones. This is true even more of public debt. During the decade preceding the depression, while the Federal debt was being reduced, State and Local debts both approximately doubled. In 1922 Federal net debt was nearly three-quarters of total governmental net debt. In 1932, when Federal debt, after reaching its lowest point in 1930, was already on the increase, the proportion had fallen to about one-half. In 1937, as Table XIII shows, it was again 66·2 per cent. State debt had risen comparatively little in the five-year interval, and Local debt had fallen more. Since then the preponderance of Federal debt has been increasing steadily, and the war promises to make it eclipse State and Local debt altogether.

Since the increase in the debt of the United States has been very largely due to deficit-financing caused by war, depression and " pump-priming ", most of it is " dead-weight " debt. This contrasts with other Federations studied in this Enquiry such as South Africa and, especially, India. In these countries a much greater proportion of the public debt, especially of that of the Central Governments, is directly productive in the sense of producing its own interest. Of course, it may be said that the productivity of the debt incurred by the Roosevelt administration before the war is to be sought in the recovery it was intended to promote rather than in interest received by the Government from investments. Nevertheless there can be no doubt that this debt will continue to be a much heavier charge on the taxpayer for decades to come than, say, is the case in India or in South Africa. The contrast is less in the case of Local Government debt. But even in the case of cities of 100,000 or more inhabitants debt of public service enterprises constituted, in 1937, only 34·3 per cent of the gross debt and 39·0 per cent of the net debt.[1]

Summary figures for debt, like those for revenues and expenditures, hide the great differences between different units of Government. There are differences both in indebtedness and in credit standing. In this connexion it will be remembered that some of the States, such as Mississippi, Florida and Alabama, have repudiated or defaulted on their debts in the past. Table 15 in Part III compares interest charges and total expenditures of State Governments in 1936-37, individually and by regions. Two features are especially striking. First, the regions whose debt charges are proportionately above the average are the South-east (very marked), the North-east and (to a lesser extent) California. Secondly, the differences between individual States, even within the same region, are far greater than those between regions. The average expenditure devoted to debt charges for all States and regions is 3·5 per cent of total expenditures. The lowest for any region is 0·9 per cent (South-west), and the highest 6·1 per cent (South-east). The lowest for any State is 0·0 per cent (Florida) and the highest 18·8 per cent (Arkansas), both in the same region (South-east). Even New York (5·4 per cent) and New Jersey (7·1 per cent), though above the average, are far below Arkansas (18·8 per cent), South Dakota (10·6 per cent) and Tennessee (10·2 per cent), while Pennsylvania (2·0 per cent) is definitely below the average.

Indirect Debt

In addition to the direct public debt of the Federal Government, the last decade has seen a new development, the guaranteed security. Many of the Federal corporations created since 1932 have been financed by the issue of their own securities, guaranteed by the Government and constituting contingent liabilities of the United States. The process began with the creation of the Reconstruction Finance Corporation in 1932. As a result of the New Deal it grew enormously between 1934 and 1941 (see Table XIV). On 30th June of the latter year, the outstanding

[1] Net debt is here defined as funded or fixed debt less sinking fund assets. In the figures quoted above it means total gross debt less net balance held by the Treasurer of the U.S.A. in the case of Federal debt, and gross debt less sinking fund assets in the cases of State and Local debts.

guaranteed liabilities of the United States totalled $6362 millions. But in October of the same year the Treasury announced that no more guaranteed securities would be issued, that those then outstanding would be converted into direct obligations of the United States, and that the Federal corporations would in future be financed directly by the Treasury. This chapter in the history of the United States debt may therefore be considered closed.[1]

TABLE XIV

CONTINGENT LIABILITIES OF THE UNITED STATES, 1934–41 [1]

($ Millions)

30th June	Home Owners' Loan Corporation	Federal Farm Mortgage Corporation	Reconstruction Finance Corporation	Commodity Credit Corporation	United States Housing Authority	Federal Housing Administration	Total
1934	747	313	236	..	..	..	1296
1935	2767	1233	251	..	..	..	4251
1936	3071	1431	253	..	..	..	4755
1937	3007	1431	257	..	..	..[2]	4695
1938	2969	1419	299	206	..	1	4894
1939	2935	1388	822	206	115	3	5469
1940	2635	1269	1097	407	114	8	5530
1941	2410	1271	1742	696	226	17	6362

[1] The figures include interest, but do not include various guaranteed obligations (*e.g.* obligations of the Tennessee Valley Authority) purchased by the Treasury and reflected in the direct public debt.
[2] Less than $500,000.

Source.—H. Walter Hargreaves, "The Guaranteed Security in Federal Finance", *Journal of Political Economy*, Aug. 1942, p. 569. (Mr. Hargreaves' figures are based on the United States Treasury's Statements of the Public Debt.)

V. CONCLUSION

It is difficult to sum up briefly the main results of this study of American finance. The first outstanding feature is the great increase in public expenditures which was marked even before the war. Higher standards for old services and large-scale expenditures on new activities are noticeable in all layers of Government, but especially in the Federal layer in recent years. Secondly, the great depression of 1929–33 was accompanied by large expenditure on relief which has made the New Deal a landmark in American public finance. Deficit budgeting became the order of the day. Recovery, as bitter experience has taught, depends on increasing purchasing power, and the merit of deficit budgeting as a remedy for depression depended on whether Government borrowing increases purchasing power and whether this increase leads to greater spending. These

[1] Cf. H. Walter Hargreaves, "The Guaranteed Security in Federal Finance", *Journal of Political Economy*, Aug. 1942.

two features of American public finance have resulted in a change in tax structures. There is considerable competition for revenues among competing authorities, mainly between Federal and State and between State and Local Authorities. The multiplicity of taxing authorities is noteworthy. They number about 175,000 and some authorities are very small, leading to the levying of unequal taxes and also to high costs of collection. The number of taxes is also large. What constitutes a separate tax depends on difference in base and rate. It would not be wrong to state that the Federal tax system runs to over 100 taxes, and in New York State there are also 38 State taxes and seven Local taxes, or a total of 145 in all.[1] Ten of these taxes produce over nine-tenths of the total revenue. The three main taxes are the property tax, the personal and corporation income taxes, and the comparatively recent pay-roll tax. In the last century the three taxes which dominated all others were customs duties, a federal source of revenue, the property tax and the poll tax a so-called democratic tax which, like a club subscription, was the same for everyone contributing to the support of Government. Customs duties were a Federal source of revenue whereas property taxes were for State and Local purposes. The Federal Government under the Constitution could levy a property tax only in proportion to the population of the various States, since it has always been regarded as a direct tax. It was levied only on rare occasions by the Federal Government, and then, too, only with indifferent success. In the present century the property tax has become in the main a local tax. In 1900 more than half of the State revenues came from the property tax, but to-day only one-twentieth does. In place of this, in order of time, the following taxes have taken their place in State taxation : the motor vehicle licence tax, the stock transfer tax, the personal income tax (a quarter of the States of the Union levy no personal income tax), the gasoline tax, the general sales tax, the pay-roll tax and the excess profits tax. Local Authorities are dependent on property taxation and their powers are delegated to them by the States. They are handicapped in three ways ; by imposition of tax limits and the extension of tax exemptions on the part of the States, and by the fact that, being small authorities, they are limited from taxing income or corporations. This third is perhaps the greatest of the restrictions.[2] On the whole, however, the limitations of Local Authorities in the field of taxation are economic, due to the restricted area of the authority and the impossibility of taxing, for example, corporations doing business elsewhere in the State. Local tax powers are delegated powers, and in recent years State Governments have been turning over to Local Governments the

[1] Cf. Mabel Newcomer, *Taxation and Fiscal Policy*, Columbia University Press, New York, 1940, p. 17.

[2] *Op. cit.*, p. 48.

property tax as an exclusively local tax. State taxes are normally added to Local taxes and collected by Local officials. With the improvement in communication the number of businesses doing interstate business is increasing, and this makes the jurisdiction of State Governments in taxation more difficult, the advantage in tax administration being with the wide jurisdiction. Overlapping taxes are numerous, *e.g.* income taxes, corporation taxes and the taxation of liquor, tobacco and gasoline, and the cost of collection of separate levies is greater than for a single levy. Sometimes one layer of Government takes little or no account of the taxation imposed by another layer, so that the double burden becomes especially heavy. It is here that systematic integration of taxes is desirable, and, as shown in Part II, conflicts arise and the obstacles to be overcome are not at all simple. The Federal Government depends mainly on the taxation of personal incomes and corporations, pay-roll taxes, customs and the taxation of drink and tobacco. Thus, in 1940 Federal taxes amounted to $5698 millions, of which *net* income taxes were personal income taxes $982 millions and corporation taxes $112 millions, pay-roll taxes $838 millions, tobacco $609 millions, alcohol $624 millions, customs $350 millions and estate duties $331 millions. Pay-roll taxes were introduced by the 1935 Social Security Act and are earmarked for old-age benefits and unemployment compensation. The Federal old-age benefit is 2 per cent of the pay-roll (1 per cent from the employer and 1 per cent from the wage-earner). The unemployment benefit tax is a combined Federal and State levy of 3 per cent on the pay-roll. In some States it is higher. The productivity of the tax is very great, but the increase in old-age benefits without increasing the rate of contribution has been such that the reserve will not increase to the extent hitherto regarded as certain.

It is of interest to compare the changes in tax collections in recent years, expressed as percentages of the whole, exclusive of pay-roll taxes.

	Tax Collections (exclusive of Pay-roll Taxes)			
	1929	1933	1937	1940
Federal	37	23	39	38
State	17	21	23	25
Cities :				
(*a*) 100,000 and over (Local Governments)	18	21	16	15
(*b*) 30,000–100,000 (Local Governments)	3	35	22	22
(*c*) Other Local Governments (Local Governments)	25	..	..	..
Local Governments (total)	46			
	100	100	100	100

If State and Local taxes as well as Federal taxes are included, taxation is now (1943) of the order of one-third of the national income excluding social security charges, as compared with 12 per cent at the end of the war of 1914–18 and 20 per cent in the late 1930s.

Another characteristic of American finance is its resiliency to the exceptional conditions of war. A few statistics in this connexion bring this out clearly. In 1940–41 total Federal expenditure was $12·7 billions, of which $6·3 was on national defence ; in 1941–42 this increased to $30·6 and $24 billions respectively ; in 1942–43 to $82 and $77 billions respectively, a remarkable increase especially since Pearl Harbour, 7th December 1941. In the year ending 30th June 1944 the Budget for war alone is anticipated to exceed $100 billions (£25,000 millions), which, according to the President, is a maximum programme for waging war. In the last war, even in the peak year 1918–19, war costs were only one-sixth of the national income, but in 1941–42 they were not far short of one-half and in 1942–43 about two-thirds, and in the current year it is of the order of three-fourths. Such prodigious expenditures meant a great leap-up in production. The index of production of the Federal Reserve Board was 77 per cent above the level of September 1939, and the index of munitions production published by the War Production Board was 382 in October 1942 (November 1941 = 100). Durable goods production was up, as compared with September 1939, 150 per cent. Agricultural production reached in 1942 a new high level, $15·6 billions, or one billion dollars above that of the previous record year, 1919. In the field of taxation there have also been surprises. In 1940–41 Federal taxation was $8·3 billions, or excluding the pay-roll tax $7·6 billions ; in 1941–42 $12·8 billions, and excluding the pay-roll tax $11·9 billions ; in 1942–43 $17·8 and $16·5 billions respectively ; and in the current year (1943–44) taxation will be seven times the level of 1939–40 taxation, the taxation revenue being estimated at $35 billions. New taxation was $7 billions in 1942–43 and $16 billions in 1943–44. But this is not the whole story. Although these large sums are being raised by taxation, there are large war expenditures financed by loans. The gross debt on 30th June was, in billions of dollars, as follows : 1919, 25; 1930, 16 (the lowest since the 1914–18 war); 1935, 29; 1936, 34; 1937, 36 ; 1938, 37 ; 1939, 40 ; 1940, 43 ; 1941, 49 ; and 1942, 71. In his message to Congress on 11th January 1943 the President stated that the Public Debt will total $135 billions in the year ended 30th June 1943, and by June 1944, $210 billions under existing revenue legislation. These are astronomical figures and reflect national effort of a magnitude without precedent in world history. Nevertheless, in spite of the concentration of the war, " there will be ", as the President stated, " sufficient volume in our bill of fare, but less variety. That may hurt our taste but not our health." Although borrowing has great psychological advantages over taxation because it seems to postpone the final reckoning of sacrifices, raises funds more quickly than taxes and makes available to Government large amounts of funds borrowed directly from the banks, yet, to avoid the inflationary and other abuses of borrowing, taxation has to be kept at the highest possible level. In this respect there has been a great advance in the financing of the present war as compared with that of the last world war. The taxes to loans ratio in 1942–43 was less than one-third as compared with one-half in Great Britain and over one-half in Canada. In the last war the United States and Great Britain met only 25 per cent of total central expenditures by taxation, France 13 per cent and Germany 10 per cent. One great difference, however, between the war burden on the United States and on Great Britain is that the United States has been able to expand output greatly without curtailing consumption below the pre-war level and without cutting the pre-war additions to capital by more than one-half. In Great Britain it was not possible to extend output in anything like to the same degree for several reasons, such as the smaller volume of unemployment, the higher proportion of man-power in the fighting services, the blockade and the air-raids. Consequently in Great Britain consumption had to be curtailed to a greater degree, and in place of a cut in the pre-war rate of investment a heavy inroad on accumulated capital had to take place. In this respect the United States has indeed been fortunate in being able to expand her war effort with so little effect on her future store of capital or on her present standard of living.

CHAPTER IV

THE PUBLIC FINANCE AND NATIONAL ECONOMY OF CANADA[1]

I. Canada's Normal National Economy

To understand Canada's financial problems we have to look to the salient features of the Canadian national economy during the three-quarters of a century that have elapsed between the passing of the British North America Act, 1867, and the present war. The most striking fact is that the Canadian national economy before the war was a highly vulnerable one. Canada, the oldest Federation of the British Commonwealth, is linked up in economic solidarity with the outside world, especially with Great Britain and the United States. In international trade she plays an extremely important part. With a population of only over 11 millions she was sixth among the countries of chief importance in foreign trade; first in the tourist trade; fourth in the volume of shipping leaving a country's ports; and fourth in railway mileage. In 1929 her national income per head was greater than that of any other country except the United States, while in 1937 owing to drought Canada was sixth or seventh. She exported wheat and other agricultural products, many forest products and minerals such as gold, silver, copper, nickel, lead and zinc. Indeed her surplus was very great. She produced five times more wheat than she consumed, ten times more newsprint and twenty times more non-ferrous metals. Her surplus of wheat was 40 per cent of the world's exports of wheat, and her surplus of non-ferrous metals is also 40 per cent of the world's exports. Her export of newsprint was two-thirds of the world's exports. Canada, therefore, was a marginal source of supply for many commodities, her own production being great and her consumption small. The result was that any reduction in the world demand profoundly affected the prices which she got and also her ability to pay interest on the large amount of capital invested. This is all to the good on a rising market because she controlled the marginal supply, but on a falling market it was quite the reverse. Her imports included such essential raw materials as coal, oil, rubber, tin, manufactured iron and steel, chemicals and

[1] I am indebted to the Report of the Royal Commission on Dominion-Provincial Relations — the Rowell-Sirois Report (Ottawa Government Printer, 1940) — and to the Dominion Statistician who has supplied the latest available data. With the exception of Table II on p. 77, the tables in this chapter are based mainly on the data of Canadian public finance made by the Royal Commission and do not correspond with the Public Accounts of the Dominion and the Provinces.

textiles. Indeed Canada was one of the largest importers of coal, oil and steel products just as she was one of the largest exporters of wheat, newsprint and non-ferrous metals. Just before the present war Canada's trade with the United Kingdom was 30 per cent of her total trade, whereas the United Kingdom's trade with Canada was only 5 per cent of her total trade. Canada's trade with the United States was 50 per cent of Canada's total trade, while the United States' trade with Canada was only 15 per cent of the total United States' trade. It will be seen, therefore, that Canada's position in her financial relations with the outside world in ordinary times was vulnerable; she was not and could not always be in a strong position when it came to bargaining. Fluctuations in gross income and in net income were large at both extremes of the trade cycle. The financial relations of the Dominion, Provinces and Local Authorities were also subject to variations. Moreover, the Canadian national economy is made up of a number of very different areas, such as the Maritimes, Quebec, Ontario, the Prairies and British Columbia, and in many instances economic interests do not coincide with regional boundaries. There are sections of Quebec which are more closely allied to the Saskatchewan than to the neighbouring regional economies. In the Prairie Province of Manitoba there are areas evolving an economy of the Ontario type. In short, the Canadian national economy in ordinary times is made up of a number of very different areas, and the income of those areas varies enormously from year to year and from area to area. This is of particular importance in public finance. Take, for example, that important sector of Canadian economy, the wheat industry. Here we have large areas dependent on the profitable production of a single product; and where distress is due, as in the great depression, to a catastrophic fall in the price of wheat and to inflated costs and similar factors, such as a series of crop failures, then large-scale intervention is necessary to prevent a complete collapse of the industry. In such cases the cost was beyond the taxable capacity of Provincial and Municipal Governments. The Dominion, therefore, apart from the Provincial Governments had to assist with emergency grants.

A large part of the surplus of the national economy is concentrated in a few specially favoured areas. Provincial Governments with their important functions conferred by the British North America Act have large powers such as the control of the public domain, responsibility for roads and other public works, the major social services and direct taxation. In recent years there have been profound changes in social policy which are likely to be permanent. When it is remembered that the total income of the Prairies fell almost by one-half and income from agriculture by almost four-fifths taking the average of the years 1930 to 1937 as compared with the average of the years 1926 to 1929, it will be seen how important the problem of the employable unemployed became. During the great depression of 1929–32 there were parts of the Prairie Provinces that threatened to become depressed areas. Widespread drought, recurring from time to time, also made widespread relief necessary both for families and for stock. The disparities in the impact of the depression ranged in a loss of income varying from 72 per cent in Saskatchewan to 36 per cent in Nova Scotia. The Prairie Provinces suffered most as they were dependent almost entirely on the export of wheat. The catastrophic changes brought about by the depression of 1929–36 have put enormous strains on the economy, on the constitutional division of powers and the economic policies of the Dominion Government. The manner in which the fall of income was distributed over the various Provinces was of much significance in the Federation.

Two other factors must be mentioned. The Dominion Government, which invested $3000 millions in railways together with an investment of considerably over $1000 millions in a privately owned railway, on the assumption that railways would have a monopoly of land transportation, had now to face serious competition from rival railways in some areas and from the newer method of road transportation falling exclusively or nearly exclusively within the jurisdiction of the Provinces. This made for rigidity in debt structures which becomes very serious in times of strain, as interest has to be paid. There is not only competition between the two railway systems themselves but also competition between railways and roads. The Provinces are developing means of transportation which may ultimately destroy the solvency of the railways, and there is the likelihood of over-investment in roads as in the past there was over-investment in railways, with the result that there may be even a still heavier burden upon the Canadian economy. There is also the question of tariffs which brought a relative increase in costs and worsened the conditions under which the exporting industries were operating at a time when the prices for wheat and other primary products were drastically falling. The result was that the standard was reduced and the defaulting of debt became more general.

To sum up: Canada's pre-war economy, depending as it did on a few specialised exports, was vulnerable. The large changes in income and the rigidities of the cost structure as a whole were obvious. The increased costs were brought about for national and political reasons, and further increased the vulnerability of the economy. There have been widespread disparities between the various regions which have been more or less constant; in times of depression, however, these have been greatly intensified as between certain regions. This made it impossible for some Provincial Governments to weather the storm, and so gave rise to problems of Provincial and Local finance. On the one hand there have been elements making for national integration ; on the other hand elements making for disintegration. The implications of the economic and social changes which have occurred in Canada in recent years have been of far-reaching importance in public finance. The Dominion Government has found it necessary to accept responsibilities of a character not foreseen at the time of Confederation. Several Provincial Governments have found themselves with resources insufficient to discharge their constitutional responsibilities, including the payment of fixed charges on their outstanding debt and including the cost of unemployment and other social services. Local Authorities have been confronted with the same problems and they have been compelled to make heavy levies on real estate and to impose other taxes which have not always been realised. The relations between Provinces and Local Authorities are an essential problem of Provincial finance. New constitutional responsibilities have to be undertaken, new revenue sources tapped or governmental burdens reduced, increased or adjusted to meet changes in circumstances.

II. The British North America Act

Before we proceed to analyse the distribution of the revenues under the Canadian system it is necessary very briefly to refer to the British North America Act, 1867, sections 91 and 92. The Statute of Westminster, 1931, section 7 (1), it will be remembered, does not " apply to the repeal, amendment or alteration of the British North America Acts, 1867 to 1930, or any order, rule or regulation made thereunder ". A minute examination of the British North America Act so far as it related to Federal finance is beyond the scope of this Enquiry : it would involve an excursion into Dominion constitutional law and numerous Privy Council decisions. Under section 91 the Dominion has power " to make laws for the peace, order and good government of Canada, in relation to all matters not coming within the classes of subjects by this Act assigned exclusively to the legislatures of the Provinces ". By this clause the residue of powers not expressly given to the Provinces is reserved to the Dominion. The Dominion is also given unlimited powers of taxation (the raising of money by any mode or system of taxation). Section 92 (2) gives the Provinces power to levy " direct taxation within the Province ". Section 92 (9) is not clear, as it is not certain whether indirect as well as direct taxation is authorised by the words " shop, saloon, tavern, auctioneer and other licences ". Can, too, licences be made to cover any kind of business activity or does it apply to a limited genus of which those specifically mentioned are examples ? This is not really important, because the chief source of Provincial revenues is direct taxation under section 92 (2). The Privy Council has put a restrictive interpretation on section 91, viz. that the Dominion has power to make laws "for the peace, order and good government of Canada" only in temporary and overwhelming emergencies such as war, pestilence or famine. A deep-rooted social malaise, such as unemployment, is beyond the power of the Dominion unless it is comprised in the enumerated heads of section 91. This means that most of present-day legislation on the social services (which was never contemplated or expressly provided for by the North America Act, 1867) must be enacted by the Provinces. "There is much truth", says the Royal Commission on Dominion-Provincial Relations,[1] "as well as some exaggeration, in the contention that the 'Property and Civil Rights in the Provinces' clause[2] has become the real residuary clause of the Constitution." The Privy Council's decisions of 1937 on a number of Dominion measures, known as the Bennett "New Deal", again emphasised the wide range of Provincial powers in social security legislation. It was held that the Acts of the Canadian Parliament dealing with the weekly day of rest in industrial undertakings, with minimum wages and with the limitation of hours of work went beyond the Dominion Parliament's powers as they affected "Property and Civil Rights in the Provinces" under section 92 (13). For the same reason the Employment and Social Insurance Act providing for a national system of unemployment insurance in specified industries and financed by compulsory contributions from employers and employees and by contributions from the Federal Government was also held to be unconstitutional. Uniformity of standards in many kinds of social security and labour legislation is desirable, but the Dominion Government must leave this to the Provinces, and the Provinces were limited by the financial provisions in section 92 of the British North America Act. For a quarter of a century the Dominion had overcome the difficulty by giving conditional grants to the Provinces, but administrative co-operation had not resulted in efficient co-operation. The Privy Council also declared the Natural Products Marketing Act invalid. This Act provided for the marketing and distribution of products by a Dominion Marketing Board. The Privy Council held that the Federal power to regulate trade and commerce under section 91 (2) did not extend to the regulation of trading transactions completed within a single Province. The Dominion's power was confined to interprovincial and international aspects of trade. The decision of the Privy Council brought home again the fact that the power to regulate the economic life of Canada is divided between the Dominion and the Provinces, and neither the Dominion nor the Provinces can encroach upon the sphere of the other. At the same time the Dominion has extensive powers of economic regulation enumerated under section 91. It can

[1] Book I, The Constitution Today, chap. ix, p. 247.

[2] Section 92 (13).

control companies with Dominion charters; the grain trade by declaring local works to be for the general advantage of Canada under section 92 (10c); banks, monetary matters, transportation, shipping, etc. (under the enumerated heads of section 91); and it can prohibit economic or industrial practices, *e.g.* certain kinds of trade combination, under the criminal law as a pretence or pretext to encroach upon Provincial powers. As the Constitution is now, it is doubtful whether or not delegation of legislative power is constitutionally possible. The delegation of power by a Province to the Dominion and vice versa would be a device for overcoming in practice the difficulties arising in regard to economic activities from the division of legislative power between the Dominion and Provinces of the Federation. It has recently been declared by the Supreme Court of Canada that Parliament or a Provincial legislature may authorise "delegation in depth" to the limits of their respective powers so long as Parliament or the legislature retains (as it must, premising its continued existence) the ability to withdraw the delegated authority.[1] Close and continuous co-operation is taking place and is in contrast with the original conception of federalism in which there was a clear-cut division of powers. It is doubtful, as already noted, whether such co-operation is sound from the viewpoint either of administration or of public finance. The history of the administration of conditional grants reinforces this. The constant danger of Dominion-Provincial friction affects spheres of joint administration. The Royal Commission on Dominion-Provincial Relations was of opinion that "Where legislative power over a particular subject matter is divided, it is ordinarily desirable that these powers should be pooled under the control of a single government in order to secure unified effort in administration".[2]

III. Government Revenues before the War

The summary tables below are intended to bring out the essential features of the revenue system, the public expenditures and public debt of Canada in the pre-rearmament year 1937. Data for war years have also been compiled, as has been done for the crisis years during the depression 1929–36 in order to study crisis finance in its various aspects. Further details are given in the general tables in Part III of the Enquiry.

The most arresting fact underlying all these tables is the greatly increased cost of government in Canada in recent years. Governments, Dominion, Provincial, and Municipal or Local, have been extending their services in all directions. This is clearly seen in the very rapid growth

[1] *Vide* Supreme Court of Canada in "Reference *re* Regulations (Chemicals) under War Measures Act" (*Canadian Bar Review*, Toronto, Feb. 1943).

[2] Report, Book I, p. 259.

in expenditures connected with social security and with development. With the growth in expenditures there has been increasing competition for revenues on the part of the various layers of Government. The following table shows this growth at a glance :

TABLE I

GOVERNMENT EXPENDITURES AND REVENUES IN CANADA [1]

(Fiscal year nearest to calendar year)

A. *Expenditures*

	$ millions						Percentage Increase, 1940 over—	
	1913	1921	1926	1930	1937	1940	1913	1937
Dominion .	131	381	314	419	514	1278	875	149
Provincial .	49	91	127	188	261	276	463	6
Municipal .	100	206	240	285	282	279	179	−1
Total .	280	678	681	892	1057	1833	554	73

The relatively large increase in Dominion expenditure as compared with those of Provincial and Local expenditures is striking. To meet these expenditures the following revenues were necessary :

B. *Revenues*

	$ millions						Percentage Increase, 1940 over—	
	1913	1921	1926	1930	1937	1940	1913	1937
Dominion .	148	360	391	345	500	763	416	53
Provincial .	46	91	136	178	247	286	522	16
Municipal .	110	230	271	317	309	313	185	1
Total .	304	681	798	840	1056	1362	348	29

[1] The figures in this table are gross expenditures and revenues and do not therefore agree with the figures in the following tables, where net figures are given and double counting has been eliminated. The figures for 1940 are taken from *Comparative Statistics of Public Finance, 1936–1940*, compiled for the Dominion-Provincial Conference of Jan. 1941, on the same basis as those of the Rowell-Sirois Report.

The table also brings out the effect of the war in further increasing the preponderance of the Dominion and in creating a substantial Dominion deficit. This is further illustrated by Table II in which Government revenues and expenditures are compared with the national income. It also shows the growing importance of defence expenditures.

TABLE II

GOVERNMENT REVENUES AND EXPENDITURES EXPRESSED IN TERMS OF THE NATIONAL INCOME [1]

	1937–38	1940–41	1941–42
National Income [2] ($ millions)	4404	5345	6500
Revenues :			
(*a*) $ millions :			
Dominion	517	872	1488
Provincial	288	305	305 [3]
Municipal	309	314	313
Total	1114	1491	2106
(*b*) Per cent of the national income :			
Dominion	12	16	22
Provincial	6	6	5
Municipal	7	6	5
Total	25	28	32
Expenditures :			
(*a*) $ millions :			
Dominion	535	1250	1885
Provincial	274	273	274 [3]
Municipal	311	314	309
Total	1120	1837	2468
(*b*) Per cent of the national income :			
Dominion	12	23	29
Provincial	6	5	4
Municipal	7	6	5
Total	25	34	38
Defence or War Expenditure : [4]			
$ millions	33	778	1,382
Per cent of the national income	1	15	21
Per cent of Dominion expenditure	6	62	73
Per cent of total expenditures	3	42	56
Population (thousands)	11,120	11,385	11,420
Per capita ($) :			
National income	396	470	569
Revenues	100	131	184
Expenditures	101	161	217
Defence or war expenditure	3	68	122

[1] This table is based on figures supplied by the Dominion Statistician. They correspond to the public accounts, and not to those of the Rowell-Sirois Report.
[2] Tentative figures for the calendar years 1937, 1940 and 1941.
[3] Estimated.
[4] See also Table 11, Part III.

Table III gives the main heads of revenue in millions of dollars under four main groups — Group I, Progressive Taxes; Group II, Taxes on Property; Group III, Mainly Taxes on Business; Group IV, Mainly

TABLE III

THE REVENUE SYSTEM OF CANADA, ALL GOVERNMENTS, 1937
($ millions)

	Dominion	Provincial	Municipal	Total
GROUP I. *Progressive Taxes*:				
Personal income taxes	51	12	2	65
Succession duties	..	36	..	36
Total, Group I	51	48	2	101
GROUP II. *Taxes on Property*:				
Property taxes on real estate	..	3	144	147
Property taxes on buildings	..	3	112	115
Business property taxes	..	..	14	14
Public domain	2	21	..	23
Total, Group II	2	27	270	299
GROUP III. *Mainly Taxes on Business*:				
Corporation taxes	72	34	..	106
Company fees, licences, etc.	2	8	10	20
Total, Group III	74	42	10	126
GROUP IV. *Mainly Consumption Taxes*:				
Customs (including $7 millions on liquor)	112	..	..	112
Excise (including $20 millions on liquor)	52	..	..	52
Other Similar Taxes and Licences:				
Manufacturer's taxes	17	..	..	17
Sales taxes	138	2	4	144
Gasoline tax	..	39	..	39
Liquor control (other than customs and excise)	..	30	..	30
Automobile licences	..	26	..	26
Amusements	..	3	..	3
Sub-total, Other Taxes and Licences	155	100	4	259
Surplus Utility Earnings	7	1	6	14
Miscellaneous (taxes and receipts)	12	5	17	34[1]
Total, Group IV	338	106	27	471
Dominion subsidies to Provinces[2]	..	21	..	21
GRAND TOTAL	465	244	309	1018
Less duplications (mainly subsidies)	22	..	..	22
NET TOTAL	443	244	309	996

[1] Including duplication amounting to $1·5 millions.
[2] Provincial subsidies to municipalities have been deducted from off-setting expenditures in the Report of the Royal Commission.

Consumption Taxes. The shares of Dominion, Provincial and Municipal Governments are shown. The classification is, as explained in Chapter II, not an ideal one but the best possible to bring out the characteristics of a Federal system of taxation. No clear line of demarcation is possible in every instance. Thus the taxation of foreign dividends in recent years may be classified as a tax on income or as a tax on corporations. Although Dominion loans are exempt under the Act, Provincial Government loans are not, and if the tax on foreign dividends were placed in Group III under business taxes this fact would have to be remembered. Again, taxes classified as progressive are not always completely progressive in all incomes. Very high rates are levied on large incomes and on large estates, and less is taken from medium incomes and medium estates. Canadian taxation is progressive as between medium and large incomes, but, at any rate in 1937, regressive as between small and medium incomes.

As in the previous chapter it is convenient to express the data in the above tables in the form of percentage showing the percentage share of each Government in each tax and also the percentage which each tax bears to the revenue of each Government. This is given in Table IV.

From Tables III and IV the following characteristics emerge. The tax system is predominantly regressive. The Dominion Government, for example, has a very productive source of revenue in a comparatively high sales tax. This tax in 1937 yielded $138 millions out of a total Dominion revenue of $465 millions, as compared with $112 millions from customs and $52 millions from excise. In the second place, only 10 per cent of the total taxation of Canada (all Governments) is in the first group — progressive taxes. The personal income tax produces only 11 per cent of the Dominion revenue and 5 per cent of total Provincial revenues. This was the position before the war. These percentages require further analysis in order to see how far the principle of progression is applied. Three-quarters of this 10 per cent comes from incomes over $10,000 and proportionately large estates and 35 per cent from incomes of $50,000 and over. The Dominion income tax in 1937 was, on very large incomes, one of the highest in the world, and when combined with Provincial income taxation in the four Western Provinces was perhaps the highest in the world. In Alberta, for example, the combined Dominion-Provincial income tax reached, before the war, 105 per cent of the total income of $1 million. A table given below and published in the Report[1] shows a variation on the highest incomes varying from 33 per cent of the total income in Nova Scotia (Halifax) and Quebec to 58 per cent in Saskatchewan (Regina). In addition to these differences there are also major differences in

[1] On Dominion-Provincial Relations, Book II, p. 111.

TABLE IV

THE REVENUE SYSTEM OF CANADA, ALL GOVERNMENTS, 1937

(Percentage distribution)

	Percentage Share of each Government in Total Revenues				Percentage Distribution of each Government's Revenues			
	Dominion	Provincial	Municipal	Total	Dominion	Provincial	Municipal	Total
GROUP I. *Progressive Taxes :*								
Personal income taxes .	79	18	3	100	11	5	1	6
Succession duties . .	..	100	..	100	..	15	..	4
Total, Group I . .	50	48	2	100	11	20	1	10
GROUP II. *Taxes on Property :*								
Taxes on real estate . .	..	2	98	100	..	1	47	15
Taxes on buildings . .	..	3	97	100	..	1	36	12
Business property taxes .	..	..	100	100	..	..	5	1
Public domain . .	10	90	..	100	..	9	..	2
Total, Group II . .	1	9	90	100	..	11	88	30
GROUP III. *Mainly Taxes on Business :*								
Corporation taxes . .	68	32	..	100	15	14	..	11
Company fees, licences, etc.	11	39	50	100	..	3	3	2
Total, Group III	59	34	7	100	15	17	3	13
GROUP IV. *Mainly Consumption Taxes :*								
Customs	100	..	..	100	25	..	..	13
Excise	100	..	..	100	11	..	..	4
Other Similar Taxes and Licences :								
Manufacturer's taxes .	100	..	..	100	4	..	..	2
Sales taxes . . .	96	1	3	100	30	1	1	14
Gasoline taxes . .	..	100	..	100	..	16	..	4
Liquor control (other than customs and excise) .	..	100	..	100	..	12	..	3
Automobile licences . .	..	100	..	100	..	11	..	3
Amusement taxes . .	..	100	..	100	..	1	..	..
Sub-total, Other Taxes and Licences .	60	38	2	100	34	41	1	26
Surplus Utility Earnings .	50	7	43	100	3	..	2	1
Miscellaneous . . .	33	15	52	100	1	3	5	3
Total, Group IV .	70	24	6	100	74	44	8	47
Dominion subsidies to Provinces	..	100	..	100	..	8	..[1].	2
GRAND TOTAL . . .	46	24	30	100	100	100	100	102
Less duplications . .	100	..	..	100	5	..	..	2
NET TOTAL . .	44	25	31	100	95	100	100	100

[1] Provincial subsidies to Municipalities have been deduced from offsetting expenditures in the Report of the Royal Commission.

Dominion, Provincial and Municipal Income Taxes payable by a Married Man with No Children[1]

	Gross Income		
	$3000	$10,000	$100,000
Tax payable by resident of—	$ c.	$ c.	$ c.
Charlottetown, P.E.I.	61 90	821 20	38,249 15
Halifax, N.S.	30 00	546 00	32,518 50
St. John, N.B.	30 00	636 00	35,283 50
Quebec, Quebec	30 00	546 00	32,518 50
Montreal, Quebec	33 00	655 20	39,022 20
Toronto, Ontario	44 55	778 70	39,920 54
Winnipeg, Manitoba	77 04	993 28	46,864 62
Regina, Saskatchewan	71 50	1034 25	58,230 90
Edmonton, Alberta	65 00	1036 00	58,228 50
Victoria, B.C.	60 00	1051 00	55,513 50
New York, U.S.A.	28 00	655 00	38,274 00
London, England	283 13	1910 63	50,120 00
Paris, France	579 00	3564 00	54,239 00

[1] Assuming all earned income in $3000 and $10,000 brackets, and $14,000 earned income in $100,000 bracket. Rates prior to Sept. 1939.

exemptions and in the determination of taxable income. An equitable tax in every sense of the term is almost an impossibility, but when the variations are as great as those quoted they are very unsatisfactory from the individual taxpayer's point of view. It cannot be said that tax justice obtains where an individual is taxed twice on the same income by two taxing authorities, such as, for example in Alberta and British Columbia where the income paid to the Dominion is not allowed as an exemption. The following table shows the percentage of the gross income taken in British Columbia and Alberta in contrast with the percentage taken in Ontario, where the provincial rate is half the Dominion rate and where the income tax paid to the Dominion is allowed as an exemption :

TABLE V

Percentage of the Gross Income taken by the Provincial Income Tax

(Married man with no dependants — prior to Sept. 1939 Dominion Income Tax increase)

Income, $	British Columbia	Alberta	Ontario
100,000	23	26	7·4
500,000	27	29	7·8
1,000,000	27	30	7·7

Source.—Report of the Royal Commission on Dominion-Provincial Relations, Book II, p. 158.

It is clear that equity as between individuals and as between different regions is not possible in such circumstances. It was for this reason that the Royal Commission recommended that among other things the Dominion should be conceded the exclusive right to levy taxes on personal incomes, a recommendation accepted by the Dominion Government. An income tax for the Dominion as a whole could not otherwise be developed. Six Provinces and a number of Municipalities were levying income tax in addition to the Dominion. The Dominion has made good, as will be seen below, to the Provinces the revenue from income tax previously received by them from that source. For the duration of the war all the Provinces concurred with this arrangement.[1]

If, as recommended by the Royal Commission, the taxes which lend themselves most readily to progression (viz. the personal income tax and succession duties) were (permanently) entrusted to the Dominion Government and made uniform throughout Canada, each Provincial Government would be in a position to provide directly or through Local Authorities normal educational and other social services and development without having to impose very heavy taxation. The most outstanding inequality in Canadian taxation is territorial, and it is in the least wealthy Provinces that the percentage of taxes to total and surplus income is highest. With the Dominion Government in possession of the progressive taxes *par excellence* it would be possible to find the funds for the National Adjustment Grants, payable to those Provinces whose need is great, without resort to types of taxes which reduce the national income. At the same time there is the danger, a real danger in a Federation, of centralisation leading to the loss of real provincial self-government. This is analysed further in Chapters VIII and IX.

The high regression of the Canadian system before the war is well seen from the high proportion of taxes on consumption (Group IV) and also of those taxes in Group III which are not levied on income. The high regressive nature of the system is also seen in an examination of the taxes in those groups. Thus the Canadian sales tax of 8 per cent takes a much higher proportion of income than the sales taxes of most other countries. It has been estimated that it takes from $3\frac{1}{2}$ to $5\frac{1}{2}$ per cent of the income according to the distribution of consumption. Its great merit is its productivity. On the other hand, while it collects for the Government 8 per cent of the manufacturer's price, it takes from the ultimate taxpayer approximately the same percentage of the retail price. The tax is pyramided, since each buyer calculates his profit on the price at which he buys, a price which includes the tax.

[1] In the Budget for 1942–43 the Dominion Government assigned $84,428,000 to the Provinces as compensation for their loss of income tax.

Another criticism of the Canadian revenue system is that the burden of taxation is on costs rather than on surplus. Taxes which increase costs of production tend to eliminate the marginal firm or industry and to interfere with investment. The result of the tendency of marginal firms to disappear and of the tendency of potential investors to refrain from engaging in new enterprises, is that both labour and capital resources will be thrown out of employment and that the national income will be correspondingly diminished. Out of this diminished national income a larger revenue than before will have to be raised, as the unemployed will have to be maintained at the public cost. If, in order to raise the larger revenues, new taxes are imposed which bear on costs, the vicious circle will be completed. The alternative to taxes which increase business costs lies in taxes falling on profits or other surpluses. In the long run this means that the latter taxes should be replaced by an expansion of the personal income tax.[1] Among taxes on costs are the taxes in Group IV and also taxes on corporations in Group III other than those on net income, because they have to be paid regardless of the fact that net income has been earned or not — such as taxes on capital stock, the number of branches and other fixed taxes on corporations. In short, the Canadian system has been criticised as not collecting a given amount of revenue with the least burden on the national income. The very high proportion of the tax burden that falls on costs rather than on profits, together with the lack of co-ordination in tax policy among the competing tax authorities, reduce the national income by restricting marginal investment, production and employment. Three-quarters of the total taxes before the war have no direct relationship to net income and at any rate, under the pre-war division of revenue powers, could not be so adjusted.

Lastly, as will be seen, the revenue sources of the Provinces and the Municipalities are limited, while within the framework of the Constitution these layers of Government have a very important position especially with respect to social security. This means that they cannot efficiently perform what is in this respect required of them. The position is all the more difficult because of the load of dead-weight debt which the Provinces and Municipalities carry, the equivalent of one-fifth of the total Municipal-Provincial expenditures. The shares of the Provinces and Municipalities in the various revenues are shown in the following table :

[1] Report of the Royal Commission on Dominion-Provincial Relations, Book II, p. 161. As to the extent this has been achieved in Dominion war finance, see section on The Canadian Economy in War-Time — section vii below.

TABLE VI

THE DISTRIBUTION OF PROVINCIAL AND MUNICIPAL REVENUES, PER CAPITA AND PER CENT, 1937 [1]

	Provincial	Municipal	Provincial and Municipal	
	$ per capita	$ per capita	$ per capita	per cent
GROUP I. *Progressive Taxes :*				
Personal income taxes	1·07	0·17	1·24	2
Succession duties . . .	3·22	..	3·22	7
Total, Group I . . .	4·29	0·17	4·46	9
GROUP II. *Taxes on Property :*				
Real property taxes . . .	0·53	22·07	22·60	45
Public domain . . .	1·90	..	1·90	4
Total, Group II . . .	2·43	22·07	24·50	49
GROUP III. *Taxes on Business :*				
Corporation taxes . . .	3·06	..	3·06	6
GROUP IV. *Mainly Consumption Taxes :*				
Sales taxes	0·17	0·40	0·57	1
Gasoline taxes	3·50	..	3·50	7
Motor vehicles	2·34	.. [2]	2·34	5
Liquor control	2·68	..	2·68	5
Other licences, permits and fees .	0·74	0·94	1·68	3
Amusement taxes . . .	0·26	..	0·26	1
Miscellaneous services . . .	0·09	..	0·09	..
Surplus utility earnings . . .	..	0·56	0·56	1
Miscellaneous revenues . . .	0·55	3·70	4·26	9
Total, Group IV . . .	10·33	5·60	15·94	32
Dominion Subsidies to Provinces .	1·91	..	1·91	4
GRAND TOTAL	22·02	27·84	49·87	100

[1] These figures are based on those in Book III of the Rowell-Sirois Report, whereas Tables III and IV are based on those in Table 84, p. 211 of Book I. The two sets of figures differ in their classification of revenues, though not in the totals.
[2] Particulars not available ; included under "Other Licences, Permits and Fees".

PROVINCIAL REVENUES

The detailed table showing the data for each Province is given in Part III of the Enquiry (Table 5). Considerable care has to be taken in comparing these, as they have to be analysed in relation to the Provincial income, especially the free or taxable surplus income and the amount of services supplied by governmental agencies. There are other special circumstances to be considered in making comparisons between Provinces, as these differ so much in the division of responsibility for the social services, including education, and for the upkeep of roads. Not only does the proportion borne for each of these services by Provinces differ widely in the same year but also in the same Province between different periods. In Prince Edward Island, for example, where there is a small agricultural economy combined with a lack of industrial and urban development, there is a Federal subsidy three times the average *per capita* for all Provinces and one-third of the total Provincial-Municipal expenditures. In Nova Scotia small-scale subsistence industry and a vulnerable economy make for low taxable capacity. As compared with other Provinces, the low return from property taxation and the relatively high proportion of revenues from the Federal subsidy are striking. In New Brunswick, " the best-watered country in the world ", as in the other Maritime Provinces, real property taxation is below the average and progressive taxation is negligible. The latter is left to Municipalities and levied on a frequently arbitrary assessment at the local real property tax rate with exemptions varying according to local conditions. It combines a small poll tax and a rough approximation of a property tax. In Quebec, which conforms to the average revenue system, income and sales taxes are levied by Municipalities rather than by the Provincial Government. Developed progressive taxes are absent from Provincial income. The Church has a unique position in Quebec, since it carries out functions, *e.g.* in education and social welfare, performed in other Provinces by Provincial and Local Governments. Hence the Quebec taxpayer contributes more for such services than appears from the public accounts. This falls especially on real estate, partly because the greater part of church property is exempt from taxation. This is also one of the factors which have caused some Local Authorities to turn to income and sales taxes and to corporation taxes (licences and fees). In Ontario, in 1937, subsidies from the Dominion Government were less than 2 per cent of Provincial-Municipal revenue, and Provincial subsidies to Municipalities are 20 per cent of those. Since the depression Quebec's financial position has suffered, as its economy depended to a large extent on world trade. Ontario's tax policy is affected by Federal tax policy to a greater extent than in other Provinces, and in progressive taxation her action is limited to Federal policy. The high level of property taxation has provided the Municipalities with considerable revenue. The revenue system of Manitoba is one of the soundest in Canada. Not only is the yield of real property taxation large, especially in Winnipeg, but there is an emphasis on direct taxation such as the Provincial income tax and succession duties. In 1937 these were 20 per cent of total Provincial revenues. This is perhaps due to a large portion of Prairie surplus revenue being centred in Winnipeg. The *per capita* income of Saskatchewan is, with the exception of Prince Edward Island, the lowest in Canada. There are no urban centres or corporations in the Province where surplus income accumulates and consequently Provincial taxation is unsatisfactory. In emergencies the existing system, depending as it does on a major industry, wheat, is in a particularly unfortunate position. The tax sources tend to yield much less than the Canadian average. The sales tax, however, is an effort to broaden the basis of taxation and has been productive to a degree few other taxes could have been in the circumstances. In Alberta the Provincial real property tax still prevails, as in Saskatchewan, to a distinctive degree. Progressive taxation in spite of high rates is below the average for all Provinces. Corporation taxes were increased during the period under review on grounds perhaps other than of revenue. The *per capita* revenue of British Columbia is nearly double the Canadian average. Municipal revenues there are at the Canadian average although the proportion of municipally organised areas is much smaller than in most Provinces. Corporation taxation and revenues from the public domain are three times the Canadian average. British Columbia is rich in resources and to exploit these resources corporation organisation is greatly developed. The high Provincial income makes it possible to provide Government services well above the average Canadian standard.

This brief survey of Dominion, Provincial and Municipal revenues would be incomplete without some reference to the revolutionary changes in the economic and social role of Government which have necessitated an immense increase in Government revenues and new kinds of revenue. The proportion of the national income spent by Governments has risen from less than 10 per cent at Confederation to 25 per cent or more in 1937, and taxes used in 1874 would have provided but one-half of all Government receipts in 1937, including the property taxes which have continued to support almost the whole of the great increase in Municipal services. The Dominion Government has expanded its income by a heavy sales tax, by the taxation of business and by the personal income tax, the fairest of taxes. In 1937 the Provinces, which had been given power to levy direct taxation, receipts from the public domain, licences and fees, and were expected to rely to some extent on fixed unconditional Federal subsidies under the Constitution, obtained less than one-fourth of their income from these sources. The great bulk of new sources for the Provinces could not have been foreseen at the time of Confederation, sources which have been interpreted as falling within Provincial jurisdiction. In the words of the Royal Commission, “ Some of these sources are directly competitive with those employed by the Dominion ; many of the others constitute onerous or uneconomic levies on consumption and the costs of production". With the joint occupation of the field of direct taxes, neither the Dominion nor the Provinces nor both together have been able to employ the progressive taxes to the extent which is economically and socially desirable. It is clear that the present situation in Canadian public finance represents a wide departure from the conception of the Fathers of Confederation and from the spirit of the financial settlement which they devised. Costly Government responsibilities which have become national in scope are being supported by Regional and Local revenue. Revenue sources which have become national in character are being employed by Regional and Local Governments to the complete or partial exclusion of the Central authority.[1] It is interesting to compare these views with the position that has resulted from the war.[2]

IV. Public Expenditures before the War

Next we turn to public expenditures. The most outstanding features of the division of Government expenditures between the Dominion, Provinces and Municipalities in 1937 are brought out in the following two tables, VII and VIII, on pp. 88 and 89.

The main features of these tables are as follows:

(1) The large recurring expenditure on debt charges — 27 per cent of the total expenditure of all Governments, and 61 per cent of the total is on Dominion debt.

(2) The primary functions of Government, including debt charges, account for 52 per cent of the total, and the secondary functions — the social services and development including transportation — account for the remaining 48 per cent.

(3) Relief expenditures, mainly unemployment but also advances to farmers, are the legacy of the great depression. Excluding debt charges they account for 13 per cent of the expenditures, but including debt charges for this function alone they account for 15 per cent of the total.

(4) Development, including transportation, accounts for 12 per cent of the expenditures excluding debt charges, but 30 per cent including developmental debt charges; from 1867 onwards the main object of public loan policy has been the provision of transportation facilities, railways, canals, public works and harbours. The unification of railways, waterways and harbours was the enormous task of the Dominion Government under the British North America Act, 1867. With the advent of the motor car millions of dollars have been spent on the construction of roads.

[1] Report, Book I, chapter viii, pp. 245-6.
[2] See section vii below, page 93.

TABLE VII

PUBLIC EXPENDITURES FROM REVENUE IN CANADA, ALL GOVERNMENTS, 1937

($ millions)

	Dominion	Provincial	Municipal	Total
1. *Primary Functions:*				
Legislation, administration and justice	52	33	65	150
National defence	34	..	..	34
Military pensions and aftercare .	54	..	..	54
Miscellaneous	..	9	..	9
Debt charges	167	51	55	273
Total, Primary Functions . .	307	93	120	520
2. *Secondary Functions:*				
(1) Social Services:				
Education	..	32	77	109
Unemployment relief . . .	66	43	18	127
Other public welfare . . .	44	44	36	125
Sub-total, Social Services .	110	119	131	361
(2) Developmental:				
Agriculture and public domain .	20	21	..	41
Transportation	20	25	31	76
Sub-total, Developmental . .	40	46	31	117
Total, Secondary Functions .	150	165	162	478
Subsidies to Provinces . . .	21	..[1]	..	21
GRAND TOTAL	478	258	282	1018
Less duplications	22	..	..	22
NET TOTAL	456	258	282	996

[1] Provincial subsidies to Municipalities have been deducted from offsetting expenditures in the Report of the Royal Commission.

Two-thirds of the total net debt charges in 1937 were for development, mainly transportation.

(5) Unconditional subsidies paid to the Provinces account for only 4 per cent of the total expenditure of the Dominion Government.

(6) Education accounts for 12 per cent of Provincial, 27 per cent of Municipal and 11 per cent of total expenditures.

It is of interest to compare the main group of expenditures including and excluding debt charges for each main group. In other words, in the

TABLE VIII

PUBLIC EXPENDITURES FROM REVENUE IN CANADA, ALL GOVERNMENTS, 1937
(Percentage distribution)

	Percentage Share of each Government in Total Expenditures				Percentage Distribution of each Government's Expenditure			
	Dominion	Provincial	Municipal	Total	Dominion	Provincial	Municipal	Total
1. *Primary Functions :*								
Legislation, administration and justice	34	22	44	100	11	13	28	15
National defence	100	..	..	100	7	..	..	3
Military pensions and aftercare	100	..	..	100	12	..	..	6
Miscellaneous	..	100	..	100	..	4	..	1
Debt charges	61	19	20	100	35	20	20	27
Total, Primary Functions	60	17	23	100	65	37	48	52
2. *Secondary Functions :*								
(1) Social Services :								
Education	..	29	71	100	..	12	27	11
Unemployment relief	55	34	11	100	14	16	5	13
Other public welfare	34	36	30	100	9	17	9	12
Sub-total, Social Services	33	33	34	100	23	45	41	36
(2) Developmental :								
Agriculture and public domain	49	51	..	100	4	8	..	4
Transportation	27	33	40	100	4	10	11	8
Sub-total, Developmental	34	39	27	100	8	18	11	12
Total, Secondary Functions	31	35	34	100	31	63	52	48
Subsidies to Provinces	100	..[1]	..	100	4	..[1]	..	2
GRAND TOTAL	47	25	28	100	100	100	100	102
Less duplications	100	..	..	100	5	..	..	2
NET TOTAL	46	26	28	100	95	100	100	100

[1] Provincial subsidies to Municipalities have been deducted from offsetting expenditures in the Report of the Royal Commission.

former case the debt charges are apportioned to the expenditure group concerned and in the latter the debt charges are lumped together under primary functions. The results are given in the first of the small tables overleaf. The large capital expenditure on railways accounts for the discrepancy between the last two columns there. The percentage distribution of each Government's expenditures including the appropriate debt charges is given in the second of the small tables overleaf.

	Percentage of Expenditures in 1937—	
	Including Debt Charges	Excluding Debt Charges
Primary Functions . . .	29	52
Secondary Functions :		
1. Education	12	11
2. Public welfare :		
Unemployment relief . .	15	13
Other	14	12
3. Development and transportation	30	12
Total, Secondary Functions .	71	48
TOTAL EXPENDITURES . . .	100	100

	Dominion	Provincial	Municipal	Total
Primary Functions	35	18	28	29
Secondary Functions :				
1. Education	..	13	32	12
2. Public welfare :				
Unemployment relief . .	17	19	7	15
Other	9	18	16	14
3. Development and transportation	35	32	17	30
Total, Secondary Functions .	61	82	72	71
Subsidies to Provinces . . .	4	..	..	2
GRAND TOTAL	100	100	100	102
Less duplications . . .	5	..	..	2
NET TOTAL	95	100	100	100

The detailed tables of relief expenditure on current and capital account will be found in Part III of the Enquiry (Tables 8 and 9). They show as clearly as the noonday sun the remarkable effect of the economic blizzard of 1929–32 on Dominion finance and on the finance of the nine Provinces.

The fall in the price of wheat was an uncontrollable external factor, and this, with internal rigidities of overhead costs, brought great distress. Tariff policy, directed to maintain employment in certain regions, threw an even greater burden on primary producers. Local vested interests sprung up and depression burdens were very unevenly distributed. The increase in " Other Public Welfare " (old-age pensions, hospitals, asylums and public health) was only in part due to the depression. It was also due in large part to the economic and social evolution which is taking place in Canada. When the Act of Federation was passed, the provision of minimum social standards was never contemplated, nor was the transfer from Municipalities to the Dominion Government of a large part of the cost. The effect of large transfer expenditures [1] on the distribution of the national income and on the tax structures has sometimes been overlooked. It resulted in the collapse of the once accepted division of powers in a Federation; it shattered the old theory that the individual should be responsible for his own welfare and that of his dependants.

V. The Public Debt of Canada before the War

An analysis of the public debt of Canada for the year 1937 shows clearly the large amounts incurred for developmental purposes and in recent years for public welfare. The total debt of all Governments was $7863 millions, and of this $1413 millions was represented by liquid assets (*e.g.* cash), investments which were completely self-supporting and the capitalised value of interest earned by partially self-supporting assets. The following table shows how the balance of public debt was incurred:

TABLE IX

Canada's Public Debt in 1937: Portion not Directly Self-supporting
($ millions)

	Dominion	Provincial	Municipal	Total
Debt incurred for—				
1. *Primary Functions* of Government, including war expenditures .	1818	80	..	..
Less cumulative current surplus before special charges .	1233	..	..	..
Total, Primary Functions .	585	80	225	890
2. *Secondary Functions:*				
(1) Social Services:				
Education	..	50	180	230
Public welfare . . .	420	235	175	830
(2) Development and transportation	3250	975	275	4500
Total, Secondary Functions .	3670	1260	630	5560
Grand Total	4255	1340	855	6450

Source.—Report of the Royal Commission on Dominion-Provincial Relations, Book I, Table 78.

[1] In 1937 transfer expenditures of all Governments, *i.e.* expenditures on public welfare, mainly unemployment relief and war pensions, and interest on unproductive debts, were $406 millions out of a total expenditure of $996 millions.

The interest on this debt was $271 millions,[1] or about 27 per cent of all Government expenditures. Of this $100 millions was the cost of servicing accumulated deficits, war expenditures, capitalised unemployment relief and capitalised losses. The balance, $171 millions, was paid on debts incurred for development.

TABLE X

ANNUAL DEBT CHARGES OF CANADA, 1937

($ millions)

	Dominion	Provincial	Municipal	Total
1. *Primary Functions* . . .	23	3	14	40
2. *Secondary Functions* :				
(1) Social Services :				
Education	..	2	12	14
Public welfare . . .	16	9	11	34[1]
(2) Development and transportation	128	37	18	183
Total, Secondary Functions .	144	48	41	231[1]
GRAND TOTAL	167	51	55	271[1]

[1] After elimination of double counting.

VI. The Royal Commission on Dominion-Provincial Relations

This section of the chapter would be incomplete without a reference to the recommendations of the Royal Commission on Dominion-Provincial Relations, 1940.[2] These have been accepted by the Dominion Government. At a Dominion-Provincial Conference held in Ottawa in January 1941, the premiers of three Provinces — Ontario, Manitoba and British Columbia —suggested postponement until after the war. As already noted, an Unemployment Insurance Act for the whole of Canada has been passed, and the Provinces have withdrawn during the war from the field of personal income taxation. The Royal Commission held that the maintenance of the employable unemployed could not be efficiently performed on a Provincial basis or by Local Authorities. In this view the Commission agreed with the National Employment Commission and La Commission des Assurances Sociales de Québec. They were also of opinion that assistance to farmers when operating cost advances had to be given in times of widespread disaster, and could not be left to these Governments. The Dominion Government, therefore, should assume direct administration

[1] Excluding provision for amortisation.
[2] See Appendix I for Summary of Recommendations.

and financial responsibility rather than render indirect assistance by way of advances to the Provinces. The administration of non-contributory old-age pensions, to which the Dominion Government was already paying as high a proportion of the cost as it reasonably could without assuming control of the administration, should continue to remain with the Provinces, and no further financial help was recommended. If, however, non-contributory old-age pensions were to be superseded or supplemented by a contributory system, the Commission recommended that such a system should be under the control of the Dominion. It was also suggested that the Dominion should take over all Provincial debts and that each Province should pay to the Dominion a sum equal to the interest which it now receives from its investments. In view of the peculiar case of the Province of Quebec, where the *per capita* debt is low as compared with that of other Provinces on account of the fact that the Municipalities perform duties discharged elsewhere by Provincial Governments, the Dominion should take over 40 per cent of the combined Provincial and Municipal net debt. The Provinces should surrender their subsidies and receive an annual national adjustment grant which should be appraised by a small permanent Commission (which might be called the Finance Commission) assisted by an adequate technical staff. The system of grants should be reconsidered every five years and would be irreducible during this period. For special emergencies, as in the case of Saskatchewan, special provision would be made annually.

The Provinces on their part would renounce the tax on personal incomes and taxes imposed on corporations which individuals or partnerships carrying on the same businesses as the corporations would be required to pay. This transfer would include all such taxes, except a bona-fide licence fee which would remain with the Province. The Provinces should also forgo various forms of succession duty. This would put an end to grievances that the differences of rate in the various Provinces where such duties are levied are inequitable and distort investment because of the differences in rates between Provinces and the dangers of double taxation. Many Provinces, it was held, had a grievance because estates built up by investment throughout Canada were taxed not for national purposes but for the benefit of favourably situated Provinces. Finally, the existing Dominion subsidies to the Provinces would be abolished and replaced by the system of grants recommended by the Commission.

VII. The Canadian Economy in War-Time

Canada's war-time economy falls into two periods — that prior to May 1940, when the Dominion was called on to supply increasing quantities of food and raw materials, and the period subsequent to that date when Canada became in addition a supplier of large quantities of explosives, chemicals, shells, small-arms ammunition, bombs, tanks, vehicles, aircraft, ships and other munitions of war. It was natural, therefore, that the War Supply Board should have been superseded in April 1940 by the Department of Munitions and Supply which has had such an important part in the acceleration of the war effort in all directions. It remodelled the Canadian economy to meet the intensified needs of the Allies after France fell. When it was decided that the Dominion Government should finance and own the required capital equipment, the Department came forward with a programme of capital assistance to industry by which the greater part of capital equipment has been achieved after June 1940. Not only have new factories been erected, equipped and financed, but private concerns have been enlarged and machinery labelled as Government property installed in privately owned factories. Branches within the Department of a quasi-autonomous nature were also set up to deal with all kinds of munitions production, and these, with two other forms of administration — Controllers and Government Corporations — have been made the chief means of organising the Canadian economy for war. The War-Time Prices and Trade Board, the National Labour Supply Council and the Department of Finance have also assisted in the supremely important task of war regimentation.[1] In 1943 war production had reached a remarkably high level. In January 1943 the business placed by the Department of Munitions and Supply exceeded $6 billions. In 1942 war industrial production was at the rate of $2·6 billions, and for 1943 it is estimated to reach $3·7 billions. In 1942 one-half of the output of munitions was sent to the British theatre of war and to Russia, and 20 per cent to the United States and Pacific war zones, including China. War production was the main reason of the increase in the net national income to a new high record — $7·5 billions in 1942 as compared with $4·6 billions in 1939, an increase of no less than 61 per cent. By 1943 the country's productive capacity was no longer adequate to support a parallel expansion in the output of both munitions and consumers' goods. The production of the latter, therefore, had in an increasing degree to be held in check by a system of controls and priorities, including the direct control of prices and production, and by the restriction and diversion of civilian expenditures by taxation, thereby releasing resources required for war purposes. Finance in war-time provides the money required to

[1] Cf. *Mobilizing Canada's Resources for War*, Plumptre (Toronto, The Macmillan Co., 1941); *Canadian War Economics*, edited by Parkinson (Toronto, University of Toronto Press, 1941); "War Finance and the Canadian Economy, 1914–20", *Deutsch Canadian Journal of Economics and Political Science*, vol. vi (1940); *An Approach to War Finance*, Plumptre, *op. cit.* vol. vii (1941).

mobilise the human and material resources for war and prevents the spending of money on non-war purposes so that civilian activities do not interfere with or frustrate the war effort. The State, therefore, must tax adequately as well as it must borrow the savings of both individuals and companies or corporations. It must sometimes expand or add to credit and currency by borrowing from the banks; and if there is not full employment such expansion may be helpful, since it may stimulate production without inflation. If production is getting to its maximum and industry cannot expand, more credit or currency will result in an increase, not in production, but in prices.

The outstanding features of Canadian public finance in war-time, as will be seen from the tables in Part III, are:

(1) The great growth in *Federal* (or Dominion) expenditures, which in 1943 was eight times above the pre-war level.

(2) The enormous increase in *war* expenditures.

(3) The growth in *Federal* revenues, most noticeably in the taxation of personal incomes and the incomes of corporations, in federal succession duties, in customs duties and excise duties, especially on liquor and tobacco, and also in sales taxation; the burden of personal income taxation is greater than that of the United States and similar to that of Great Britain. This emphasis on progressive taxation is one of the most interesting changes in Canadian war finance.

(4) The withdrawal of the Provinces from the field of personal income and corporation taxes during the war. In 1943–44 the compensation paid to the Provinces was $84 millions on this account.

(5) The policy of the Federal Government to meet half the expenditure from taxes and half from borrowing.

(6) The comparative stability in provincial and in municipal finance as compared with the remarkable changes in Federal finance.

(7) The increase in the Dominion Public debt from $3153 millions in the pre-war year to $6182 millions (net) in 1942–43,[1] despite the great decrease in sterling indebtedness as the country turns from being a debtor to a creditor country. It is true that Canada in 1943 is running up a debit balance with the United States, but this process has, since the Hyde Park Agreement of 1941, slowed down. Under this agreement the United States charges to its British Lend-Lease account such exports to Canada as are to be used for Canadian war products exported to Britain, and the United States buys more from Canada. Meanwhile Canada accumulates sterling balances on a large scale. By December 1942 the total sterling

[1] For 1943–44 the borrowing needs were estimated at $2748 millions. The third Victory Loan of Oct. 1942 had a minimum objective of $750 millions, but produced $991 millions from 2 million subscribers.

balances had reached $2770 millions. Of this over $800 millions were used for repatriating sterling debt, public and otherwise. $250 millions were covered by British sales of gold to Canada, and the remaining $1700 millions, by an interest-free loan to Britain of $700 millions and by a gift of $1000 millions made early in 1942 under the United Kingdom Financing Act. This sum of $1000 millions was included in the Dominion expenditure figure. A similar gift of $1000 millions was put into the Budget for 1943–44.

In Part III of this Enquiry Canadian Tables 1 to 4 and 7 show the tax structures, public expenditures and the public debt of Governments in Canada after the outbreak of war. It will be noted how great has been the increase in the total expenditures of all layers of Government. Before the war this was 25 to 30 per cent of the national income and often included large expenditures for urban and agricultural relief. In 1941–42 the deficit of the Canadian national railways disappeared and there was also a fall in the expenditure on unemployment and relief, now a small item. The demands made on the railways during the last three years have already much exceeded the operations of the first world war, and in 1942 the increase over 1939 was of the order of 60 per cent. The increase in the returns of the sales tax, a regressive tax, in 1942–43 and 1943–44, was noticeable. Thus in 1938–39 the Federal sales tax was $122·1 millions, the Provincial sales taxes $2·4 millions and the Municipal sales taxes $4·3 millions, or a total of $128·8 millions. In 1942–43 the yield was $218, $14·7, $6·7 and $239·4 millions respectively. Other Federal regressive taxes also increased, thus miscellaneous Federal taxes increased from $22·9 millions in 1938–39 to $76·8 millions in 1943–44.

The most striking changes brought about by the war are summarised opposite and overleaf.

The figures show that the expenditures on education and highways have not decreased or remained constant on account of the war. The large expenditures on public welfare have, owing to the better employment, decreased in 1942–43 as compared with the pre-war year 1938–39.

It will be seen from what has been said that the war has been financed by taxation, by borrowing from the public the savings of individuals and corporations and also by credit expansion under the banking system. These methods have been supplemented by special controls such as import quotas and prohibitions, price-fixing, exchange control and rationing. The Government realised early in the war the advantages of taxation and of skimming off the savings of the people and corporations. The war effort would have been sadly cramped had civilian demand been allowed to compete with war requirements both as regards man-power and materials. An all-out war effort and a rising standard of living are not good bed-

DOMINION FINANCE

($ millions)

	Fiscal Years (1st April–31st March)		
	1938–39 (Pre-war Year)	1942–43	1943–44
War expenditures	34 [1]	3724 [2]	4890 [2]
Non-war expenditures	439 [1]	663	610 [3]
Total expenditures	473 [1]	4387 [2]	5500 [2]
Total revenues	426 [1]	2249	2752

[1] Cf. Statistical Summary, Bank of Canada, Oct.–Nov. 1942, p. 85.
[2] Includes $1000 millions for the allocation of war supplies to the Allied Powers.
[3] Includes $84 millions as compensation to Provincial Governments for assigning proceeds of the income and corporation taxes to the Federal Government during the war.

($ millions)

	1938–39	1942–43
Income tax	47	505
Taxes on corporation profits	85	770
Other corporation taxes	2	16
Succession duties	..	15
Withholding taxes on dividends, interest	10	28
Excise duties and taxes on liquor and tobacco	53	156
Import duties and taxes	94	231
Sales taxes	122	218
Miscellaneous taxes	23	77

PROVINCIAL FINANCE *

($ millions)

	Fiscal Years (1st April–31st March)	
	1938–39	1942–43
Expenditure	266	276
Revenue	246	300

MUNICIPAL FINANCE *

($ millions)

	1938–39	1942–43
Expenditure	288	286
Revenue	312	318

Source.—Statistical Summary, Bank of Canada, Oct.–Nov. 1942, pp. 84-5.

EXPENDITURE ON EDUCATION, PUBLIC WELFARE AND HIGHWAYS AND OTHER AIDS TO TRANSPORT *

($ millions)

	1938–39	1942–43
Education :		
Federal	2·3	2·2
Provincial	17·2	21·4
Municipal	96·0	110·1
Total	115·5	133·7
Public Welfare :		
Federal—General	5·2	22·8 [1]
Old-age pensions	..	..
Relief [2]	13·2	2·6
Provincial—General	42·5	50·4
Old-age pensions	39·3	43·8
Relief	26·9	6·1
Municipal—General	28·0	28·5
Old-age pensions	..	..
Relief [2]	61·8	9·9
Total—General	75·7	101·7
„ Old-age pensions	39·3	43·8
„ Relief [2]	101·9	18·6
Total	216·9	164·1
Highways, etc. :		
Federal	23·4	21·9
Provincial	24·2	27·7
Municipal	32·1	36·1
Total	79·7	85·7

[1] Includes $17 millions for administration of and contribution to unemployment insurance.
[2] Excludes municipal expenditure on relief works and provincial expenditure on provincial relief works.
* *Source.*—Statistical Summary, Bank of Canada, Oct.–Nov. 1942, pp. 84-5.

fellows. At first the financing of the war was of a credit expansion nature, as when, for example, after the outbreak of war a loan of $200 millions was raised from the banks. A controlled expansion of credit was desirable to assist production and to decrease unemployment which was 12 per cent,[1] but once this took place a public loan for $200 millions was floated and in the second war Budget heavier taxation was levied. A second

[1] The percentage of total wage-earners unemployed was 2 per cent in 1928, a maximum of 26 per cent in 1932, 9 per cent in 1937 and 12 per cent in 1939 (Dominion Bureau of Statistics — The Unemployment Situation).

public loan for $300 millions was successfully floated. Early in 1941 a short-term loan for $250 millions from the banks was raised. In the third war Budget heavier taxation was levied with a Victory Loan offered to the public in June 1941. This was successful. The tax structure, however, has been made to bear the maximum load, and the taxation of incomes, corporations and excess profits but not the sales tax (because it is regressive) have brought in much grist to the mill. On 23rd June 1942, for example, very sharp increases of income and national defence taxes took place and were henceforth to be collected at source wherever possible. The tax was steeply progressive. Exemptions for married persons and children were lowered but a proportion of the tax was treated as compulsory savings returnable with 2 per cent interest after the conclusion of hostilities. A married man, for example, with two children and an annual income of $5000 who hitherto paid $735 had to pay $1062 as income tax and compulsory savings. In March 1943 " pay as you earn " was introduced but without complete cancellation of the balances due on last year's taxes. Only half of the tax liability on the earned income of individuals (but not of corporations) and on income from investment up to $3000, for the year 1942, was " forgiven ", and of the amount remaining one-third had to be paid by 30th June and two-thirds on 31st December 1943. Half of the income tax on investments for 1942 was deferred until the death of the taxpayer on the basis that, while wages and salaries cease on death, there is capital from which to pay deferred taxes on the death of the taxpayer. Special concessions were given to farmers. They paid tax on only two-thirds of their estimated income before the end of the calendar year, and the balance was to be paid when the actual income was established by the end of March 1944. Farmers when suffering a loss in any year may deduct from the income in either of the next two years.

The financial policy laid down in the first war Budget in September 1939 is being followed: (1) the pay-as-you-go policy as far as is practicable; (2) the insistence of the principle of equality of sacrifice on the basis of ability to pay; and (3) the levying of taxes to the highest possible point. Taxes could not be carried beyond that point where production efficiency would be interfered with, " but ", said the Minister of Finance, " we are not prepared to be timid or light-hearted in judging where this point lies ". This principle is seen not only in the taxation on the income of individuals but also on the taxation of corporate incomes where the rate has been raised sharply. In the Budget presented in June 1942 an interesting change was made. Previously company profits were first subject to a flat rate of 18 per cent corporate income tax, and then paid 75 per cent of the excess profits under the Excess Profits Tax Act over the standard profits or 22 per cent of the total profits, whichever was the greater. Now under the new Excess Profits Tax Act a company pays a flat rate of 12 per cent on its total profits in addition to the 18 per cent corporation income tax, and thereafter 100 per cent of excess profits or 10 per cent of its total profits, whichever is the greater. This means that the 100 per cent excess profits tax becomes the greater when the company earns more than 116·6 per cent of its standard profits, compared with 156·7 per cent under previous legislation. A company or corporation as before pays at least 40 per cent of its total profits in taxation. It cannot retain under the new legislation more than 70 per cent of its standard profits as calculated for purposes of excess profits tax. Standard profits are calculated after payment of income tax. It is, therefore, estimated that, allowing for the 20 per cent refund or excess profits tax, a corporation with standard profits at the level of the 1936–39 average taxable profits can retain about seven-eighths of its average profits for those years, the years on which the standard is based. The tax refund has borne income tax and is payable without interest after the war.

A conspectus of Canadian public finance is given in a table furnished by the Dominion Statistician, Ottawa, showing the revenues and expenditures of the war years, as compared with those of the pre-rearmament year 1937–38, expressed as a percentage of national income and per head of population, together with the war expenditures also expressed as a percentage of national income and per head of population. This will be found in Part III, Table 11. It shows that in 1941–42 as compared with 1937–38 Government revenues (Dominion, Provincial and Municipal) had increased from 25·6 per cent to 32·3 per cent of the national income, Government expenditures from 25·7 per cent to 37·9 per cent, and the expenditure on the war from 0·7 per cent to 21·2 per cent, a truly remarkable change in Canadian public finance.

VIII. Conclusion

To-day Canada is the most highly developed Dominion both industrially and financially. The advance which the Dominion has made in recent years, especially since the Bank of Canada commenced business in March 1935 after the passage of the Bank of Canada Act in 1934, is most striking. A quarter of a century ago Canada was without a broad tax structure and there was no domestic money market from which to borrow. There was no central bank to control or to co-ordinate the financial life of the country.[1] Before the outbreak of the present war Canada no longer depended on London for loans as in 1914, for in that

[1] Cf. Plumptre, *Central Banking in the British Dominions,* Toronto University Press, 1940.

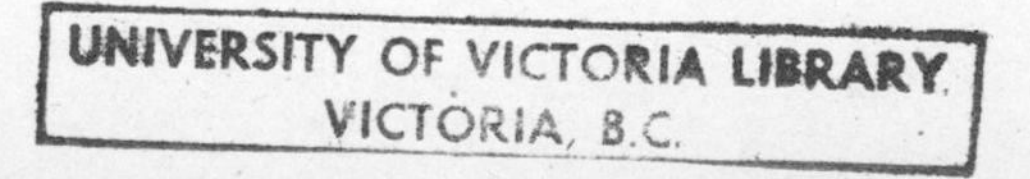

year, be it remembered, less than $1 million of Canada's funded debt was held by Canadians. Between 1914 and 1920 Canada's war expenditures rarely exceeded 10 per cent of the national income, and her tax structure was in 1939 no longer the primitive tax structure of customs and excise duties of twenty-five years earlier. Nevertheless war expenditure was only a fraction of 1 per cent before the outbreak of the present war, and this is a rough measure of the unpreparedness of the Dominion for total war. The war expenditure increases described in the previous section are almost too great to be believed. These have been possible because of the large real resources of the country of man-power and equipment. Employment of each of these since September 1939 has been upward, as may be measured by the increase of national income as long as that is an increase of real production and not only an increase in prices. Diminished consumption for non-war purposes and diminished investment in new equipment were other real sources of Canada's war effort. The tax structure was improved beyond all recognition to meet the new expenditures. To distribute the burden of war as fairly as possible a resort to direct taxes was made. Before the war more than two-thirds of all tax revenues came from indirect taxes. To-day, on the other hand, more than half is from direct taxation (personal income taxes, the national defence tax, the corporate income tax, the excess profits tax less payments to provinces for tax transfer, succession duties, and taxes on dividends and interest). Canadian taxes on personal incomes are higher than those in the United States and more or less conform to those in Great Britain. The increase in progression through income taxation is very noticeable. But the burden of indirect taxation is, all things considered, heavier in Canada than in Great Britain (Table 11, Part III). New taxes to restrict incomes have been levied. Among these are the excess profits tax, the national defence tax, succession duties, a gasoline tax, a passenger transportation tax and entertainments taxes on motion pictures. Other taxes to conserve resources include the automobile tax, the tax on radio valves and wireless sets. The whole policy of Canadian war finance, as illustrated in what has been said above, is best summarised in the Minister of Finance's own words in the Canadian House of Commons: "The task of finance is to provide the funds which are used to pay for war services. But in a deeper sense the task of finance is, by taxation and borrowing, to restrict the civilian demand for economic resources in order that they will be free when the defence or supply departments need them. . . . If finance proceeds more rapidly in curtailing civilian demand than defence proceeds in making use of the resources thus set free, there will be unemployment and waste, while, on the other hand, if finance lags behind the defence services, they will be faced by shortages and delays, and the competition between military and civil demands will bring about inflation."[1] Tax as high as you can and mobilise savings by an intensive campaign and avoid the inflationary gap brought about by bank borrowings, are the aims of the Dominion Treasury in 1943–44.

[1] The Hon. J. L. Ilsley, Canadian House of Commons Debates, 30th July 1940, p. 2272. Cf. Plumptre, *Mobilizing Canada's Resources for War*, Toronto, The Macmillan Co., 1941, p. 122.

CHAPTER V

THE PUBLIC FINANCE AND NATIONAL ECONOMY OF AUSTRALIA

I. THE NATIONAL ECONOMY

THE Commonwealth of Australia is over thirty-one times the size of the United Kingdom but has only about one-seventh of its population. Its size is roughly the same as that of the United States, but the United States has nineteen times Australia's population. As compared with Canada, Australia's area is about three-quarters of a million square miles less, but her population is approximately 7 millions as compared with Canada's 10 millions. Australia, however, owing to scarcity of rainfall, cannot support a population of anything like the size of that of the continental United States. The whole continent of Australia is a large and irregular plateau, part of which is below sea level. Round this plateau there is a mountainous coastline with intervals of sandy shores on the north, west and south. On the east coast there are good harbours and rivers, while in the west there is a coastline with poor inland water communication. Of the six States of the Commonwealth three are greatly superior to the other three in the production of wealth — Victoria, New South Wales and Queensland being much more prosperous on the whole than what may be called the marginal States — South Australia, Western Australia and Tasmania. This diversity in natural resources, size, population and state of development gives rise to differences of standards in financial administration as shown in the Budgets, even when these are corrected to make allowances for items brought into account in some but not in others, and adjustments made to eliminate the effects of emergency expenditure and variations in accounting practice. These differences are mainly in (1) the standard of expenditure in regard to the costs of administration and the scale of social services, (2) the maintenance of capital equipment and (3) the taxable capacity of the States and the standard of effort by the States and Local Authorities in raising revenue.

Population cannot be settled in vacant spaces unless there are available resources. Unless there is a rainfall of about ten inches in the area, cultivation is hardly possible. Wheat cannot be successfully grown if the rainfall is below ten inches, and settlement is impossible unless minerals or some special industrial or commercial opportunities exist. Methods of dry farming with an annual rainfall of this amount, eight inches falling within the growing period, and wheat-breeding have made it possible to grow wheat under difficult conditions, and the discovery of plenty of land suitable for the merino sheep — Australia is the chief producer of wool in the world — has led to the production of much wealth from arid and semi-arid areas. In Queensland, New South Wales and Victoria the rainfall, which is much heavier between the mountains and the coast than it is on the inner side of the Divide, varies in the coastal belt from 160 inches a year in Northern Queensland to 25 inches in Western Victoria. In Queensland sugar, wool, tropical fruit and dairy produce are the chief products ; in New South Wales wool, wheat, dairying and the production of fruit are the main primary industries, while in Victoria wheat-farming, wool-raising and dairying with cultivation of vines and citrus fruits in the Murray irrigation areas and of apples in the south are the chief occupations. Cattle and sheep are grazed, and forestry is carried on among the foothills of the Great Divide. On the plateaus mining and cattle-grazing are the chief industries.

When we turn to the marginal States we see the mistake made by Australians and outsiders alike of overestimating the natural wealth of the continent, although the achievements in developing pastoral and wheat-growing industries have been noteworthy. In the marginal States there is a large area which is difficult to cultivate and to develop. South Australia, out of a total area of 380,000 square miles, has an area of 311,000 square miles with a rainfall under 10 inches ; Western Australia, out of a total area of 976,000 square miles, has 487,000 square miles with a similar rainfall. Tasmania, although her rainfall exceeds in parts 100 inches per annum and in no part is less than 20 inches, is mountainous, particularly on the west, and the productive area is not large. One-third of the island has no population, and only over 6 million acres out of some 17 millions have been alienated. The economy of South Australia is based largely on wheat and wool produced under conditions more difficult than the average, and she is vulnerable to price depressions. She lacks coal, but in spite of this has retained a surprising amount of secondary industry. Western Australia also specialises in wheat and wool, and in addition in the production of gold. Unfortunately her finances have been seriously affected by reckless financing of wheat in an area well suited for this crop, and by an attempt to settle migrants in the extreme south-west for dairying. With a small population and limited resources capable of development, Tasmania has more difficult problems than those of the other five States. Her unproductive assets, for example, are a growing burden and her taxable capacity is low. Loan losses per head are relatively very high[1] and are a heavy burden on the State finances. Indeed they are much higher than those of South Australia and Western Australia. The main factors contributing to this are losses on railways, roads and bridges, and land settlement.

[1] See Table 15, Part III.

These variations in the economic position between States led the Commonwealth Grants Commission to lay down the fundamental principle that " Special Grants from the Commonwealth Government are justified when a State through financial stress from any cause is unable efficiently to discharge its functions as a member of the federation and should be determined by the amount of help found necessary to make it possible for that State by reasonable effort to function at a standard not appreciably below that of other States ".[1] A Federation, in short, cannot work on a strict book-keeping system, and it must be elastic in providing for change by constitutional amendment and for co-operation in supplementing the Constitution. Financial adjustments are necessary in the case of the units against whom the financial scheme of Federation may work unfavourably. The Centre and units more fortunately placed must make their contribution to the common cause of Federation. It cannot be expected that each of the units, economically or geographically, can be identical, and national policy may affect some of the units more detrimentally than others. It is necessary for the Centre to intervene so that the citizens in the Federation should have a minimum standard of social and other services. In this way the financial inequality of the units is remedied and the effective working of the Federation made possible.

We have referred to the development by the States of a policy of protection to rural production through subsidies and similar assistance, a policy of extending and intensifying settlement. This was a policy for the development of primary industry by State assistance. It clashed with the claims of secondary industry for protection by tariffs. The tariff was used as an instrument of development because it tended to produce a larger population and a better balanced economy. It imposed, however, a burden on exports ; yet in spite of it the main exports, wool and wheat, have increased. Tariff policy has raised the prices of protected goods, and these include the primary products butter, sugar and tobacco. According to the Commonwealth Grants Commission, " all sheltered products and activities, such as potatoes, bricks, transport and retailing, adjust their prices to the new level of costs. Unsheltered industry, which in Australia is predominantly export industry, is subject to world demand, and cannot raise its prices. In Australia, higher costs of consumption goods are nearly all passed on quickly, and often automatically, to wages and the costs of industry. It follows that the greater part of the cost of protection is passed on and finally borne, not by the consumer, but by the export industry."[2] States which have a large amount of unsheltered industry are Western Australia and South Australia, which had respectively

[1] Commonwealth Grants Commission, Third Report (F. 2251, 1936), Chap. vi, p. 75.

[2] *Ibid.*, p. 64.

60 and 47 per cent out of the total production of such industry in 1932–33 ; the percentage for all States was 35 per cent, for Queensland 24 per cent, for Victoria 29 per cent, for New South Wales 36 per cent and for Tasmania 39 per cent.[1] By unsheltered production is meant the production of primary products including minerals. Western Australia has always alleged that it is almost impossible to set up factory industries in competition with those of the Eastern States : Interstate free trade has exposed her infant industries to the competition of similar industries in the Eastern States. " If such industries ", the Government of Western Australia stated, " could have been established successfully, our population would have been greater, the avenues of employment increased, and the [State's] national income augmented to an extent that cannot be measured only by the excess cost of imports from the Eastern States." [2]

The ideas behind the policy of protection which is followed by the Commonwealth, ideas typical of not always very clear protectionist arguments, are best stated in *The Australian Tariff, An Economic Enquiry*, by Professors Copland, Giblin and Brigden and Messrs. Dyason and Wickens.[3] It is a report of an informal Committee invited by the Prime Minister to study the tariff problem. It pointed out that Australia's exports were primary products, the products of agriculture and mining, while her imports were mainly manufactured goods. Protection had conferred a double benefit. First, it had diverted resources from the primary industries where diminishing returns are in operation and where declining export prices would have resulted. Resources were diverted into secondary industry. A shift of the terms of international trade would have occurred without protection. To produce as great a national income under free trade as under protection it would have been necessary to expand primary industry already producing at increasing costs, and any addition to exports would, without doubt, depress prices. The issue did not, it may be noted, arise from protection to agriculture as in Great Britain, but from protection to manufactures. Secondly, the permanent policy of protection had added to the national income by increasing the share of wages where the largest number of people was supported on more generous lines. The tariff, in short, had subsidised labour at the expense of landowners. Opportunity for employment had increased and a higher standard of living was the result. " The advantage of protection

[1] Commonwealth Grants Commission, Third Report, Appendix 19, p. 206.

[2] Statement of Case, quoted by the Commonwealth Grants Commission, Fourth Report (F. 1816, 1937), p. 49.

[3] *The Australian Tariff, An Economic Enquiry* (Melbourne University Press in association with Macmillan & Co. Ltd., second edition, 1929). Cf. Copland, " A Neglected Phase of the Tariff Controversy ", *Quarterly Journal of Economics*, Feb. 1931. For a criticism of the Australian case see Anderson, " Protection and the Historical Situation : Australia ", *Quarterly Journal of Economics*, Nov. 1938.

is in the maintenance of a larger population than could have been expected at the same standard of living without the protective tariff." [1] The Committee did not attempt to estimate the net benefit or the net burden to the six States separately and was unable to adopt the provisional estimates made previously by two of their number.[2] The Committee estimated that Australian products which are protected cost, in 1926–27, £36 millions, more than the same goods could have been imported for, duty free. Protected manufactured goods cost about £26 millions more than free imports and protected primary products about £10 millions, a total of £36 millions, or £6 per head of population.

"In so far as the establishment of secondary industry involves a subsidy from the community, which falls with especial severity on export industry, there is a clash of interest between secondary industry and the interests which depend upon primary industry. Moreover, the secondary industries tend to be developed in the Eastern States. These are nearer the great coal-fields, and have the larger populations, and as they had an early start, the modern tendency to concentration makes these industries even larger. The more sparsely settled outer States could never establish these industries except at great cost to themselves. As a result the clash between the interests of primary and secondary industries tends to grow into a conflict between the more closely populated Eastern States of Victoria and New South Wales and the sparsely settled marginal States of South Australia, Western Australia and Tasmania. Queensland occupies a middle position because of her enormous pastoral wealth, the small proportion of really arid country, and the high return of the sugar industry, protected by an embargo and price agreement which is now equivalent to a duty of about 250 per cent." [3] Table I overleaf shows the production by States in 1937–38.

Another noteworthy feature of Australian national economy is the high *per capita* income which prevails in spite of the policy of protection, and which is responsible for some of the arguments quoted above (cf. pp. 105-6). Australia belongs to the high national income group of countries, the other countries being the United States, Canada, New Zealand, Great Britain and the Argentine. With a population of only about 7 millions the national income in 1937–38 was £796 millions, or £113 per annum per head of the total population, or over £2 per week, a large figure. If the breadwinner alone be taken, Australia's national income per head, like others of the £2 a week group, is double that amount. But, however, this group contains only 10 per cent of the world's population. No

[1] *Op. cit.*, p. 140.
[2] *Ibid.* Appendix W (The Effects of the Tariff upon State Finances), p. 229.
[3] Commonwealth Grants Commission, Third Report (F. 2251, 1936), para. 65, p. 39.

TABLE I

PRODUCTION BY STATES, 1937–38 *

(£ millions)

State	Agriculture, Dairying, Poultry, Bees, Forestry and Fisheries	Pastoral	Mining	Total Primary Industry	Manufactures (Secondary Industry)	Grand Total
New South Wales	31·1	35·3	12·0	78·4	85·2	163·6
Victoria . .	30·5	19·5	2·3	52·3	64·9	117·2
Queensland .	21·9	16·2	3·6	41·7	18·6	60·3
South Australia .	12·3	5·1	2·6	20·0	13·8	33·8
Western Australia	8·8	4·5	9·4	22·7	8·6	31·3
Tasmania . .	4·4	1·6	2·3	8·3	5·4	13·7
Total . .	109·0	82·2	32·2	223·4	196·5	419·9

* Compiled from data in Appendix 10, Commonwealth Grants Commission, Eighth Report (1941).

less than 81 per cent of the world's population has an average income per breadwinner below £2 a week, so that the world as a whole is poor in comparison with the first group of countries above. An intermediate group covering 9 per cent of the world's population includes the principal industrial countries of Europe with an average income per breadwinner of between £2 and £4 weekly.[1] Australia's income in 1937–38, the pre-rearmament year, was higher than in the pre-depression year 1928–29, and very much higher than in 1931–32. This is clearly brought out in the following table :

TABLE II

THE NATIONAL INCOME OF AUSTRALIA *

Year	National Income (£ millions)	Index Numbers (100=1928–29)
1928–29	768	100
1929–30	730	95
1930–31	566	74
1931–32	528	69
1932–33	550	72
1933–34	609	79
1934–35	632	82
1935–36	704	92
1936–37	760	99
1937–38	796	104
1938–39	788	103
1939–40	863	112
1940–41	925	120

* Cf. Colin Clark and J. G. Crawford, *The Australian National Income*, Commonwealth Grants Commission, Seventh, Eighth and Ninth Reports.

[1] Cf. Colin Clark, *The Conditions of Economic Progress.*

The table also shows the effect of the change-over from a peace-time to a war-time economy. In 1939–40, for example, as compared with the previous year, there was an increase of 9 per cent, and in the following year of 8 per cent. Among the factors making for an increase, the most important was the great drive to increase the production of munitions of war with the consequent demand for labour and the rise in wages, especially in the industrial States of New South Wales and Victoria. The trend towards increasing productivity with the aid of machinery and the better organisation of labour-power and resources has been marked in recent years in Australian as in British industry. This has been specially intensified since 1939–40. On the other hand, there have been the adverse influences arising from the dislocation of overseas trade. Owing to war demands on shipping, Great Britain has been unable to absorb the normal imports from Australia. This has severely affected the States which were most dependent on primary production, such as South Australia and Western Australia in regard to wheat and Tasmania in regard to fruit.

Australia's prosperity, indeed her very existence, depends on making the most of her specialised resources and on exchanging them on as advantageous terms as possible for her other requirements. Australia, as we have seen, is the world's largest producer of wool, and she is also one of the world's important producers of wheat. Out of a total export trade of £A157·6 millions in 1937–38 the exports of wool amounted to £47·0 millions, wheat and flour to £26·9 millions, meat to £12·3 millions, butter to £10·8 millions, hides and skins to £6·2 millions, fruit to £6·0 millions and sugar to £4·0 millions. Of minerals export gold amounted to £13·9 millions, and lead and spelter to £5·7 millions. On the other hand, her imports were mainly manufactured goods which she could not make so cheaply. Of her imports from abroad, amounting to £114·0 millions sterling, some of the most important were piece goods £12·0 millions, motor cars, chassis, bodies and parts £7·8 millions, iron and steel £5·0 millions, electrical machinery, cable and wire £5·0 millions, motive power machinery other than electric £3·7 millions, drugs, chemicals and fertilisers £5·3 millions, tea £2·4 millions, tobacco, cigarettes and cigars £2·0 millions. The greater part of Australia's customs and excise revenue, normally over 60 per cent, is the result of the policy of protection, and this, it may be noted, makes it impossible to adjust revenue easily to meet the needs of the Commonwealth. Moreover, business conditions and, in war-time, shipping have a great effect on it, a much greater effect than on any other major branch of taxation. In 1930–31 customs and excise revenue fell by 32 per cent, while direct taxation, Commonwealth and State, actually increased in that year. Even inclusive of the sales tax the fall in total indirect taxation in 1930–31 was 25 per cent. Incidentally, were the Commonwealth to confine itself to customs and excise it would be in an uncertain position, and as the Commonwealth Grants Commission has more than once pointed out, any nice adjustment of taxing powers to responsibilities would be impossible in practice.

Conclusions on the National Economy

Australia's economy is very dependent on international trade, which accounts for a considerable proportion of her national income. Her resources are such that she specialises on primary products, in several of which she is one of the world's biggest producers. Nevertheless, she has for a long time pursued a policy of high and increasing protection, especially to secondary industry. This has resulted in a more diversified economy. The national income is very high, but the policy of protection has intensified the effects of the great physical and economic differences between the more populous and prosperous States of New South Wales, Victoria and Queensland, and the marginal States of South Australia, Western Australia and Tasmania. These differences, together with financial policies that have not always been very prudent in the past, have necessitated financial assistance in the form of annual special grants from the Commonwealth to the marginal States. The grants are intended to enable these States, with reasonable effort on their own part, to provide social and other services at a level similar to that of the other States.

II. The Constitutional Background

By the Commonwealth of Australia Constitution Act, 1900,[1] which came into force in the following year, the Australian Parliament has the "power to make laws for the peace, order and good government of the Commonwealth with respect to (*inter alia*) taxation; but so as not to discriminate between States or parts of States".[2] At the time of federation the Commonwealth was given limited financial powers. It was granted under the Constitution (section 88) exclusive power to levy indirect taxation in the form of customs and excise. But under section 87, known as the Braddon clause, only one-fourth of the net revenue from these duties was allocated annually to Commonwealth expenditure during the years 1901 to 1910, the remainder being handed over to the States. Alternatively, it could have been "applied towards the payment of interest on debts of the several States taken over by the Commonwealth".

[1] 63 & 64 Vict. chap. 12, amended in 1928 by the addition of section 105A giving effect to the powers conferred on the Commonwealth by section 105.
[2] Section 51.

During the last war, however, in 1915–16, the Commonwealth levied a direct tax in the form of an income tax. Before this date, viz. in 1910–11, it had levied the land tax and in 1914–15 estate duties, both direct taxes. In 1930–31 its indirect taxing powers were extended to sales taxes levied on home-manufactured and imported goods. The Constitution gives the Commonwealth the widest taxing powers, both in direct and indirect taxation. The States, having agreed to assign to the Central authority under the Constitution customs and excise taxes (including sales taxes), have been left almost entirely with direct taxes. During the last four decades balance between the revenues of the Commonwealth and States has been maintained by recurring and non-recurring grants to the States from the Commonwealth which amounted during the period 1901–1941 to the large total of £385 millions.[1] In Federations, especially at certain stages of development, redistribution of revenue is to some degree inevitable, and Australia is no exception to the rule. Experience showed that inequalities as between the States occurred and it was found that certain States could not discharge, without assistance, their functions efficiently. The Commonwealth Grants Commission, under section 96 of the Constitution,[2] laid down the principle mentioned on p. 107 above.

In the pre-rearmament year, 1937–38, apart from invalid and old-age pensions financed by the Commonwealth Government and costing £15·8 millions, the Commonwealth made the following payments to or for the States: interest on States' debts £7·6 millions, sinking fund on States' debts £1·5 millions, special grants under section 96 of the Constitution £2·4 millions, Federal Aid road grants £4·1 millions, other grants £0·5 million: total £16·1 millions.[3, 4] In 1942–43 invalid and old-age pensions were estimated to be £22·4 millions, and payments to the States from Consolidated Revenue £41·1 millions.[5]

At the various conferences of Commonwealth and State ministers and in the press it has sometimes been claimed that there has been invasion of a field of taxation reserved by the Constitution for the States. But a careful examination of the proceedings of these conferences and the reports of the Commonwealth Grants Commission as well as of the Constitution Act itself proves that no such invasion took place. There is

[1] Amount paid from Consolidated Revenue Fund, excluding payments for relief of primary producers, medical research, etc.

[2] Section 96 reads, "During a period of ten years after the establishment of the Commonwealth and thereafter until the Parliament otherwise provides, the Parliament may grant financial assistance to any State on such terms and conditions as the Parliament thinks fit".

[3] See Table 19, Part III.

[4] Excluding relief of primary producers.

[5] Excluding relief of primary producers, but including £27·8 millions for income tax and entertainments tax reimbursement.

certainly nothing in the Constitution which would justify this contention. The States, for example, were never given the entire field of direct taxation for themselves. The steadily widening field of Federal activity and the increasing cost of defence from the first decade of the present century made any such separation of revenues impossible even at the time when the Commonwealth had only just embarked on a national programme. Customs and excise revenues would have been quite inadequate to finance the 1914–18 war and the Commonwealth, therefore, had to resort to direct taxation.[1] Total war always throws added gigantic burdens and responsibilities on a Federal Government.

These points may be made clearer by a short survey of the salient changes in the financial history of the Commonwealth. These may be grouped conveniently into four stages: (1) the period of the Braddon clause — section 87 of the Constitution — which covered the years 1901 to 1910; (2) the period from 1910–11 to 1926–27, the period of the *per capita* payments; (3) the period from the Financial Agreement Act, 1928, to 1942, the period when the Commonwealth took over the debts of the six States and the Loan Council was formed; and (4) the period of the ascendancy of the Commonwealth Government from the passing of the legislation to implement the uniform income tax plan, *i.e.* from 4th June 1942 to the present time. Each of these periods corresponds to major changes in financial policy.

(1) *Period I* (1900–1901 to 1909–10).—In regard to the first of these periods, from 1901 to 1910, monthly payments to the States of all the surplus revenue of the Commonwealth were provided for in sections 87, 89, 93 and 94 of the Constitution. Each State was credited with the Commonwealth revenue collected in that State and debited with the expenditure incurred on its behalf in the transferred departments, and also with a share of the new expenditure of the Commonwealth on a *per capita* basis. This is generally known as the "book-keeping system". This was, under the Constitution, to continue until 1906–7 (the expiry of the first five years provided for in section 93), or until "Parliament otherwise provides". The "book-keeping system" could thus be changed by the Commonwealth Parliament at any time after 8th October 1906, the date of the expiry of the five-year period. Payments to the States of surplus revenue of the Commonwealth ceased when the Commonwealth began to pay invalid and old-age pensions. This gave rise to criticism. In 1907–8 the Commonwealth paid its surplus revenue into a trust account as a reserve for these pensions, a procedure which was

[1] The Commonwealth Grants Commission clearly shows that it would have been impossible for the Commonwealth to vacate the field of direct taxation even if it had discontinued the *per capita* payments (*vide* table on p. 23, First Report, F. 3390, 1934).

challenged by the State of New South Wales, but upheld by the High Court. The State of Western Australia was permitted under section 95 of the Constitution to impose for five years customs duties on goods passing into that State and not originally imported from beyond the Commonwealth, such duties being collected by the Commonwealth. It may be noted that in the Constitution as it came from the final Convention in Melbourne the provision that three-fourths of the revenue from customs should go to the States was a permanent one. But free-traders believed that the raising of a customs revenue four times greater than was required by the Commonwealth Government would mean a victory for protection, and others were uncertain of the future of State revenues. Owing to these fears a compromise was made limiting the payments to the States to ten years. Section 96 was also inserted providing for special grants during these first ten years of Federation, and thereafter if Parliament thought these to be necessary.

(2) *Period II* (1910–11 to 1926–27).—In 1910 a scheme of *per capita* payments was adopted by the passing of the Surplus Revenue Act of that year, and payment became effective from 1st July. A special payment to Western Australia of £250,000 per annum in the first year, thereafter progressively decreasing by £10,000 each year, was included in this Act.[1] No constitutional amendment took place when it was passed, and thus the position of the States was insecure. A constitutional referendum was indeed taken, but it was rejected as it was thought the proposed amendment might "leg-rope the Commonwealth". The various Governments continued, however, to honour the agreement for *per capita* payments. The Act of 1910 provided that it should continue for ten years from 1st July 1910, and thereafter until Parliament otherwise determined. *Per capita* payments continued until 1926–27.

(3) *Period III* (1927–28 to 1941–42).—The Commonwealth Government was under no obligation to continue the *per capita* payments and the Surplus Revenue Act was repealed. The States, faced with the loss of *per capita* payments, accepted certain proposals incorporated in the Finance Agreement of 1927, and hence in the Financial Agreement Act of 1928. This has improved the credit of the States as a whole.[2] Independent borrowing by the States increased the cost of loans, and since 1923 borrowing programmes have been considered from time to time at conferences at which the Treasurers of the Commonwealth and of the States formed themselves into an advisory but not an executive body — the Australian Loan Council. Between 1923 and 1927 it arranged for the amounts

[1] See Table 20, Part III.

[2] The interest contributions of the Commonwealth, however, will not increase as population increases and, therefore, the position of the States may grow less favourable as time goes on.

to be borrowed by the Commonwealth and the six States. By the Financial Agreement Act of 1928 this advisory body officially became the Australian Loan Council. It was the Central authority which arranged within prescribed limits all borrowings, conversions, renewals, redemptions and consolidations of the public debts of the Commonwealth and of the States. The Commonwealth took over the public debts of the States but left them to find the interest. The Commonwealth shared among the States an annual sum of £7,584,912, the equivalent of the *per capita* payments for 1926–27, as a contribution towards interest on these debts. It also paid for certain sinking fund contributions. The Constitution was amended (by section 105A, added in 1928) to give effect to the powers originally conferred on the Commonwealth in section 105 of the Constitution and used in the Financial Agreement of 1927. Section 105A is as follows:

(i) The Commonwealth may make agreements with the States with respect to the public debts of the States, including:
- (*a*) the taking over of such debts by the Commonwealth;
- (*b*) the management of such debts;
- (*c*) the payment of interest and the provision and management of sinking funds in respect of such debts;
- (*d*) the consolidation, renewal, conversion and redemption of such debts;
- (*e*) the indemnification of the Commonwealth by the States in respect of debts taken over by the Commonwealth; and
- (*f*) the borrowing of money by the States or by the Commonwealth, or by the Commonwealth for the States.

(ii) The Parliament may make laws for validating any such agreement made before the commencement of this section.

(iii) The Parliament may make laws for the carrying-out by the parties thereto of any such agreement.

(iv) Any such agreement may be varied or rescinded by the parties thereto.

(v) Every such agreement and any such variation thereof shall be binding upon the Commonwealth and the States parties thereto notwithstanding anything contained in this Constitution or the Constitution of the several States or in any law of the Parliament of the Commonwealth or of any State.

(vi) The powers conferred by this section shall not be construed as being limited in any way by the provisions of section one hundred and five of this Constitution.

The period from the Financial Agreement of 1927 to 1942 separates into two well-marked divisions — that before the depression of 1930 and that from the depression to 1942. Before the depression the total deficits were not high. Indeed, in Victoria and Queensland they were low. After the depression the deficits were very abnormal in the States, at any rate until 1935–36. An examination of the surpluses and deficits of the

Commonwealth shows between 1929–30 and 1939–40 a net surplus of £6·5 millions in the Commonwealth accounts. In nine of the eleven years there were surpluses. In 1930–31 there was an abnormal deficit of £10·8 millions, but in the succeeding years there was a surplus of £18·8 millions. In the same period the net deficit of New South Wales was £43·6 millions, that of Victoria £7·8 millions, that of Queensland £8·1 millions, that of South Australia £6·5 millions, that of Western Australia £6·0 millions and that of Tasmania £0·9 million. The total net deficit for the period 1929–30 to 1939–40 was £72·8 millions for all States combined and £66·3 millions for Commonwealth and States.[1] The losses on loan works in the States rose to a very high figure. "It is obvious", said the Commonwealth Grants Commission, "that the depression has been the chief factor in increasing the deficits of the States. The depression affected the Commonwealth in a most striking way, owing chiefly to the great reduction in customs revenue. This led to an increase of Commonwealth taxation in the form of a drastic impost on property incomes, a primage duty on imports and the sales tax, which is a form of excise taxation and therefore not open to the States.[2] The Commonwealth was also helped very much by the suspension by the British Government of payments in respect of war debt."[3]

In 1933 the Commonwealth Government appointed the Commonwealth Grants Commission of three members to enquire into and report upon claims made by any State for a grant of financial assistance under section 96 of the Constitution. The grants recommended in 1937–38 were as follows: South Australia £1,200,000; Western Australia £575,000; Tasmania £575,000; making a total of £2,350,000. In 1942–43 they were £550,000, £800,000 and £575,000 respectively, making a total of £1,925,000.[4]

(4) *Period IV* (from 1942 onwards).—It is not possible to demarcate with accuracy the beginning of the fourth period which for convenience is placed as from 1942. This year has been selected as it marks the passing of the uniform income tax law by the Australian Parliament and the High Court's judgment validating it. It is, in short, a landmark in Australian constitutional and financial history.

It will be recalled that in Canada in April 1941 the Minister of Finance offered compensation to the Provincial Governments in respect of personal and corporation income taxes and the guarantee of gasoline tax revenues, if they would vacate the personal and corporation income tax fields for

[1] See Commonwealth Grants Commission, Eighth Report (F. 1357, 1941), Appendix 20, p. 125.

[2] In 1932–33, in the depth of the depression, Federal, State and Local Authority taxation was 20 per cent of the national income; in 1939–40 the proportion was 18·2 per cent.

[3] Commonwealth Grants Commission, Third Report (F. 2251, 1936), p. 29.

[4] See Table 20, Part III.

the duration of the war in order that a uniform tax may be levied throughout the Dominion on persons and corporations. The Provinces accepted the proposal, the Dominion-Provincial Taxation Agreement Act was passed, and in the Budget for 1942–43 $84,428,000 were provided for compensation. An effective and equitable tax policy during the war was thus made possible. In Australia the highest amount of taxation was imperative to finance the war, but the Commonwealth Government was severely handicapped in getting a reasonable return from the taxation of income by the high rates of income tax prevailing in some States. In January 1941 the Commonwealth Government submitted to the States alternative proposals for the reduction of all State income tax to the level of the most lightly taxed State or an increase to the level of the most heavily taxed. In the former case the States were to be compensated for their sacrifice of revenue by Commonwealth grants, and in the latter case the increased taxation was to be lent to the Commonwealth. The States rejected these proposals. On 27th June 1941, at a meeting of the Loan Council, the Commonwealth put forward a fresh proposal that the States should vacate the income tax field for the duration of the war in favour of the Commonwealth, and accept £30 millions annually in compensation, of which £24·5 millions would be distributed on a basis of £3 : 10s. per head of the population, the balance to be divided on any basis to which the States could agree. The Treasurer (Mr. A. W. Fadden) said that the Commonwealth must make the maximum demand on the taxpayer (who is the same taxpayer both in regard to Commonwealth and State taxation), and that the claims of the Commonwealth must come first. Otherwise, the varying incidence of State taxation may have to be overlooked by raising the Commonwealth taxation on high incomes (which were already heavily taxed in some States), or by abolishing the allowances on State income tax, such as the deduction which is allowed for Commonwealth tax purposes, and also many other concessions enjoyed by taxpayers. Either course would affect the State differentially. Thus Victoria, with an income tax of £2 : 11 : 4 per head of population, would not be affected to the same degree as Queensland, where the rate was £5 : 12 : 2 per head, or as New South Wales, where it was £5 : 10 : 7. The alternative course might be acceptable to Queensland but Victoria might regard it as unfair. With the exception of the Premier of South Australia all the State premiers opposed the proposals of the Commonwealth Government as imposing unconstitutional and crippling burdens. The Premier of Victoria protested that his State would be penalised for its long record of prudent finance to relieve the improvident States. If the State vacated the income tax field there would be a huge increase in Commonwealth taxation on low and medium-sized incomes in Victoria to bring the total taxation to that payable by Queensland and New South Wales. The Premiers of Queensland and Western Australia, on the other hand, held that the lower rates in Victoria have been made possible, not by better financial methods, but by the high protection policy of the Commonwealth. This, in their view, has made it easier to maintain a balanced Budget in the highly industrialised States than in those dependent almost entirely on primary production and disastrously sensitive to world price fluctuations.

War finance exigencies continued to force the issue of financial readjustments for the duration of the war, in spite of the States' cry that State sovereignty was endangered by what was called " unification by finance ". A Committee, appointed to consider a scheme of uniform income taxation for the Commonwealth, consisting of Professor R. C. Mills, of the University of Sydney, Mr. Scullin and Mr. Spooner, presented a report early in April 1942. They recommended the retirement of the States from the field of income taxation for the duration of the war and one year thereafter, the substitution of the Commonwealth as the one income-taxing authority as from 1st July, and compensation to the States for loss of revenue. On 22nd April the Premiers' Conference representing the Governments of all the States and of the Commonwealth rejected by a decisive majority the Commonwealth Government's proposal. This was done although the Commonwealth Prime Minister had clearly stated that the Commonwealth must have complete freedom of action over the whole field of income tax throughout the war, with the right to take all additional proceeds of the increasing national income or the increased rates of taxation, and the States should limit their share of income taxation to £34·5 millions annually during the war. Three weeks later the Commonwealth Treasurer (Mr. Chifley) introduced into the House of Representatives three bills for a uniform tax throughout Australia — one bill provided for the temporary transfer to the Commonwealth of the trained staffs, accommodation and equipment of the States used for the collection of income tax, a second bill provided the payment for that assistance and for income tax to be equalised throughout the Commonwealth according to ability to pay, and a third bill provided that the payment of Federal income tax should have priority over the States income tax during the war and for one year thereafter. The Commonwealth estimated an additional yield of from £12 millions to £15 millions for war purposes. The States were to receive grants based on their average income tax collections for the last two years. The bills passed both Houses — the House of Representatives on 29th May and the Senate on 4th June. The new measures were to come into force on 1st August. The Governments of Victoria, Queensland, South Australia and Western Australia applied to the High Court for a decree invalidating the Acts as *ultra vires* under the Commonwealth Constitution. The case was heard before a full Bench of the High Court on 22nd June, and on 23rd July the Commonwealth Acts were held, in a majority judgment, to be valid in their entirety. It was held that these Acts were a genuine exercise of Parliament's defence power. It was essential for the effective prosecution of the war, which was being carried on to preserve the very existence of the Commonwealth and the States, that the entire resources of the country should be marshalled in the war effort. The Commonwealth, therefore, must have command of the sinews of war, of which income tax was a very important one. On 11th August at a Premiers' Conference the Commonwealth Prime Minister (Mr. Curtin) announced that the Commonwealth proposed to levy an entertainments tax which hitherto had been a State source of revenue, and he assured the premiers that the Commonwealth did not propose any further encroachment. This was regarded by the States as another inroad on the States' taxation field. Mr. Curtin said that the Commonwealth would levy a uniform tax yielding £3 millions a year as against £0·75 million raised by five States, Queensland at present not imposing an entertainments tax. The Commonwealth would refund to the States what they received from the tax in the current financial year. The Treasurer of Queensland said that his Government proposed to introduce an entertainments tax because of the imposition by the Commonwealth of a uniform income tax. All the State premiers, with the exception of Tasmania (who accepted the proposal for the war only), opposed the Commonwealth's scheme. Mr. Curtin informed the Conference that the Treasurer would submit the proposal to each State separately, and, if the States did not agree, the Commonwealth would impose on the States' entertainments taxes a uniform Federal tax. It should be noted that the Commonwealth levied an entertainments tax from 1916–17 to 1932–33. Mr. Curtin said the proposed tax was a luxury tax enforcing the required approach to austerity. Finally all the States agreed to withdraw from the entertainments tax field and were compensated on the basis of the previous year's revenue from this source. The new Commonwealth tax was a steeply graduated one rising to as much as 5s. 10d. on 12s. 6d., which is the cost of admittance to race meetings.

It is now possible to summarise the financial scheme of the Constitution :

(1) The Commonwealth has the widest powers of taxation under the Constitution, Federal taxation taking priority over State taxation. It has exclusive power to impose customs and excise duties, including sales taxes, a form of excise taxation. Its main source of revenue is customs and excise, and since the outbreak of war income and sales taxation has been extended. Other sources of revenue are estate duties, the land tax and,

in 1942, the entertainments tax to which it was decided to revert, reclassified as a direct tax. From 1916–17 to 1932–33 the Commonwealth had levied an entertainments tax, and from 1930–31 onwards a sales tax. In 1937–38 Commonwealth taxation was £69·0 millions. Indirect taxes yielded £56·4 millions (£8 : 4 : 4 per head of population) and direct taxes £12·6 millions (£1 : 16 : 10 per head of population) — a total of £10 : 1 : 2 per head of population.

(2) Except in regard to customs and excise including sales taxation, both the Commonwealth and the States have full powers of taxation. The main sources of State taxation are the income tax (including the dividend tax and other taxes on income), probate and succession duties, other stamp duties, the land tax, lotteries (in Queensland and Tasmania), the taxation of racing, motor vehicles, liquor and entertainments, and licences.

Taxation by the States in 1937–38 amounted to £49·7 millions, or £7 : 5 : 2 per head of population, of which £35·9 millions was direct and £13·8 millions indirect.

(3) The Commonwealth makes very considerable payments from revenue to the States in connexion with States' debts, grants for Federal Aid roads and works, special grants, grants for local public works, medical research and other items. In addition, assistance is given for relief of primary producers in the form of assistance to the wheat and other industries and of bounties. Primary producers also receive payments from the loan fund. Payments from revenue made direct to the States and excluding assistance for the relief of primary producers in 1937–1938 amounted to £16·1 millions. Of this, £9·9 millions, or 11·5 per cent of the revenue of the States in that year, enters into the Consolidated Revenue and similar accounts included in Tables VI and VII on pp. 128-9 and 130-31.[1]

(4) Special grants under section 96 of the Constitution are made to three of the six States — to Western Australia since 1910–11, to Tasmania since 1912–13 and to South Australia since 1929–30. The fundamental principle, laid down by the Commonwealth Grants Commission and quoted above, is that such grants are necessary when a State is unable to perform efficiently its functions as a unit of the Federation, and the grant is determined by the amount required to make it function, with reasonable effort, on a standard not appreciably below that of other States. The aim is to produce Budget equilibrium without impairing State responsibility. This necessitates the measurement of relative financial position, which entails Budget corrections on account of variations in accounting practice, and adjustments on account of economy in expenditure, severity of taxation,

[1] See also Tables 3, 4, 18 and 19 in Part III.

and maintenance of capital equipment. Such grants are required in a Federal system mainly for three reasons. In the first place, it is impossible to relate finance to function, and there is consequently maladjustment between the Centre and the units in the distribution of constitutional powers. Secondly, in a Federation there is always specialisation, which increases the differences between the units and benefits some more than others. It may even benefit the Centre at the expense of the units if their specialisation is due to tariff protection; the Eastern States of the Commonwealth are a good example. These are permanent factors. A less permanent factor is that the weaker States in a time of depression are an embarrassment to the Federation unless they are assisted. This is especially so where the loan policy of the States has been unwise, as in the case of some States of the Commonwealth. The 1942 Acts of the Commonwealth Parliament on uniform income tax throughout the Commonwealth, with the High Court's judgment upholding these Acts, show the overriding power of the Australian Parliament in taxation. During the forty years of Australian Federation the Commonwealth has greatly increased its governmental functions, and this has required the raising of greater revenues. This tendency has been very much accelerated by the war, as it was, though to a lesser extent, by the war of 1914–18. Total war adds enormously to the burdens and responsibilities of the Federal Government. The judgment of the High Court makes it clear that the Commonwealth's power to pass legislation virtually depriving the States of their taxation powers does not depend on the existence of a state of war in which the Commonwealth may exercise unlimited emergency powers. The Rt. Hon. William Hughes, K.C., holds that the judgment is the "final answer to the States' pretensions to sovereign powers", and the Rt. Hon. R. G. Menzies, K.C., a former Attorney-General of the Commonwealth Government, believes the judgment to be the beginning of a new era in which the Federation of Australia must be regarded as much more a unitary form of government and much less a Federal system than it was thought to be. In this respect, therefore, it is becoming similar to that of the Union of South Africa, and should a change in the Constitution take place after the war it is not unlikely that this will be on the South African model. Forty years' working of the Constitution shows that it requires revision, and public opinion, when it thinks about the matter at all, increasingly thinks of Australia as a whole. The questions of investing the Australian Parliament with greater functions, of the division of the States into many more Provinces with modest Provincial Councils, and of the increase in the membership of Parliament, are outside the scope of this Report. These points, however, have gained new importance in view of recent happenings in the financial relations of the

Commonwealth and the States. Without sound finance, sound government is not possible, and without sound government, sound finance is also impossible.

The trend towards increased importance of the Commonwealth in the constitutional framework has been strikingly demonstrated by the recent provisions for post-war reconstruction. On 22nd September 1942 Mr. Curtin, the Commonwealth Prime Minister, announced that the Cabinet had decided to initiate legislation authorising a referendum on the Federal Constitution. It was intended to give the Commonwealth wide powers in the economic and social field, with the object of enabling it to take effective action for reconstruction after its war-time powers had lapsed. A Convention, made up of representatives of the Governments and Oppositions of the Commonwealth and of the six States, was called to consider the proposals. As was to be expected, objections were raised on the part of the States, which complained that the measures were unificationist, and on that of the Opposition, which complained that the Commonwealth Government were using the war as a pretext for carrying out the Labour policy. But in the end unanimous agreement was suddenly reached. On 2nd December it was announced that the Convention had accepted the re-drafted bill, and that the State premiers had agreed to introduce it in their Parliaments before the end of January and to do everything in their power to secure its passage. It was hoped that this would obviate the necessity for a referendum, which would have been undesirable in war-time. The bill provided for the transfer by the States to the Commonwealth of specified powers for a period of five years after the cessation of hostilities. It would enable the Commonwealth to make laws for the purpose of post-war reconstruction on the following subjects: the conditions of Service men and the dependants of those who are killed or disabled; employment and unemployment; the organised marketing of commodities; the codifying of company law and the law regulating trusts, combines and monopolies; profiteering and prices (exclusive of prices or rates charged by the State or semi-governmental or local governing authorities for goods and services); production (other than primary) and the distribution of goods with the consent of the State Executive Council; primary production (provided that no legislation under this paragraph shall discriminate between the States); control of oversea exchange; oversea investments and the regulation of the raising of money in accordance with such plans as the Australian Loan Council approves; air transport; the uniformity of railway gauges; national works (provided that the consent of the State Executive Council shall be obtained before each work is undertaken and that it is carried out in co-operation with the State); national health in co-operation with the State; family allowances;

and aborigines. The bill was passed by all the State Parliaments, with two exceptions. The Victorian Parliament inserted a clause making its operation dependent on its being passed in all the other States, and the Tasmanian Legislative Council (or Upper House) rejected it altogether. It is to be re-submitted to them, and if it is rejected again, there may have to be a referendum.

It is evident that the exercise of these powers would involve far-reaching co-operation between the Commonwealth and State administrative machineries. It is even more evident that the transfer to the Commonwealth of all these functions, and the comprehensive reconstruction policy which they are designed to make possible, would be bound to have most important repercussion on the financial relations between the Federation and the units.

III. Government Revenues and Expenditures

General Trends

The increased cost of government in Australia in recent years is brought out in the table on the opposite page.

The expenditure figures include expenditures from revenue, including gross expenditure of business undertakings, of the Commonwealth and the States, less duplication due to grants and other intergovernmental payments. The revenue figures include tax revenues paid into the Consolidated Revenue or corresponding funds and gross revenues from business undertakings, less duplication as in the case of expenditures. Comparable figures of Local Authority expenditures and revenues are not available for any of the years given except 1937–38. For that year they have been shown in the footnote to the table.

The trends exhibited by the figures are clearly marked, and are very similar to those prevailing in the other Federations studied in this Enquiry. Both in the case of the Commonwealth and in that of the States there was a very considerable rise in expenditures and revenues during the war of 1914–18. After the first adjustments to a peace-time economy had been made, there was a further rise, more gradual but unmistakable, until the depression of 1930. This for a time caused a fall in the revenues and expenditures of both Commonwealth and States, though State expenditures did not fall until 1932–33. After the depression the tendency to rise reasserted itself, being reinforced after a few years by the period of rearmament. With the outbreak of war Commonwealth revenues and expenditures both increased enormously, whereas the rise was much less marked in the case of the States. With the exception of the depression years, Commonwealth expenditures, and consequently revenues, have in

TABLE III

Government Expenditures and Revenues in Australia [1]

(£ millions)

	1912–13	1922–23	1928–29	1931–32	1933–34	1937–38	1940–41	Percentage Increase		
								1937–38 over 1912–13	1940–41 over 1912–13	1940–41 over 1937–38
A. *Expenditures :*										
Commonwealth . .	16	54	67	60	62	76	141	375	781	86
State . . .	44	89	118	120	108	125	138	185	214	10
Total . .	60	143	185	180	170	201	279	235	365	39
B. *Revenues :*										
Commonwealth . .	22	63	73	70	73	89	150	305	582	68
State . . .	37	81	106	91	91	116	129	213	249	11
Total . .	59	144	179	161	164	205	279	248	374	36

[1] Duplication due to intergovernmental grants and similar payments has been eliminated. (This accounts for the large apparent surpluses of the Commonwealth roughly equal in most years to the apparent deficits of the States.) Commonwealth figures for 1912–13 and State figures for 1912–13, 1922–23 and 1928–29 are on a slightly different basis from those for later years. Local Government figures are not available in comparable form for any of the years given, except 1937–38. In that year they were as follows :

Expenditures and Revenues of All Governments, 1937–38

(£A millions)

	Expenditures	Revenues
Commonwealth . .	76	89
State . . .	125	115
Local . . .	25	18
Total . .	226	222

Source.—Finance, Bulletin of the Commonwealth Bureau of Census and Statistics.

TABLE IV

Government Revenues and Expenditures expressed in Terms of the National Income

Commonwealth and States

	1928–29	1931–32	1933–34	1937–38	1940–41
National Income [1] (£ millions)	768	528	609	796	925
Revenue : [2]					
(*a*) £ millions :					
Commonwealth	73	70	73	89	150
State	106	91	91	116	129
Total	179	161	164	205	279
(*b*) Per cent of the National Income :					
Commonwealth	9	13	12	11	16
State	14	17	15	15	14
Total	23	30	27	26	30
Expenditure : [2]					
(*a*) £ millions					
Commonwealth	67	60	62	76	141
State	118	120	108	125	138
Total	185	180	170	201	279
(*b*) Per cent of the National Income :					
Commonwealth	9	11	10	10	15
State	15	23	18	15	15
Total	24	34	28	25	30
Defence Expenditure :					
£ millions	4	4	4	6	66
Per cent of the National Income	1	1	1	1	7
Per cent of Commonwealth Expenditure	6	6	6	8	47
Per cent of Total Government Expenditure	2	2	2	3	24

All Governments

	1937–38
National Income [1] (£ millions)	796
Revenue : [3]	
(*a*) £ millions :	
Commonwealth	89
State	116
Local	18
Total	223
(*b*) Per cent of the National Income :	
Commonwealth	11
State	15
Local	2
Total	28
Expenditure : [3]	
(*a*) £ millions :	
Commonwealth	76
State	125
Local	25
Total	226
(*b*) Per cent of the National Income :	
Commonwealth	10
State	15
Local	3
Total	28
Defence Expenditure :	
£ millions	6
Per cent of the National Income	1
Per cent of Commonwealth Expenditure	8
Per cent of Total Government Expenditure	3

[1] Produced income, as given in the Seventh and Ninth Reports (1940 and 1942) of the Commonwealth Grants Commission.
[2] See Table III.
[3] See Table III, footnote.

the long run tended to increase more than those of the States and Local Authorities.

These tendencies are further illustrated by the table on p. 124, which compares Government revenues and expenditures, and defence expenditures separately, with the national income. It shows that the Commonwealth finances were more sensitive in the short run to changes in the national income during the depression than were those of the States. Moreover, with respect to her war effort Australia did not get fully into her stride until after the period covered by the figures given there.

The Tax Structure

It will have been noticed that in the above tables the Commonwealth appears to be shown to have continuous large surpluses, and the States deficits usually of similar magnitude. This is due to the transfer to the States of revenues collected by the Commonwealth, which has been dealt with in more detail in section II of this chapter (" The Constitutional Background "). The following table and diagrams illustrate the transfer of revenues since the last war (the figures refer to tax revenues only) : [1]

TABLE V

TAX REVENUES AVAILABLE TO COMMONWEALTH AND STATES

(£ millions)

	Year ended 30th June—							
	1920	1925	1930	1935	1938	1939	1940	1941
Total tax receipts :								
Commonwealth .	42	53	58	59	69	74	90	126
States . . .	14	23	34	36	50	51	54	56
Payments by Commonwealth to or for States * .	7	8	11	14	16	16	16	15
Total tax revenue available :								
To Commonwealth	35	45	47	45	53	58	74	111
To States . .	21	31	45	50	66	67	70	71
Total tax revenues, Commonwealth and States .	56	76	92	95	119	125	144	182

* Excluding payments for industries, non-recurring grants, and payments for medical research, etc.

[1] Since 1931–32 the Commonwealth has also made payments to the States from Loan Fund. Table 18 in Part III gives in summary form Commonwealth payments to or for the States from revenue and from Loan Fund from 1930–31 to 1941–42, Table 19 gives details of the payments made in 1937–38, while Table 20 gives special grants from 1910–11 to 1942–43.

CHART I

Tax Revenues collected by and available to Commonwealth and States

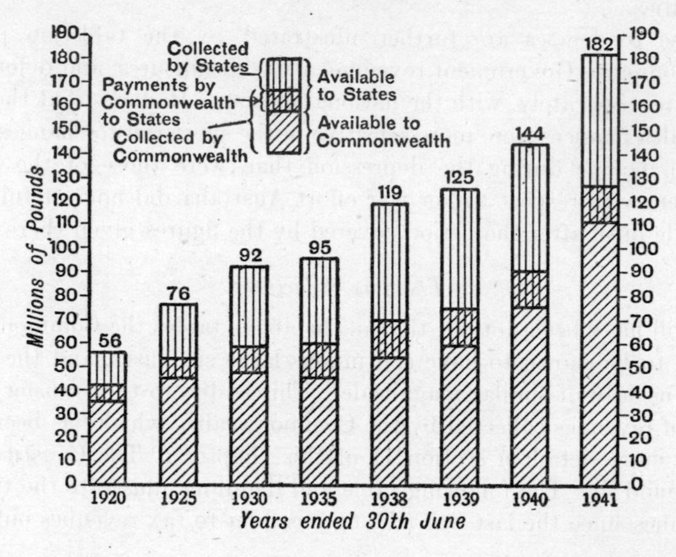

CHART II

Proportion of Total Tax Revenues available to Commonwealth and States

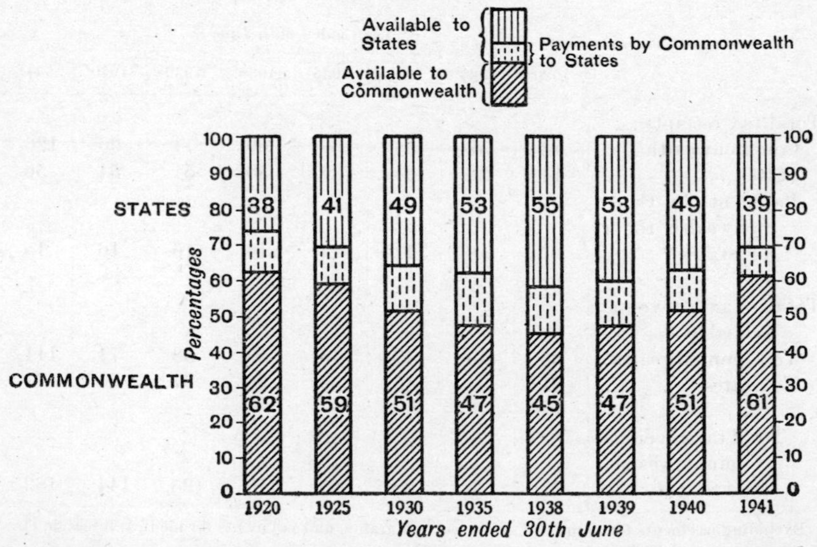

Note.—The proportion of total tax revenues collected by the Commonwealth but made available to the States in the form of grants and similar payments was as follows:

	Year ended 30th June—							
	1920	1925	1930	1935	1938	1939	1940	1941
Grants, etc., as a percentage of total tax revenues .	12	11	12	14	13	13	11	8

The figures, and especially the percentages in Chart II, show that during the twenties and thirties of the present century, up to the rearmament period, the tendency for Commonwealth revenues to rise relative to those of the States was for a time reversed, at any rate in the case of tax revenues. This phase was specially marked during the depression when the receipts from indirect taxation, on which the Commonwealth largely relied, fell considerably, while those from direct taxation, the main source of revenue of the States, increased [1] (see pp. 109-10 above). It came to an abrupt end with the advent of rearmament and war, and the expansion of Commonwealth revenues again outstripped that of State revenues, as the Commonwealth came to rely more and more on direct taxation (see pp. 115-22 above, and compare Table VII below with Table 1 in Part III).

Tables VI and VII give the main heads of revenue of Commonwealth, States and Local Authorities in 1937–38 in thousands of pounds and in percentages. The items are divided into the four main groups: I, Progressive Taxes; II, Taxes on Real Property; III, Taxes on Business; and IV, Mainly Consumption Taxes. The figures are, in the main, taken from those published by the Commonwealth Bureau of Census and Statistics in their bulletin *Finance*. These refer to the Consolidated Revenue Accounts of the Commonwealth and the States, except that in the case of New South Wales several special funds are included because they cover fields included in other States in the Consolidated Revenue Fund. The other main funds, the Loan and Trust Funds, are excluded from the tables.[2]

The figures differ, however, from those in *Finance* in several respects. To begin with, net revenues only of business undertakings have been included, as these alone are comparable to taxes. Net losses incurred by some States or by the Commonwealth have not been deducted from net revenues of others in arriving at the totals, but have been included in the

[1] Commonwealth revenue from customs and excise amounted to £41·8 millions in 1929–30, £28·3 millions in 1930–31, £28·4 millions in 1931–32, £48·4 millions in 1937–38, £53·8 millions in 1940–41, and was budgeted to be £47·6 millions in 1941–42, though it turned out to be £56·8 millions. In 1937–38 it accounted for 70 per cent of Commonwealth tax revenues, whereas income taxes accounted for 60 per cent of State tax revenues.

[2] The Commonwealth Loan Fund came into existence in 1911–12. In the last war it was divided into a General Loan Fund, mainly for public works, and a War Loan Fund for war purposes. The State Loan Funds are debited with all loan moneys raised by the States and credited with the expenditure therefrom on public works or other purposes. Payments into the Trust Fund of the Commonwealth include those for invalid and old-age pensions under the Commonwealth Invalid and Old-Age Pensions Act, 1908. State Trust Funds include the amounts held in trust by the State Governments for various purposes, *e.g.* savings bank funds, municipal sinking funds placed in the hands of the Governments, the sums deposited with the Governments by life insurance companies in cash or approved securities as required by law, and various other accounts such as suspense and superannuation accounts.

TABLE VI

THE REVENUE SYSTEM OF AUSTRALIA, ALL GOVERNMENTS, 1937–38 [1]

(£ thousands)

	Common-wealth	State	Local	Total
GROUP I. *Progressive Taxes :*				
Taxes on individual income [2] . . .	5,753	24,272	..	30,025
Probate, estate and succession duties .	1,873	3,951	..	5,824
Total, Group I	7,626	28,223	..	35,849
GROUP II. *Taxes on Real Property :*				
Land tax	1,368	1,157	..	2,525
Local rates and penalties [3] . .	..	..	13,295	13,295
State non-tax revenue from lands .	..	4,507	..	4,507
Total, Group II	1,368	5,664	13,295	20,327
GROUP III. *Taxes on Business :*				
Taxes on company income [2] . . .	3,645	..	..	3,645
War-time (1914–19) profits tax .	–1	..	..	–1
Stamp duties	..	2,938	..	2,938
Licences and miscellaneous State taxes	..	331	253	584
Non-tax revenue under Group III .	358	..	..	358
Total, Group III . . .	4,002	3,269	253	7,524
GROUP IV. *Mainly Consumption Taxes :*				
Customs	32,973	..	..	32,973
Excise :				
Liquor [4]	8,473	..	..	8,473
Tobacco (including cigars and cigarettes)	5,592	..	..	5,592
Other	1,345	..	..	1,345
Sub-total, Excise	15,410	..	..	15,410
Other Similar Taxes and Licences :				
Sales tax	8,024	..	..	8,024
Flour tax	3	..	..	3
State liquor taxes	..	701	..	701
Motor vehicles	..	5,417	..	5,417
Entertainments	..	515	..	515
Racing	..	1,131	..	1,131
Lotteries	..	473	..	473
Other taxes (local)	..	..	45	45
Sub-total, Other Taxes and Licences	8,027	8,237	45	16,309

TABLE VI—(*continued*)

	Commonwealth	State	Local	Total
Revenue from Business Undertakings, Public Works and Services : [5]				
Post Office	2,789	..	..	2,789
Railways, tramways and omnibuses	..	12,844	..	12,844
Harbours, rivers and lights	..	1,649	..	1,649
Water supply, sewerage, irrigation, drainage, etc.	..	1,758	1,090	2,848
Other State business undertakings	..	937	..	937
Local council properties	..	..	1,622	1,622
Street construction	..	..	596	596
Other local works and services	..	..	253	253
Local business undertakings	..	..	351	351
Sub-total, Business Undertakings, Public Works and Services	2,789	17,188	3,912	23,889
Miscellaneous :				
Territories [6]	331	..	..	331
Interest [7]	1,044 [8]	5,921	..	6,965
Other	1,488	7,818	839	10,145
Sub-total, Miscellaneous	2,863	13,739	839	17,441
Total, Group IV	62,062	39,164	4,796	106,022
Grants and similar intergovernmental payments	..	9,906	6,379	16,285
GRAND TOTAL	75,058	86,226	24,723	186,007
Less grants, etc.	9,906	6,379	..	16,285
NET TOTAL	65,152	79,847	24,723	169,722

[1] *These figures differ from those in " Finance " (bulletin of the Commonwealth Bureau of Census and Statistics) in that they include net revenue only of Commonwealth and State business undertakings. For other details, especially on State taxation figures, see text.*

[2] Complete separate data are not available for individual and company income taxation. The (known) total of Commonwealth income taxation has therefore been split up in the proportion of assessments for the year in question, and that of State income taxation has been given in Group I without being split up. The figure for State individual income taxation thus includes company taxation.

[3] Separate figures of rates and penalties are not available for Queensland and South Australia. In the other States penalties are very small in proportion to rates (see Part III, Table 7).

[4] State liquor taxes are given under " Other Similar Taxes and Licences ".

[5] Net revenues only for business undertakings. Total receipts for local public works and services.

[6] Excluding railways.

[7] Commonwealth and States.

[8] Excluding balance of interest on States' debts payable by States.

TABLE VII

The Revenue System of Australia, All Governments, 1937–38 [1]

(Percentage distribution)

	Percentage Share of each Government in Total Revenues				Percentage Distribution of each Government's Revenue			
	Common-wealth	State	Local	Total	Common-wealth	State	Local	Total
Group I. *Progressive Taxes:*								
Taxes on individual income [2]	19	81	..	100	8	28	..	18
Probate, estate and succession duties	32	68	..	100	2	5	..	3
Total, Group I	21	79	..	100	10	33	..	21
Group II. *Taxes on Real Property:*								
Land tax	54	46	..	100	2	2	..	1
Local rates and penalties [3]	..	..	100	100	..	..	54	8
State non-tax revenue from lands	..	100	..	100	..	5	..	3
Total, Group II	7	28	65	100	2	7	54	12
Group III. *Taxes on Business:*								
Taxes on company income [2]	100	..	..	100	5	..	..	2
War-time (1914–19) profits tax	100	..	..	100	..	..	..	..
Stamp duties	..	100	..	100	..	3	..	2
Licences and miscellaneous State taxes	..	57	43	100	..	..	1	..
Non-tax revenue under Group III	100	..	..	100	..	..	..	..
Total, Group III	53	44	3	100	5	3	1	4
Group IV. *Mainly Consumption Taxes:*								
Customs	100	..	..	100	44	..	..	19
Excise:								
Liquor [4]	100 [4]	..	..	100	11	..	..	5
Tobacco (including cigars and cigarettes)	100	..	..	100	7	..	..	3
Other	100	..	..	100	2	..	..	1
Sub-total, Excise	100	..	..	100	20	..	..	9
Other Similar Taxes and Licences:								
Sales tax	100	..	..	100	11	..	..	5
Flour tax	100	..	..	100	..	..	..	..
State liquor taxes	..	100	..	100	..	1	..	1
Motor vehicles	..	100	..	100	..	6	..	3
Entertainments	..	100	..	100	..	1	..	..
Racing	..	100	..	100	..	1	..	1
Lotteries	..	100	..	100	..	1	..	..
Other taxes (local)	..	..	100	100	..	..	..	..
Sub-total, Other Taxes and Licences	49	50	1	100	11	10	..	10

TABLE VII—(*continued*)

	Percentage Share of each Government in Total Revenues				Percentage Distribution of each Government's Revenue			
	Common-wealth	State	Local	Total	Common-wealth	State	Local	Total
Revenue from Business Undertakings, Public Works and Services : [5]								
Post Office	100	..	..	100	4	..	..	2
Railways, tramways and omnibuses	..	100	..	100	..	15	..	8
Harbours, rivers and lights	..	100	..	100	..	2	..	1
Water supply, sewerage, irrigation, drainage, etc.	..	62	38	100	..	2	4	2
Other State business undertakings	..	100	..	100	..	1	..	1
Local council properties	..	..	100	100	..	..	7	1
Street construction	..	..	100	100	..	..	2	..
Other local works and services	..	..	100	100	..	..	1	..
Local business undertakings	..	..	100	100	..	..	2	..
Sub-total, Business Undertakings, Public Works and Services	12	72	16	100	4	20	16	15
Miscellaneous :								
Territories [6]	100	..	..	100	..	..	..	..
Interest [7]	15 [8]	85	..	..	2 [8]	7	..	4
Other	15	77	8	100	2	9	3	6
Sub-total, Miscellaneous	16	79	5	100	4	16	3	10
Total, Group IV	59	37	4	100	83	46	19	63
Grants and similar intergovernmental payments	..	61	39	100	..	11	26	10
GRAND TOTAL	40	46	14	100	100	100	100	110
Less grants, etc.	61	39	..	100	13	7	..	10
NET TOTAL	38	47	15	100	87	93	100	100

Note.—For footnotes see Table VI.

expenditure tables (Tables XI and XII) on pp. 139-40 and 141-2. Secondly, only a certain proportion of total State tax collections[1] is included in the Consolidated Revenue accounts as given in the above-mentioned bulletin, the remainder being paid to various special funds differing in nature

[1] Total revenues from taxation of all Governments in 1937–38 by States are given in Tables VIII and IX below.

and extent as between different States. It was necessary to use the figures from *Finance* in order to obtain comparable totals. On the other hand, the actual proportion of State tax revenues derived from various sources had to be given in order to present a fair and comparable picture of the revenue system. For this reason the figures of State tax collections from different sources have been reduced proportionately so as to add up to the amount actually paid to Consolidated Revenue. This accounts for the differences between the figures in Table VI and those in Table VIII below.

A caveat should be noted, especially in making comparisons with other chapters of this Enquiry. It has not been possible to obtain separate figures of individual and company income taxation for all the States, and for this reason the whole of State income tax collections has had to be given under Group I (Progressive Taxes, item "taxes on individual income"). This means that the totals of Group I for State revenues and for all Governments are above the true figure, while the corresponding totals of Group III are below it.

The Australian revenue system, as shown in these tables, has three important characteristics. The first of these is its "regressivity" or high degree of regression. Group IV (Mainly Consumption Taxes) comprises no less than 63 per cent of total revenues, of which 19 per cent represents customs, 9 per cent excise, 10 per cent other similar taxes and licences, 15 per cent revenue from business undertakings, public works and services, and 10 per cent miscellaneous items (including interest receipts). Progressive taxes accounted for 21 per cent, of which 18 per cent represented taxation of individual income and the remaining 3 per cent probate, estate and succession duties. (But it must be remembered that anything between one-quarter and one-half of the income tax figure may be represented by State company income taxation.) Group III (Taxes on Business), other than State company income taxation, represented 4 per cent, mainly Commonwealth tax on company income and State stamp duties. Groups I and III together accounted for 25 per cent of the total revenues of all Governments combined. Group II (Taxation of Real Property) accounted for 12 per cent, chiefly local rates.

The regression of the system is most conspicuous in the case of Commonwealth revenues. This brings us to the second important characteristic. In contrast to other Federations studied in this Enquiry (except Canada), the States, or units, and not the Federation, are the progressive element in the revenue system. This is due to historical causes which have been alluded to in section II of this chapter. In the United States the predominance of the Federal Government in financial matters was well established by the time that progressive taxation began to be developed, but this was not the case to anything like the same extent in Australia. Hence the Commonwealth still relied, in 1937–38, on customs for no less than 44 per cent of its revenue, on excise for 20 per cent and on the sales tax for 11 per cent. Business Undertakings (the Post Office) and miscellaneous items each accounted for another 4 per cent, making a total for Group IV of no less than 83 per cent. (This is higher than in any other of the Federations studied here, with the exception of India (87 per cent), where the heavy reliance of the Provinces on property taxation makes their revenue system even more regressive than that of the Centre.) Group II (Taxes on Real Property) accounted for 2 per cent; Group I (Progressive Taxes), mainly individual income tax, for 10 per cent, and Group III (Taxes on Business), represented by company income tax, for the remaining 5 per cent.

The picture is very different in the case of State revenues. Taxes on income represent 28 per cent of the total, probate and succession duties 5 per cent (making a total for Group I of 33 per cent), taxes on business other than company income tax 3 per cent, making a total for Groups I and III of 36 per cent as compared with 15 per cent in the case of Commonwealth revenues. Group II (Taxes on Real Property) represents 7 per cent of State revenues, most of which is strictly not taxation but non-tax revenue from lands. Group IV (Mainly Consumption Taxes) represents 46 per cent, of which various consumption taxes and licences account for 10 per cent, business undertakings (especially railways) for 20 per cent, and miscellaneous items (including interest) for 16 per cent. Grants and similar payments from the Commonwealth account for the remaining 11 per cent, although it must be noted that not all Commonwealth payments to or for the States, even from revenue, are included in this figure.

Local Government revenues exhibit the usual feature of reliance on property taxation, mainly in the form of rates (Group II comprises 54 per cent of the total). Licences, the only item in Group III, account for only 1 per cent, business undertakings for little more, but revenues from various works and services and from local council properties swell the sub-total "Business Undertakings, Public Works and Services" to 16 per cent, making, together with 3 per cent of miscellaneous revenues, a total of 19 per cent for Group IV. Grants from the higher layers of Government comprise 26 per cent of the total.

All this brings us to the last of the three outstanding characteristics, namely, the comparative unimportance of Local Authorities in the revenue system. They account for only 15 per cent of the net total of Government revenues, as compared with 47 per cent in the case of the States, and 38 per cent in that of the Commonwealth. This is largely due to the fact that Australia is a new country, largely developed with the help of State aid, whereas Local Authorities only gradually came into being.

This last fact accounts for a feature which is not brought out by the above tables, but must be discussed here — the differences between States, both in regard to tax structure and in regard to the distribution of functions between the State and Local Governments and other authorities. Some of these differences are brought out by Tables VIII and IX, which give the revenues of all Governments from taxation in 1937–38, by States, in thousands of pounds and in percentages.[1]

It is evident from these tables that there are considerable differences between the States with regard to the progression of their tax systems, and with regard to the proportion which Local Government taxation bears to State taxation. When comparisons are made between the revenue, expenditure and debt of States it is necessary to remember that the functions of State Governments differ, some performing municipal or semi-municipal functions. The States render many public services which in Great Britain are left either to municipal or private enterprise. Gross receipts from business undertakings represent a very considerable proportion of State revenues as given in the official accounts, although in our tables, for reasons already explained, net revenues only have been included.

Transport is a case in point. In New South Wales and Western Australia tramways are controlled by the State Government, whereas in other States they are run by boards or trusts or private companies. In Tasmania transport has been vested in a Transport Commission since 1st July 1939. Financial responsibility for roads varies between the State and Local Government authorities. The cost of State highways [2] is borne by the State in New South Wales, Victoria and Tasmania, while in Queensland Local Authorities are responsible for a proportion not exceeding 50 per cent of maintenance cost. Main roads in Western Australia and Tasmania are maintained by the State, whereas in New South Wales and Victoria Local Authorities are responsible for one-quarter and one-third respectively and in Queensland for not more than 20 per cent. In South Australia the contribution of Local Authorities is only a small proportion of the total expenditure on main roads. For water supply and sewerage there is a considerable divergence in financial responsibility. In New South Wales and Victoria, for example, it is divided between State, Local and semi-Governmental authorities such as boards or trusts. In Queensland and Tasmania Local Authorities carry the burden. In South Australia responsibility rests with the State Government, while in Western Australia

[1] See also Tables 3 to 10 in Part III.

[2] Roads for which the States bear the whole or part of the financial responsibility are divided into several classes, of which State highways are the first and main roads another.

TABLE VIII

Revenues from Taxation, All Governments, by States, 1937–38

(£ thousands)

Collecting Authority and Item	New South Wales	Victoria	Queensland	South Australia	Western Australia	Tasmania	Total
Commonwealth :							
Income tax [1]	4,090	3,095	840	660	517	196	9,398
Estate duty [2]	670	918	126	91	43	24	1,872
Land tax [3]	689	424	65	90	82	18	1,368
Customs [4]	13,044	8,959	4,791	2,845	2,203	1,131	32,973
Excise [4]	6,096	4,187	2,239	1,330	1,029	529	15,410
Sales tax [4]	3,174	2,180	1,166	693	536	275	8,024
Other tax revenues [4]	1	1	.. [5]	.. [5]	.. [5]	.. [5]	2
Total, Commonwealth	27,764	19,764	9,227	5,709	4,410	2,173	69,047
States :							
Income taxes	13,330	5,912	5,652	2,033	2,085	743	29,755
Probate and succession duties	2,233	1,431	636	244	102	108	4,754
Land tax	2	498	405	325	124	84	1,438
Stamp duties	1,369	953	632	278	281	79	3,592
Motor vehicles	2,587	1,825	819	673	429	148	6,481
Other tax revenues	984	1,028	395	445	286	535	3,673
Total, States	20,505	11,647	8,539	3,998	3,307	1,697	49,693
Local Authorities :							
Rates [6]	5,411	3,738	2,266	871	673	335	13,294
Other tax revenues	117	88	33	30	20	10	298
Total, Local Authorities	5,528	3,826	2,299	901	693	345	13,592
Grand Total	53,797	35,237	20,065	10,608	8,410	4,215	132,332

[1] Includes Central Office collections allocated to States in proportion to State Office collections of Federal income tax.
[2] Includes Central Office collections allocated to States on basis of dissection of returns for 1936–37.
[3] Total collections apportioned to States on basis of assessments for 1936–37.
[4] Allocated to States on population basis.
[5] Less than £500.
[6] Including a small proportion of penalties.

TABLE IX

Revenues from Taxation, All Governments, by States, 1937–38

(Percentage distribution)

Collecting Authority and Item	New South Wales	Victoria	Queensland	South Australia	Western Australia	Tasmania	Total
Commonwealth :							
Income tax	7·6	8·8	4·2	6·2	6·1	4·7	7·1
Estate duty	1·3	2·6	0·6	0·9	0·5	0·6	1·4
Land tax	1·3	1·2	0·3	0·9	1·0	0·4	1·0
Customs	24·2	25·4	23·9	26·8	26·2	26·8	24·9
Excise	11·3	11·9	11·2	12·5	12·3	12·5	11·7
Sales tax	5·9	6·2	5·8	6·5	6·4	6·5	6·1
Other tax revenues	..[1]	..[1]	..[1]	..[1]	..[1]	..[1]	..[1]
Total, Commonwealth	51·6	56·1	46·0	53·8	52·5	51·5	52·2
States :							
Income taxes	24·8	16·8	28·2	19·2	24·8	17·6	22·5
Probate and succession duties	4·2	4·0	3·2	2·3	1·2	2·6	3·6
Land tax	..[1]	1·4	2·0	3·1	1·5	2·0	1·1
Stamp duties	2·5	2·7	3·1	2·6	3·3	1·9	2·7
Motor vehicles	4·8	5·2	4·1	6·3	5·1	3·5	4·9
Other tax revenues (mostly consumption)	1·8	2·9	2·0	4·2	3·4	12·7	2·8
Total, States	38·1	33·0	42·6	37·7	39·3	40·3	37·6
Local Authorities :							
Rates and penalties	10·1	10·6	11·2	8·2	8·0	7·9	10·0
Other tax revenues (mostly licences)	0·2	0·3	0·2	0·3	0·2	0·3	0·2
Total, Local Authorities	10·3	10·9	11·4	8·5	8·2	8·2	10·2
GRAND TOTAL	100·0	100·0	100·0	100·0	100·0	100·0	100·0
Distribution among States :							
Commonwealth	40·2	28·6	13·4	8·3	6·4	3·1	100·0
States	41·3	23·4	17·2	8·0	6·7	3·4	100·0
Local authorities	40·7	28·2	16·9	6·6	5·1	2·5	100·0
GRAND TOTAL	40·6	26·6	15·2	8·0	6·4	3·2	100·0

it is divided between the State and Local Authorities. For this reason payments for water supply and sewerage have been excluded from the following table (taken from the Seventh Report of the Commonwealth Grants Commission (F.3600), 1940, p. 74). The other differences between the figures in it and those in Table VIII above are due to the exclusion from the latter of charges for public utility services. (The figures in Table VIII are taken from *Finance*, the bulletin of the Commonwealth Bureau of Census and Statistics.)

TABLE X

LOCAL GOVERNMENT TAXATION, 1937–38

(Excluding payments for water supply and sewerage)

State	Total	Per Head of Population
	£ thousands	s. d.
New South Wales .	6,070	44·11
Victoria . .	3,960	42·6
Queensland . .	2,681	53·11
South Australia .	915	31·6
Western Australia .	764	33·5
Tasmania . .	357	30·4
Total .	14,747	43·2

There is a fair equality of service for items included under Local Government activity, but the debt charges in the last three States in the above table are very much less than in the first three. There is evidence that one of the chief causes for the low level of Local taxation in the last three States in the table is that the Governments of South Australia, Western Australia and Tasmania raise loans for local purposes which in the first three States devolve upon Local Authorities. In other words, the States of South Australia, Western Australia and Tasmania shoulder burdens which, being for Local purposes, should fall on Local Authorities.

We have already seen that Local Government financial statistics in Australia are not very satisfactory. This makes it difficult at times to make accurate comparisons, either between States or especially between years. But the matter is complicated by the fact that functions are not equally distributed in the several States, and for some purposes it would perhaps be best to add State and Local figures when making comparisons between States. Moreover, as we have already seen in connexion with the State taxes included in Tables VI and VII above, difficulties are caused by the fact that various States have special funds apart from the Consolidated Revenue Fund, and that the fields covered by these funds (and the corresponding statistical figures) are not the same as between different States, nor as between different periods in the same State.

Public Expenditures

Tables XI and XII below give public expenditures from revenue of all Governments in 1937–38, in thousands of pounds and in percentages. The figures, like those in Table VI above, are taken for the most part from *Finance*, the bulletin of the Commonwealth Bureau of Census and Statistics. They refer, in the case of the Commonwealth and the States, to expenditures from the Consolidated Revenue Fund,[1] although in the case of New South Wales several special accounts have been included to make the data comparable with those of the other States. But there are certain differences between our figures and those in *Finance*. In the first place, they have been arranged in the usual groups: 1, Primary Functions; 2, Secondary Functions — (1) Social Services, (2) Developmental Expenditure, (3) Miscellaneous; and grants and similar intergovernmental payments. Secondly, net expenditure only on Commonwealth and State business undertakings has been included. (*Finance* gives net profits only of Local Government undertakings, just as we do.) For this purpose, net losses incurred by the various authorities have been given, and any net profits made by other authorities have not been deducted but given in the revenue tables (Tables VI and VII above). Thirdly, Commonwealth expenditure from excess receipts (*i.e.* from surplus revenue of the previous financial year) has been included. Lastly, Commonwealth expenditure on pensions and debt services has been eliminated from the *Finance* figures of the cost of the various departments other than business undertakings and Territories, and given separately. It should be noted that no separate details of expenditure on pensions by Local Authorities are available, and that, in contrast to other chapters of this volume (except Chapter VI on South Africa), figures for debt services include not only interest payments but sinking fund payments, redemption and conversion expenses, and exchange. It has not been possible to eliminate grants to Local Governments from State expenditure figures. This is why the totals of primary and secondary functions in the last column of Table XII add up to 104 per cent (of the net total for all Governments).

The most outstanding feature of these tables is the enormous proportion of expenditure, especially State expenditure, which is devoted to debt services. It must be remembered that the figures are appreciably swollen by the inclusion of items which, as indicated above, have been omitted in most of the other chapters. Nevertheless, the contrast with the other Federations studied here is too great to be explained away by this. An

[1] Hence loan expenditure of all kinds is, of course, excluded.

TABLE XI

PUBLIC EXPENDITURES FROM REVENUE, ALL GOVERNMENTS, 1937–38 [1]

(£ thousands)

	Commonwealth	State	Local	Total
1. *Primary Functions :*				
Legislation, administration and justice	3,338	4,659	1,906	9,903
Public safety [2]	..	4,608	225	4,833
Defence [3]	6,061	..	..	6,061
Pensions [4]	8,278	2,386	..	10,664
Debt services [5]	13,590	39,477	4,277	57,344
Total, Primary Functions	31,267	51,130	6,408	88,805
2. *Secondary Functions :*				
(1) *Social Services :*				
Education	114 [6]	12,154	..	12,268
Public health (including hospitals)	377	4,734	2,496 [7]	7,607
Invalid and old-age pensions	15,799	..	..	15,799
Relief of the aged, indigent, etc.	..	1,951	..	1,951
Unemployment relief	..	5,817	..	5,817
Repatriation and War Service Homes Commission	923	..	..	923
Child welfare	..	620	..	620
Maternity allowances	400	..	..	400
Family endowment	..	1,470	..	1,470
Miscellaneous	151	562	..	713
Sub-total, Social Services	17,764	27,308	2,496	47,568
(2) *Developmental :*				
Post office [8]	1,000	..	..	1,000
Railways	705	213	..	918
Shipping and mail services	70	..	..	70
Roads, streets and bridges [9]	4,150	..	11,253	15,403
Street lighting	..	..	706	706
Civil aviation	123	..	..	123
Miscellaneous State business undertakings	..	2	..	2
Lands and survey	..	1,646	..	1,646
Agriculture	..	1,684	..	1,684
Forestry	..	406	..	406
Bounties	276	..	..	276
Research and publicity [10]	661	..	..	661
Relief to primary producers	262	..	..	262
Local council properties	..	..	2,553	2,553
Other public works and services	3,665 [11]	1,568	588	5,821
Sub-total, Developmental	10,912	5,519	15,100	31,531

[*Table continued overleaf*

TABLE XI—(*continued*)

	Common-wealth	State	Local	Total
(3) *Miscellaneous :*				
Territories	1,057	..	..	1,057
Other	..	2,290	958	3,248
Sub-total, Miscellaneous	1,057	2,290	958	4,305
Total, Secondary Functions	29,733	35,117	18,554	83,404
Grants and similar intergovernmental payments	11,840	..[12]	..	11,840
GRAND TOTAL	72,840	86,247	24,962	184,049
Less grants, etc.	11,840	6,379[13]	..	18,219
NET TOTAL	61,000	79,868	24,962	165,830

[1] *These figures differ from those in "Finance" (bulletin of the Commonwealth Bureau of Census and Statistics) in that they include net expenditure only on Commonwealth and State business undertakings, and that Commonwealth expenditures include expenditure from excess receipts. For other details see text.*
[2] Includes police, penal establishments, Local Authority grants to fire brigades, and other items.
[3] Includes £104,758 of miscellaneous expenditure on account of the war of 1914–18.
[4] Excludes business undertakings and Territories. No separate details are available for Local Authorities.
[5] Interest, sinking fund, redemption and conversion expenses, and exchange. Business undertakings and Territories are excluded. The Commonwealth figure includes £276,558 of expenditure from excess receipts in reduction of deficits.
[6] Soldiers' children education scheme [war (1914–18) services expenditure] and National Library.
[7] Health administration, sanitary and garbage services, hospitals and ambulances, and other charities.
[8] Expenditure on Post Office works out of Excess Receipts.
[9] Commonwealth: payments to States for Federal Aid roads. The total for all Governments probably includes duplication amounting to about £2 millions due to grants to Local Authorities. It has not been possible to eliminate this, since no details are available for Western Australia and since neither Commonwealth payments for Federal Aid roads nor road expenditure or grants to Local Authorities appear in the State Consolidated Revenue Fund accounts as given in *Finance*.
[10] Includes scientific research included under "Education" in the State figures and in other chapters of this Enquiry.
[11] New works £3,551,776, and miscellaneous £113,318.
[12] State grants to Local Authorities are not given separately in *Finance*.
[13] Of this, £5,691,747 was for unemployment relief and roads (divided in a ratio of about 3 : 2). See also footnote 9. It is probable that some of these grants should be subtracted from Commonwealth rather than from State expenditures in arriving at the net totals.

examination of Table 6 in Part III, which gives the percentage distribution of the expenditure from revenue of the individual States in 1937–38, shows that the different States vary considerably with regard to the proportion of their expenditure devoted to debt services. It is highest in the case of Western Australia, South Australia and Queensland. One reason is deficit financing such as occurred during the great depression — we have already noticed that although State revenues declined at that time, expenditures only followed the downward course of Commonwealth expenditures after some delay. But there are more important reasons, connected with the fact that in Australia the States perform functions elsewhere entrusted to Local Government authorities or left to private enterprise. The State debts, therefore, have increased markedly with the

TABLE XII

PUBLIC EXPENDITURES FROM REVENUE, ALL GOVERNMENTS, 1937–38 [1]

(Percentage distribution)

	Percentage Share of each Government in Total Expenditures				Percentage Distribution of each Government's Expenditure			
	Common-wealth	State	Local	Total	Common-wealth	State	Local	Total
1. *Primary Functions :*								
Legislation, administration and justice	34	47	19	100	5	5	8	6
Public safety [2]	..	95	5	100	..	5	1	3
Defence [3]	100	..	..	100	8	..	..	4
Pensions [4]	78	22	..	100	11	3	..	6
Debt services [5]	24	69	7	100	19	46	17	35
Total, Primary Functions . .	35	58	7	100	43	59	26	54
2. *Secondary Functions :*								
(1) *Social Services :*								
Education	1 [6]	99	..	100	..	14	..	7
Public health (including hospitals) .	5	62	33 [7]	100	1	5	10 [7]	5
Invalid and old-age pensions .	100	..	..	100	22	..	..	9
Relief of the aged, indigent, etc. .	..	100	..	100	..	2	..	1
Unemployment relief . . .	..	100	..	100	..	7	..	4
Repatriation and War Service Homes Commission	100	..	..	100	1	..	..	1
Child welfare	..	100	..	100	..	1	..	..
Maternity allowances	100	..	..	100	1	..	..	..
Family endowment	..	100	..	100	..	2	..	1
Miscellaneous	21	79	..	100	..	1	..	..
Sub-total, Social Services	37	58	5	100	25	32	10	28
(2) *Developmental :*								
Post office [8]	100	..	..	100	1	..	..	1
Railways	77	23	..	100	1	..	..	1
Shipping and mail services . .	100	..	..	100	..	..	..	..
Roads, streets and bridges [9] . .	27	..	73	100	6	..	45	9
Street lighting	..	..	100	100	..	..	3	..
Civil aviation	100	..	..	100	..	..	..	..
Miscellaneous State business undertakings	..	100	..	100	..	..	..	..
Lands and survey	..	100	..	100	..	2	..	1
Agriculture	..	100	..	100	..	2	..	1
Forestry	..	100	..	100	..	..	..	..
Bounties	100	..	..	100	..	..	..	..
Research and publicity [10] . . .	100	..	..	100	1	..	..	..
Relief to primary producers . .	100	..	..	100	..	..	..	..
Local council properties . . .	..	..	100	100	..	..	10	2
Other public works and services .	63 [11]	27	10	100	6 [11]	2	2	4
Sub-total, Developmental .	35	17	48	100	15	6	60	19

[*Table continued overleaf*

TABLE XII—(*continued*)

	Percentage Share of each Government in Total Expenditures				Percentage Distribution of each Government's Expenditure			
	Commonwealth	State	Local	Total	Commonwealth	State	Local	Total
(3) *Miscellaneous:*								
Territories	100	..	..	100	1	..	..	1
Other	..	70	30	100	..	3	4	2
Sub-total, Miscellaneous	25	53	22	100	1	3	4	3
Total, Secondary Functions	36	42	22	100	41	41	74	50
Grants and similar intergovernmental payments	100	..[12]	..	100	16	..[12]	..	7
GRAND TOTAL	39	47	14	100	100	100	100	111
Less grants, etc.	65	35[13]	..	100	16	7[13]	..	11
NET TOTAL	37	48	15	100	84	93	100	100

Note.—For footnotes see Table XI. In the above table, aggregate expenditures of all Governments (last column, primary and secondary functions) add up to 104 per cent (of the net total). The reason for this is that it has not been possible to eliminate grants to Local Authorities (4 per cent of the net total) from the expenditure of the higher layers of Government.

gradual development of Australia. Yet there is more to it than that. The Commonwealth Grants Commission has on several occasions in its annual reports commented unfavourably on the heavy unproductive debt of the States, especially of the three States claiming special grants from the Commonwealth — South Australia, Western Australia and Tasmania. The Commission also believed that " there is strong evidence . . . that the claimant States do not compel the local authorities to bear their burden of loans for local purposes in the same way as the non-claimant States ".[1] " The proportion of unproductive loan expenditure in Western Australia and Tasmania is such that it should be a matter of considerable concern. . . . No adequate provision, either by way of amortisation of debt or by charges for services, has been made to relieve the losses appearing in the State budget." [2] The Commission also showed in what way past policy had been extravagant or mistaken. For instance, loan expenditure is not always made on a plan by which all loan charges are met by charging the cost to the beneficiaries, or by which the loan is liquidated by depreciation and sinking fund charges.

[1] Commonwealth Grants Commission, Fourth Report, p. 59. Cf. also Fifth Report, pp. 59-65.

[2] Commonwealth Grants Commission, Eighth Report (1941), pp. 72 and 73. See also Table 15 in Part III.

Another feature of the tables is the comparatively high proportion of Commonwealth expenditure devoted to secondary functions. In this respect Australia resembles the United States more than the other Federations studied here, although the expenditure in question is concentrated on a fairly narrow field. Apart from payments to States with respect to Federal Aid roads, the only important item of Commonwealth expenditure on secondary functions was invalid and old-age pensions. Education is mainly a matter for the States, and so are poor and unemployment reliefs. Responsibility for public health and similar items is divided between the States and Local Authorities. The Commonwealth spent £400,000 on maternity allowances in 1937–38. The State of New South Wales spent £1,470,000 on family endowment. Since July 1941 there has been a more comprehensive Commonwealth system of family endowment, covering all States. The scheme provides for a payment of 5s. a week in respect of all children under 16 years of age, irrespective of the amount of family income. In the Commonwealth Budget for 1941–42 £13 millions were provided for this purpose. This provision promised temporarily to reverse the war-time trend of Commonwealth expenditure from revenue on primary functions to increase in proportion to expenditure on secondary functions (see Table 2 in Part III). As we have seen (p. 121), family allowances are among the subjects over which the Commonwealth is to be given power under the recent agreement with respect to post-war reconstruction. In general, the terms of this agreement mean that after the war there will be a further tendency for the Commonwealth to spend a greater proportion of its revenue on secondary functions.[1]

The tables also illustrate the transfer of revenue from the Commonwealth to the States by means of grants and other payments, although not all of these are included in the item " Grants and similar intergovernmental payments ". For instance, payments for Federal Aid roads have been given under road expenditure. Unfortunately the figures in *Finance* do not include the State road funds ; neither do they show separately grants by the higher layers of Government, such as the States, to Local Authorities. For this reason the figure for total road expenditure in the tables probably includes a certain amount of duplication in respect of Local expenditure from grants, while it does not include State expenditure not financed from Commonwealth grants. Commonwealth payments to or for

[1] This has been further borne out by the social security plans now being introduced. The first stage, announced by the Commonwealth Treasurer on 11th Feb. 1943, is the creation of a national welfare fund. This is to be financed from an annual contribution from Commonwealth revenues amounting to £30 millions, or one-quarter of the receipts from individual income tax, whichever is the lower. The benefits to be paid from the fund include higher maternity allowances, funeral benefit for old-age pensioners, and allowances for dependent wives and all unendowed children.

the States in 1937–38, from revenue and from loan fund, are given in detail in Table 19 in Part III.

IV. Public Debt

On 30th June 1938 the public debt of all Governments in Australia was as given in Table XIII, pp. 145–46.

Debt maturing in Australia is given in Australian pounds in the official accounts; debt maturing in London in pounds sterling; debt maturing in New York in pounds into which the dollar figures have been arbitrarily converted at the rate of £ = $4·8665; debt maturing in New Zealand in pounds; and total debt represents the total "face" or "book" value of the debt, *i.e.* no account has been taken of the differences in the various pounds in adding up debt maturing in different centres.

Since the Commonwealth took over the debts of the States under the Financial Agreement Act, 1928, the public debt of Australia as given in the Commonwealth Budget Accounts comprises both debt for Commonwealth purposes and debt on account of the States. The corresponding figures for 1941 have been given in Table 11, Part III (Commonwealth and State Debt, 30th June 1941). Owing to the differences between States with respect to the functions of State, Local and semi-Governmental authorities, the debt of the latter has been included in Table XIII below.

The Commonwealth debt is much more recent than the State debt. New South Wales, for example, began borrowing in 1842. The Commonwealth Government first entered the loan market as a borrower in 1915, although previous to that, in 1911, it had taken over transferred properties, and the liabilities of the Northern Territory and of the Port Augusta–Oodnadatta Railway amounting to £5·9 millions. Some property (buildings, etc.) was taken over from the States at the time of Federation, and the Commonwealth paid 3½ per cent on the value of the property so transferred. Other debt was incurred for works and various purposes, but it is war that has been mainly responsible for the growth of the Commonwealth debt. Debt on account of the war of 1914–18 represented more than two-thirds of the total debt for Commonwealth purposes on 30th June 1938. By 30th June 1941 the present war had swollen the proportion of Commonwealth debt due to war to three-quarters, and the aggregate of such debt by nearly a third.

State debts have been incurred very largely for various developmental works. As we have seen, the State Governments undertake functions performed in other countries by Local Authorities or private enterprises, and this has caused their debts to increase with the development of the States. The net loan expenditure incurred by the States up to 30th June 1938 was as given in Table XIV, p. 146.

TABLE XIII

Public Debt of Australia, All Governments, 30th June 1938

	Maturing in—				
	Australia £ thousands (Australian)	London £ thousands (Stg.)	New York £ thousands ($4·8665)	New Zealand £ thousands	Total £ thousands [1]
For Commonwealth Purposes :					
(1) War Debt (1914–19) :					
Stock and bonds	178,876	11,020	..	..	189,896
Miscellaneous	183	..	..	..	183
Indebtedness to United Kingdom	..	79,724	..	..	79,724
Sub-total, War Debt	179,059	90,744	..	..	269,803
(2) Works and other Purposes :					
Stock and bonds	26,606	61,965	16,081	..	104,652
Short-term debt [2]	..	5,495	..	..	5,495
General Trust Fund investments [3]	10,692	..	..	..	10,692
Balance of loans taken over from South Australia :					
(i) Northern Territory	29	149	..	..	178
(ii) Port Augusta Railway	15	10	..	..	25
Sub-total, Works and other Purposes	37,342	67,619	16,081	..	121,042
Total, Commonwealth Purposes	216,401	158,363	16,081	..	390,845
On Account of States :					
Stock and bonds	423,144	200,539	28,549	..	652,232
Short-term debt [2]	46,598	23,155	..	..	69,753
Balance of debts of States taken over by Commonwealth and still represented by State securities	..	162,195	..	..	162,195
Total on Account of States	469,742	385,889	28,549	..	884,180
Total Commonwealth and State Public Debt	686,143	544,252	44,630	..	1,275,025
Local Governments :					
Due to Central Government	15,602	..	..	..	15,602
Due to banks (net overdraft) [4]	1,402	..	..	..	1,402
Due to public creditor	53,527	12,723	5,501	31	71,782
Total, Local Governments	70,531	12,723	5,501	31	88,786
Grand Total, All Governments	741,072 [5]	556,975	50,131	31	1,348,209 [5]

[Table continued overleaf

TABLE XIII—(*continued*)

	Maturing in—				
	Australia £ thousands (Australian)	London £ thousands (Stg.)	New York £ thousands ($4·8665)	New Zealand £ thousands	Total £ thousands [1]
Semi-Governmental and Other Public Authorities :					
Due to Central Government . .	41,140	..	..	..	41,140
Due to banks (net overdraft) [4] .	1,701	..	..	..	1,701
Due to public creditor . .	79,367	10,658	1,442	..	91,467
Total, Semi-Governmental Authorities . . .	122,208	10,658	1,442	..	134,308
Total, Local and Semi-Governmental Authorities . .	192,739	23,381	6,943	31	223,094
GRAND TOTAL, ALL GOVERNMENTS AND SEMI-GOVERNMENTAL AUTHORITIES	822,140 [6]	567,633	51,573	31	1,441,377 [6]

[1] Total "face" or "book" value of the debt without adjustment on account of relative currency change since the loans were floated.
[2] Short-dated Treasury bills and debentures.
[3] Other Treasury bills.
[4] Aggregate of net overdrafts of all funds. The credit balances of other authorities which do not carry overdrafts have not been deducted.
[5] Excludes Local Government debt to Central Governments.
[6] Excludes debts to Central Government of Local and semi-Governmental authorities.

TABLE XIV

NET LOAN EXPENDITURE INCURRED BY THE STATES UP TO 30TH JUNE 1938
(£ millions)

Public Works, Services, etc. :			
Railways and tramways			371
Roads, bridges, harbours, rivers, and lighthouses			89
Public buildings			36
Housing advances			12
Primary production :			
Settlement	95	Sub-total	160
Water conservation, irrigation and drainage	30		
Other	35		
Water supply and sewerage			103
Electricity supply			27
Other public works and services, including industrial undertakings and immigration .			13
Loans and grants to local bodies			21
Unemployment relief			26
Other purposes			13
Total, Public Works, Services, etc. . .			871
Deficits and other items			99
GRAND TOTAL			970

These figures refer to the amounts actually spent, and exclude those still unpaid. They show the nature of the debt, whether productive or unproductive. No data are available by which it would be possible to show the actual proportion of productive debt for all States.

Details of the debts of the States, Local Governments and semi-Governmental authorities are to be found in Tables 12 to 14 in Part III.

Public Debt Charges

The debt charges of all Governments for 1937–38 are set out in the following table, which is analogous in its arrangement to Table XIII (see above, pp. 145-6). Both table sshow the predominance in peace-time of State debt, and the high proportion of the debt charges which is payable abroad, mostly in London.

Public debt charges and net losses of the several States, in 1937–38 and 1940–41, are set out in Table 15 in Part III, and the interest payable by Local Government and semi-Governmental authorities respectively in 1937–38, by States, is set out in Tables 16 and 17.

Special interest attaches to Table 15, which gives interest, sinking fund and exchange charges of the several States, in millions of pounds and per head of the population, as well as the net losses on these charges after deducting earnings. It fully demonstrates the great difference between New South Wales and Victoria and the other States, but especially between the former and the "claimant" States of South Australia, Western Australia and Tasmania. The net losses per head of the population are much higher in the three last named than in the other States. Especially is this true of Tasmania, where the debt charges per head are comparatively moderate — only those of Victoria are lower — but where the proportion of these charges given as net losses is phenomenal, making such losses per head the highest for all States. On the other hand, it must be admitted that the regular occurrence of substantial net losses in all States, including the eastern ones, shows that none of them has in the past pursued a policy of what may be strictly termed "sound finance" according to old-fashioned principles.

The losses arise from works partially or wholly unproductive and from deficits financed from loan funds. The Commonwealth Grants Commission has examined the position with special reference to South Australia, Western Australia and Tasmania, and concluded that "no irrigation, land settlement or railway authority charges consumers sufficient to cover its costs, and the combined deficits of these undertakings have an unstabilising effect on political conditions and on public finance. There is a further more cogent reason why the system of not making adequate charges for economic services is unsound. If the deficiency is charged to

TABLE XV

DEBT CHARGES OF AUSTRALIA, ALL GOVERNMENTS, 1938 (INTEREST PAYABLE ON 30TH JUNE)

Interest on Debt of—	Payable in— Australia £ thousands (Australian)	London £ thousands (Stg.)	New York £ thousands ($4·8665)	New Zealand £ thousands	Total £ thousands [1]
Commonwealth :					
War (1914–19) . . .	7,150	426	..	..	7,576
Works and other purposes .	1,152	2,775	785	..	4,712
Total, Commonwealth .	8,302	3,201	785	..	12,288
States :					
New South Wales . .	6,211	5,943	627	..	12,781
Victoria	4,085	2,412	222	..	6,719
Queensland . . .	1,966	2,794	408	..	5,168
South Australia . .	2,312	1,675	87	..	4,074
Western Australia . .	1,673	1,695	101	..	3,469
Tasmania . . .	468	492	11	..	971
Total, States .	16,715	15,011	1,456	..	33,182
Total, Commonwealth and States	25,017	18,212	2,241	..	45,470
Local Governments :					
To Central Government .	649	..	..	..	649
To banks (net overdraft) [2] .	63	..	..	..	63
To public creditor . .	2,328	656	294	2	3,280
Total, Local Governments	3,040	656	294	2	3,992
GRAND TOTAL, ALL GOVERNMENTS . . .	27,408 [3]	18,868	2,535	2	48,813 [3]
Semi - Governmental and Other Public Authorities :					
To Central Government .	1,540	..	..	..	1,540
To banks (net overdraft) [2] .	42	..	..	..	42
To public creditor . .	3,134	470	79	..	3,683
Total, Semi-Governmental Authorities . .	4,716	470	79	..	5,265
Total, Local and Semi-Governmental Authorities . . .	7,756	1,126	373	2	9,257
GRAND TOTAL, ALL GOVERNMENTS AND SEMI-GOVERNMENTAL AUTHORITIES	30,584 [4]	19,338	2,614	2	52,538 [4]

[1] Nominal amount of interest payable, taking no account of exchange.
[2] Aggregate of net overdrafts of all funds. The interest on the credit balances of other authorities which do not carry overdrafts has not been deducted.
[3] Excludes interest due from Local to Central Governments.
[4] Excludes interest due from Local and semi-Governmental authorities to the Central Governments.

the taxpayer, it will fall mainly on the higher grades of taxable income. The benefit of the lower charges on economic services goes predominantly to the larger user, but in this case he is usually the landowner. This applies to the main services on which loan money is spent in Australia, viz. roads, land settlement, railways and water supply. Charges for these services, which are less than the annual cost, and which make no adequate levy on the persons benefited, act as a subsidy to land values. High land values in a community dependent on primary production are a definite hindrance to such production."[1]

To sum up: the debt charges of the Commonwealth are mainly on unproductive debt resulting from two great wars, whereas those of the States are due to the investment of Australian and foreign capital in productive enterprises of many kinds and also in unproductive works. The loan policy of the States is not above criticism, for reasons stated above, especially in South Australia, Western Australia and Tasmania, which receive special grants from the Commonwealth to assist them in trying to maintain Budget equilibrium.

V. War Changes

As in other Federations studied here, the war has considerably increased the relative importance of the Commonwealth in Australian finance. Its expenditure has become paramount. Tables 1 and 2 in Part III give the Commonwealth revenues and its expenditures from Consolidated Revenue in 1940–41 (actual figures) and 1941–42 (Budget figures). A comparison of these tables with Tables VI, VII, XI and XII will show some of the changes that have taken place. The Commonwealth expenditure from revenue budgeted for in 1941–42 is more than twice as large as that of 1937 38 — the increase is 109 per cent. The proportion of the total devoted to defence or war has risen from 8 to 44 per cent. In 1940–41, before the proportion of secondary functions was temporarily swelled by the introduction of Commonwealth child endowment, the proportion of expenditure from revenue devoted to war was 49 per cent. The increase in Commonwealth loan expenditure was much more phenomenal. Omitting redemptions it amounted to £4·5 millions in 1937–38 and to £151·7 millions in 1941–42 (Budget estimate) — an increase of 3234 per cent. The loan expenditure on defence rose from £1·7 millions to £149·1 millions. Expenditure from Consolidated Revenue and Loan Fund combined has risen from £77·7 millions in 1937–38 to £303·7 millions in 1941–42, or, if the official totals are adopted, from £90·9 millions to £321·9 millions. Expenditure on defence or war from revenue

[1] Commonwealth Grants Commission, Eighth Report (F. 1357, 1941), pp. 75-81.

and loan rose from £7·7 millions to £215·7 millions. In introducing the Budget for 1943–44 in the House of Representatives Mr. Chifley, the Commonwealth Treasurer, showed that half the whole National Income is being devoted to the war, and taxation in the current financial year is expected to reach £270 millions as compared with £74 millions in 1938–39. Up to 30th June 1943 the total cost of the war to Australia reached £1107 millions, of which £363 millions were provided by taxation, £474 millions by loans from the public and £259 millions by discounting Treasury Bills with the Commonwealth Bank.

At the same time, the greatest possible economy is taking place in civil expenditure. Loan expenditure is confined as far as practicable to war needs. There has been a considerable contraction of loan expenditure on public works other than defence. The Loan Council, held in Melbourne on 11th August 1942, sanctioned a programme involving the expenditure of £12·9 millions, a saving of no less than £6·7 millions on the programme of the preceding year. All works sanctioned were directly or indirectly for defence, or subject to inescapable commitments or of special character. A substantial reduction took place in loan expenditure on State and semi-Governmental works.

As elsewhere, the increase in expenditures has led to an increased predominance of the Centre in the field of taxation, and to greater progression in the revenue system. We have already seen (pp. 117-19) that the Commonwealth has for the period of the war displaced the States from the income tax and entertainments tax field. Commonwealth revenues have risen from £75·1 millions in 1937–38 to £152·0 millions (Budget estimate) in 1941–42, or by 102 per cent. At the same time, Group I (Progressive Taxes) rose from 10 to 23 per cent of total Commonwealth revenues, and income tax (on individuals and companies combined) from 13 per cent to 33 per cent, or 41 per cent if pay-roll tax and war-time company tax and supertax are included. These figures are previous to the surrender of State income taxes, which took place in 1942.

Thus a high and increasing proportion of the national income is diverted to the war effort, though Table IV on page 124 shows that this process only got fully under way after some delay. Meanwhile that income is rising in spite of the interruption of oversea trade and the consequent effect on " primary " exports.[1] Industrial reorganisation to meet war needs is having a special advantageous effect on the industrial States, New South Wales and Victoria. These factors will not remain without repercussions in the field of finance.

[1] The latter has meant, among other things, that Australia has not been able to repatriate her sterling debt to the same extent as Canada and India.

CHAPTER VI

THE PUBLIC FINANCE AND NATIONAL ECONOMY OF SOUTH AFRICA

I. The National Economy

The Union of South Africa has an area of somewhat less than half a million square miles. It is, therefore, four times the size of Great Britain and twice that of France. Its population is 9·6 millions, of whom a shade over 2 millions are European. The mainspring of its economic activity at the present time is gold mining. In recent decades agricultural and pastoral production has been considerably increased with a view to supplying not only the Union's own requirements but also the demand for export abroad. This has been combined with an enormous expansion in manufactures which has been especially noticeable in recent years. Prior to 1925 the tariff was mainly a revenue one, but under the revised tariff of that year a policy of protection for industries in the Union was systematically undertaken. South Africa is fortunate in being the producer of a commodity which is always in general demand — gold, which has been mined there since 1886 and in considerable quantities since 1896. She produces about one-third of the world's gold and is easily the greatest producer.[1] From 1923 to 1929 there was prosperity combined with expansion in the Union. The years 1929 to 1932 were depression years, but after 1932 the price of gold leapt up to new high records, and this not only gave an enormous impetus to mining itself but revived to a very substantial degree the economic activity of the Union. The large imports of capital, mainly British, have been due to expansion in mining, chiefly diamonds and gold, and in transportation, mainly railways. Professor Frankel in his comprehensive study on *Capital Investment in Africa* [2] brings this out clearly. In dealing with the economic structure of the Union he shows that South Africa is largely dependent, as we have shown Canada to be, on a very restricted number of exportable products. There are few countries in the world so dependent on foreign trade as is the Union. In 1937 all mineral exports accounted for 75·3 per cent of the total export trade (diamonds for 2·8 per cent and gold exports for 69·3 per cent); wool exports for 10·6 per cent; and all agricultural and pastoral exports 23·5 per cent.

[1] *Vide* G. Findlay Shirras, "The Position and Prospects of Gold", *Economic Journal*, June–Sept. 1940. Since the peak year 1940 this percentage has increased to over that figure: 14 million fine oz. in 1940 out of an estimated world production of 40·5 millions, and in 1942 14·8 million fine oz. out of a world production of 36 millions.

[2] Issued by the Committee of the African Research Survey under the auspices of the Royal Institute of International Affairs. Oxford University Press, London, 1938.

Thus mineral and agricultural, including pastoral, exports account for 98·8 per cent. Over the thirty years gold alone has formed nearly 60 per cent of the total, and it is on the mineral industry that the modern economy of the Union has been built. To an ever-increasing extent the finances of the Union depend on the direct and indirect taxation of gold mining. The Minister of Finance, Mr. Hofmeyr, stated in September 1942 that the fact that the maintenance of gold production was essential not only for South Africa's war effort but for the cause of the United Nations had come to be appreciated generally. " In the last financial year ", he said, " the gold-mining industry contributed directly over 30 per cent of all the State income on revenue and loan accounts and a good deal more indirectly." The severity of taxation on gold-mining income was illustrated by the Transvaal Chamber of Mines in its evidence to the Departmental Committee on Mining Taxation in 1935 by the following approximate rate of similar taxation expressed as a percentage of taxable profits in other gold-producing countries : Union of South Africa 42 ; Rhodesia 23 ; Australia 18 ; U.S.A. 14 to 18 ; Canada 13 to 19 ; West Africa 12. Another characteristic of the Union economy is the degree to which agriculture is assisted for the benefit of Europeans engaged in that industry. A large part of the burden falls on those export industries, such as gold, which do not receive off-setting advantages and cannot shift the tax. The burden has also grown on mines because of the protection granted to manufacturing industry since 1925. Except in the case of wool there is no important agricultural commodity which is not dependent on the maintenance of an artificial internal price structure or on some similar kind of protection. While anxious not to give a one-sided or *ex-parte* view I agree, generally, with Professor Frankel when he says, " There has grown up in the Union a system of tariffs, subsidies, quotas, price regulating and marketing schemes, which is remarkable in its wide ramifications, contradictions and complexities. Nearly every important agricultural commodity for which an appreciable local market exists has now to be sold at internal prices above the corresponding world prices. Moreover, the rates structure of the railways has been mainly devised to conform with the system whereby agricultural, particularly export products are subsidised by means of artificially low transport charges. Since Union too, very large sums have been spent on the construction of unpayable branch lines in order to stimulate farming, often in quite unsuitable areas. The low contribution made by agriculture to the direct revenues of the Central Government is due both to the special exemptions under the Income Tax Acts and to the low net incomes obtained from agricultural operations."[1] Thus, in spite of the efforts of the Government to put

[1] Frankel, *Capital Investment in South Africa*, Oxford University Press, 1928, pp. 121-2.

" European " agriculture on a secure basis, it is more dependent that ever on the remainder of the Union economy. More than one-half of the Union's native population is on farms, and of these 70 per cent is occupied in European areas. The policy is to pluck the golden goose with as little squealing as possible to enable agriculture and industries to be in a position sufficiently sound to hold their own when the Union will no longer be primarily dependent on gold.

The total amount of foreign capital invested between 1870 and 1936 in the Union of South Africa is approximately £523 millions. Of this price capital is £250 millions, of which two-thirds is in mining, and of the remainder three-fifths is in landowning, banking, insurance and investment companies and two-fifths in commerce, industry and agriculture.[1] These estimates show that, in return for the gold, diamonds, etc., the Union has become equipped with foreign capital in the form of machinery and other paraphernalia of an advanced industrial economy. When it is remembered how small the population is, and how the development of the Union has been determined to a very large extent by the interests of the white population, these foreign capital investments are remarkably high. Nevertheless, investments have not resulted so far in a high standard of living for the population as a whole, white, native or coloured. The entire population is not employed at the optimum level, *i.e.* at a level which would maximise the national output. Therefore the national income is still low per head of total population, and up to the outbreak of war, the flow of capital continued at such a rate that there were few, if any, signs of the Union ever becoming a creditor country. A debtor country should eventually increase its own national income so that it no longer requires capital from abroad, as has been seen recently in other parts of the British Commonwealth. The Union (except in mining — three-quarters of the foreign capital is invested in mines and in urban centres serving these mines) is a good example of a country in which the marginal efficiency of capital is low in most enterprises. This large investment of capital from abroad obscures the poverty of the great part of the population, native, coloured and European. The most urgent problem in the Union economy to-day is to increase the national income or to increase production, a gigantic task, and this means the development of non-material as well as material resources among all classes of the population, including coloured and poor whites. This development, as one authority somewhere phrases it, depends " on opening the doors of personal opportunity ". But in South Africa these doors remain closed to a large section of the population — coloured, native and European.

[1] Frankel, *op. cit.* Table 28.

II. The South Africa Act

The Union brought about by the South Africa Act, 1909, was not the first attempt to federate the four main political divisions of South Africa. The first attempt was mooted in 1857, and again in 1877 when a permissive South Africa Act was passed by the British Parliament. It failed, but Sir Bartle Frere, Governor of Cape Colony and the first High Commissioner of South Africa, pushed on the idea of Federation. In 1880 the Sprigg ministry definitely formulated proposals for union to be considered by the delegates of the various States. The proposals again fell through, and after the battle of Majuba, 1881, the British Government abandoned the Transvaal. Even before this Cecil Rhodes had the idea of a federated South Africa under British rule with the assent of the Cape Dutch. Rhodes, who died at the comparatively early age of forty-nine, leaving some £6 millions to the public service, endowing 170 scholarships at Oxford for students of the Colonies, U.S.A. and Germany, and leaving £100,000 to his old College, Oriel College, Oxford, belonged to a group of statesmen who will live in the history of South Africa — Lord Milner, 1854–1925 ; Jan Hendrik Hofmeyr, 1845–1909 ; Sir L. S. Jameson, 1853–1917 ; General Louis Botha, 1852–1909 ; and Lord Selborne, High Commissioner of South Africa in 1907. Lord Milner, after being Under-Secretary for Finance in Egypt (1890–92) and Chairman of the Board of Inland Revenue in London (1892–97), became High Commissioner of South Africa in 1897 and continued in office until 1905. Milner had a great and strong mind and saw, in a way few of his contemporaries did, the advantages of a political union of the South African States. It was he, too, who saw the undoubted advantages of a customs union, realised in 1903, and of a unified transport system, railways, harbours and ports.[1] He saw, too, the advantages of a policy for agriculture, for industry and for education. He had a peculiar genius for finance, as figures were "real counters of thought to him and a balance sheet as lucid as a page of print". Milner, in short, prepared the way for Selborne, his successor, who wrote a *Memorandum on the Closer Union of the South African Colonies*. After the Peace of Vereeniging, 31st May 1902, all four political divisions of South Africa were British colonies and in consequence their federation

[1] "Lord Milner had also taken advantage of every opportunity to terminate or minimise the injurious competition between the various railway systems in South Africa for the trade of the Rand. The railways of the Transvaal and the Orange River Colony were united under one management, the Inter-Colonial Council, administered as a joint concern; and agreements were concluded with the Cape and Natal Governments at the Railway Rates Conference of 1905. This movement of closer railway union contributed in no small way towards the attainment of political union" (M. H. de Kock, *The Economic Development of South Africa*, London, P. S. King & Son, 1936).

was easier than hitherto. In 1909 the National Convention met, first in Durban and then in Capetown, and had representatives of all the South African colonies. The South Africa Act, 1909, resulted and on 31st May 1910, *i.e.* on the eighth anniversary of the Peace of Vereeniging and thirty-three years after the Permissive Federation Act of 1877, the four colonies finally entered upon the complete union of the wide Dominion of to-day.

The Act itself is of special interest to the student of Federal Finance. It differs from the Canadian and Australian Constitutions in that the Provinces of the Union have no written Constitution superior to ordinary law which guarantees their rights, as in the cases of the Provinces of Canada and of the States of Australia. The Union Parliament could abolish the provincial system if or when it likes. There is nothing in the Statute of Westminster applicable to the Union of South Africa which guarantees the Constitution. It cannot, therefore, be said that the relationship of the Union Government to the Provinces is really federal in character. Two things seem clear in this connexion. In the first place, the provincial system in the South Africa Act, 1909, was, as it were, a sop to those in favour of a federal form of government. In the Act it is the unitary system that is really established. Secondly, the continuance of the provincial system at the present time is to be explained as due to fears still entertained in some parts of the Union, notably in Natal, of the domination of the Union Parliament and the Union Government, rather than to any functions which the Provincial Governments perform. Direct taxation granted to the Provinces under section 85 (i) was withdrawn from them by Act No. 46 of 1925, amending the financial relations between the Union and the Provinces, as set out in the Financial Relations Act of 1913.[1] From the first the Provinces have relied on subsidies from the Union to a very large extent. In 1937, for example, 52 per cent of their total revenue was from subsidies (*vide* Table IV below) as compared with 8 per cent in Canada. For this reason more than any other perhaps, the Provinces have not been genuinely self-governing. The Provinces and *not* Local Authorities are entrusted with elementary education, hospitals, poor relief, roads and bridges, racing, betting, game and fish preservation. Under section 85 (vi) Provinces are also in charge of " municipal institutions, divisional councils and other local institutions of a similar nature ", and so the Provincial Government is of immediate concern even to a town council of the size of Johannesburg.[2] On the other hand,

[1] This Act was modified by Acts No. 9 of 1917, No. 6 of 1920, No. 5 of 1921, No. 5 of 1922, No. 21 of 1924, No. 46 of 1925, No. 39 of 1927 and No. 50 of 1935.

[2] Cf. Maud, *City Government, the Johannesburg Experiment*, Oxford, Clarendon Press, 1938.

problems relating to native affairs, to the public health of the country as a whole, to defence, justice, higher and technical education, agriculture, commerce and industry, railways and harbours are administered exclusively by the Union Government. The Union Parliament has "full power to make laws for the peace, order and good government" of South Africa under the South Africa Act. The financial powers of the Provinces are limited and they are, in effect, as the Provinces of Canada and the States of Australia are not, pensioners of the Union Government instead of sovereign Governments. The Municipalities differ from those in practically every other country of the world. In most countries it is usual for Municipalities to obtain grants for education, police, health and other purposes, and the grants are dependent on a satisfactory standard of performance by the Local Authority. In South Africa not only is the scope of Municipal Government limited but Local Authorities have practically no help or supervision from the Union or Provincial Governments. The Municipalities, therefore, have been forced to finance themselves by profits from public utilities (water, transport, electricity, etc.), and even on sewerage and sanitary services profit is frequently made. Only about half their annual revenue in 1937 was met by the taxation of property, as will be seen from Table IV below. Rating differs from the English model, as owners bear the whole burden, occupiers being exempt, and the rating power of Local Authorities is limited to an annual maximum by legislative enactment.[1] The English method of assessment, the basis being annual rental value, is not followed in South Africa, where land and improvements are assessed separately on the capital or selling value in each case. Since education, poor relief and hospital administration do not fall definitely within the sphere of South African Municipalities, they do not generally provide for the social or cultural municipal life, although the bigger Municipalities have housing schemes to provide for the needs of the poorer classes, both European and native;[2] nor do they make regular provision for poor relief. It is sometimes said that the urban native can relieve his own destitution by retiring to the rural areas reserved for native occupation or by relying on assistance from his family or friends.

The financial provisions of the Constitution are contained in sections 117 to 133 of the South Africa Act, 1909. A Consolidated Revenue Fund and a separate Railway and Harbour Fund were constituted under section 117: "All revenues, from whatever source arising, over which the

[1] *Vide* Rating Proclamation (No. 38 of 1902). Maud, *op. cit.* p. 54.

[2] Johannesburg, for example, has built the Orlando Native Township, and it has announced that it intends spending another million pounds or more on another big housing scheme to take the place of the one on the Pretoria Road.

several Colonies have at the establishment of the Union power of appropriation, shall vest in the Governor-General-in-Council. There shall be formed a Railway and Harbour Fund, into which shall be paid all revenues raised or received by the Governor-General-in-Council from the administration of the railways, ports and harbours, and such fund shall be appropriated by Parliament to the purposes of the railways, ports and harbours in the manner prescribed by this Act. There shall also be formed a Consolidated Revenue Fund, into which shall be paid all other revenues raised or received by the Governor-General-in-Council, and such fund shall be appropriated by Parliament for the purposes of the Union in the manner prescribed by this Act, and subject to the charges imposed thereby." From the date of the Constitution of the Union, May 1909, until April 1913, when the Financial Relations Act came into force, the funds required by the Provinces were provided by grants from the Union Exchequer. The Act of 1913 transferred to the Provinces certain taxes and fees, *e.g.* totalisator taxes, fees (school and hospital fees), licences (dog licences, licences for game hunting, trading and professional licences), auction dues and other receipts connected with provincial matters as defined in section 85 of the South Africa Act. At first little use was made of these powers but later, with the growth of provincial expenditures, resort to them became indispensable. The proceeds of the transfer duty on fixed property, licences for the sale or supply of liquor and native pass fees are collected by the Union and assigned to the Provinces under the Financial Relations Act. These revenues are, in the words of the Report of the Provincial Finances Commission, 1923, " revenues over which the Provinces have no control and in regard to the levying of which the Provinces have no responsibility ". These revenues are uncertain and, while encouraging expenditure in good years, they have caused, by their shrinkage in years of depression, great difficulties. The Financial Relations Act, 1913, based the amount of subsidy on the expenditure for any year — it was to be one-half of such expenditure — but if the expenditure for any year exceeded the expenditure of the previous year by more than 7½ per cent, that Province was to get one-third instead of one-half of that excess as subsidy. A special subsidy of £100,000 per annum was granted to Natal and the Orange Free State, as they were less favourably placed than the other two Provinces. The expenditure of Local bodies within a Province ranked as ordinary expenditure of the Province itself. This provision was necessitated by the predominance of Local expenditure in the Cape Province. The Provinces were also permitted to include the annual interest and debt redemption payments as part of their ordinary expenditure for the assessment. Owing to the increase in expenditures mainly on education, roads, hospitals and poor relief, the Provinces were given in 1917 additional powers to raise taxation in respect of licences for places of amusement, and an increase of 15 per cent was permitted in the assessment of the subsidy for education, the largest item, and 5 per cent for other expenditures. In the post-war crisis of 1921 the cutting-down of subsidies led Provincial Governments to resort to their powers of taxation, but this met with opposition from their legislatures and the deficits were met largely by borrowing. In 1922 the Baxter Provincial Finances Commission was appointed to report on the whole system of financial relations of the Provinces with the Union. In its Report the Commission recommended a new basis for subsidies, viz. by reference to the number of pupils in average attendance. It also suggested somewhat radical changes in taxation which were adopted in the Provincial Subsidies and Taxation Powers Amendment Act, 1925. This Act withdrew from the Provinces the general power of direct taxation, derived under section 85 (i) of the South Africa Act, 1909, as direct taxation on the part of the Provinces had given rise to a large number of cases on the validity of the taxing ordinances read in the light of the Constitution. The Provinces were given the power under the Act to raise taxes on vehicles, including motor vehicles ; a wheel tax ; an amusements tax ; taxes on persons other than companies and on the incomes of persons other than companies, subject to certain limits ; a tax on companies other than mutual life insurance companies ; a tax on the ownership of immovable property ; the taxation of racing and betting and the dissemination of betting information ; licences including (1) licences for dogs outside urban areas, (2) licences to own or drive any motor and other mechanical vehicles, (3) licences on the importation for sale within the province of goods from beyond the borders of the Union. Licences in respect of trade, professions and occupations were taken over by the Union Government but the proceeds were transferred to the Provinces together with the proceeds of transfer duty, liquor licences and native pass fees. Under Act 17 of 1938 the Provincial Governments may authorise the carrying-out of professions and callings without payment and are then reimbursed by the Union Government for the loss of such revenue. Under Act 33 of 1939 the Cape Provincial Administration is paid an annual subsidy of £160,000 in lieu of importers' licences. A Consultative Committee consisting of the Administrator and the Executive Committee of each of the four Provinces was appointed under Act No. 50 of 1935 as a result of the Roos Provincial Finance Commission which reported in 1934.[1] The Minister of the Interior is the permanent President. The Committee meets to discuss matters common to the Provinces. The Act of 1935 also provided that the outstanding capital loans made to the

[1] U.G. No. 46, 1934.

provinces prior to the 1st April 1935 to meet deficits on revenue account were, together with interest charges upon these loans, assumed by the Union Government. As the annual subsidy to Natal was increased from £75,000 to £125,000, the Provincial Council of Natal could pay to the city of Pietermaritzburg compensation for the loss of prosperity through its having ceased to be a seat of Government. By the National Roads Act [1] the Provincial taxpayer was given considerable relief, as the National Road Board took over the payment of interest and redemption charges on loans raised prior to 1st April 1935. The National Road Board votes the grants for the construction, repair and maintenance of roads payable to the Provinces whose duty it is to carry out this work in accordance with plans approved by the Board. This is interesting as yet another indication of the control of the Centre over the units in the sphere of public finance.

III. Government Revenues and Expenditures

The following table, which is in two parts, shows the increase in Government expenditures and revenues in the Union of South Africa : [2]

TABLE I

Government Expenditures and Revenues in South Africa *

(£ millions)

	1913–14	1921–22	1926–27	1930–31	1937–38	1940–41	Percentage Increase, 1940 over—	
							1913–14	1937–38
A. *Expenditures :*								
Union . .	11	21	22	24	33	65	491	97
Provincial .	3	9	10	12	17	19	533	8
Total .	14	30	32	36	50	84	500	68
B. *Revenues :*								
Union . .	13	24	29	29	44	55	323	25
Provincial .	1	4	4	5	8	9	800	13
Total .	14	28	33	34	52	64	357	23

* Financial years beginning 1st April.

If we take the national income of South Africa and express the Union, Provincial and Municipal revenues and the total Union expenditures from revenue and from loan as a percentage of it, we find that South Africa, as compared with the United States, Canada and Australia, is in a favourable position from the viewpoint of the burden of taxation. The national

[1] No. 42 of 1935.

[2] Municipal data are not available.

income estimates are those of Professor Frankel and his collaborators.[1] They were quoted by Mr. J. H. Hofmeyr, Minister of Finance, in presenting his Budget to the House of Assembly on 25th February 1942, when he stated that " Hard though the saying may appear to be to those who are smarting under the increased burdens imposed in recent years, this country is still, by comparison with others, lightly taxed ". The estimates for 1940–41, 1941–42 and 1942–43 are our own and are based on Professor Frankel's estimate after allowing for the increase in prices and assuming that the increase in production was not less than the increase between 1939–40 and 1940–41, a safe estimate. The data are given in the following table :

TABLE II

GOVERNMENT REVENUES AND EXPENDITURES EXPRESSED IN TERMS OF THE NATIONAL INCOME

	1937–38	1940–41	1941–42	1942–43
1. *Revenues* (*£ millions*) :				
Union	40	55	80	88
Provincial	8	8	8	8
Municipal	10	10	10	10
Total	58	73	98	106
2. *Union Expenditures* (*£ millions*) :				
From revenue	35	65	75	88
From loan	19	47	54	52
Total	54	112	129	140
3. *National Income* (*£ millions*) . .	370	470	510	550
4. *Percentage of the National Income* :				
(*a*) Revenues	16	16	19	19
(*b*) Union Expenditures :				
i. Expenditures from revenue .	9	14	15	16
ii. Loan expenditures . .	5	10	10	9
iii. Total	14	24	25	25
iv. Defence only . .	1	10	14	15

Note.—For the years 1941–42 and 1942–43 it has been assumed that provincial and municipal expenditures have not increased and are approximately the same as in 1940–41. Provincial revenue figures exclude all grants and subsidies.

[1] These figures refer to revenues collected by, not to those available to, the various Governments.

The percentages in the table opposite are particularly striking when compared with those of other Federal Governments. War expenditure, it may be noted, was 10 per cent of the national income in 1940–41 as compared with 15 per cent in Canada and 40 per cent in Great Britain. In 1942–43 the percentage in the Union of South Africa is 15 per cent and in Canada over 40 per cent (including gifts to the United Kingdom).

It will aid the understanding of the tables below if the distribution of the national income is remembered. The following figures are for the year July 1938 to June 1939 (the figures in brackets are for the corresponding period of 1940–41); they are in millions of pounds. Mining 81·5 (100); manufactures 69·7 (85); commerce 53·8 (60); farming 50·0 (60); railways 23·9 (27); defence 0·0 (24); Central Government 17·5 (17); Provincial Government 15·0 (15); Local Government 8·0 (8); education, professions, etc. 12·4 (12); rent 27·3 (28); others 35·7 (36)—total 394·8 (472). The details of the national income were as follows: available for consumption 316·2 (367); net investment 56·8 (31); dividends and interest paid abroad 20·0 (19); war expenditure 1·8 (55). Note the importance of mining and then of manufactures as compared with the place taken by agriculture, which, as has been observed above, is subsidised. The increase in war expenditure by £53 millions, the decrease in net investment by £25 millions and the increase in the income available for spending by 10 per cent after allowing for war expenditure, are noteworthy.

Tables III and IV summarise overleaf the revenues of South Africa for the Union, Provinces and Municipalities in four main groups for the pre-rearmament year 1937–38.

It is sometimes said that it is difficult to discuss as a whole the tax structure of a Federal system in which a large proportion of the total governmental revenues and expenditures are provincial and local. The incidence of taxation, the services provided by the various Governments and the transfer expenditures are problems particularly complicated in such circumstances. Such a difficulty does not arise in the Union of South Africa as the Centre predominates to an unusual degree. The revenues collected by the Union in 1937–38 were as much as 66 per cent of the revenues of all Governments as compared with only 17 per cent in the case of the Provinces (excluding subsidies from the Union Government) and 17 per cent in that of Municipalities (revenues available to the Union, Provinces and Municipalities were respectively 55, 28 and 17 per cent of the total). Moreover, subsidies from the Union to Provincial Governments play a much greater part in Provincial revenues than is the case in any of the other Federal systems studied.

The system as a whole has certain well-defined characteristics. In the

TABLE III

THE REVENUE SYSTEM OF SOUTH AFRICA, ALL GOVERNMENTS, 1937–38

(£ thousands)

	Union	Provincial	Municipal	Total
GROUP I. *Mainly Progressive Taxes :*				
Income taxes on individuals	1,530 [1]	1,180 [2]	..	2,710
Supertax on individuals	2,103 [1]	.. [3]	..	2,103
Estate and succession duties	1,038			1,038
Native taxes and pass fees	629	604		1,233
Total, Group I	5,300	1,784	..	7,084
GROUP II. *Taxes on Property :*				
Taxes on land and buildings	15	936	4,728	5,679
Government property and estate	320	..	624	944
Total, Group II	335	936	5,352	6,623
GROUP III. *Taxes on Business :*				
Mining revenue (mainly income tax)	10,190	..	..	10,190
Income taxes on non-mining companies	3,046 [1]	749	..	3,795
Stamp duties and other taxes	1,496	695		2,191
Total, Group III	14,732	1,444	..	16,176
GROUP IV. *Mainly Consumption Taxes :*				
Customs	10,678	..	..	10,678
Excise	2,912	..	..	2,912
Other Similar Taxes and Licences :				
Motor vehicle licences		2,137		2,137
Other licences	..	165		165
Entertainment and racing	..	741		741
Other taxes	..	118	..	117
Sub-total, Other Taxes and Licences	..	3,161	..	3,160
Revenues from public utilities and services (net)	1,555 [4]	..	2,859	4,414
Miscellaneous	4,114 [5]	908	2,198	7,220
Total, Group IV	19,259	4,069	5,057	28,384
Grants and subsidies	..	8,955 [6]		8,955
GRAND TOTAL	39,626	17,188	10,409	67,222
Less duplications	6,791 [7]	..	..	6,791
NET TOTAL	32,835	17,188	10,409	60,431

[1] Approximate figure obtained by dividing up total collections in proportion to assessments.
[2] Includes supertax.
[3] Included under income taxes.
[4] Posts, telegraphs and telephones.
[5] Of this, £2,459,000 interest.
[6] Union Government subsidies . . . £6,319,000
Grant : South Africa Native Trust . . 817,000
,, National Road Fund . . 1,809,000
,, Other 10,000

£8,955,000

[7] Subsidies to the Provinces and interest on loans made to the Provinces.

TABLE IV

THE REVENUE SYSTEM OF SOUTH AFRICA, ALL GOVERNMENTS, 1937–38
(Percentage distribution)

	Percentage Share of each Government in Total Revenues				Percentage Distribution of each Government's Revenues			
	Union	Provincial	Municipal	Total	Union	Provincial	Municipal	Total
GROUP I. *Mainly Progressive Taxes :*								
Income taxes on individuals	56	44	..	100	4	7	..	4
Supertax on individuals	100	.. [1]	..	100	5	.. [1]	..	3
Estate and succession duties	100	..	..	100	2	..	..	2
Native taxes and pass fees	51	49	..	100	2	3	..	2
Total, Group I	75	25	..	100	13	10	..	11
GROUP II. *Taxes on Property :*								
Taxes on land and buildings	..	17	83	100	..	5	45	9
Government property and estate	34	..	66	100	1	..	6	2
Total, Group II	5	14	81	100	1	5	51	11
GROUP III. *Taxes on Business :*								
Mining revenue (mainly income tax)	100	..	..	100	25	..	..	17
Income taxes on non-mining companies	80	20	..	100	8	4	..	6
Stamp duties and other taxes	68	32	..	100	4	5	..	4
Total, Group III	91	9	..	100	37	9	..	27
GROUP IV. *Mainly Consumption Taxes :*								
Customs	100	..	..	100	27	..	..	18
Excise	100	..	..	100	7	..	..	5
Other Similar Taxes and Licences :								
Motor vehicle licences	..	100	..	100	..	12	..	4
Other licences	..	100	..	100	..	1	..	..
Entertainment and racing	..	100	..	100	..	4	..	1
Other taxes	..	100	..	100	..	1	..	..
Sub-total, Other Taxes and Licences	..	100	..	100	..	18	..	5
Revenues from public utilities and services (net)	35	..	65	100	4	..	28	7
Miscellaneous	57	13	30	100	11	5	21	12
Total, Group IV	68	14	18	100	49	24	49	47
Grants and subsidies	..	100	..	100	..	52	..	15
GRAND TOTAL	59	26	15	100	100	100	100	111
Less duplications	100	..	..	100	17	..	..	11
NET TOTAL	55	28	17	100	83	100	100	100

[1] Included under income taxes.

first place, it is neither highly progressive nor highly regressive, although it tends to the regression inherent in consumption taxation. Progressive taxes (all Governments) are 11 per cent and consumption taxes 47 per cent of the total revenues. The income tax is not steeply progressive as it is, for example, in Canada, and the exemption limits compare very favourably with those in many other Federal Governments. It is only to this 11 per cent that the principles of progression were applied in 1937–38 to redress the regression. At the same time, the high taxation of mining (especially gold mining) is on surplus as is the income tax on individuals, and in this respect is not on costs like indirect taxes. In 1937–38 37 per cent of the Union's revenue was from business taxation and 25 per cent was from mining. It may be argued that the South African system has some degree of balance, although regression is noticeable. Again, the South African system has also the characteristic of efficiency, not merely in its narrower sense of collecting existing taxes with economy but also in its wider sense in collecting a given amount of revenue with the least burden on the national income. There are not the divided jurisdictions, the duplicated taxation machinery and lack of uniformity that are to be found in some other Federal systems, especially in the United States, Canada and Australia. Lastly, the position of Municipalities in the tax systems is exceptional. The Municipalities do not have to finance, as is customary elsewhere in Federal systems, education, hospitals and poor relief, and therefore their scope is limited. Their sources of revenue are from rates and to an unusual degree from the net profits of public utilities such as the provision of gas, electricity, water, buses and tramways.

The total expenditures amounted to 15 per cent of the national income. The data exclude loan expenditures and those of the railways and harbours, which are self-supporting and separated from the Consolidated Fund under the South Africa Act. Expressing expenditures as a percentage of the national income does not give a reliable index of the burden of government, especially in comparison with other countries, unless accompanied by an analysis of expenditures. Some expenditures are on the primary functions of government, *e.g.* administration and defence. Others are on the social services, such as education, unemployment relief and public health. There is also the important group of developmental expenditures including transportation, which in the case of South Africa is of considerable importance. Expenditures may also be classified into collective services and transfer expenditures. To the former group belong most expenditures on primary functions and such expenditures on secondary functions as education and developmental expenditures including transportation. In 1937–38 non-transfer expenditures amounted to £40

TABLE V

PUBLIC EXPENDITURES FROM REVENUE IN SOUTH AFRICA, ALL GOVERNMENTS, 1937–38

(£ thousands)

	Union	Provincial	Municipal	Total
1. *Primary Functions :*				
Legislation, administration and justice	5,868	458	1,154	7,480
Defence	1,788	..	..	1,788
Pensions	2,636	..[1]	226	2,862
Debt services [2]	5,348	673	4,181	10,202
Total, Primary Functions . .	15,640	1,131	5,561	22,332
2. *Secondary Functions :*				
(1) *Social Services :*				
Education	1,356	9,611	..	10,967
Unemployment expenditure . .	313	..	..	313
Old-age pensions . . .	2,050	..	..	2,050
Blind persons' pensions . .	75	..	..	75
Other public welfare [3] . .	2,342	1,515	903	4,760
Sub-total, Social Services . .	6,136	11,126	903	18,165
(2) *Developmental :*				
Lands and agriculture . .	3,713	..	..	3,713
Commerce and industry . .	280	..	..	280
Mining	550	..	..	550
Native affairs	850 [4]	..	..	850
Public works, roads and bridges .	1,314	4,385	1,768	7,467
Sub-total, Developmental . .	6,707	4,385	1,768	12,860
(3) *Miscellaneous*	501	930	1,183	2,614
Total, Secondary Functions .	13,344	16,441	3,854	33,639
Grants and subsidies	6,315	..	..	6,315
GRAND TOTAL	35,299	17,572	9,415	62,286
Less duplications	6,787 [5]	..	..	6,787
NET TOTAL	28,512	17,572	9,415	55,499

[1] No separate figures are given in the Official Year Book of the Union of South Africa.
[2] Includes redemption and other payments as well as interest.
[3] Includes public health and benefits on account of miners' phthisis.
[4] Includes grant of £340,000 to South African Native Trust.
[5] Union subsidies to Provinces and interest paid to Union Government on loans to Provincial administrations.

Note.—Expenditures on public utilities have been deducted from the corresponding revenues in arriving at the net figures in Tables III and IV.

millions, or 73 per cent of the total, or the equivalent of 11 per cent of the national income. Transfer expenditures (pensions, relief and other public welfare and interest on unproductive debt, *i.e.* debt that does not produce its own interest) were £15 millions, or 27 per cent of the total, or the equivalent of 4 per cent of the national income. Transfer expenditures

TABLE VI

PUBLIC EXPENDITURES FROM REVENUE IN SOUTH AFRICA, ALL GOVERNMENTS, 1937–38

(Percentage distribution)

	Percentage Share of each Government in Total Expenditures				Percentage Distribution of each Government's Expenditures			
	Union	Provincial	Municipal	Total	Union	Provincial	Municipal	Total
1. *Primary Functions :*								
Legislation, administration and justice	79	6	15	100	17	2	12	14
Defence	100	..	..	100	5	..	..	3
Pensions	92	..[1]	8	100	7	..[1]	3	5
Debt services	52	7	41	100	15	4	44	18
Total, Primary Functions	70	5	25	100	44	6	59	40
2. *Secondary Functions :*								
(1) *Social Services :*								
Education	12	88	..	100	4	55	..	20
Unemployment expenditure	100	..	..	100	1	..	..	1
Old-age pensions	100	..	..	100	6	..	..	4
Blind persons' pensions	100	..	..	100	..	..	..	..
Other public welfare	49	32	19	100	6	8	10	8
Sub-total, Social Services	34	61	5	100	17	63	10	33
(2) *Developmental :*								
Lands and agriculture	100	..	..	100	10	..	..	7
Commerce and industry	100	..	..	100	1	..	..	1
Mining	100	..	..	100	2	..	..	1
Native affairs	100	..	..	100	2	..	..	2
Public works, roads and bridges	17	59	24	100	4	25	19	12
Sub-total, Developmental	52	34	14	100	19	25	19	23
(3) *Miscellaneous*	19	36	45	100	2	6	12	5
Total, Secondary Functions	40	49	11	100	38	94	41	61
Grants and subsidies	100	..	..	100	18	..	..	11
GRAND TOTAL	57	28	15	100	100	100	100	112
Less duplications	100	..	..	100	19	..	..	12
NET TOTAL	51	32	17	100	81	100	100	100

[1] No separate figures are given in the Official Year Book of the Union of South Africa.

are comparatively small because of the small importance of unemployment relief.

The expenditures on the traditional "primary functions" of Governments, *i.e.* on legislation, administration and justice, defence, pensions and debt charges accounted for 40 per cent of total public expenditures in the Union of South Africa. Law and police and defence are expenditures of the Union and not of Provincial and Municipal Governments (except for Municipal expenditures on police in Cape Province, Natal and the Transvaal). Debt charges are not high, 18 per cent for all Governments as compared with, for example, 27 per cent in Canada. Defence in 1937–38 was 5 per cent of the Union expenditure and 3 per cent of all governmental expenditures. Since the outbreak of war it has increased by leaps and bounds, the expenditure from revenue alone rising to 38 per cent in 1940–1941, 39 per cent in 1941–42 and 46 per cent in 1942–43. If loan expenditures were also included, the total cost of defence expressed as a percentage of the total expenditures would be as follows: 1937–38 4 per cent, 1939–40 8 per cent, 1940–41 42 per cent, 1941–42 55 per cent, 1942–1943 57 per cent.

Expenditures on education amounted in 1937 to 20 per cent of total expenditures. The Union is responsible for higher education, *i.e.* that above matriculation standard, including grants to universities and for agricultural education, research stations and the like. It spent £1·4 millions, or 4 per cent of its expenditure, on this, or 12 per cent of the total expenditure by Governments on education. Provincial Governments (which are entrusted with elementary and secondary education) spent £9·6 millions, or 55 per cent of their expenditures, or 88 per cent of the total expenditures by Governments on education.

European education is mainly State education, *i.e.* administered and financed by the State, private or local effort being very small. Non-European education, on the other hand, is only State-aided, *i.e.* partly supported and controlled by Missionary enterprise. The development of education in recent decades is set out in Table 18 in Part III of the Enquiry. It shows since Union a great increase in all branches of education. The percentage of pupils in post-primary European education has gone up from 11 per cent at the time of Union to 20 per cent in 1937, and the State has increased its expenditure from £9·65 to £24·66 per annum per pupil. Native education, on the other hand, has also considerably increased although the percentage of natives enjoying education is still small, 6 per cent in 1937 as compared with 20 per cent for Europeans. Only 2 per cent of native pupils receive some sort of post-primary education as compared with ten times that figure for Europeans. In 1937 the State spent nearly twelve times as much per pupil, and something like forty times as much per head of the population, on European as compared with native education. But it must be remembered that the discrepancy in education given is less than this because of the expenditure from Mission funds. At the same time, differences in the standard of living between Europeans and natives is very great, and this has to be remembered in comparing expenditure. It does not, however, entirely explain the great contrast between European and non-European education. The main expenditures of the Provinces are on education — 55 per cent of the total in 1937–38. Public works, chiefly roads and buildings, accounted for 25 per cent in the same year.

In Municipal expenditure the chief item is the debt charges,[1] which in 1937–38 amounted to 44 per cent of the total expenditures. This debt was incurred mainly for developmental items such as gas and electricity. This is seen in the following table:

TABLE VII

CAPITAL EXPENDITURES OF MUNICIPALITIES IN 1937

(£ thousands)

	Cape of Good Hope	Natal	Transvaal	Orange Free State	Union
Roads and bridges .	586	129	694	42	1451
Public health . .	201	80	476	4	761
Electricity supply .	1260	157	1087	118	2622
Water supply . .	432	116	256	29	833
Properties . .	410	52	2259	33	2754
Other . . .	390	483	539	41	1453
Total . .	3279	1017	5311	267	9874

We have seen that 66 per cent of the revenues of all Governments are collected by the Union itself. In relation to the Provinces — Cape of Good Hope, Natal, Transvaal and Orange Free State — this is significant. In the first place, the main sources of income that would cause inequalities in Provincial revenues, *e.g.* mining revenues, are not allowed to remain with the Provinces or the Municipalities. Secondly, the subsidies amount to 52 per cent of the Provincial income, the subsidies themselves being based on an objective basis, viz. educational needs. There is, therefore, a greater uniformity of treatment by all Governments in regard to South Africans than is perhaps usual in other Federations. Railway policy, too, subsidises agriculture by freight rates, and therefore inequalities that would arise among different areas are ironed out.

[1] The figures for debt charges in Tables V and VI include redemption and other payments as well as interest. This should be borne in mind when comparing them with the corresponding figures in other chapters of this Enquiry, of which only the Australian ones include all these items.

IV. The Public Debt

The public debt of South Africa has been incurred, as elsewhere, to meet the cost of public works and also emergencies and temporary deficits. If productive debt is taken to mean self-supporting debt which pays its full interest and amortisation charges directly, then a large part of the debt, 61 per cent of the debt in 1939, may be regarded as productive — *e.g.* the debt on railways and harbours and posts and telegraphs. The debt incurred by Municipalities for public utilities would be, to a large extent, also classified as productive. The South African railways and harbours, for example, in the year ended 31st March 1942, produced a surplus of over £6 millions which was allocated to the reduction of interest-bearing capital (£2 millions), a special contribution to the renewals fund (£1 million) and a credit to the rates equalisation fund (£2·4 millions). The remainder went to reduce the deficiency in the pension and superannuation fund (£0·5 million) and as a contribution to the railway institute fund (£0·1 million). Part of the public debt which is not directly self-supporting is represented by tangible and useful assets which increase the productive power and therefore the taxable capacity of the Union. The unproductive debts include also the dead-weight debts representing deficits or bad investments. A large part of the total debt incurred for expenditure on unproductive works has from time to time been paid off, and is, therefore, not reflected in the present unproductive debt of the Union. A feature of the debt is the proportion payable in foreign currencies : 36 per cent of the Union debt is of this nature. In recent years, as will be seen from Table 19 in Part III, there has been a reduction in this debt. It should be remembered that with exchange control as a weapon of Central Bank and national economic policy all commitments should be under the control of one body. In the Union of South Africa under section 124 of the South Africa Act, the Union took over the debts of the four Provinces and also (under sections 121–3) all cash, securities, crown lands, public works, movable and immovable property and all rights in mines and minerals. Since that date the Provinces borrow only from the Union Government and compete with each other following a procedure similar to that in Australia.

It will be seen from the table overleaf (VIII) that the greater part of the public debt of the Union of South Africa in 1939 was productive.

TABLE VIII

THE PUBLIC DEBT OF THE UNION OF SOUTH AFRICA, 1910 and 1939

	£ millions		Per Cent	
	1910	1939	1910	1939
I. *Productive Debt :*				
Railways and Harbours . . .	74	144	64	52
Telegraphs and Telephones . .	1	12	1	4
Posts and Telegraphs and other .	1	16	1	5
Total, Productive Debt .	76	172	66	61
II. *Unproductive Debt :*				
Loans to Provincial administrations and Local authorities . . .	4	18	3	6
Universities and colleges . . .	1	2	1	1
Public works and buildings . .	1	17	1	6
War and defence . . .	10	40	9	14
Other	22	30	20	12
Total, Unproductive Debt . .	38	107	34	39
GRAND TOTAL	114	279	100	100
Interest self-producing or productive	3	7	60	63
Interest to be met out of taxation .	2	4	40	37
Total	5	11	100	100

The spread of the debt between the Union, Provinces and Municipalities is seen in the following table :

TABLE IX

DEBTS OF ALL GOVERNMENTS IN 1939

(£ millions)

Union	Provinces	Municipalities	Total
279	(14) [1]	60	339
Percentages			
82	(4) [1]	18	100

[1] Provincial debt is borrowed from the Union.

The outstanding features of the public debt may be summarised thus :

(1) The public debt is increasing with the development of the Union.

With the increased costs of Governments — the Union, Provinces and Municipalities — due mainly to the great extension of governmental activity, this growth is unavoidable.

(2) The net increase in public debt is not greater than the amount of interest received by the Governments.

(3) The decrease in the external debt.

(4) The greater part of the public debt of the Union is productive. In 1939 only about 37 per cent of the interest payable in respect of the gross public debt was the cost of serving unproductive debts, accumulated deficits and war expenditures, and may be regarded as a burden.

(5) The wisdom of making provinces borrow from the Union, thus preventing borrowing of a dead-weight character.

The conclusion which we come to is that the public debt of the Union is on a firm basis.

V. The South African Tax Structure as affected by the War

Compared with the other Federations, there was not much unemployment in South Africa at the outbreak of war, nor does there appear to have been much capital equipment standing idle. Not many plants were closed down or working short time.

Only the supply of food was in a different position — great surpluses of foodstuffs had been dumped abroad for years in consequence of the great subsidies to farmers, and food consumption consequently could be increased as a result of increased employment without causing a rise in the demand for men and materials for food production.

In South Africa, Government interference in production, outside of its control of the armed forces and of a few munition plants, has been small. It was only in 1942 that the Union was swinging over to a controlled economy. The latest development can be seen at a glance in the table overleaf.

In the year 1940–41 the South African expenditure for war purposes was £56 millions. For 1941–42 it was £72 millions and for 1942–43 it was estimated at £80 millions. In the financial year 1939–40 of the total Government expenditure of £132 millions (compared with £58 millions[1] in 1937–38), £56 millions was for defence and £56 millions was on loan account (compared with £19 millions in 1937–38). In addition, loans amounting to £8·4 millions were paid off. Since then more of South Africa's sterling debt has been repatriated ; *e.g.* £40 millions of stock were covered by a British Treasury vesting order made in December 1942.

[1] Including gross expenditure on Posts and Telegraphs (£4 millions).

TABLE X

WAR BUDGET FIGURES, 1941–42 AND 1942–43

1941–42		
Revised estimate of revenue		£79,533,000
Revised estimate of expenditure		73,800,000
		£5,733,000
1940–41 surplus carried forward		494,493
Estimated surplus at 31st March 1942 . .		£6,227,493
Of which to be transferred to loan account . .		6,000,000
Leaving a net balance to be carried forward to 1942–43 of .		£227,493
1942–43		
Estimate of Expenditure	..	£88,366,170
Estimate of revenue on existing basis of taxation	£78,643,000	
Plus balance carried forward from 1941–42 .	227,493	78,870,493
Leaving a shortfall of	..	£9,495,677
Which was to be met as follows:		
Additional customs and excise duties on tobacco and petrol	£1,570,000	
Additional death duties	75,000	
Increase of gold mines special contribution from 16 to 20 per cent . . .	1,640,000	
Trade Profits Special Levy . . .	4,000,000	
Tax on individuals	640,000	
Surcharge on income tax . . .	910,000	
Land sales profit tax	450,000	
		9,285,000
Leaving an estimated deficit at 31st March 1943	..	£210,677

This means that in return for goods received in the past South Africa supplies goods now, whether gold or other commodities, and thus far eases the strain on British finances, as long as Britain wants and can use South African gold.

Thus, up to 1942 the major part of South Africa's war effort had so far been financed by loans. This was in marked contrast to Great Britain and the other Dominions, where, though large sums were raised by loans, taxation was in these years very heavy.

South African taxation was very light, and apart from increased taxation of the gold mines and normal income tax, the other tax increases have not made a serious difference to the weight of taxation. For it should be remembered that income tax rates before the war were very low in South Africa, and even a substantial percentage increase in the rates does not, therefore, mean that the absolute burden is great.

There are signs, however, that this state of affairs is going to change. In the year 1941–42 the buoyancy of the revenue was such that a surplus of more than £6 millions arose. This was used in reduction of loans. This means, in effect, that in 1941–42 one-half of the war expenditure of £72 millions had been paid out of revenue funds, whereas it was originally intended to pay £29 millions, or 40 per cent, from revenue and £43 millions, or 60 per cent, from loan. In 1942–43 a war expenditure of £80 millions was budgeted for to be paid half from revenue and half from loan, though this figure is likely to be exceeded.

The increased burden is being met by a great increase in taxation.

In Part III will be found further detailed tables of revenue and expenditure. The data are interesting because they show how, in order to meet expenditure connected with the war, taxation has been increased, notably in three directions, viz. in progressive taxation (personal income taxes and succession duties), in the taxation of companies (especially gold mines) and in consumption taxes. The requirements of the Union are now so great that the tax burden has to be widespread, and this has meant a judicious mixture as in the past of direct and indirect taxes, with the modern bias towards progressive taxes and the taxation of surplus. The present financial policy of the Union also attempts to draw off, in Mr. Hofmeyr's own words, "as much as we can of the actual surplus of purchasing power. That can be done by taxation and by certain types of borrowing. As far as borrowing is concerned, we have taken a definitely anti-inflationary step by using money borrowed in South Africa to cancel the repatriated stock held by the Reserve Bank. Moreover, we have, through the thrift movement, promoted voluntary savings with, as I have indicated, a considerable measure of success. But we have not done enough. There are far too many people who have not responded to the appeal to spend less and save more. There is still far too much money which is being spent lightly and unthinkingly without regard to the interests of the community as a whole. The time would seem to have come to consider the use of compulsory savings as a means of drawing off the surplus to which I have referred. The third method is taxation."[1]

War taxation in the Union has been on the whole well distributed. The total expenditure has risen steeply since 1939, until in 1942–43 on Revenue and Loan Accounts it reached £140 millions, of which £88,366,000

[1] Budget Statement by Mr. J. H. Hofmeyr, Minister of Finance, House of Assembly, 26th February 1942.

are on Revenue Account. The method of meeting an estimated deficit of about £9½ millions is of special interest.

The existing Excess Profits Duty, which was raised in 1941–42 from 10s. in the £ to 13s. 4d., continues, but there is an ingenious tax, called the Trade Profits Special Levy, which is estimated to bring in £4 millions. Like the excess profits duty it is a deduction in calculating normal and super income tax. The rate of levy is a progressive one. Payers of excess profits duty may pay the duty on the difference between their present income and either their pre-war standard of income or a statutory percentage (8 per cent for companies and 12 per cent for individuals) on the capital employed by them in their business. The levy is charged on the difference between the statutory percentage and the actual profits earned. The result is to remove certain inequalities which have existed in the rate of taxation as between established companies and companies which have sprung up since the war and have no pre-war standard of profits. A company with a capital of £20,000 and a pre-war standard profit of £3000 is now required to pay no excess profits duty if its profit does not exceed £3000 and if it elects to be assessed on the basis of its pre-war standard. If, however, the test is the statutory percentage and not the pre-war standard, the company will pay excess profits duty on the difference between its present income (£3000) and 8 per cent of its capital of £20,000, *i.e.* on £1400. The Trade Profits Special Levy will amount to not more than half the rate of the excess profits duty (6s. 8d.). The increase of the gold mines special contribution from 17 to 20 per cent in 1942–43 will bring in £1,640,000 and is further proof of the great extent to which the Union is dependent upon its revenue from gold mines. The rate was increased early in 1943 to 22½ per cent, yielding an additional £910,000.

Another tax which was new to South Africa was the tax on profits arising from the sale of land as given in Table X, page 172. Any profit derived from the sale of fixed property which was purchased since October 1939 was liable to this tax, which was at the rate of 6s. 8d. in the £ if the property were bought between 1st October 1939 and 25th February 1942, and at the rate of 13s. 6d. after that date. The tax was estimated to bring in £450,000. Income tax is increased in two ways, though it is still light as compared with that in other Dominions and Great Britain. In the first place there is a tax on individuals — a flat-rate tax resembling the familiar personal tax payable to the Provinces — of £1 (£2 : 10s. on incomes over £250). All single persons earning £250 and over pay £2 : 10s., while married persons earning between £250 and £300 pay £1 and married persons earning over £300 pay £2 : 10s. Secondly, there is a 10 per cent surcharge on the amount of income tax and supertax paid during the year 1942–43. A small addition to succession duties (death duties) was estimated to bring in an additional £75,000. Consumption taxes on cut tobacco and petrol were estimated to bring in £1,570,000.

Despite these new duties and taxes war expenditure is the equivalent of about 15 per cent of the national income as compared with 61 per cent in Great Britain and 90 per cent in Germany.[1] The percentages of the national income to revenues and expenditures for the years 1937–38, 1940–41, 1941–42 and 1942–43, are given in Table II on page 160 above.

The conclusion is that, expressed in terms of the national income, the burden of taxation is still light and the public expenditures, even in war-time, are not strikingly high.

[1] For Germany see H. W. Singer, *The German War Economy*, Manchester Statistical Society, 1943, p. 24.

CHAPTER VII

THE PUBLIC FINANCE AND NATIONAL ECONOMY OF INDIA

I. Conditions governing Indian Finance

In none of the Federations studied in this book is an analysis of the national economy so important to the understanding of the financial structure as in the case of India. The sub-continent, inhabited by many races and tribes speaking over one dozen main languages and over two hundred minor dialects, is more than twenty-five times the size of England and Wales. It covers an area of 1·5 million square miles of which 0·8 million square miles is British India and the remaining 0·7 million square miles are the Indian States. Two-thirds of the population lives on one-fourth of the area, and at the last Census, taken on 1st March 1941, it reached a total of 388·8 millions, excluding Burma (which ceased to be part of the Indian Empire on 1st April 1937). The population of India thus is 70 per cent of the population of the British Commonwealth. The increase in population was 15 per cent over the previous census and compares favourably with the increase of more than 10 per cent in the Census of 1931 as compared with its immediate predecessor, the Census of 1921. If we accept Professor Willcox's estimate of the population of China,[1] the statement of Herodotus is true — " Of all nations that we know, it is India that has the largest population ".

The population is anything but homogeneous. The Sikh and the Bengali, the Madrasi and the Bhil all differ from each other more than do the inhabitants of different parts of Europe. Nevertheless, after one hundred and seventy years of British rule, there is a noteworthy feeling of national unity among educated classes and a pride in India. Two-thirds of the population profess Hinduism in one form or another and over one-fifth are followers of Islam. The difference between the two is an age-long one. It is not only a difference of religion in the stricter sense,

[1] *Vide* F. W. Willcox, *International Migrations*, vol. ii, pp. 33-82 (National Bureau of Economic Research, New York, 1930). Professor Willcox says that careful estimates regarding the population of China are much below the figure which had been guessed at. There has been no census in China and, by an examination of the number of households and similar statistics, he gives a figure of 342 millions in place of 450 millions in 1929.

Note.—In the Indian system of notation large numbers are expressed in crores and lakhs and not in millions.

1 crore of rupees = Rs. 10,000,000 = £750,000.

1 lakh of rupees = Rs. 100,000 = £7500.

1 rupee = 16 annas ; 1 anna = 12 pies ; 13⅓ rupees = £1 ; 1 anna = 1⅛d.

but also one of law and culture. Indeed, they may be said to represent two distinct and separate civilisations. Hinduism is distinguished by the phenomenon of caste which leads to a degree of social disunity to which no parallel can be found in human history, while at the same time it has produced great cultural stability. The religion of Islam, on the other hand, is based on the conception of the equality of man and, unlike Hinduism, is monotheistic and iconoclastic. In addition to these two great communities and to Indian Christians (which number over 7 millions [1]) there is an infinite variety of other religions and sects ranging from the mystical speculations of Buddhism and Jainism to the simple beliefs of Animism.

The outstanding characteristic of the population, a characteristic which is of great importance in Indian finance, is its dependence on agriculture. The structure of public finance is moulded to a large degree by economic and social conditions, and this is certainly true in the case of India, which is so predominantly rural in character. It has 700,000 villages, a striking contrast with Great Britain where four-fifths of the people live in towns. Seven-tenths of the population depend on agriculture for a living as compared with 7 or 8 per cent in Britain. It is well known that a country which is so very greatly dependent on agriculture must needs be poor as compared with the industrialised countries of the West. Indeed, in European countries the net output per person engaged in manufacture and measured at the world price of the product so that the effects of protection are eliminated, is from 60 to 100 per cent greater than the output per male worker in agriculture and mining similarly measured.

In this connexion a caveat must be entered. Unless the individual worker is assisted by the two powerful factors of production, capital and organisation, the value of his output will be relatively low. The great increase in British industry and in agriculture from the early twenties of the present century was due in a large degree to the increased amount of capital per person.

Not only are the Indians dependent on agriculture but on an uncertain agriculture. Indian agriculture, to an extent scarcely realised by Western peoples, depends on rainfall. More than four-fifths of the cultivated areas of the country is dependent upon this precarious rainfall, and the livelihood of five-sixths of the population depends, it has been estimated, on the South-West monsoon. As the time comes round each year in June when the monsoon is due, its arrival is a subject of deep concern. The proverbs of the people confirm this. The peasant of Marwar, for example, knows when

[1] 7,250,000 in the 1941 Census; 6,300,000 in the 1931 Census.

August's here, no sound of thunder,
Sky is clear, and weather fine ;
Wife ! 'tis time for us to sunder,
You to your folk, I to mine.

The timely rainfall producing a bumper crop gives rise to the proverb in Bihar :

One shower in Swati — friend, behold !
The Kurmi's earrings turned to gold !

The danger of widespread famine is ever present, and dates from the very dawn of Indian history. During recent years, however, famine has not been either so frequent or so widespread because of the extension of railways and irrigation, the growth of industries (which draw the workpeople temporarily from the villages to the towns in times of such unemployment), the greater mobility of labour, and last but not least, the improvements in preparations for dealing with it and with famine relief generally. An unfavourable monsoon affects the Budget of the Central Government as well as that of the Provinces, as it reduces purchasing power, diminishes the volume of imports, the profits of commerce and the receipts from transport so that the revenue from customs, income tax and railways are involved. In the Provinces it means expenditure on famine relief, remissions of land revenue and a fall in returns from excise revenue. It thus affects the revenues of both the Central and Provincial Governments. Another fact governing Indian finance is the low national income of the country. Although the aggregate of goods and services produced in a twelvemonth is great, it has to be divided among a large population and the resulting *per capita* figure is exceedingly small, especially when compared with that of advanced industrial countries like Great Britain and the United States.

Another caveat may also be mentioned here. We are accustomed to think, in making comparisons in national income between one country and another, in terms of the national income of the most advanced industrial countries. But these countries are exceptional. The world in this respect is really a very poor place. A standard of living below £2 or $9 a week per breadwinner would fit 81 per cent of the world's population. The standard of living double this amount would be found only in the United States, Canada, Australia, Great Britain and Argentina, *i.e.* among 10 per cent of the world's population. The remaining 9 per cent of the world's population is in the principal industrial countries of Europe with an average per breadwinner per week of from £2 or $9 to double that amount.[1] The four industrial countries of U.S.A., Great Britain, France

[1] Cf. G. Findlay Shirras, "*National Income*", *Review of the International Institute of Statistics* (The Hague, 1936); also Colin Clark, *The Conditions of Economic Progress* (Macmillan & Co.), 1940.

and Germany contain 13 per cent of the world's population, but produce 40 to 50 per cent of the world's output. Poverty, therefore, is very unequally distributed over areas as it is between social classes.

The average national income per head (man, woman and child) in India is at the present time only one-twentieth of that of Great Britain. In 1931, when the value of primary products had fallen, it was one-fifteenth, but we should not be far out if we say that the income per head of the United Kingdom is between fifteen and twenty times greater than that of British India. The national income per head of British India is next below that of the whole of Soviet Russia and of Bulgaria. Unfortunately statistics are not available for China where, it is believed, the income per head is even lower. At the present time, the Indian income amounts to £7 per head per annum.[1] In making comparisons one has to take into consideration the different standards of value which obtain in regard to the necessaries of existence and efficiency, and even to comforts and luxuries. Those in a hot country differ considerably, as, for example, in clothing and fuel, from those of a colder climate. A well-known writer, Rabindranath Tagore, has expressed it thus : " We have as far as possible made our food and clothing unburdensome, and this our very climate has taught us to do. We require openings in the walls more than the walls themselves. Light and air have more to do with wearing apparel than the weaver's loom : the sun makes for us the heat-producing factors, which elsewhere are required from foods. All these natural conditions have moulded our life to a particular shape which I cannot believe it will be profitable to ignore."

Not only is the income low per head, but it varies very much more from year to year than is the case in an industrial country, so that this is also a factor to be considered in regard to taxable capacity. Nothing is so striking to the Westerner than the low standard of living on which the mass of the Indian population exists and the extent of the poverty. There has, it is true, been considerable economic progress in recent years, but the smallness of the national income is still very striking. It is only by a long-term policy of industrialisation and more widespread education in the villages up and down the countryside that the problem may be solved. The influx of industrial workers from the villages to the towns even in a short space of time, as the worker is not yet divorced from his home in the village, tends to lower the standard of living of workers in industry. " Whereas only a few years ago it was said to be difficult to obtain labour

[1] For a detailed study of the national income of India, see G. Findlay Shirras, *The Science of Public Finance*, vol. i., chap. xv (Macmillan & Co., 3rd edition, London, 1936) ; also G. Findlay Shirras, *Poverty and Kindred Economic Problems in India* (Government Press, Delhi, 2nd edition) ; G. Findlay Shirras, " The National Income of British India, 1931–32 " — a Review, *Economic Journal*, June–Sept. 1941, p. 325.

in industry, that complaint is not heard to-day. On the contrary, during the recent boom in the cotton trade, Bombay, Cawnpore and Ahmedabad were able to recruit, with no difficulty whatever, the tens of thousands of additional workers needed to run a night-shift. At Jamshedpur, remote though it is from the large centres of population, the steel-works turned away hundreds every day. The number of men wanting to go to sea is so great that the unions have been urging a system of engagement by rotation on the shipowners of Bombay and Calcutta. In fact, there is probably no industry in the country that could not recruit all the unskilled labour it required within a few days or weeks. This is primarily due to the low wages, the under-employment and the poor conditions of life in the villages." [1]

Another characteristic of the national economy is the great disparity in the incomes of different classes of people in India. The large number of small incomes and the comparatively small number of very large incomes is striking, as was shown in a study of the Pareto law and the distribution of income.[2]

The plain fact is that the majority of the population in India is chiefly concerned with getting a living. Religion and the pursuit of wealth as we know them in Western countries is not what they are in the East. The villager is content to produce enough to live. He also wishes to be allowed to worship his gods as he desires and, in a country of universal marriage, to marry his daughter as soon as she reaches puberty, and to take part in local village ceremonies. Marshall puts it thus: "Man's character has been moulded by his everyday work, and the material resources which he thereby procures, more than by any other influence unless it be that of his religious ideals; and the two great forming agencies of the world's history have been the religious and the economic. Here and there the ardour of the military or the artistic spirit has been for a while predominant; but religious and economic influences have nowhere been displaced from the front rank even for a time; and they have nearly always been more important than all others put together. Religious motives are more intense than economic, but their direct action seldom extends over so large a part of life. For the business by which a person earns his livelihood generally fills his thoughts during by far the greater part of those hours in which his mind is at its best; during them his character is being formed by the way in which he uses his faculties in his work, by the thoughts and the feelings which it suggests, and by his

[1] Harold Butler, *Problems of Industry in the East*. International Labour Office, Geneva, 1938.

[2] G. Findlay Shirras, "The Pareto Law and the Distribution of Income", *Economic Journal*, 1935, vol. xlv, p. 663.

relations to his associates in work, his employers or his employees."[1] How true of India!

It must not be thought that changes are not taking place. To-day, economics is knocking at the door of ethics in the East, and we are witnessing the shifting of the line between the sphere of religion and that of secular business, especially in the more advanced areas of the countryside. For centuries the life of the country has been dominated by religion, or as we may more correctly say, by custom, which if not religious in origin has in the process of time become largely religious in sanction.

The spread of communication by motor transport among the villages and the spread of irrigation are breaking through the isolation of centuries and making for a higher standard of living. The problem, however, for the Hindu is getting the sacred cow back from the temple to the field. Nothing is so sacred to the Hindu as the cow. Nevertheless in some of the more advanced areas of the Punjab, when a cow can no longer give milk, it is sold to the butcher. If this were done in the less advanced districts, the owner would be outcasted. Similarly, the Sikh who cannot grow tobacco because of the religious sanction against smoking, is now in some parts growing tobacco as crop. In other areas the Sikh practises family limitation, because as one Sikh said, " Too much rain reduces the crop ; too many sons bring reproach." They believe that every son comes with a share written on his forehead. In the country where holdings are so small as to become uneconomic and where each son is entitled to a share in his father's land, one can understand why a child appears with a share written on his forehead. Similarly the Mahomedans are beginning to take interest because of the fact that credit is indispensable to all undertakings, and there are not a few students of Islam who hold that Islam has been profoundly at a disadvantage from a wealth point of view by this prohibition to take interest.

We have noted some of the salient features of the Indian economy such as the dependence upon agriculture, the low national income and the inequalities in the distribution of wealth and income. There are other factors of vulnerability which must be mentioned to complete the picture. These are the backwardness of industry and, in foreign trade, the dependence on world prices for India's few specialised exports. Such dependence leads, unfortunately, to sharp fluctuations in the national income.

First, as regards Indian industry. To meet war demands, India's industries are undergoing a rapid expansion and it is necessary to plan ahead to prevent deterioration after the war. Nothing will increase the standard of living so much as widespread industrialisation and this is bound up with increased production in agriculture. Competent authorities

[1] Marshall, *Principles of Economics*, vol. i, chap. i. 5th edition, Macmillan & Co.

estimate that, by means of better methods of cultivation, agricultural output can be improved by 25 per cent without any increase in capital expenditure, and a further 25 per cent could be added, at very little cost, by factors such as better seed, fencing and the consolidation of holdings. During the last fifty years the population has been increasing at the rate of 0·8 per cent per annum, while agricultural production has been increasing at the rate of 0·4 per cent per annum. Unless production is increased considerably, a deterioration in the already low standard of living is likely to take place. Agriculture alone cannot maintain the rural population. As the Famine Commission of 1880 pointed out, the numbers who have no other employment than agriculture are greatly in excess of what is required for cultivation. Since that date the position has not, owing to the great increases in population in the last few decades, improved, notwithstanding the development of industry together with a policy of discriminating protection introduced in the early twenties. In 1913–14, for example, India imported 60 per cent of the total consumption of cotton piece goods, 20 per cent was supplied by Indian mills, and 20 per cent by hand looms. In 1936–37 only 13 per cent was imported, and 61 per cent was supplied by Indian mills and 26 per cent by hand looms. The expansion of the Indian cotton-mill industry has been at the expense of foreign mills and not of the indigenous hand-loom industry, which has maintained its production. The production of cotton textiles averaged, during the years 1914 to 1917, 325 million lb. per annum and in 1937–38 rose to 715 million lb. Sugar production in the same period had risen from 20,000 tons to 1,072,000 tons, and India is one of the greatest sugar-producing countries of the world, being the chief producer of cane sugar. Before 1932–33 India depended on imports for approximately half of her domestic consumption and by 1936–37 had become self-sufficient in sugar. The present output of coal is approximately 30 million tons and geological surveys have shown that there are unlimited supplies of high-quality coal. One field in the Central Provinces alone is estimated to contain a supply of 17,000 million tons. A single district in the province of Bihar is estimated to contain over 3000 million tons. The reserves of good coking and high-grade coal are not high, but this may be more than compensated for by the immense sources of water-power in the Himalayas and elsewhere. The Tata Hydro-Electric system, the Mysore Hydro-Electric Works, two systems in Madras and those in the United Provinces, the Punjab and Kashmir are examples. With the aid of protection imports of iron and steel goods have been halved as compared with the 1913–14, and the Tata Iron and Steel Works at Jamshedpur are the largest steel-works in the British Empire. The output of finished steel is more than 50 per cent above the pre-war level and the industry is producing a great variety of finished steels. Iron ore has increased from 409,000 tons, the average of the years 1914–18, to 2,871,000 tons in 1937–38; manganese ore from 577,000 tons to 1,052,000 tons and petroleum from 7,325,000 gallons to 75,658,000 gallons. Three-quarters of the world's supply of sheet and block mica comes from Indian mines. India is the world's largest supplier of oil seeds and of jute, the second largest supplier of tea and the third largest producer of tobacco. With the exception of the U.S.S.R. she is the largest producer of manganese and is also an important producer of chromite. One-third of the world's cattle population is in India and vast quantities of hides and skins are produced every year. Ordnance factories, railway workshops and hundreds of other factories are now working to maximum capacity. All things considered, the development of industry has great possibilities. At the same time it must be remembered that only 10 per cent of the population is engaged in industry, and of this the great majority is still employed in small-scale industries. About 3 or 4 millions, or about 1 or 2 per cent, of all occupied persons are in large-scale industry. In 1939 less than 2 million persons were employed in factories under the Factory Acts. Nevertheless India with her large numbers in industry is one of the eight countries of chief industrial importance.

Under the Government of India Act, 1935, the main responsibility for the development of industries rests with the Provinces, the Central Government being responsible only for "the development of industries, where development under Federal control is declared by Federal law to be expedient in the public interest". The Centre is also given the "regulation of mines and oilfields and mineral development to the extent to which such regulation and development under Federal control is declared by Federal law to be expedient in the public interest". While Government initiative in recent decades has been considerable, it cannot be compared with, for example, a second-rate industrial power like Japan in organisation. In Japan the Government built up key industries in the late nineteenth and early twentieth centuries. To-day it not only operates arsenals and munition plants, but also shipyards, telephone services, and monopolies of tobacco, salt and camphor. Even before the war with China there were what has been called public-private enterprises in banking, communications and colonial development, and the Government controls the policies and personnel of many private concerns. The Mitsui, Mutsubishi and Sumitomo concerns nevertheless possess considerable initiative, but there has been nothing in India, so far as State organisation goes, to compare with that in Japan since the invasion of Manchuria in 1931, especially in the heavy industries. By extensive powers during the last decade, and especially since the outbreak of war with China, the Japanese Government has shown what the East can do in harnessing foreign trade to the war machine, in closing the capital market to non-essential industries, in controlling practically the whole of economic life, in great concentration of production, especially in ships, tanks, aeroplane production, in chemicals, metals and machinery, and in the building-up of large stocks of commodities, especially those which have to be imported, such as iron ore, scrap iron, steel, coal and oil.[1] Since 1941, however, great strides have been made in Indian industry, so that the country may become much more highly organised as an arsenal for the United Nations.[2] The implications of this policy on the national income and the raising of the standard of living and the increasing taxable capacity are obvious.

In foreign trade, India ranks about ninth or tenth among the countries of the world. The *per capita* value is exceedingly small, but this does not mean that India's foreign trade is unimportant. On the contrary, it indicates that there are unexploited possibilities. With the development of communications — India has the third largest railway mileage in the world [3] — exports of grains and raw materials grew and manufactured goods were imported in return. The present century has seen a great development in foreign trade. India's chief exports are tea, leather and hides, raw cotton, oil seeds, jute and jute manufactures. These few specialised exports make her vulnerable and any fall in world prices hits the producer of primary products. Her imports, on the other hand, are mainly manufactured goods — machinery, mineral oils, cotton goods, iron and steel, chemicals, dyes, woollen goods, motor cars and other vehicles, electrical instruments and hardware. Grain and pulse, however, are also imported, *e.g.* rice from Burma. Again, her position both as to her trade and financial relations with the outside world is largely that of her position in relation to Great Britain, which in 1937–38 took 34 per cent of India's exports and in 1941–42 31 per cent. India, on the other hand, took from Great Britain 30 and 21 per cent respectively of her total imports from abroad in those years.

The changes in the direction of trade in the present century are striking. Since the Fiscal Autonomy Convention of 1921 India has had the power to determine her own tariffs and has followed a protective policy, with the result that British exporters have lost markets now supplied by India's industries. Imports of Lancashire piece-goods, which had averaged 2,550 million yards per annum before 1914, had fallen

[1] Cf. G. P. Allen, *The Industrialization of Japan and Manchukuo, 1930–40*, edited by E. B. Schumpeter (New York, Macmillan & Co., 1940); K. Mitchell, *Japan's Industrial Strength* (New York Institute of Pacific Relations, 1942); and L. K. Rosinger, *Japan as an Economic Power* (Foreign Policy Report, Foreign Policy Association, April 1942).

[2] Cf. *India's Progress in Industrialisation*, Bulletin of International News, 13th June 1942 (London, Royal Institute of International Affairs).

[3] India has the third largest railway mileage and ranks after the U.S.A. and Russia and before Canada.

to 205 million yards by 1939, or less than one-twelfth of the imports of a quarter of century earlier. A great steel industry has been built up behind a tariff wall, the Tata Steel Works being the largest single unit manufacturing steel in the British Empire. To-day, more than 25 per cent of the total exports from India are goods manufactured in India. The vast bulk of the manufactures is consumed within the country. As will be seen in the table below, India's imports of British goods has fallen from 63 per cent to 30 per cent in 1937–38 and to 21 per cent in 1941–42, whereas Great Britain in 1941–42 took 31 per cent of India's exports as against 34 per cent in 1937–38 and 25 per cent the pre-war average. Great Britain just before the war was actually buying more goods from India than Great Britain sold to her. Great Britain, before the war, took Rs. 555 millions of India's exports and India took Rs. 520 millions worth of British goods.

INDIA'S FOREIGN TRADE

(In percentages)

(A) *Imports*

From—	Average, 1909–14	1937–38	1941–42
United Kingdom	63	30	21
Rest of British Empire	7	25	40
U.S.A.	3	7	20
Japan	2	13	7
Java	6	0·2	1·1
Germany	6	9	..
Other Countries	13	15·8	10·9
Total	100	100·0	100·0

(B) *Exports*

To—	Average, 1909–14	1937–38	1941–42
United Kingdom	25	34	31
Rest of British Empire	16	18	30
U.S.A.	8	10	21
Japan	8	10	2
France	7	3	..
Germany	10	6	..
Other countries	26	19	16
Total	100	100	100

The general conclusion is that British manufacturers must realise that most of the world is going to be able to make for itself the old staple goods of British industry after the war and that Great Britain must concentrate on (1) special qualities of older types; (2) newer types of production; and, above all, (3) on what has been called British "experience in the production and installation of capital plant, on good salesmanship, and reliability and promptitude of delivery." British manufacturers can provide, therefore, capital goods for industrial expansion and re-equipment, and consumers' goods of the more specialised kinds.

II. The Indian Financial System

The Federal system of finance came into existence with the introduction of the Reforms in 1921–22 following the passing of the Government of India Act, 1919. Before that date, Indian finance was highly centralised, although by a policy of gradualness it became less so. Between 1870 and 1912 devolution grew slowly. It was for this reason that the authors of the Report on Indian Constitutional Reforms, usually known as the Montagu-Chelmsford Report, said: "Our task is not like that of the Fathers of the Union in the United States and Canada. We have to demolish the existing structure at least in part, before we can build the new. Our business is one of devolution, of drawing lines of demarcation, of cutting long-standing ties. The Government of India must give and the provinces must receive; for only so can the growing organism of self-government draw air into its lungs and live. It requires no great effort of imagination to draw a future map of India which shall present the external semblance of a great new confederation within the Empire. But we must sedulously beware of the ready application of federal arguments or federal examples to a task which is the very reverse of that which confronted Alexander Hamilton and Sir John Macdonald."[1] The Reforms brought about a separation of the sources of revenue and assigned some to the Centre and others to the Provinces. It avoided the inconveniences arising from a system of heads of revenues shared between the Centre and the Provinces and also the system of "doles" from the Centre to the Provinces.

It is not possible, for reasons of space, to show in detail how the transformation from a Centralised to a Federal system took place. A few outstanding facts, however, may be mentioned. The East India Company Act, 1773, provided that every President and Council of Madras and Bombay should "constantly and diligently" transmit to the Governor-General and Council of Bengal "advice and intelligence" on all transactions and matters "whatsoever that shall come to their knowledge relating to the Government, revenues or interest of the said United Company". By the Charter Act of 1833, the Governor-General of Bengal became the Governor-General of India and was invested with complete control over the revenues of Bombay, Madras and other subordinate Governments. The Acts of 1853 and 1858 continued the Central Government's control over all revenues as well as expenditures. In 1870 some

[1] Report on Indian Constitutional Reforms (Cd. 9109, 1917), p. 101.

degree of financial decentralisation took place when the administration of certain departments, including education, police and medical services, was transferred to Provincial Governments. These Governments were given a fixed grant for this purpose together with departmental receipts and were permitted to allot at their discretion the revenues assigned to them, subject to certain financial rules. There was no inducement to the Provinces to develop their own revenues because of the fixed assignments. In 1877 a further step took place and important heads of revenue, such as stamp duties, excise and income tax collected in the Provinces, were provincialised. In expenditure the Provinces had their powers extended to the depths of land revenue, general administration, law and justice. Nevertheless fixed grants from the Centre continued, although in two Provinces a definite proportion of the land revenue was assigned in place of a fixed sum. From 1882 there was developed a system of what is known as "the divided heads of revenue". In 1904 the settlements were made quasi-permanent. In 1912 took place the last of the pre-Reform settlements. To meet its own expenditure, stated the Government of India's Resolution of 1912, "the Government of India retains, in the first place, the entire profits of the commercial departments and, secondly, all the revenue whose locale is no guide to its true incidence, such as the net receipts from Customs, Salt and Opium. The income derived from these sources is, however, insufficient to cover the cost of the imperial services, and an arrangement had therefore to be made by which the other sources of revenue should be distributed between the central and the various provincial governments."[1] These settlements led to much friction between the Central and the Provincial Governments. All the principal heads of revenue collected within the Provinces were divided between the Central Government and the Provinces and were supplemented by non-recurring subsidies which were part of the financial settlements to the Provinces. No general standards of needs had been worked out; the settlements were based on traditions. There were thus very different standards of administration between Provinces. The Reforms which took effect from 1921–22 avoided the inconveniences by a Federal system of finance. The Centre had certain heads of revenue and the Provinces other heads. In expenditure the Provinces had an inexhaustible field for the development of social services, such as education and public health, while the demands on the Centre, except in time of war, were far more constant. The revenues of the Centre comprised those which proved more capable of expansion, such as income tax and the commercial departments such as the railways. In a period of ordinary progress this led to a strong claim by the Provinces for a share in income tax, especially

[1] Report of the Indian Statutory Commission (Cmd. 3568, 1930), vol. i, p. 345.

on the part of the more industrialised Provinces such as Bombay and Bengal. In accordance with the provisions of section 84A of the Government of India Act, 1919, the Indian Statutory Commission conducted a constitutional enquiry in 1928 and 1929. Sir Walter Layton, its Financial Assessor, made three criticisms of the system which was introduced in 1921–22. In the first place, the Provinces had rapidly expanding needs, but the sources of revenue assigned to them were insufficient and showed no signs of increasing growth, whereas the sources of revenue of the Centre, which ordinarily had but comparatively stationary needs, were expanding or capable of expansion. Secondly, the system of devolution treated the Provinces unequally, as it gave some of them a much greater proportionate increase of revenue than others. Thirdly, it gave practically no power to the Provinces to tax industrial activities and therefore the industrial, as contrasted with the agricultural, provinces were handicapped. The Commission suggested that the Provinces might have a share of income tax and other taxes such as the export duty on jute. The British Government's proposals were published in a White Paper entitled *Proposals for Indian Constitutional Reform* [1] in which the British Government proposed, after extensive enquiries by committees, conferences and consultations in India and in England, a scheme extending over six years, an allocation of revenues between the Centre and the Provinces and the sharing of income tax, a scheme which was, with one small exception in regard to a surcharge by the Provinces, approved by the Joint Committee of both Houses of Parliament in the following year [2] and subsequently incorporated in Part 7 and Schedule 7 of the Government of India Act, 1935. Under this Act the Centre has the following sources of revenue: customs duties, excise duties on tobacco and other goods manufactured or produced in India except alcoholic liquors, opium, Indian hemp and other narcotic drugs and narcotics and non-narcotic drugs, and medicinal and toilet preparations containing alcohol; income tax other than on agricultural incomes; the corporation tax; succession duties other than on agricultural land; salt; State lotteries; fees other than fees taken in courts; terminal taxes on goods or passengers carried by rail or air; taxes on railway fares and freights; commercial stamp duties, *i.e.* stamp duties on bills of exchange, cheques, promissory notes, bills of lading, letters of credit, policies of insurance, proxies and receipts; taxes on the capital value of the assets, exclusive of agricultural land, of individuals and companies, and taxes on the capital of companies. As will be seen below in Table VI, the main sources of revenue are customs, the income tax, and com-

[1] Cmd. 4268, 1933.

[2] Joint Committee on Indian Constitutional Reform, H.L. 6 (1, Part I), H.C. 5 (1, Part I), 1934.

mercial departments, mainly railways. Several of the taxes in the above list, such as those on capital and terminal taxes, have not yet been levied. It was, however, considered desirable to make the schedules as complete as possible in the Act so as to avoid uncertainty and litigation in the Supreme Court in the future.

The most interesting fact on the Centre's sources of revenue relates to income tax. In the first place, agricultural incomes are exempt and there is no historical or other justification for this, in spite of the land tax (land revenue). Agricultural incomes were not exempt from income tax between its first introduction, in 1860, and 1873. When the tax was reintroduced by the Act of 1886 agricultural incomes were exempt from the scope of the tax, and this has continued ever since. It cannot be said that land revenue is the counterpart of income tax and that to tax agricultural incomes would be double taxation. By not levying income tax on agricultural incomes the non-agricultural incomes of those who own land are made to pay a lower rate of tax than they should. The taxation of agricultural incomes would check the tendency to put savings into land to avoid taxation. In the Government of India Act, 1935, the taxation of agricultural incomes is a Provincial subject. Secondly, the Provinces share in the total collections of income tax under section 138. This was in fact suggested by Sir Walter Layton, the Indian Statutory Commission's Financial Assessor, when he suggested that " in order to meet the claim of the industrial provinces, a substantial portion of the revenue from income tax should be assigned to the provinces according to certain principles ".[1] The British Government in its White Paper[2] and the Joint Committee of both Houses of Parliament also[3] accepted the principle. The Government of India Act provided that the allocation between the Central and Provincial Governments in India was to be settled by an Order in Council, and the British Government undertook that a special enquiry should first be held so that they and Parliament might be furnished with an independent review and technical advice. Sir Otto Niemeyer in his able Report recommended that the Provinces should receive ultimately 50 per cent of the taxes on income which, under the terms of the Act, are divisible between them and the Central Government, the amount being distributed on a basis of fixed percentages. The 50 per cent is calculated on " the net proceeds in any financial year of any such tax, except in so far as these proceeds represent proceeds attributable to Chief Commissioners' Provinces or to taxes payable in respect of Federal emoluments ",

[1] Report of the Indian Statutory Commission (Cmd. 3569, 1930), vol. ii (Recommendations), para. 293, p. 255.

[2] Proposals for Indian Constitutional Reform (Cmd. 4268, 1933), para. 139, p. 74.

[3] Joint Committee on Indian Constitutional Reform, H.L. 6 (1, Part I), H.C. 5 (1, Part I), 1934, paras. 250-53.

i.e. incomes derived from Federal sources (Federal areas or emoluments of Federal Officers) are excluded. The percentage distribution is as follows: Madras 15; Bombay 20; Bengal 20; United Provinces 15; Punjab 8; Bihar 10; Central Provinces 5; Assam 2; North-West Frontier Province 1; Orissa 2; Sind 2. These percentages were arrived at " by fixing the scale of distribution partly on residence and partly on population, paying to neither factor a rigidly pedantic deference, for which the actual data provide insufficient justification ".[1] Sir Otto Niemeyer recommended that this share should be retained by the Central Government for the first five years or until the whole, together with any General Budget receipts from the Railways, would bring the Central Government's share in the divisible total up to 13 crores, whichever was less; and for a second period of five years, in the first year five-sixths of the sum, if any, retained in the last year of the first period, decreasing by a further sixth of that sum in each of the succeeding five years. These recommendations were promulgated in the Government of India (Distribution of Revenues) Order in Council, dated 3rd July 1938. The Central Government but not Provincial Governments may impose a surcharge under section 138, 1 (b), of the 1935 Act. As pointed out by the Joint Committee, it is implicit in this proposal that the power should only be exercisable in times of serious financial stress. The Joint Committee, it may be noted, did not agree with the proposal that a Provincial Legislature should be empowered to impose a surcharge not exceeding 12½ per cent on the taxes levied on the personal income of persons resident in the Province for its own purposes, because it might lead to differential rates of tax on the inhabitants of different Provinces, and although a limit would be set, this in itself is undesirable and outweighs the elasticity which it would give to Provincial revenues. The Joint Committee also stated what has since proved to be true in more than one Federation since the war — " The rates of taxes on income are likely also to be sufficiently high to make it difficult to increase the rate by way of surcharge, and to give the Provinces such a power might well nullify the emergency power of imposing a surcharge which we think it essential that the Federation should possess ". The surcharge now in force at the Centre (1942–43) is on the highest slice of income, and equivalent to 50 per cent, and that on the supertax is also equivalent to 50 per cent. Since 1939 the basic scales have been highly progressive and the rate of progression has been steepened by the surcharge. The income tax surcharge now runs from 6 pies in the rupee on all taxable incomes of between Rs. 1500 and Rs. 5000 to 9 pies in the rupee on the next Rs. 5000, then to 1 anna and 2 pies in the rupee on the next

[1] *Indian Financial Enquiry*, Report by Sir Otto Niemeyer, G.B.E., K.C.B. (Cmd. 5163, 1936), para. 34.

Rs. 5000 and 1 anna and 3 pies in the rupee on the balance of total income. The progressive rate of tax now levied expressed as a percentage of total income ranges from 2 per cent at one end of the scale to 85 per cent at the other end, *i.e.* on 30 lakhs (£225,000) a year. While the rates are very much higher than before the war, we cannot but refer to the remarks of Sir Walter Layton and of Sir Otto Niemeyer on this point. Sir Walter Layton referred to the exemption of agricultural incomes from income tax and suggested that this should be abolished by definite stages and the whole of the proceeds of the taxation of these incomes should be assigned to the Province of origin.[1] He also pointed out that there are large accumulations of wealth on which the burden of Government taxation rests very lightly. " In spite of the widespread poverty in India, I see no reason to doubt that the public revenues of India can be substantially increased without taxation becoming intolerable, provided that its incidence is adjusted to the capacity of taxpayers to pay and that heavy additional burdens are not put upon primary necessities." [2] Sir Otto Niemeyer remarked in his Report, dated 6th April 1936, that not merely were the existing rates of income and supertax in India by no means excessive, but the general scheme of taxation (Central and Provincial) operates to relieve the wealthier commercial classes " to an extent which is unusual in taxation schemes ".[3] Even to-day this holds good in spite of the changes in progressive taxation.

The Provinces, apart from the share of income tax noted above, depend on their own sources of revenue, which are mainly land revenue, excise and stamps. Forests and irrigation in some Provinces are important heads of revenue. The list of taxes set out in the Seventh Schedule of the 1935 Act, in addition to those just mentioned, includes taxes on " lands and buildings, hearths and windows ", taxes on mineral rights, subject to any limitations imposed by any Act of the Federal Legislature relating to mineral development, capitation taxes, taxes on professions, trades, callings and employments, taxes on animals and boats, taxes on the sale of goods and on advertisements, cesses on the entry of goods into a local area for consumption, use or sale therein, taxes on luxuries, including taxes on entertainments, amusements, betting and gambling, tolls and fees, but not fees taken in any court. Taxes on agricultural income and duties in respect of succession to agricultural land are also listed as Provincial sources of revenue, if or when levied. There are three sections of Part VII of the Act, sections 137, 140 and 142 which are of special

[1] Report of the Indian Statutory Commission, vol. ii (Recommendations) (Cmd. 3589, 1930), p. 277.

[2] *Op. cit.* p. 208.

[3] *Indian Financial Enquiry*, Report (Cmd. 5163, 1936), para. 31, p. 17.

interest. The first of these sections deals with a category of taxes in which the power to impose the tax is vested solely in the Centre, although the proceeds would be distributed to the Provinces, subject to the right of the Federation to impose a surcharge for Federal purposes. These taxes include succession duties in respect of succession to property other than agricultural land, such stamp duties as are mentioned in the Central or Federal list, terminal taxes on goods and passengers by land and air, and taxes on railway fares and freights. The second of these sections introduces new features for the division of resources. Salt duties, Federal duties of excise and export duties are to be collected by the Federation, " but, if an Act of the Federal Legislature so provides, there shall be paid out of the revenues of the Federation to the Provinces and to the Federated States, if any, to which the Act imposing the duty extends, sums equivalent to the whole or any part of the net proceeds of that duty, and these sums shall be distributed among the Provinces and those States in accordance with such principles of distribution as may be formulated by the Act ". It is also provided that the net proceeds of any export duty on jute or jute products shall be shared with the producing Provinces or Federated States in proportion to the amount of jute grown. The percentage of the net proceeds assigned to certain Provinces recommended by Sir Otto Niemeyer and fixed by an Order in Council was 62½ per cent. The main object of section 140 is to give elasticity to the financial scheme. The sharing of the taxes may also be an incentive to their introduction where they do not at present exist.

The last of the three sections, section 142, deals with subsidies, which are not high as compared with those in Canada or the Union of South Africa. These subsidies or grants-in-aid were fixed in 1936 by Order in Council on Sir Otto Niemeyer's recommendation as follows : Sind — 105 lakhs of rupees annually for a period of ten years (*i.e.* till 1946–47 inclusive) to be diminished by 25 lakhs a year for the next twenty years, by 40 lakhs a year for the next five years, by 45 lakhs a year for the next succeeding five years, and thereafter, until the whole Barrage debt is repaid, by 50 lakhs a year : North-West Frontier Province — 100 lakhs, to be reconsidered after five years ; Orissa — 40 lakhs, increased to 47 lakhs in the first year and to 43 lakhs in the second, third, fourth and fifth years ; Assam — 30 lakhs ; the United Provinces — 25 lakhs for five years. Thus Sir Otto Niemeyer, while of opinion that the extent to which the Provinces are likely to be dependent upon Central assistance was exaggerated, owing to fallacious deductions made from their financial records during the depression, recommended that eight out of the eleven Provinces should receive grants of assistance of varying amounts.

An aspect of Indian finance which has been much neglected by students of public finance is the inadequate development of Local taxation, both municipal and rural. Indeed, Local finance is one of the principal features of the Indian Fiscal system to-day. In rural areas public revenues and expenditures are woefully insufficient, and since the Reforms came into force in 1921 this aspect of Federal finance has been almost overlooked as attention has been concentrated on the relations between the Centre and Provincial Governments. Before the Reforms Local self-government in India was rather of the Continental type. It was deconcentrated rather than decentralised. The principal Local official was the official of the Provincial Government. The District Officer or Collector was, like the French Prefect of a Department, an officer of the Government operating locally. "As Chairman of the District Board, and often of one or more Municipalities, he was carrying out the will of his judicial superiors. He was just as much the eyes, ears and arms of the provincial Government as when functioning as revenue officer or district magistrate. Local self-government was just one of his many activities. He regarded his staff as available to assist him in all branches of his work. A single will operated in all spheres of activity in the district."[1] It therefore cannot be said that the British system of Local self-government was the type. Local bodies with wills of their own did not generally exist. They did not carry out their own policies, policies subject only to certain powers of control retained by the Central Government. Local self-government in the financial sphere since the Reforms, which brought about elected Chairmen and an extended franchise, showed up the weakness of not having, as in the British system, a competent and well-paid service of professional administrators who, while they follow out the policy of the elected representatives, are their advisers and executive officials. The Ministry of Health by its system of grants-in-aid given on conditions to ensure efficiency, by insisting on standards of competence and by numerous administrative devices, has steadily raised Local administration standards in this country. In India the only real power of the Provinces is for the Minister to suspend or to dissolve a Local Authority, and this leaves him powerless when less drastic treatment is called for. The resources of Municipalities and the District and Local Boards are frequently inadequate for the services to be performed, and this is one of the reasons for lack of trained personnel. There is, too, the great reluctance of elected members to impose local taxation and to insist on its collection. The giving of grants to Local Authorities, often without conditions, has divorced control of policy from financial responsibility. The Indian Statutory Commission summed up the position thus: "While the rural authorities have the advantage of the machinery of revenue for the collection of their basic

[1] Indian Statutory Commission, Report (Cmd. 3568, 1930), vol. i, p. 301.

source of income, cess on land, Municipalities adopt a variety of expedients for raising revenue. The most disturbing feature, however, is the failure to collect the direct taxes imposed. In Great Britain, a Municipality expects to collect up to 98 or 99 per cent of the rates imposed by it, and a drop in collection to 95 per cent would be the subject of a very close enquiry. But in Municipalities in India since the Reforms, uncollected arrears have been mounting up to very large sums. This feature is referred to by almost every provincial Government in reviewing the work of the Municipalities, and it is clear that there is great laxity in this respect. Another very general criticism is directed to the prevalence of embezzlement by employees. This is clearly to some extent the result of the failure to pay salaries sufficiently high to secure trustworthy officials. But it is also due to carelessness, want of system and inefficient supervision. Generally speaking, the management of the finances of Local Authorities has deteriorated since the Reforms, and this laxity is not adequately corrected by such powers of audit as the provincial Governments possess." [1]

Municipalities have a wide choice of taxes. Some levy a water-rate to cover more than the actual costs of water supply and supplement this by the taxation of vehicles or other taxes. Some have special taxes for education and other services. The taxes include terminal taxes, octroi duties, property taxes, taxes on professions and taxes on personal income. Rural authorities depend mainly on a cess or surcharge on the land revenue (or land tax) which in many of the Provinces is subject to a maximum of one anna in the rupee, *i.e.* one-sixteenth, a rate that has remained unchanged for over sixty years. This is sometimes supplemented by taxes on professions and on companies and by tolls or taxes on vehicles. A large proportion of the revenue of these authorities is given as grants-in-aid for particular services and in the form of capital sums for public works.

III. Government Revenues and Expenditures

As in other Federations, the costs of government have increased. This is shown in Table I below, which indicates the increase since the Reforms. As Burma ceased to be part of the Indian Empire from 1st April 1937, figures for it have been omitted from the totals of Provincial and Local expenditures and revenues previous to that year. The increase in the pre-rearmament year 1937–38 over that of 1921–22 is 19 per cent in the expenditure of the Provinces and 38 per cent in that of Local Government (Municipalities, District and Local Boards). Unfortunately, it has not been possible to eliminate the effect of the separation of Burma from Central Government revenues and expenditures. In 1937–38, for example,

[1] Cmd. 3568, 1930, vol. i, p. 313.

the net loss to Central Government revenues on the Budget was estimated at Rs. 2⅓ crores. If we take the reduction in expenditures to be of similar magnitude, the *decrease* in Central Government expenditure of India *including* Burma between 1921–22 and 1937–38 was 13 per cent.

TABLE I

EXPENDITURES AND REVENUES OF ALL GOVERNMENTS [1]

	1921–22	1924–25	1926–27	1931–32	1937–38	1941–42	Percentage Increase, 1941–42 over	
							1921–22	1937–38
A. *Expenditures* (Rs. millions)								
Central .	1428	1318	1317	1334	1226	1852 [2]	30	51
Provincial .	702	681	783	774	832	962	37	16
Local . .	248	296	320	315	341	350 [3]	41	3
Total .	2378	2295	2420	2423	2399	3164	33	32
B. *Revenues* (Rs. millions)								
Central .	1152	1375	1317	1216	1224	1680 [2]	45	37
Provincial .	612	710	759	733	858	960	57	12
Local . .	224	265	296	307	343	350 [3]	56	2
Total .	1988	2350	2372	2256	2425	2990	50	23

[1] Burma has been excluded as it is no longer part of the Indian Empire. But it has not been possible to eliminate from Central expenditures and revenues the effect of the separation of Burma before 1937–38. For that year the estimated net loss to Indian Central Government revenues arising from the separation of Burma was Rs. 2⅓ crores (Rs. 23 millions) on the Budget of 1937–38.

[2] Revised estimate. [3] Estimate.

The fall in governmental expenditures in the years following the great depression is very noticeable, as will be seen from the following table :

TABLE II

EXPENDITURES OF THE CENTRAL AND PROVINCIAL GOVERNMENTS, 1929–36 [1]

Year beginning 1st April	Rs. millions		Index Numbers (1929=100)	
	Central	Provincial	Central	Provincial
1929–30	1324	938	100	100
1930–31	1362	942	103	100
1931–32	1334	867	101	92
1932–33	1239	857	94	91
1933–34	1194	859	90	92
1934–35	1218	854	92	91
1935–36	1211	887	91	95
1936–37	1196	916	90	98

[1] These figures include Burma.

In 1937-38 and in previous years the expenditures of the Central Government were greater than those of the Provinces and Local Authorities combined. Owing almost entirely to the war, the expenditure of the Centre charged to revenue in 1941–42 increased by 51 per cent, and in 1942–43 was budgeted to show an increase of 85 per cent over the expenditure of the year 1937–38.

The figures for revenue in 1937–38 show that the percentage increase in the Central Government's revenue is less than the increases in Provincial and Local revenues as compared with the first year of the Reforms, 1921–1922. The percentage increases of Central revenues in 1941–42 and 1942–43 over those of the year 1937–38 are 37 per cent and 56 per cent respectively. Provincial Governments have benefited since 1937–38 by the sharing of personal income taxation and, in the case of the jute-growing Provinces, by obtaining 62½ per cent of the export duty on jute. Table I is also of interest as showing that Provincial revenues and expenditures have increased more than either those of Central or Local Governments between 1921–22 and 1941–42.

It is of interest to compare these expenditures and revenues with the national income. The general conclusion to be drawn from Tables III and IV is the comparative lightness of the burden of taxation and of expenditures. The burden of taxation, it will be seen, was much heavier in the depression years 1931–32 and 1932–33 than it was in 1941–42.

The table, in short, brings out the truth of the statement that the public revenues can be increased without making the burden of taxation unduly heavy, a fact noted by Sir Walter Layton and Sir Otto Niemeyer above. The burden in its lightness compares very favourably with the other Federations studied in the Report, even with the Union of South Africa where the burden is far from heavy. It must not be forgotten that in India as in South Africa the burden of expenditure on the social services such as unemployment relief is small. Both the revenues and the expenditures of all Governments in 1937–38 were the equivalent of only 13 per cent of the national income. In 1941–42 these percentages had fallen to 10 per cent in the case of revenues, and 10 per cent in that of expenditures.

Tables V and VI give the revenue system of India, all Governments, both in millions of rupees (Table V) and in percentages (Table VI).

The main conclusions that may be drawn from these tables with regard to the revenue system are as follows :

(1) The system as a whole is regressive. One may say markedly regressive. Consumption taxes form an important part of the revenue of all Governments. Progressive taxation in the form of personal income tax and supertax is only 4 per cent of the total, while company income tax and company supertax (corporation tax) are 2 per cent. Taxes on

real property account for 18 per cent of the whole, and of this by far the major part is land revenue, land revenue being 12 per cent of the total revenue of all Governments taken together.

(2) As the taxation is largely on consumption the taxes enter in the main into costs and are not in a large degree on surplus, even if it be argued that the land tax is on surplus.

(3) The revenue of the Centre is derived mainly from customs (35 per cent) and railways (27 per cent). Other sources of revenue are income tax (6 per cent), taxes on business (5 per cent), salt (8 per cent), excise (6 per cent) and miscellaneous (13 per cent). It will thus be seen that the Centre depends to a very large degree on consumption taxes and to a comparatively small extent on the taxation of income and of business. It receives, too, a large source of revenue from railways. Railway finance was separated from the general finances in 1924. There is a fixed annual contribution from railways to general revenues of 1 per cent of the capital outlay, and this is a first charge on the net receipts of railways. In addition to this, a proportion, generally one-fifth, of the net surplus profits is credited to general revenues and the remainder transferred to a railway reserve fund. The large figures of revenue and expenditure which appear in the tables under railways are the net revenue, *i.e.* gross receipts less working expenses, and under expenditure the debt charges only.

(4) Provincial revenues are mainly from taxes on real property 36 per cent (land revenue 31 per cent and forests 4 per cent), from excise 17 per cent, stamps 12 per cent, irrigation 11 per cent, share of the export duty on jute 3 per cent, share of income tax 1 per cent, miscellaneous (entertainment, betting, electricity duties, etc.) 16 per cent and subsidies from the Centre 4 per cent.

(5) Local revenues to the extent of one-third of the total are derived from taxes on real property, viz. lands and houses. The remainder is derived mainly, if not entirely, from consumption taxes on goods and services. Taxes on real property yield 32 per cent, taxes on consumption 35 per cent, grants-in-aid 4 per cent, taxes on business 1 per cent, and miscellaneous sources 28 per cent of Local Government revenues ; Group IV $= 35 + 28 = 63$.

(6) A comparison with other tax structures shows that there is not as large a scope for income and business taxation as in an advanced industrial country. The chief source of revenue must be the relatively simple consumption taxes and the taxation of property, of which land taxation is the chief. Subsidies from the Centre since the Reforms do not play an important role — 4 per cent of the total revenue of the Provinces as compared with 8 per cent in Canada. In Local finance India depends on property taxes — one-third of her total Local revenue as compared with

TABLE III

British India: Revenues and Expenditures of All Governments expressed in Terms of the National Income

	1921–22	1924–25	1926–27	1929–30	1931–32	1932–33	1937–38	1938–39	1939–40	1940–41	1941–42
National Income: (Rs. millions)[1]	29,500	32,000	27,500	29,000	17,000	16,000	19,000	18,000	21,000	25,000	30,000
Revenues:											
(*a*) Rs. millions:											
Central	1152	1375	1317	1327	1216	1254	1224	1211	1258	1451	1680[3]
Provincial	704	813	864	946	832	843	858	851	914	985	960
Local	239	282	319	343	327	328	343	350[2]	350[2]	350[2]	350[2]
Total	2095	2470	2500	2616	2375	2425	2425	2412	2522	2786	2990
(*b*) Percentage of National Income:											
Central	4	4	5	5	7	8	6	6	6	6	6
Provincial	2	3	3	3	5	5	5	5	4	4	3
Local	1	1	1	1	2	2	2	2	2	1	1
Total	7	8	9	9	14	15	13	13	12	11	10
Expenditure:											
(*a*) Rs. millions:											
Central	1428	1318	1317	1324	1334	1239	1226	1217	1258	1517	1852[3]
Provincial	792	784	902	938	867	857	832	859	892	954	962
Local	265	315	339	350[2]	335	323	341	350[2]	350[2]	350[2]	350[2]
Total	2485	2417	2558	2612	2536	2419	2399	2426	2500	2821	3164

(*b*) Percentage of National Income :											
Central	5	5	5	5	8	8	7	6	6	6	6
Provincial	3	2	3	3	5	5	4	5	4	4	3
Local	1	1	1	1	2	2	2	2	2	1	1
Total	8	8	9	9	15	15	13	13	12	11	10
Defence Expenditure chargeable to the Revenue of the Government of India (net) :											
(*a*) Rs. millions	698	556	560	551	518	467	473	462	495	736	1024
(*b*) Percentage of national income .	2	2	2	2	3	3	2	3	2	3	3
(*c*) ,, central expenditure	49	42	43	42	39	38	39	38	39	49	55
(*d*) ,, total expenditure .	28	23	22	21	20	19	20	19	20	26	32

[1] Estimates, as shown in "National Income" (*Review of the International Institute of Statistics*, The Hague, 1936), *Poverty and Kindred Economic Problems of India*, pp. 42-3, and *The Science of Public Finance*, vol. i, chap. xv, p. 247 (Macmillan & Co.), by G. Findlay Shirras. For recent years the data were extrapolated by the same method. Cf. footnote on page 179. [2] Estimated. [3] Revised estimate.

TABLE IV

Revenues of All Governments per Head of Population, 1937–38 (Rs.)

	Bombay	Bengal	Madras	United Provinces	Punjab	Bihar	Orissa	Assam	Central Provinces and Berar	Sind	N.W.F.	Coorg	Total
Central Government .	14·13	4·65	2·24	0·79	0·63	0·56	0·25	1·83	0·10	14·00	0·28	0·26	4·5
Provincial Governments .	6·30	2·59	3·45	2·56	5·10	1·96	3·49	3·19	2·93	10·05	7·58	9·81	3·1
Municipalities . .	7·69	4·43	6·10	5·19	6·12	3·37	3·26	6·12	4·81	12·38	7·52	4·44	8·1
District and Local Boards	1·18	0·34	0·93	0·48	1·04	0·50	0·38	0·44	0·50	1·25	0·62	0·92	0·5

Note.—Bombay City 28·44; Calcutta City 20·81; Madras City 11·58.

TABLE V

The Revenue System of India, All Governments, 1937–38

(Rs. millions)

	Central	Provincial	Local [1]	Total
Group I. *Progressive Taxes :*				
Personal income taxes	75·8	12·5	..	88·3
Supertax (personal)	14·7	..	..	14·7
Total, Group I	90·5	12·5	..	103·0
Group II. *Taxes on Real Property :*				
Land revenue	1·9	264·0	..	265·9
Provincial rates	..	..	51·8	51·8
Taxes on houses and other real property	..	..	50·2 [2]	50·2
Forests	1·6	28·5	..	30·1
Rents and sale of land	..	11·4	7·6 [2]	19·0
Total, Group II	3·5	303·9	109·6	417·0
Group III. *Taxes on Business :*				
Company income tax	36·5	..	..	36·5
Company supertax (corporation tax)	18·8	..	..	18·8
Tax on professions and trades	..	..	3·4 [2]	3·4
Total, Group III	55·3	..	3·4	58·7
Group IV. *Chiefly Consumption Taxes :*				
Customs :				
Imports :				
Liquor	20·8	..	..	20·8
Motor spirit	45·6	..	..	45·6
Other	345·4	..	..	345·4
Exports	17·7	26·5	..	44·2
Miscellaneous	1·6	..	..	1·6
Sub-total, Customs	431·1	26·5	..	457·6
Excise :				
Central :				
Sugar	33·3	..	..	33·3
Matches	20·0	..	..	20·0
Motor spirit	12·2	..	..	12·2
Other	11·1	..	..	11·1
Sub-total, Central Excise	76·6	..	..	76·6
Provincial :				
Liquor	1·4	103·4	..	104·8
Opium	0·4	20·1 [3]	..	20·5
Other	0·3	20·4	..	20·7
Sub-total, Provincial Excise	2·1	143·9	..	146·0
Sub-total, Excise [4]	78·7	143·9	..	222·6

TABLE V—(*continued*)

	Central	Provincial	Local [1]	Total
Other Similar Taxes and Licences :				
Octroi	..	..	14·5 [2]	14·5
Salt	83·9	0·1	.	84·0
Tobacco duties	..	2·4	..	2·4
Opium	5·1	..	..	5·1
Entertainment and betting	..	4·6	..	4·6
Automobile licences	0·3	15·0	..	15·3
Other taxes, licences and fees	..	..	34·0 [2]	34·0
Stamps :				
Non judicial	0·6	36·5	..	37·1
Judicial	0·8	70·4	..	71·2
General	2·3	..	..	2·3
Registration	0·1	11·6	..	11·7
Sub-total, Other Taxes and Licences	93·1	140·6	48·5	282·2
Revenue from Public Utilities :				
Railways (net)	326·5	0·2	..	326·7
Posts and telegraphs (net)	12·9	..	..	12·9
Irrigation (net)	0·2	93·2	..	93·4
Civil works (roads and bridges)	3·2	23·3	27·6	54·1
Electricity duties and lighting rates	..	3·2	4·0 [2]	7·2
Water rate	..	..	21·9 [2]	21·9
Conservancy rates and receipts [5]	..	..	10·6 [2]	10·6
Miscellaneous	..	..	8·4 [2]	8·4
Sub-total, Revenue from Public Utilities	342·8	119·9	72·5	535·2
Defence Receipts	52·5	..	..	52·5
Miscellaneous	70·9	79·1	96·0	246·0
Total, Group IV	1069·1	510·0	217·0	1796·1
Contributions from States	6·4	..	..	6·4
Grants-in-aid, etc.	..	31·7 [6]	12·5 [2]	44·2
GRAND TOTAL	1224·8	858·1	342·5	2425·4
Less duplications	31·6 [7]	15·8 [8]	..	47·4
NET TOTAL	1193·2	842·3	342·5	2378·0

[1] Municipalities, District and Local Boards.
[2] Municipal only.
[3] Including duplication amounting to Rs. 4·64 millions (see note 8).
[4] Excluding salt (given separately below).
[5] Charges for removal of night soil : a quasi-sewerage charge.
[6] Consists of Rs. 31·4 millions of grants-in-aid from the Central Government and Rs. 0·3 million of miscellaneous adjustments.
[7] Consists of Rs. 31·4 millions of grants-in-aid to the Provinces and Rs. 0·16 million of miscellaneous adjustments.
[8] Consists of Rs. 11·13 millions of grants-in-aid to Municipalities and Rs. 4·64 millions for opium sold by the Central to the Provincial Governments.

Note.—We have not been able to obtain figures for District and Local Boards as detailed as those for other Governments, partly because of the lack of uniformity in the presentation of the accounts in the various Provincial Reports on Local Authorities.

TABLE VI

The Revenue System of India, All Governments, 1937–38 [1]

(Percentage distribution)

	Percentage Share of each Government in Total Revenues				Percentage Distribution of each Government's Revenue			
	Central	Provincial	Local	Total	Central	Provincial	Local	Total
Group I. *Progressive Taxes :*								
Personal income taxes	86	14	..	100	6	1	..	3
Supertax (personal)	100	..	..	100	1	..	..	1
Total, Group I	88	12	..	100	7	1	..	4
Group II. *Taxes on Real Property :*								
Land revenue	1	99	..	100	..	31	..	12
Provincial rates	..	..	100	100	..	..	15	2
Taxes on houses and other real property	..	..	100	100	..	..	15	2
Forests	5	95	..	100	..	4	..	1
Rents and sale of land	..	60	40	100	..	1	2	1
Total, Group II	1	73	26	100	..	36	32	18
Group III. *Taxes on Business :*								
Company income tax	100	..	..	100	3	..	..	1
Company supertax (corporation tax)	100	..	..	100	2	..	..	1
Tax on professions and trades	..	..	100	100	..	..	1	..
Total, Group III	94	..	6	100	5	..	1	2
Group IV. *Chiefly Consumption Taxes :*								
Customs :								
Imports :								
Liquor	100	..	..	100	2	..	..	1
Motor spirit	100	..	..	100	4	..	..	2
Other	100	..	..	100	28	..	..	14
Exports	40	60	..	100	1	3	..	2
Miscellaneous	100	..	..	100	..	..	..	..
Sub-total, Customs	94	6	..	100	35	3	..	19
Excise :								
Central :								
Sugar	100	..	..	100	2	..	..	1
Matches	100	..	..	100	2	..	..	1
Motor spirit	100	..	..	100	1	..	..	1
Other	100	..	..	100	1	..	..	..
Sub-total, Central Excise	100	..	..	100	6	..	..	3
Provincial :								
Liquor	1	99	..	100	..	13	..	4
Opium	2	98	..	100	..	2	..	1
Other	1	99	..	100	..	2	..	1
Sub-total, Provincial Excise	1	99	..	100	..	17	..	6
Sub-total, Excise	35	65	..	100	6	17	..	9

[1] See notes to Table V.

TABLE VI—(*continued*)

	Percentage Share of each Government in Total Revenues				Percentage Distribution of each Government's Revenue			
	Central	Provincial	Local	Total	Central	Provincial	Local	Total
Other Similar Taxes and Licences :								
Octroi	..	..	100	100	..	..	4	1
Salt	100	..	..	100	8	..	..	3
Tobacco duties	..	100	..	100	..	..	..	..
Opium	100	..	..	100	..	..	..	..
Entertainment and betting	..	100	..	100	..	1	..	..
Automobile licences	2	98	..	100	..	2	..	1
Other taxes, licences and fees	..	..	100	100	..	..	10	2
Stamps :								
Non-judicial	2	98	..	100	..	4	..	2
Judicial	1	99	..	100	..	8	..	3
General	100	..	..	100	..	..	..	..
Registration	1	99	..	100	..	1	..	..
Sub-total, Other Taxes and Licences	35	54	11	100	8	16	14	12
Revenue from Public Utilities :								
Railways (net)	100	..	..	100	27	..	..	15
Posts and telegraphs (net)	100	..	..	100	1	..	..	1
Irrigation (net)	..	100	..	100	..	11	..	4
Civil works (roads and bridges)	6	43	51	100	..	3	9	2
Electricity duties and lighting rates	..	44	56	100	..	..	1	..
Water rate	..	..	100	100	..	..	6	1
Conservancy rates and receipts	..	..	100	100	..	..	3	..
Miscellaneous	..	..	100	100	..	..	2	..
Sub-total, Revenue from Public Utilities	64	22	14	100	28	14	21	23
Defence Receipts	100	..	..	100	4	..	..	2
Miscellaneous	29	32	39	100	6	9	28	10
Total, Group IV	60	28	12	100	87	59	63	75
Contributions from States	100	..	..	100	1	..	..	..
Grants-in-aid, etc.	..	72	28	100	..	4	4	2
GRAND TOTAL	51	35	14	100	100	100	100	101
Less duplications	67	33	..	100	3	2	..	1
NET TOTAL	50	36	14	100	97	98	100	100

nine-tenths in Canada — and on consumption taxes and services — 63 per cent as compared with 8 per cent in Canada. Municipalities obtain, as in the Union of South Africa, a considerable revenue from public utilities.

Public Expenditures

Tables VII and VIII analyse the various categories of Government expenditures and the division between the Centre, Provinces and Local Authorities. As Government activity and the public finance system have developed, these tables are of considerable interest. The analysis of the nature of expenditures is also important, as is the variation in the standards of Provinces in regard to expenditures.[1] Several interesting conclusions may be drawn from the data.

It is unnecessary to refer to the various categories of Government expenditures as these have been described in Chapter II of the Enquiry. The primary functions, regulative and protective, amounted to the high figure of 58 per cent of the (net) total, 67 per cent of Central expenditures, 54 per cent of Provincial expenditures and 24 per cent of Local expenditures. In the same year in South Africa primary functions were 40 per cent and in Canada 52, and India, therefore, incurred expenditure on the primary functions of Government at least as high in proportion to her wealth and income as advanced countries in the West and elsewhere. On the other hand, expenditure on the social services, such as education and public health, was only 15 per cent as compared with 36 per cent in Canada, 33 per cent in the Union of South Africa, 29 per cent in Australia and about 41 per cent in the United States. India has none of the expenditures which have transformed the expenditure structures of some Federations since the great depression — expenditures on unemployment relief. Expenditures on development are relatively high. Transfer expenditures which do not directly add anything to the national income (*e.g.* expenditures on relief and other public welfare, pensions, and interest on unproductive debts) are small.

It is necessary to refer to certain heads of expenditure in some detail. Defence is high — 22 per cent of the expenditures of all Governments and 43 per cent of the Central Government's expenditure. In the same year (1937–38) defence expenditure (gross) was 2·8 per cent of the national income. (Net defence expenditure, *i.e.* defence expenditure net of defence receipts, as given in Table III, was 2·5 per cent of the national income, 20 per cent of total, and 39 per cent of Central Government expenditure.) The ratio of 22 per cent is high in part because other kinds of expenditure, *e.g.* on relief and on unproductive debt, are low. The heaviness of the tax burden depends very largely on the nature of public expenditures. Wise expenditure, for example, on the social services, especially on education and public health, may increase the productive power and, therefore, the taxable capacity of the country. Defence expenditure is, of course,

[1] See also Part III, Tables 5 and 6.

TABLE VII

Public Expenditures from Revenue, All Governments, 1937–38

(Rs. millions)

	Central	Provincial	Local [1]	Total
1. *Primary Functions :*				
Civil administration, legislation and justice	121·7	369·9	80·9	827·8 [2]
Pensions	29·0	62·9		
Debt services	150·0	13·4		
Defence	526·0	..		526·0
Total, Primary Functions	826·7	446·2	80·9 [2]	1353·8
2. *Secondary Functions :*				
(1) *Social Services :*				
Education	9·2	117·2	87·7	214·1
Public health	4·4	51·9	83·9 [3]	140·2
Other	..	..	1·6	1·6
Sub-total, Social Services	13·6	169·1	173·2	355·9
(2) *Developmental :*				
Railways	299·0	..	..	299·0
Aviation	2·1	..	..	2·1
Posts and telegraphs	7·6	..	..	7·6
Broadcasting	1·4	..	..	1·4
Civil works [4]	25·0	83·2	60·3	168·5
Agriculture and irrigation	6·7	88·2	..	94·9
Industries	0·8	10·1	..	10·9
Co-operation	0·1	6·2	..	6·3
Other	..	..	7·3	7·3
Sub-total, Developmental	342·7	187·7	67·6	598·0
(3) *Miscellaneous*	10·2	29·5	19·8	59·4
Total, Secondary Functions	366·5	386·3	260·6	1013·3
Grants and contributions [5]	31·6	..	..	31·6
Grand Total	1224·8	832·5	341·5	2398·7
Less grants and contributions	31·6	11·1 [6]	..	42·7
Net Total	1193·2	821·4	341·5	2356·0

[1] Municipalities and District and Local Boards.

[2] We have not been able to obtain figures for District and Local Boards as detailed as those for other Governments, partly because of the lack of uniformity in the presentation of the accounts in the various Provincial Reports on Local Authorities.

[3] Includes water supply, drainage and conservancy (removal of night soil).

[4] Roads, bridges and buildings.

[5] This sum excludes the shares of income tax and of the export duty on jute which belong to the Provinces as of right (see Table V). The share of income tax was Rs. 12·5 millions and that of the export duty Rs. 26·5 millions for 1937–38. The figure for "Grants and Contributions" includes Rs. 31·43 millions of grants-in-aid from the Central to Provincial Governments and Rs. 0·16 million of miscellaneous adjustments between the Central and Provincial Governments. Grants from Central and Provincial to Local Governments are not shown as separate headings in the Finance and Revenue Accounts.

[6] Grants from Government to Municipalities (see footnote 2).

TABLE VIII

PUBLIC EXPENDITURES FROM REVENUE, ALL GOVERNMENTS, 1937–38 [1]

(Percentage distribution)

	Percentage Share of each Government in Total Expenditures				Percentage Distribution of each Government's Expenditure			
	Central	Provincial	Local	Total	Central	Provincial	Local	Total
1. *Primary Functions :*								
Civil administration, legislation and justice	..	..	..	100	10	44		
Pensions	..	..	..	100	2	8	24 (Civil administration to Defence, bracketed)	36 (Civil administration to Debt services, bracketed)
Debt services	..	..	..	100	12	2		
Defence	100	..	..	100	43	..		22
Total, Primary Functions	61	33	6	100	67	54	24	58
2. *Secondary Functions :*								
(1) *Social Services :*								
Education	4	55	41	100	1	14	26	9
Public health	3	37	60	100	..	6	25	6
Other	..	..	100	100	..	..	..	..
Sub-total, Social Services	4	47	49	100	1	20	51	15
(2) *Developmental :*								
Railways	100	..	..	100	24	..	..	14
Aviation	100	..	..	100	..	..	..	..
Posts and telegraphs	100	..	..	100	1	..	..	..
Broadcasting	100	..	..	100	..	..	..	..
Civil works	15	49	36	100	2	10	17	7
Agriculture and irrigation	7	93	..	100	1	11	..	4
Industries	7	93	..	100	..	1	..	..
Co-operation	1	99	..	100	..	1	..	..
Other	..	..	100	100	..	..	2	..
Sub-total, Developmental	57	32	11	100	28	23	19	25
(3) *Miscellaneous*	17	50	33	100	1	3	6	3
Total, Secondary Functions	36	38	26	100	30	46	76	43
Grants and contributions	100	..	..	100	3	..	..	1
GRAND TOTAL	51	35	14	100	100	100	100	102
Less duplications	74	26	..	100	3	1	..	2
NET TOTAL	51	35	14	100	97	99	100	100

[1] See notes to Table V.

necessary for the security required for the development of production. Unless, as in Germany and Russia, the making of munitions is conducted on so large a scale that it leads to full employment, such expenditure does not increase productive power. In India, however, since 1941, 1500 engineering workshops, including 23 railway workshops, have been producing on a large scale. Such defence expenditure now shows a stimulated production, employment and taxable capacity similar to those in the above mentioned countries. Although the present daily rate of expenditure on defence is Rs. 40 lakhs (£300,000) as given in the Budget speech for 1942–43, such stimulation will not be comparable with that in Western countries where the *per capita* expenditure is at least 200 times as great. The net expenditure figure for defence in Table III (as well as the figure in Table VII) gives the expenditure from revenue only. In this connexion it may be of interest to note that "the gross expenditure on defence services and supplies expected to be brought to account in India's books for the year 1941–42 amounts in all to Rs. 300 crores, of which, after India's share as shown above has been deducted, the balance of nearly Rs. 200 crores is borne by His Majesty's Government. This latter figure does not include the value of equipment supplied and other services rendered by His Majesty's Government without charge."[1]

TABLE IX

INDIAN DEFENCE EXPENDITURES COMPARED WITH THOSE OF OTHER COUNTRIES, 1937–38

	Percentage of Government Expenditures	Percentage of National Income
India . .	22	3
Great Britain .	26	5
U.S.A. . .	13	1
Canada . .	6	1
Australia . .	7	1

The burden of defence is absolutely and relatively large and a very important factor in the Indian financial situation.

India's expenditure on *education* is 9 per cent of the total Government expenditures, 14 per cent of Provincial expenditures and 26 per cent of Local expenditures. This is relatively, as compared with other Federations, a low figure. The expenditure fell after the depression and some Provinces have been spending less than others on this great nation-building department. As will be seen from the tables compiled — Tables 6 and 13 of Part III — the inequalities between Province and Province

[1] Finance Member's speech on introducing the Budget proposals for 1942–43, *Gazette of India*, 28th February 1942, para. 18, p. 288.

are obvious. Even making allowances for the fact that with a scattered population it costs more to run a Province than one in which there is a dense population, because more teachers are required per head of population and other costs are correspondingly higher, the disparity in expenditures per head of population is so great that it cannot be due entirely to these considerations. The raising of the standard of living and of production by more and better education cannot be done merely by expenditure on education, as better teachers, etc., are required. The Report of the Indian Statutory Commission's Auxiliary Committee on Education pointed this out clearly. There is a great wastage, as, for example, only a small proportion of those who are at the primary stage reach Class IV in which the attainment of literacy may be expected. Moreover " Powers have been devolved on local bodies in such a way that the Ministers responsible to the legislatures have no effective control of the expenditure of money voted for mass education ".[1] The development of education is thus a policy requiring great discrimination. At the Census of 1931, it may be recalled, the number of literates per 100 males of 5 and over was 15·6 and per 100 females 2·9, and literacy means the ability to read and write a postcard in any language. Literacy in England in the same Census covered only 3·25 million males and 0·39 million females. As compared with the other Federations studied in this book, it will be seen that the percentage expenditure by Provinces and Local Authorities is very small, and in no sphere of expenditure is there likely to be so great a change after the war as in the sphere of education — primary, secondary, technical and university. There will be indeed a revolution of thought in this which will have wider and deeper results than the Reformation. As Cardinal Richelieu wrote of France in the seventeenth century : " When I have regard to the majority of those who profess to teach, and the multitude of children who are taught, I seem to see an infinite crowd of sick who need nothing but a draught of clear, sweet water for their healing. Yet so uncontrolled is the thirst which affects them that, accepting indifferently all cups which are presented to them, the greater part of them drink from tainted, and some even from poisoned, sources ; thus increasing their thirst and their malady, in place of assuaging both." It is the clear sweet water of real education that is required to-day.

Table 13 (India) in Part III shows at a glance the expenditure on education by Provinces in 1937–38. The inequalities in revenue and in expenditure are very striking, and they are further brought out in Table X opposite, which shows the total expenditures, together with the percentage increase since the Reforms, on education, medical relief and

[1] Education Report (Cmd. 3407, 1929), pp. 345 and 347.

public health in the three principal agricultural Provinces and in the two chief industrial Provinces. The smaller Provinces show the same lack of development as Bengal.

TABLE X

TOTAL EXPENDITURES AND THE EXPENDITURES ON EDUCATION, MEDICAL RELIEF AND PUBLIC HEALTH IN THE THREE PRINCIPAL AGRICULTURAL PROVINCES AND THE TWO CHIEF INDUSTRIAL PROVINCES

A. *Lakhs of Rupees*

Province	1921–22			1937–38		
	Total	Education [1]	Medical Relief and Public Health	Total	Education [1]	Medical Relief and Public Health
Madras . .	1274	143	84	1583	258	139
Punjab . .	881	87	41	1147	160	66
United Provinces.	1149	151	52	1234	206	57
Bengal . .	1048	119	74	1183	137	83
Bombay . .	1502	171	74	1214	168	68

B. *Percentages*

Province	Percentage of Total Expenditure				Percentage Increase		
	Education		Medical, etc.		Total	Education	Medical
	1921–22	1937–38	1921–22	1937–38			
Madras . .	11	16	7	9	24	80	65
Punjab . .	10	14	5	6	30	84	61
United Provinces.	13	17	5	5	7	36	10
Bengal . .	11	12	7	7	13	15	12
Bombay . .	11	14	5	6	– 19	– 2	– 8

[1] These figures exclude expenditure on scientific departments.

The Indian Statutory Commission pointed out that to say that the system of public education in India was top-heavy was an old standing complaint. The fact that Bengal spends more on university than on primary education is significant in this connexion. It is also pointed out by the Commission that " the system of higher education is not adjusted to the social and economic structure of the country, and that its educated or partly educated output is greatly in excess of the country's capacity to absorb it, whether in public employment, or the professions, or commerce and industry, and consequently that it leads to great disappointment and discontent ".[1] The Indian Statutory Commission considered that there

[1] Report of the Indian Statutory Commission, 1930 (Cmd. 3568, 1930), vol. i, p. 388.

was much evidence of waste and ineffectiveness in mass education and of defects of direct control and administration to which such waste was attributable. " In the field of secondary education ", said the Commission, " the problem of guiding the system into the profitable channels of a good general education is complicated by the peculiar patronage exercised over the high schools by the universities in respect of their recognition, resulting in an undesirable dominance over both objective and curriculum. The narrowness and uniformity of high-school courses is largely attributable to university influence. But a consideration of the last quinquennial reviews issued by the provincial education departments indicates that, even on the narrow and unfruitful lines which are too commonly followed, the instruction is not effective and that the educational value obtained for public money and effort is proportionately small. Many pupils are admitted and retained and promoted from class to class in high schools, who are incapable of profiting by the instruction provided. The pay and conditions of service and the qualifications of the teachers are often very unsatisfactory, and complaints of their attitude towards their work are numerous. The impression, indeed, is left that the education departments have had little success in their attempts to improve the curriculum and teaching in secondary schools and are far from satisfied with the existing standards." [1]

Local Expenditures

Local expenditures are mainly for social services — 51 per cent, of which education is 26 per cent and public health 25 per cent of the total. Civil works (roads, bridges and buildings) account for another 17 per cent. Of the remainder 24 per cent is on administration, pensions and debt services, 2 per cent on various municipal undertakings and 6 per cent on miscellaneous items. In Part III of the Enquiry — Tables 7 to 10 — will be found the detailed tables on Municipalities and on District and Local Boards.

A description of the striking features of Indian Local expenditure would require a volume in itself. Unfortunately this is a branch of Indian public finance which, so far, has been neglected. It has been most difficult to get at the facts of Local finance in each Province and the figures in the preceding paragraph and in the tables mask the great and interesting differences in Local finance which space forbids us to set out. We are driven to the conclusion that a specialised study of Indian Local finance as it applies to certain Municipalities and to particular Provinces or to a particular part of a particular Province would not only yield new facts, but new kinds of facts. There is a considerable difference in the expendi-

[1] *Op. cit.* p. 388.

tures of Municipalities, District and Local Boards by Provinces, as will be seen especially in Table 10 of Part III. There is also a considerable difference in the expenditures of such large Municipalities as those of Calcutta, Bombay, Cawnpore and Ahmedabad as compared with those of smaller Municipalities. The expenditure from revenue of Municipalities, of which there were 758 with a population of about 22 millions, was Rs. 180·1 millions in 1937–38. The corresponding figure for District and Local Boards was Rs. 161·3 millions. It would be better in studying Local expenditures to consider them in relation to Provincial revenues and to the amount of services supplied through public, rather than private, agencies. There are certain special circumstances which may make direct comparison between two Provinces misleading. In order to provide an accurate picture of the financial position, Provincial and Local revenues and expenditures should be combined. This is particularly necessary if comparisons are to be made between Provinces, owing to variations in the division of responsibility for such functions as education and road maintenance. Although variations in the division of responsibility for the social services and roads are not so great as in Canada, they vary widely both as between Provinces and in a Province as between different periods. There is a trend to the assumption of an increasing share of the cost and increasing responsibility for administration by the higher layers of Government. This feature, however, is noticeable in other Federations studied in this Enquiry. Nevertheless, Local expenditure is of great importance, and its inadequate development, particularly in rural areas, is one of the characteristics of the Indian financial system.

Debt Charges

Debt charges amount to about 8 per cent of Government expenditure — 12 per cent of the Central expenditures, 2 per cent of Provincial expenditures and roughly 5 per cent of Local expenditures. Of the funded and unfunded debt of India,[1] which amounted at the end of 1937–38 to Rs. 12,331 millions (£925 millions), Rs. 4798 millions (£360 millions) was contracted in England. The greater portion of the debt has been used for financing the construction and acquisition of railways and the carrying-out of irrigation works, so that most of India's public debt is productive. On 31st March 1938 and 1941 the public debt of India was as follows :

[1] These figures refer to debt and obligations of the Central and Provincial Governments only. Cf. Table XI.

TABLE XI

Debt and Other Obligations of the Central and Provincial Governments of India

	31st March 1938	31st March 1941
A. Central Government (the Government of India):		
I. *Interest-bearing Obligations:*		
1. In India: (*a*) Public Debt:	Rs. millions	Rs millions
Permanent debt [1] .	4,384	5,746
Floating debt [2] .	380	849
Total Public Debt [3]	4,764	6,595
(*b*) Other Obligations:		
Unfunded debt [4] .	2,181	1,989
Depreciation and reserve funds [5] .	233	449
Total Other Obligations . . .	2,414	2,438
Total in India .	7,178	9,033
	£ millions	£ millions
2. In England: (*a*) Loans . . .	298	209
(*b*) Other Items [6] . .	62	50
Total in England	360	259
Total in England, converted into Rs. at £1 = Rs. 13⅓ (approx.) . . .	Rs. millions 4,798	Rs. millions 3,448
Total Interest-bearing Obligations	11,976	12,481
II. *Non-interest-bearing Obligations* [7] . . .	4	28
A. Total, Central Government	11,980	12,509
B. Provincial Governments: [8]		
Debt of the Provinces	1,374	1,444
Unfunded debt [9]	224	256
Total Obligations of the Provinces	1,598	1,700
Less Loans from the Central Government	1,247	1,206
B. Total Net Obligations of the Provinces	351	494
Grand Total—Debt and Other Obligations of the Central and Provincial Governments	12,331	13,003

[1] "Permanent Debt" is debt raised by Government in the open market which, at the time when it is raised, has a currency of more than twelve months.

[2] "Floating Debt" is debt with a currency of not more than twelve months, including Ways and Means Advances from the Reserve Bank of India.

[3] Excluding non-interest-bearing items.

[4] Includes Post Office savings bank deposits, Post Office certificates, State provident funds, deposits of Service funds in India and similar accounts.

[5] Includes various railway and lighthouses and lightships reserve funds.

[6] Includes liability for British Government 5 per cent War Loan taken over by India, railway annuities and deposits of Service funds in England.

[7] Includes unclaimed balances of old loans notified for discharge, and in 1940–41 Rs. 23·4 millions of interest-free defence bonds.

[8] Including the Coorg Administration.

[9] Mainly provident funds.

There is more in the philosophy of this table than is dreamt of by the ordinary reader. In the first place, behind this debt is the earning capacity of the commercial departments — the railways, posts and telegraphs, irrigation (which is a provincial subject), ports, canals, etc. The public debt in this sense is productive and is only a formal obligation of the Government of India. The concerns, in short, meet the interest, and often much more than the interest, on the capital invested. A Memorandum on the Public Debt of India, prepared in 1942 by the Financial Department of the India Office, points out that out of the Rs. 1248 crores of interest-bearing obligations of the Government of India as on 31st March 1941, Rs. 732 crores represent capital invested in the railways, Rs. 31 crores that invested in the other quasi-commercial departments, Rs. 121 crores interest-bearing loans to the Provincial Governments, and Rs. 19 crores other interest-bearing loans, including advances to Indian States. Thus the Rs. 1248 crores (£936 millions) of interest-bearing obligations of the Government of India are covered by interest-yielding assets to the extent of Rs. 903 crores (£677 millions), or 72 per cent. But over and above this, the commercial departments yield a substantial profit to the Government, which in the case of the railways alone amounted to about Rs. 19 crores in 1941–42, and is estimated at Rs. 20 crores for 1942–43. To quote the Memorandum :

The gross interest on all obligations of the Government of India (rupee and sterling combined) in 1941–42 was Rs. 40 crores. The amount of interest charged to railways and other commercial departments and to Provincial Governments and other bodies to whom interest-bearing advances have been made, was Rs. 34 crores. The net interest left to be met from general revenues was thus only Rs. 6 crores — £4½ millions. Against this, however, there accrued to general revenues a net profit from railways and other commercial departments (arrived at after charging them with full interest) amounting to Rs. 22 crores — £16½ millions. It will thus be seen that the interest payable on the whole of the public debt of India in the widest sense is much more than covered by the interest plus the additional net revenue derived by the Government of India from its various interest-earning assets.

It is true that in the case of the Central Government "productive" is here taken to include interest-bearing loans to Provinces and Indian States, which, from the point of view of the latter, may or may not be productive in the sense of producing their own interest. In point of fact, however, the position is as follows : On 31st March 1941 the total debt of the Provinces (other than provident funds and similar unfunded debt) was Rs. 144·4 crores, of which Rs. 120·6 crores consisted of loans from the Central Government. Against this, the Provinces had Rs. 124 crores invested in productive irrigation works and electricity schemes which, during

1940–41, yielded a net revenue (including interest) of Rs. 9¼ crores. The Provinces, like the Central Government, make a gain over and above their debt charges. Table XIII shows that in 1937–38 Madras, Bengal, the Punjab, the Central Provinces and Sind made a profit out of interest on their invested capital even after paying the fixed charges on their own obligations of all kinds. The following tables give the debt charges for the Central Government (Table XII), and for the Governments of the eleven Provinces and the Coorg Administration (Table XIII):

TABLE XII

CENTRAL GOVERNMENT OF INDIA, DEBT CHARGES [1]

(Lakhs of Rs.)

	1937–38	1940–41
A. Interest on Ordinary Debt:		
1. Rupee debt	1885	1942
2. Sterling debt	1661	1605
Total, Ordinary Debt	3546	3547
B. Interest on Unfunded Debt [2]	1016	656
C. Interest on Other Obligations [3]	98	172
Total, Gross Interest on all Obligations	4660	4375
D. Transfers (to be deducted):		
1. Amount transferred to commercial departments in respect of interest on capital:		
Railways	2807	2767
Posts and telegraphs	72	69
Irrigation	8	7
Salt	4	4
Other departments	3	3
Total Interest transferred to Commercial Departments	2894	2850
2. Interest paid by Provincial Governments	494	524
3. Commuted value of pensions	24	23
Total Transfers	3412	3397
BALANCE, being Net Interest on Debt and other Obligations of the Central Government	1248	978

[1] *Source.*—Combined Finance and Revenue Accounts of the Central and Provincial Governments in India for the years 1937–38 and 1940–41.
[2] See Table XI, note 4.
[3] See Table XI, note 5.

TABLE XIII

Provincial Governments Debt Charges, 1937–38 [1]

(Lakhs of Rs.)

	Coorg	Madras	Bombay	Bengal	U.P.	Punjab	Bihar	C.P. and Berar	Assam	N.W.F.	Orissa	Sind	Total
A. Interest on Ordinary Debt	..	37	138	..	108	110	..	16	..	1	..	129	539
B. Interest on Unfunded Debt [2]	..	14	13	16	12	10	6	6	4	1	1	2	85
C. Interest on Other Obligations [3]	..	..	..	..	..	..	..	..	..	..	..	..	1
Total Interest on Public Debt and other Obligations of the Provincial Governments	..	51	151	16	120	120	6	22	4	2	1	131	625 [5]
D. Transfers:													
To commercial departments (mainly irrigation)	..	99	42	22	110	158	..	25	..	1	..	134	591
Other transfers	..	..	4	2	3	4	..	5	1	..	..	..	19
Total Transfers to be deducted	..	99	46	24	113	162	..	30	1	1	..	134	610
Balance, being Net Interest on Debt and other Obligations of the Provincial Governments [4]	..	− 48	105	− 7	7	− 42	6	− 8	3	1	1	− 3	15 [5]

[1] *Source.*—Combined Finance and Revenue Accounts of the Central and Provincial Governments in India for the year 1937–38.
[2] Consists of interest on State provident funds, special loans and Treasury notes.
[3] Consists of interest on advances from the famine relief fund, deposits of depreciation reserves of Government commercial undertakings and other items.
[4] A minus sign means a surplus on balance and not an obligation.
[5] Includes C. Interest on other obligations (1 lakh of Rs.).

Repatriation of Sterling Debt

India like some of the self-governing Dominions has been extinguishing her external debt at a greatly accelerated rate as a result of the war. India in this respect takes pride of place. The only other country comparable with India is South Africa which has reduced her sterling debt from £101 millions (1939) to £21 millions (1943). Most of the sterling has been repatriated by the cancellation of sterling loans and their replacement by rupee loans. India's sterling debt was incurred, it may be remembered, for the creation of productive enterprises such as the Government-owned railways and the irrigation schemes which have added 32 million acres to the fertile land of India. Surplus of receipts has exceeded the interest payable on the debts and India, by loans, has acquired permanent assets yielding a return that relieves the taxpayer of interest on debt. No other country in the world is in so favourable a position. This process has been rendered possible as a result of the accumulation of sterling balances by the Reserve Bank of India owing to payments by the British Government for war purposes. By means of various vesting orders made by the British Treasury (by which the Treasury takes over various Indian sterling loans from holders in Great Britain), and repayments by the Government of India of loans falling due, the greater part of India's sterling stocks were liquidated by 31st March 1943. Before the war the sterling debt of the Government of India, including railway debentures, stocks and annuities, was of the order of £370 millions. By the end of the financial year on the 31st March 1941, this had been reduced to £240 millions. After the repayment of the $3\frac{1}{2}$ per cent sterling stock on 5th January 1943, the total was reduced to £66·2 millions. As a result of the repayment or redemption of various railway debentures announced in January 1943, this total is reduced by a further £27·25 millions. The arrangement with the British Treasury whereby a lump sum has been paid to it to provide the service of the railway annuities reduces the outstanding sterling debt by a further £27 millions. The balance outstanding on the 31st March 1943 was therefore only £12·25 millions, a negligible sum. The Finance Member, in pointing out this historic fact in his Budget speech of 27th February 1943, stated that " India has completed the transition from a debtor to a creditor country and extinguished within the brief space of about three years accumulations over decades of its public indebtedness to the United Kingdom ". The sterling interest charges, which amounted to £13 millions in 1936–37, to £$12\frac{1}{2}$ millions in 1937–38 and to £12 millions in 1940–41,[1] have been reduced to about £$2\frac{3}{4}$

[1] £12 millions is " Total Interest on Sterling Debt ", as shown in the Finance and Revenue Accounts, but only £11 millions is actual interest paid in sterling.

millions in 1943–44.[1] The total interest paid on the sterling debt in the year ended 31st March 1939 was, it may be noted, £12·5 millions. The sterling debt, therefore, was slightly less than the amount of interest paid on the sterling debt in 1938–39. The sterling balances are mounting so high and at so rapid a rate that it is now possible to consider the capitalising of the liability for pensions payable in sterling. This would be to the advantage of India which would not have to meet a recurring future liability and would thus avoid remittances from India to Great Britain.

The Effects of War on the Financial System

The Budget of the Government of India for 1942–43 reflects the effects of the war on the Indian national economy and on the system of public finance. There were, as Tables I and III show, increases in both public expenditures and public revenues, notably at the Centre. There were, however, no spectacular changes as in Great Britain and in the United States. There were, for example, no taxation of agricultural incomes and no system of death duties or, as in Canada and Australia, sales taxes at the Centre. The war brought great increases in taxation but it did not lead to great changes in the tax structure or in the financial relations between Federal and Provincial authorities or between Provincial Governments and Local Authorities. It did lead, however, to changes in the public debt structure as has been shown in the immediately preceding paragraphs. Like Britain, India is relying on its peace-time tax structure, supplemented by such emergency taxes as the excess profits tax and increased rates in regular taxes and duties, notably in the field of income tax and surcharges on customs. Owing to the large, very large, expenditures in India in connexion with the war (in 1937–38, the pre-rearmament year, such expenditures would have been considered as beyond the bounds of possibility), and to the resulting increase in national income and purchasing power, it has been practicable to increase the burden of taxation even on comparatively low incomes. Precautionary measures were taken to minimise or prevent inflation owing to the probable effects of the pressure of enhanced purchasing power on an insufficient supply of goods and services for private consumption. The existing surcharge on income was increased on a graduated scale and compulsory saving was introduced, especially in the taxation of lower incomes. Although incomes from Rs. 1000 to Rs. 2000 were made liable to taxation, the liability is regarded as discharged if the person assessed deposits one and a quarter times the amount of tax in defence savings, which will be repayable with interest

[1] Cf. *Memorandum on the Public Debt of India, 1942,* Financial Department of the India Office.

one year after the war. The burden of taxation is being apportioned, as it should be, with the least possible offence to the general sense of equity. The ideal tax to-day is one which, without creating a feeling of injustice or privation beyond a minimum, brings excess purchasing power in no small degree into Government coffers and which curtails the material resources and labour spent on non-essentials of war in such a way that morale does not suffer. Such taxes are difficult to devise and recourse must be had to taxes other than the ideal tax. An excess profits tax on the British model has been introduced. It contains the familiar characteristic of blocking business profits, although in a slightly modified form meant as an incentive to economy in business administration. A contribution is made by the Government of an amount up to one-tenth of the tax paid to reserve for the re-equipment of industry after the war, provided the assessed person doubles the amount. His contribution is repayable one year after the war, with 2 per cent simple interest. Excess profits taxation has a tendency to operate very unfairly, penalising some businesses very heavily and letting others off too lightly. It tends to put up the cost of production by encouraging extravagance, and it does not make sufficient allowance for the future needs of firms which are now engaged on munitions of war. Such firms will require reserves for the reconditioning after the war, and it is Government policy to encourage them to build up such reserves. An emergency surcharge of one-fifth has been levied on all customs import duties with the exceptions of petrol, the tax on which has been increased from 12 to 15 annas a gallon, and of raw cotton, the tax on which has been doubled; the excise duty on kerosene has been raised to the level of the enhanced import duty. There have been increases in postal and telegraph rates but no increase on that productive tax—salt. Railways, an important source of revenue, has brought grist to the mill. In the year 1942–43 the total additional revenue was estimated at Rs. 120 millions, and this must be added to the estimated revenue at the previous levels of taxation — Rs. 1794·8 millions. The total estimated expenditure is Rs. 2265·5 millions, leaving a deficit of Rs. 350·7 millions to be included in the Government's borrowing programme. For the next year, 1943–44, the estimated revenue on the existing level of taxation was placed at Rs. 199 crores 30 lakhs and expenditure at Rs. 259 crores 59 lakhs, leaving a deficit of Rs. 60 crores 29 lakhs. Of this prospective deficit it is estimated to cover one-third by new taxation and the remainder by borrowing. India's own defence expenditure (*i.e.* excluding that incurred and paid for by the United Kingdom and other Allies) now touches over Rs. 40 lakhs, or £300,000 daily. Defence estimates are three times their normal size. The scale of expenditure of the British Government in India is more than three times that of India's own expenditure and is increasing. The two outstanding features of Indian public finance at the present time are the increase in national income resulting from the intensive development in India's resources with the resultant large expenditures on the war and the tremendous accession of strength brought about by the conversion of external to internal debt, and also by its being paid off. A third feature, already referred to, is the beneficial effects of the increased revenue from income tax on the Provinces. For 1942–43 the share of income tax which goes to the Provinces is estimated at Rs. 8 crores 37 lakhs as against Rs. 7 crores 39 lakhs for 1941–42. "This is considerably more than the total sum which, at the time of the Niemeyer Award, the Provinces were expected to receive at the end of the ten-year devolution period or than ever appeared to be possible before the outbreak of war."[1]

In the Budget of 1943–44 increases in income tax and also in new direct taxes were announced. Of the Rs. 20 crores to be raised by taxation direct taxation accounts for Rs. 7 crores. Income tax increases affecting incomes over Rs. 5000 per annum, and a uniform surcharge amounting to $66\frac{2}{3}$ per cent over the basic rates of income tax, are imposed. The supertax surcharge on incomes exceeding Rs. 25,000 per annum is raised by one-half an anna in the rupee, so that the surcharge on supertax runs from two annas in the rupee on the smallest incomes to ten and a half on the largest. The corporation tax is raised by half an anna to two annas in the rupee, and the excess profits tax is extended to cover the profits of a further period of one year, but the rate of $66\frac{2}{3}$ per cent remains unchanged. The two new indirect taxes were an all-India excise duty upon tobacco and on the vegetable product known as vanaspati, used for adulterating ghee (or clarified butter). The scale of tobacco duties will mean an average increase of 20 per cent in retail prices and will bring in an additional Rs. 10 crores in the first year, and the yield of the vanaspati tax is estimated at Rs. 1 crore 40 lakhs. There has also been an increase in postal and telephone rates, estimated to yield approximately Rs. 1 crore 20 lakhs. It is interesting to see how in this Budget taxation has been increased mainly by indirect taxes and to a less extent by direct taxes. Nevertheless by May 1943 inflationary tendencies of a serious nature (judged by an alarming upward turn of the price level, reckless speculation, profiteering and widespread hoarding) were evident. War taxation was not sufficiently drastic to draw off even a substantial portion of the increase in spending power brought about by the needs of a gigantic war machine. War savings were not sufficiently high. In a primitive and loosely integrated economy, such as obtains in India, the controls used by more highly developed Western countries could not be imposed without great difficulty.

[1] Finance Member's speech on introducing the Budget proposals for 1942–43 (*Gazette of India Extraordinary*, 28th February 1942), para. 24, p. 290.

Drastic action was called for in both the monetary and commodity fields. Surplus purchasing power was mopped up by an intensive effort of taxation, especially on war profits,[1] and by borrowing on the part of both the Central and Provincial authorities. Various forms of commodity control were adopted, such as the Cloth and Yarn Control Scheme, the prohibition of advances of money against security of food grains except to licensees under the Food Grains Control Order (*i.e.* legitimate traders) and to producers of food grains. Forward contracts in cotton were stopped on current crops in May; no new company was to be formed without Government permission so that the formation of mushroom companies was no longer possible. The prohibition of bank advances against commodities, including bullion, resulted in a shake-out of many speculative positions.

Owing to the impossibility of applying the methods of rationing and price control, as in other belligerent countries, the rise of prices and inflation have been greater than in the United States and in the great countries of the British Commonwealth. As mentioned above, the British Government has, since the beginning of the war, spent more in India than has the Government of India. Between September 1939 and April 1943 the British Exchequer paid £438 millions and India herself spent £320 millions (a large sum for India) on India's defence. This cash payment from outside led to the absorption of goods and services within India and increased the amount of purchasing power competing for a reduced volume of goods and services available for civilian consumption. The expenditure by the Indian and British Governments leads to inflation and it might have been wiser, all things considered, for the British Government to have skimmed off excess purchasing power by raising rupee loans. By the end of July 1943 the campaign against inflation was beginning to bear fruit in several quarters. The inflationary trend in prices was checked and in some cases actually reversed. But it is not yet enough to solve the problem.

Another characteristic of Indian public finance is the great growth in sterling balances. The sterling balances are an asset of considerable potential value, and a Reconstruction Fund is being considered to provide for the financing of post-war reconstruction, including the rehabilitation and re-equipment of industry. Although the war has given much impetus to long-term industrial development, it will make it possible for the country to go ahead quickly with industrial development after the war when considerable re-equipment will be essential, and it will enable exporters in Great Britain to complete post-war programmes

[1] Twenty per cent of the profits liable for E.P.T. has to be deposited with the Government under the new regulations.

without worrying about remittance. It also makes it possible for the Government, as already noted, to arrange for future remittances of pension, which are between £5 and 6 millions a year. The scheme under consideration is on the lines of the arrangement made for sterling railway annuities, and may be described as the purchase of a tapering annuity. The capital sum involved if those charges were capitalised would be considerable.[1]

In conclusion, the war has led not only to the extinction of India's external Public Debt, but also to a change which, in the future, will affect the character and direction of her foreign trade. She has turned from the status of a debtor to that of a creditor country.

[1] Finance member's Budget Speech (1943–44), paragraphs 45–49 : " The arrangement . . . would amount to the investment of a capital sum in return for which the Government of India would at stated intervals receive sums of sterling with which they would be in a position, as far as can be estimated, to meet these sterling obligations."

PART II

CHAPTER VIII

THE GENERAL PROBLEM OF INTERGOVERNMENTAL FINANCIAL RELATIONS

CERTAIN conclusions emerge from the analysis in Part I of the Public Finance and National Economy of the United States and the Federal Self-Governing Dominions and India. These Governments, Federal, State and Local, are taking a larger portion than ever before of the national income and the character of the taxation system has assumed great economic importance. It was for this reason that the taxes were classified as they were, to show those which were on surplus and those which were on costs. This classification has been useful in judging the degree of regression of the structure as a whole. Expenditures have increased not only because of new services, especially those dealing with social security, which have markedly increased since the permanent ravages of the great depression of 1929–32 and subsequent years. War has also had its effects, especially on Federal Governments which have had to finance the most expensive of expensive wars. Assuming present trends to continue, the impact of Federal policy in the future on the units, especially Local Authorities, is likely to be greater than in the past. The tightening of the Federal grip on economic life is bound to lead to conflicts with State Governments and Local Authorities, and the need of realistic, exhaustive and precise enquiry is greater than before. The cost of government is rising over long periods in all layers of Federal Governments. More and more demands are made on Governments. Higher standards are demanded for old services and at the same time new services are insisted upon. There is no possibility of the return of Government expenditures to the level, say, of a decade ago. Social security, high expenditure on education, sanitation and roads and growing armaments have come to stay. Even the last of these cannot be excepted from the rule. Intergovernmental financial (or to use the American term, fiscal) relations must be analysed.

The Rising Cost of Government and the Competition for Revenues

All this has increased the competition for revenues among Federal, State or Provincial, and Local authorities. Conflicts have been between Federal and State authorities, between Federal and Local authorities, between State or Provincial and Local authorities, between State and State and also between nations. There has been a noticeable tendency for the overlying Government, by its larger tax powers, to curtail or control the underlying Government. In the control of large-scale business, for example, as well in the sphere of stabilisation of employment and production and the maximisation of national income, the Federal Government is, as compared with other layers of Government, in the strongest position. This, however, does not and should not mean the weaning of State and Local Governments. "Fiscal independence is a large sector of general independence, and the latter a large part of local self-government which, in turn, has important democratic values. It has been suggested that another major war might put an end to federal systems everywhere. Whether or not this be true, it appears that a large degree of State and local fiscal independence does carry values of a very high order, and that they should not be sacrificed until the necessity is clearly demonstrated. It is not believed that such is yet the case."[1] Decentralised government has a real value, and in large countries such as Canada, the United States, and Australia, government through the various Governments, whether Federal, State or Local, allows for diversity of local conditions, the development of citizenship and leadership and for the curtailment of bureaucratic methods connected with red tape and inefficiency. States or Provinces are responsible for many governmental services affecting the welfare of its citizens, as are Local Authorities. It is natural that, however carefully a constitution is drawn up, there will be at some point or points overlapping and conflict as each authority is resentful of encroachment by the other. A logical or clear-cut solution of financial relations is impossible in a Federal Government which is itself, of course, a compromise. No single panacea in financial relations is possible and no single method for co-ordination is possible.[2] Little progress has been made in the past by thinkers on the problem because they have tended to be too drastic or too grandiose and have not taken into consideration sufficiently the historical or practical aspects and the co-operative aspect of the problem. With the development of income taxes in Federations the overlapping of tax powers has greatly increased in recent years, and to-day in the United States, for example, about nine-tenths of combined Federal and State taxes come from common tax bases: only customs duties under the Constitution are denied to the States, and the property tax and perhaps the motor vehicle licence to the Federal Government. This common base applies in a less degree to State and Local taxes, as the States in recent years have been giving up the property tax to Local Governments as an

[1] Senate Document No. 69, 78th Congress — Report of the Committee on *Intergovernmental Fiscal Relations* — Major Conclusions and Recommendations. Treasury, Washington, D.C., 1943, vol. i, chap. i.

[2] In this connexion see Harold M. Groves, *Financing Government*, New York, 1939.

exclusive source owing to the introduction of gasoline and similar taxes. Local tax powers being delegated powers in the United States handicap Local Authorities in two ways—by limiting tax rates rigidly and also by extending tax exemptions. The greatest limitation, however, to Local Authorities arises from economic limitations owing to smallness of area. An income tax or a tax on companies could be easily evaded if imposed by a small Local Authority especially in these days of easy communication. As has been shown recently in Canada and Australia, a heavy overlapping tax, such as a State tax on income, may deter the Federal Government from developing fully a Federal source of revenue, and it is for this reason that Provinces and States were, for the duration of the war, precluded from this means of revenue. In any integration of Federal, State and Local taxation we must realise squarely the difficulties and the fact that no single system will be the best for all layers of Government. Miss Newcomer has emphasised that the larger jurisdiction would be in the long run the most efficient, and this would concentrate the revenues with the Federal Government. This would mean, unless we were willing to entrust the Federal Government with the administration of practically all functions, that new problems of redistribution of revenues would have to be faced, a fact overlooked by some enthusiasts for efficient tax administration. In aiming at co-ordination we must remember the increasing national economic integration and interdependence, arising especially from inter-State trade, increased communications, and the growth of large corporations. These have increased problems of inter-State competition and multiple taxation.

The Co-ordination of Public Revenues and the Reallocation of Functions

What, then, are the methods of solving this problem of increased conflicts due to overlapping and competitive tax systems? In the first place there is separation of revenues. This has been tried at various times in the history of Federal Governments. It has, for example, been tried in India, but even in the field of income tax which was at first almost entirely Federal, Provincial Governments were given, as we have seen, a share under the Niemeyer award and the 1935 Government of India Act. The great merits of separation are that it avoids the difficulties of double taxation and the collecting authority spends the proceeds of the tax. Its disadvantage is that it produces rigidity in the tax structure and therefore makes it less adaptable to changing circumstances. Apart from this fact, there is the practical difficulty. It is too revolutionary a change. Would, for example, in the United States either the Federal or State Governments give up personal income taxation, corporation taxes, death taxes, liquor or tobacco taxes? Would the Federal Government give up, too, the gasoline tax? It might, if State Governments would forgo the taxation of tobacco. The problem has only to be stated in this form to emphasise its inherent difficulties. The fact that Federal Governments are not static but dynamic is often overlooked. The first Constitution of the United States, for example, gave the Federal Government no independent sources of revenue and was supported by grants or requisitions from the various States, requisitions because the Federal Government made periodical requisitions upon the States. This failed, and the new Constitution gave the Federal Government independent revenues. Similarly the German Government were given certain independent sources, but these, being inadequate, had to be supplemented by grants from States known as Matricular-Beiträge. As the Central Government acquired greater authority, greater independence and vitality, such arrangements became out of date. To-day the importance of income taxation in the Federal field of taxation has only to be mentioned to be realised. It would be unwise at the same time to ask States or Provinces to withdraw from the income tax field as this would discourage access to progressive and personal taxation. No tax, moreover, is so fair as the progressive personal income tax, as it comes nearest to the best standard of ability. It increases progressively with income, and the nature of income and the size of the family are taken into consideration in the determination of the amount of tax. In short, tax-paying ability is more closely followed than in any other tax. These facts must be considered in the problem of the integration of Federal and State revenues. Mutual adjustment has to be considered. To abolish every form of competition in intergovernmental financial relations is impossible.

A second solution is the sharing of the same revenues between layers of Government, due attention being paid to the interests of the taxpayers. This reduces conflicts between jurisdictions, although it may be argued with some force that it sacrifices independence. In practice, however, there are more similarities in taxation practice than is generally recognised. It is more common to emphasise dissimilarities than similarities. The common form of sharing is a single collecting agency and for a division of the yield among the layers of Government. The great advantages are economy coupled with simplicity. On the other hand, there is loss of independence and a sense of inferiority on the part of the smaller authorities. There is also the uncertainty of what the yield will be from year to year. Lastly, there is always the difficulty of the basis of the distribution whether it should be population or taxable capacity or what. It is sometimes suggested in this respect that supplements or additions agreed on after consultation should be adopted, the Federal Government being the primary collecting agent and the State having the power to add supplements or additions of its own. There are, combined with the advantages of supplements such as economical administration, absence of compulsion and of duplication of taxes and the feasibility of increasing or decreasing the supplements to suit particular needs, disadvantages arising from diversity of conditions in the separate States making for diversity in the pattern of the tax. The most that can be hoped for is the combination of the greatest number of advantages with the least number of disadvantages. The late Professor E. R. A. Seligman was a believer in supplements and additions as a plan of co-ordination because the State could lighten the burden of the particular tax on localities to the extent thought desirable, and with a spread in the burden over a wider area a due balance between direct taxation such as that on real property and indirect taxation would be possible. "A survey," he said, "of the entire situation cannot fail, with moderation and goodwill on both sides, to bring about mutual adjustment, as workable as it is equitable." [1] Central administration of taxes side by side with decentralisation of Government is rapidly gaining ground. Federal aid to States and Provinces and State and Provincial aid to Local Authorities has in recent years been noticeable in the United States and Australia. A modified form of sharing, sometimes regarded as a separate device, is to have a single administration for the tax and to leave such jurisdiction to fix its own rate on a uniform base. Thus economical administration and a uniform base are combined with independence on the part of each layer of Government for the amount of the tax. Its drawback is again rigidity. The base may be inadequate. This device is sometimes, and perhaps rightly, regarded as a separate method for reducing conflicts.

Another device is the system of grants which have been developed in some Federations, as for example in Australia, more than in others. Provided the grants-in-aid do not curtail local self-government, they are an advantage. On the other hand, cases are known in which these grants-in-aid have led to extravagant and unwise expenditure and control. The system of grants from the centre is in origin British and is over a century old. It is to be found in the North America Act and at the end of last century it began in the United States, for example New York where the State attempted to lighten the burden of the local property tax. Federal grants came later and have developed with the demand for better services, especially roads. As these Federal grants do involve a certain degree of subordination, certain States have looked at this system with some misgiving. It is, however, a system which has proved, especially in the self-

[1] Seligman, "The Co-ordination of Public Revenues", p. 579, *Economic Essays in Honour of Gustav Cassel*: London, George Allen & Unwin, 1933. Cf. G. Findlay Shirras, *The Science of Public Finance*, vol. ii, p. 736; London, Macmillan & Co., 1936.

governing Dominions, worthy of extension and the Committee on Intergovernmental Fiscal Relations in the United States has suggested that Federal grants-in-aid, to effect a national minimum in various services by which a minimum standard should be provided throughout the States of the Union without over-straining Local resources and differential aids, should start with elementary education. It is true that education in Federal Constitutions is usually by the Constitution a matter for State and Local Governments, but with the movement for more and better education Federal assistance becomes more insistent, and in some Federations, especially Australia and India, is overdue. "With few exceptions", says the Committee of Intergovernmental Fiscal Relations, "the States lowest in financial ability are making the greatest relative effort to support public education. The poorer areas usually show the highest birth rates and the under-privileged individuals frequently migrate in later life to areas of greater economic opportunity. The importance of public education in raising the level of consumption and production in sub-average areas and its possible effect in reducing future outlays for relief, health, welfare and rehabilitation are also stressed. Citizenship interests in minimum standards for education are obvious. Consideration of local tax relief also enters the argument. . . . It is not an acceptable feature of our way of life to keep large sections of the population in ignorance. Of all the functions of government which might be candidates for national minimum status general education has the strongest claim. . . . Wise Federal leadership with regard to educational development in the United States can make an impressive contribution to the economic, political and cultural life of the country."[1] The Federation, in secondary and higher education, especially the latter, might assist individuals rather than institutions through scholarships, but no hard-and-fast rules can be laid down as to assistance from Federal funds for either secondary or higher education. In South Africa and in the United States the average expenditure per pupil in average daily attendance varies very widely between whites and negroes, and such wide differences raises the problem of the effectiveness of Federal assistance alone making educational opportunity more equal. On this matter consultation by the Federal Government with the units should produce beneficial results.[2]

[1] Senate Document No. 69—Report of the Committee on *Intergovernmental Fiscal Relations*, vol. i. Treasury Department, Washington, D.C., June 1943.

[2] Nothing has been brought out so clearly in this Study as the wide variations in the standards of education provided by the units of the federations studied. These variations are also to be observed between Federations. It is the duty of the Federal Government to see that no unit falls below a certain minimum since education enables citizens or potential citizens to be and to do something. It is indeed a preparation for living by the citizen and is dynamic, *i.e.* it requires to be brought up to date from time to time. The advantages of more and better education in relation to a higher national income are

Another system of co-ordination is to be found in the system of credits which has been most developed in the United States. It is a comparatively recent device and was introduced to meet the problem of death duties. It has worked smoothly and merits wider extension. It has, however, been criticised as it involves some compulsion, because to obtain the credit the State should have an identical system of tax. Some States had no death duties or had duties collected on a different system, as, for example, an inheritance tax or a tax on each share inherited. To-day, except Nevada, all States in the United States have fallen in with the Federal system of estate taxation. When anyone pays the Federal tax he is credited with 80 per cent which may be payable to the State. The State tax, therefore, costs the State and the taxpayer nothing. Similarly with the pay-roll tax credit. Pay-roll taxes, as shown elsewhere, were introduced under the Social Security Act and are for old-age pensions and unemployment benefits. If the system of credits were extended it might lead to bad spending since the States are not responsible for the tax.

It will thus be seen that in all the Federations studied there is competition among taxing authorities. None of these Federations is of the Soviet or German type. In the Soviet Republic finance is centralised to a high, a very high degree, the Central Government in Moscow controlling the finance of the States. In the Reich there is almost complete centralisation of finance. In the old Federation of Switzerland, on the other hand, there have been at work methods of smoothing over competition among taxing authorities. The Federal Government gained more power in direct taxation which previously had rested with the Cantons, and the Cantons, by assignments of revenue or subsidies, were won over to this centralisation. Indeed the Cantons may be said to rely far too much on the Federal Government. From the viewpoint of competition among taxing authorities the Federal Governments of Mexico and of the South American Republics and China repay study but are somewhat outside the scope of the present chapter. What is crystal-clear is that Federations being in their origin a compromise, the democratic Federations of the United States and the

obvious. In the United States, to quote but one example, the educational advance of California, New York, Wisconsin and New Jersey is much greater than in many of the States of the west and south. "The number of individuals enrolled in elementary schools includes 96 per cent of all persons in the State (of New York) between the ages of six and thirteen years; the number enrolled in secondary schools includes 78 per cent of all persons between fourteen and seventeen years of age; and the number enrolled in advanced and professional schools includes 17 per cent of all persons between the ages of eighteen and twenty-one years" (cf. Luther H. Gulick's Report, *Education for American Life*, The Regents of the University of the State of New York: New York, M'Graw Hill Book Company, 1938, p. 7). The necessity of improving school district organisation is dealt with in the same Report, chap. iv. The duties of Federal and State or Provincial Governments in educational finance after the war are obvious, especially in Australia and India.

self-governing Dominions have to meet this competition for revenues not by any single method but by a combination of methods promising the greatest benefits, and the future rests in a system of co-ordination of public revenues. Separation of sources, sharing of revenues, grants-in-aid, credits, supplements, joint administration and reallocation of functions will not individually achieve the desired results under all conditions and each method will have to be tried out. Each country has its own problems and no clear-cut solution, as already noted, is possible. Each problem has to be considered on its own merits, and this demands intergovernmental co-operation in no ordinary degree. A full and genuine co-operation free from suspicion of every sort is called for. This is no easy matter where, as in the United States, the number of taxing authorities is at least 175,000, and where overlapping is prevalent especially among hopelessly small authorities.

The methods of reducing conflicts among competing jurisdictions as described above are not in themselves able to solve all difficulties. There are problems unconnected with overlapping Governments but among co-ordinate governmental units, for example those in which the Federal Government competes with State or Provincial Governments in the taxation of income and of business. City often competes with city or Province or State with Province or State in attracting industries with the bait of limited tax exemption for a number of years. With the rise in taxable values as a result of this policy there is often a rise in the cost of Government, as, for example, in the social services. The competition of States, too, is well known especially in the United States, where the attraction of a taxless paradise may result in the drift to the State of wealthy tax-dodgers attracted by such advertisements as " Friendly Florida, where escape from the rigors of northern winters may be combined with freedom from double taxation " cannot *pace* credits for death duties, etc., always be given effect to. There are, too, the taxation of inter-State income of companies, State income taxation of non-residents, favourable taxation of stock transfers, State tariffs designed not so much for tax revenue protection as for the protection of industries in the State itself such as taxes on liquor, tobacco and gasoline. These and similar conflicts do not admit of any clear-cut solution but rather to beautiful compromises and to solutions by the Federal Court interpreting the Constitution to suit changed times. *Tempora mutantur, nos et mutamur in illis.* Since the great depression of 1929–32 in the United States, Canada and Australia there have been revolutionary changes in Federal functions and powers and, as one Committee has phrased it, " The legal boundaries of ' interstate commerce ' have been and are still being broadened ; a new element of flexibility in the interpretation of the Federal Constitution has appeared ;

and precedents for the use of the Government as an instrument for dealing with depressions and unemployment have been established." Nevertheless each problem must be settled on its merits — its advantages and disadvantages. In Australia and India the Federal Government almost certainly should provide a larger portion of the cost of education by a generous grant-in-aid system, and in the United States and Canada the Federal Government, apart from a limited number of relief works, should participate in outlays for direct relief to a larger degree. Unemployment and social security generally are national problems and much is to be said in favour of the Federal Government taking a leading position in this respect. But in the large Federations what may suit one State may not suit another and so local experimentation to suit local diversities may be advantageous. Were social security to be inaugurated now it is probable that it would be best done by the Federal authority. But historical and constitutional reasons in some Constitutions make this at present out of the question and little is to be gained by threats to federalise. Hastening slowly is the best policy. Similarly, as a solution of inter-State competition for the incorporation of companies a Federal Charter would be advisable and is a change long overdue, especially in the United States where States with the weakest regulations for the incorporation of businesses have got most of the business. Similarly, too, re-allocation of functions may be advocated in regard to the States (or Provinces) and Local Authorities in the control of education, roads and welfare. There is still much work to be done here, since in the Federations studied there is a dearth of statistical and other information on the relative efficiency of the various units in regard to such services. With the revolutionary changes noticeable in all the Federations in the powers of the Federal Government — in many cases by a flexible interpretation of the Federal Constitution to meet the change of circumstances — the reallocation of functions and powers has assumed new importance.

Three further points remain to be discussed — problems of inter-State relations, financial policy in relation to full employment, and the general solution to the general problem of intergovernmental financial relations, effective machinery for a close and continuous co-operation.

Problems of Inter-State Relations

Multiple taxation on personal and corporate income, on death duties, on railways and on capital stock by which two or more States impose a similar tax on the same base, could be reduced by agreement among States or Provinces: the main directing force should be the Federal authority in the Federation. Multiple taxation is as it were a trade barrier and should be prevented by the Federal Government. The

American Committee on Intergovernmental Fiscal Relations summed up the position thus: "While the States can and should do something through reciprocal legislation to reduce the amount of multiple taxation, the main impetus for improvement will have to come from the Federal Government. This means some interference with State and local fiscal independence, but in the long run it will support such independence. It is a case of amputating a finger to preserve the arm. The Federal Government should seek to acquire the right of determining State jurisdiction to tax by means of favours and subsidies extended to the States. It may be questioned that Congress and administrators are wise enough to perform successfully a role which is now gradually being abandoned by the Supreme Court. But there is fair agreement concerning many matters of jurisdiction — a proper allocation formula for corporation income, for instance — and the States, with one or two exceptions, have no very high stake in jurisdictional vested interest. Some jurisdictional problems will have to be settled by compromise. Increasing multiple taxation acts as an unfortunate penalty upon cosmopolitan ownership and business, a sort of trade barrier, which it is the natural role of the Federal Government to prevent. It should not shirk its proper task in this matter." [1] This view applies to other Federations, such as Canada and Australia. Some, such as India, have a comparatively clean slate to write on and should take early action to prevent the difficulties that have arisen in the older Federation multiple taxation. In other directions, too, the Federal Government should take the initiative, for example in equalising by grants-in-aid and other ways the great differences that occur in Federations. Thus in Australia the Commonwealth Grants Commission set up in 1933 reviews annually applications made by the States of South Australia, Western Australia and Tasmania for financial assistance from the Commonwealth. The relative taxable capacity varies with the industrial development of the units. Wealth and income tend to gravitate to the centres of population. It is a duty of the Centre and of the States or Provinces also to mitigate the maldistribution of wealth and income of the various groups, including the smaller Local Authorities. There is much difference, for example, between the Western States of the Dominion of Canada and, say, the State of Ontario and in the Commonwealth of Australia between Western Australia and Victoria. In the United States the *per capita* income, as we have shown, is so high that the rate for old-age pensions in California would be out of all proportion to that in, for example, Wyoming or the poorer States or portions of the States in the South. The average old-age pension in 1939 in California was $345, and this

[1] Senate Document No. 69, 78th Congress — Report of Committee on *Intergovernmental Fiscal Relations*, June 1943, vol. i.

exceeded the *per capita* income of the poorest State by no less than 70 per cent. It was also actually above the *per capita* income of ten States in 1943. The Federal Government in Federations has, as already noted, more than a watching brief for the general good when States or Provinces by indirect means raise what are in effect barriers to trade by the taxation of margarine and liquor manufactured outside the taxing State or by the special inducements offered to industry to settle within the State, such as exemption from State taxation for a limited period and in other ways.[1] Here again there is scope for closer co-operation and continued discussion and in some cases for reciprocal legislation. There must be not only co-operation among the units, which are in reality semi-independent democracies bound together in a common tradition, but also between the Federal Government and the units. In most Federations efficient co-operation in Federal-State or Federal-Provincial relations is far from satisfactory.

National Investment Policy and Full Employment intergovernmental financial relations in recent years have been profoundly affected by the problem of full employment, and this has involved Federal, State or Provincial, and Local Governments. These revolutionary changes may be traced to the great depression of the early thirties and to a realisation of the fact that it is technically possible to secure full employment at a price that democracy can pay in peace as well as in war. Deficit financing and a national investment policy have been studied as never before, especially in the United States and in a unitary Government like Great Britain. The conception of the interests of the electorate not merely as taxpayers but as producers and consumers has led to a new emphasis on the importance of maximum public expenditures and to a study of the economic activity of a country and not only to that part of it, about one-fifth or one-quarter, covered in the Budget itself. It has also been appreciated that at least in the short run it is better to increase Investment than to reduce saving or subsidise consumption. An Investment policy is easier to control and its ultimate effect is greater, *i.e.* in Keynesian language the multiplier is larger. It is now realised that when the community spends less than is required to purchase its output, when it saves relatively more than it is investing in durable goods, cyclical depression occurs. The community is saving in money but not in real terms, or in other words is attempting to enrich itself by piling up claims on itself in preference to accumulating goods of durable value. To cure this state

[1] " Florida started her land boom of the nineteen-twenties with constitutional amendments prohibiting state inheritance and personal income taxes, and followed this up by advertising for wealthy residents. These efforts were partially nullified a short time afterward by the Federal estate tax credit " (M. Newcomer, *Taxation and Fiscal Policy*, New York, Columbia University Press, 1940, p. 58). Cp. *Facing the Tax Problem*, The Twentieth Century Fund, New York, 1937, in which the same author collaborated.

of affairs the Government can reduce unemployment by giving consumers more money to spend. The encouragement of consumption at the expense of saving is sound policy in the long run, but if the depression or unemployment results from a deficiency in Investment the solution is to increase Investment, *i.e.* to control capital creation to make it large enough and regular enough to absorb the savings of the fully-employed community. In modern industrial States such as the United States, Great Britain and Canada there is always a tendency to save too much, to save, that is, more than is invested in durable goods. By full employment we do not exclude normal minimum unemployment when men and women change their jobs and draw benefit for a week or two. There must always be some unemployment of this sort. Full employment is compatible with this. There must be a certain amount of mobility of labour. Full employment is also compatible with seasonal employment, which is different from mass unemployment. What is known as " structural unemployment " arising in particular areas or industries is also excluded, although under full or mass employment it should be possible to drain away such pockets of unemployment. " Structural unemployment " does not arise from the same cause as mass unemployment, which is caused by cyclical depressions, from the lack of balance between the voluntary savings of the community and investment in durable goods, expenditures on the maintenance and increase of the community's machinery and other physical assets. The cure must be the community's investment in capital goods to an extent that will use the savings of that community regularly from year to year. The policy should be for the Government to stimulate capital enterprise by productive enterprise (both privately and publicly owned) and then to follow this up by its own schemes called for for reasons other than the maintenance of full employment. Unproductive public works should be undertaken only when the other expedients are exhausted. In the category of " private " productive enterprise are included all concerns including public corporations financed independently of the Government. As much as possible should be financed through private individuals and corporations, including publicly-owned concerns which do not depend on Government for their finance. There will be then no danger of too rapid State control. As has been well said, " The reasons for keeping the rôle of the state as small as possible are twofold. Large-scale state financing of investment involves the stability of the monetary system ; and a gradual spreading of state control, by way of capital investment, into every corner of the economic system at the mercy of any political adventurer who can capture the political machine. Let there by all means be public ownership and collective control, but exercised by agencies other than the State itself. . . . If self-supporting business (private or public) can be assured of low interest rates and of freedom from the risk of cyclical depression, there is no reason to believe that, in most years at least, it will not freely engage in as much investment as is required. The control of that investment by the state will be necessary — but that is a different and much less dangerous matter. The second risk is the monetary one. . . . State investment, especially if it is large, almost inevitably leads to the expansion of bank credit — that is, to the creation of money."[1] As Dr. Schacht proved in Germany, there is no danger when there is no full employment, and as modern theory shows, the price level does not depend rigidly on the quantity of money in circulation. We may have to accept as the price of full employment some changes in the value of money, but there is reason to believe that a policy of full employment could be followed out without a severe change in monetary values. The greatest danger to be faced in any policy of full employment is underestimating the extent to which funds will have to be spent. In the past the problem has been only toyed with and is much greater than is ordinarily imagined. Mr. Roosevelt's pre-war deficits of $5 billions should have been something of the order of from four to five times as great, and a figure of £1200 millions would have been required in Great Britain in 1938 to have secured full employment. In that year £500 millions were spent from savings and £400 millions from depreciation funds, and another £300 millions would have been required to be spent on capital goods to have attained full employment. To get remunerative investment both direct methods, such as guarantees against risk and adjustments of taxation (*e.g.* varying the rates allowed for depreciation in the taxation of income), and indirect methods, such as the control of the rate of interest to keep it low, would be required in the attempt to equate the total of investment exactly with savings at the highest level of the employment of resources. If the policy were executed on a sufficiently large scale it could not fail to succeed. It would mean a considerable control over international trade by the stimulation of exports and by a system of priorities for imports. Capital movements also would have to be controlled to prevent flights of capital such as wrought havoc to national schemes a decade ago. The effects of severe crises abroad would also have to be guarded against. But full employment is not against an expanding international trade although it is against what may be called the automatic technique of an uncontrolled market, and when a nation keeps its purchasing power at a maximum this in itself stimulates foreign trade.

[1] *Economist*, London, 17th Oct. 1942.

Budgeting for Employment

The policy of full employment raises two other issues : (1) the creation of the "two-Budget system" and (2) the use of taxation as a means of stimulating investment. We have already referred to the comparatively new concept of the interests of the electorate not merely as taxpayers but as producers and consumers, which is a far cry from nineteenth-century Budgets which were regarded as full and true national balance-sheets. It was considered wise and sound finance to curtail expenditures, especially in times of stress and strain, just when unemployment was bad and an expansion of public expenditures most essential, and with this there was the fetish of the "balanced Budget" which meant a curtailment of expenditures to meet the fall in revenues. Obviously any such policy put the stabilisation of economic life quite out of court. The present war showed as clearly as the noonday sun that deficits are not only unavoidable but desirable in certain circumstances. Expenditure could not be confined within the limits of taxable capacity if the maximum war effort were to be attained, and this optimum expenditure or optimum deficit, after optimum taxation had been reached, could not be arrived at by the traditional methods of public finance. What was absolutely necessary was an estimate of the whole national income of the country split up under well-defined heads and not merely the activities of the Government which formed part of it. In short, financial equilibrium was not to be arrived at by ordinary budgeting between revenue and expenditure but by an equilibrium between spendable income and available resources, by seeing how far expenditure could be extended and how far it should be covered by taxation. The gap between the two is the inflationary gap and then steps were taken to close it. Budgeting on the basis of national income and national expenditure has been successful in war and in peace it will be equally necessary if full employment is to prevail, as it must. It must be possible to measure the deflationary or inflationary gap. If it is deflationary it will mean the missing capital outlay required to have full employment, the deficiency of actual loan expenditure over the potential savings of the community if the resources of the community had been fully used in production. This means up-to-date and reliable statistical information on the national income similar to that in the British White Paper [1] together with other data such as that on private construction works. It is then possible with yearly and quarterly data to have fairly reliable information on private investment, and from

[1] *An Analysis of the Sources of War Finance and an Estimate of the National Income and Expenditure in 1938, 1940, 1941 and 1942.* Command Paper 6438, 1943. London, H.M. Stationery Office.

this a policy of continuous full employment is possible. It will mean, as in Sweden, two separate Budgets annually : a revenue Budget including all current expenditures on defence, administration, interest on the National Debt, and expenditure including that on the maintenance of State-owned capital assets. This " revenue " Budget will be balanced. The capital Budget will not be " balanced " except in the sense that it will have led to the creation of additional capital assets, both productive and unproductive, and it will be met from loans. The test of expenditure in the capital Budget will be whether it will be profitable from the social point of view, *i.e.* whether the national income is raised by as much as the interest on its cost. Housing, roads, education and public health all require huge outlays and yield a return in greater productive power of the people and in greater health and happiness. Social profit in the planning of public expenditures must be the criterion for the annual capital Budget. The two-Budget system is not in any sense a device to clothe a deficit with respectability and it must be scrutinised constantly by the Government in its everyday working just as the revenue Budget must be scrutinised constantly by the Treasury or Finance Department at the Centre so that the ordinary expenditure from revenue is covered by ordinary revenue. Indeed both must be examined with care, although on different principles and by different officials. Capital expenditures after the war will have to be allotted according to a list of priorities allocated to meet national needs. Large-scale public investment will have to dovetail into private investment and this presupposes much careful planning and Government direction.

Taxation may also be used as a means of stimulating investment, or if need be the reverse. As indicated in Part I, this is an aspect of taxation policy that is a corollary to a policy of national investment for full employment. In war, taxation policy is used to skim off the greatest possible amount of purchasing power from consumers above the minimum necessary for health and morale to Government for the winning of the war and to prevent the inflation that is always likely to occur when increased purchasing power consequent on high earnings competes for a diminished stock of goods and services. In peace-time every Government worthy of the name aims at increasing the standard of comfort of its citizens ; in war-time the reverse policy has to be developed ruthlessly in order that the Government may have the maximum of goods and services at its disposal. To achieve this the highest amount of taxation possible must be levied on personal incomes and on corporate profits (see chart opposite). Sales taxation must also be so high as to prevent the purchase of goods that can be done without. Taxation must be used with rationing, prohibition of manufacture or of imports, etc., as part of a policy to divert everything to the winning of the war.[1] Each tax in the tax structure must be examined and fitted into the whole. This is not an easy matter any more than

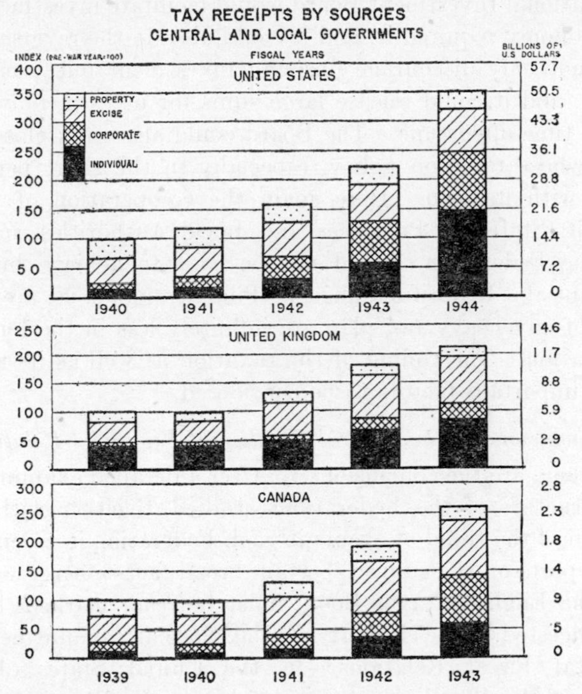

is the fitting-in of parts of a jig-saw puzzle. The central principle of policy should be to see that the total of investment exactly equals the figure carefully arrived at, neither more nor less. Taxation is one of the equalising methods and is direct and positive although its efficacy should

[1] NATIONAL INCOME, TAXES AND GOVERNMENT EXPENDITURES
(Percentages)

	Fiscal Year					
	1938–39	1939–40	1940–41	1941–42	1942–43	1943–44
Central Government taxes as percentage of expenditures:						
United States	..	61	55	39	28	42
United Kingdom	86	60	42	47	49	..
Canada	82	69	61	52*	49	..
Total taxes as percentage of national income:						
United States	..	19	20	22	24	32
United Kingdom	26	27	32	39	42	..
Canada	21	21	25	32	36	..

* Includes 700 million dollar loan to the United Kingdom not included in the Budget. If this item is excluded, the tax to expenditure ratio becomes 71.

not be exaggerated. The allowances to companies or corporations for maintenance and depreciation should be capable of change from year to year. A National Investment Board would facilitate investment when the national economy required it, and it could also do the reverse. It would, therefore, not only discourage unsound investment but would facilitate investment, and it could release large sums for investment when it considered the time opportune. The Board could also work closely with the Treasury, whose taxation policy, especially in the short period, should harmonise with its own. Here again the co-operation of the Federal Government, States or Provinces and Local Authorities, including the cities in the Federation, would not be easy to achieve but is nevertheless essential. Beautiful things, as Pindar reminds us, are hard. The hardships of any heavy tax plan are infinitely less in the long run than serious inflation. The timing of the taxation as well as its amount and nature are important factors to be considered.

Conclusions on the General Problem of Financial Relations

What, then, are the conclusions ? After a detailed examination of the financial structure of the Federations studied, together with a detailed examination of the trend of events in each Federation in recent years and of recent reports on the subject, certain broad facts emerge which, in the words of the English Prayer Book, must be read, marked, learned and inwardly digested. The Report of the Special Committee on Intergovernmental Fiscal Relations[1] in the United States (June 1943), the Report of the Royal Commission on Dominion-Provincial Relations in Canada in three volumes with several appendices,[2] the Reports of the Commonwealth Grants Commission issued annually since the passing of the Australian Commonwealth Grants Commission Act, 1933, not to mention the decisions of the Loan Council, referred to in Chapter V, together with official and non-official Reports on South Africa and India, lead to the irresistible conclusion that no single plan to solve intergovernmental financial relations is possible. There are some who favour complete centralisation on the ground that recent history proves that State or Provincial and Local independence has outlived its usefulness. There are others who emphasise that Federalism means State and Local freedom, and the price paid for this is the friction between taxing authorities which at present obtains. There is a third school which thinks it possible to have a completely perfect system but without any change in the functions of the various layers of Government. Examples of all three schools of thought may be illustrated from the Reports already quoted and, in the British Commonwealth, also from Budget speeches and from the proceedings of Premiers of the States or Provinces with the Federal Government.

[1] See Appendix II. [2] See Appendix I.

The devices of co-ordination referred to in this chapter cannot be applied under all conditions and the special historical accidents in each country cannot be overlooked. Another conclusion is that constant readjustment of financial relations will be essential and no one solution suitable for all time is possible. Thirdly, the Federal systems studied recognise the value of decentralised government although in very varying degrees, and they have a tradition behind them based on a Constitution and interpreted by a Federal Court or the Privy Council to suit changed conditions. These Federations cover a wide territory with divergent conditions and viewpoints. It is, therefore, reasonable that a decentralised form of government should be recognised, and this is, all things considered, preferable to any centralised administration. Each layer of Government has its important function. Thus with the increased development of social security, large-scale business and national activities generally the Federal Government has a most important part to play, but this should not be at the expense of the States or Provinces, cities or other Local Authorities. Financial independence, it is rightly said, is part of general independence and the latter is important in local self-government. In recent years, and especially in war, Federal administration has made tremendous strides in the field of public expenditures and in taxation, and this has meant a severe strain on the other layers of Government. The United States, Canada and Australia in the 'thirties are examples and the German Federation is an extreme example. The Nazis have been believers in extreme centralisation and the foundations of Federalism have been most seriously weakened. In the emergency of war the Provinces and the States in Canada and Australia have vacated a large part of the tax field in giving up income taxation during the war, but these Federations are more centralised than is that of the older Federation of the United States. In Australia especially there has been a highly developed system of grants from the Centre to the States, and State income taxes have been high. Moreover the autonomy of the States and Local Authorities is less developed than in the United States, so that we come back to the fact that no single solution of financial co-ordination is possible. The alternative, under present trends to central administration, is close and continuous co-operation and the Federal Government, being in a strong strategic position, must be the leader in most instances. It has many relations with each of the States or Provinces and in a variety of ways, especially with its wide taxing powers, achieves leadership.[1] This, as is often forgotten, need never be at the cost of the States and Local Authorities. Nationalism need

[1] Cf. G. Findlay-Shirras, *Science of Public Finance*, "The Distribution of Central, Provincial and Local Revenues": London, Macmillan & Co., Book III, chap. xvi. Hubbard, *Soviet Money and Finance*: London, Macmillan & Co.

not be the enemy of Federalism. In Part I the relative increase of Federal, State, and Local Authorities' expenditures and revenues has been set out and there can be only one conclusion. The States are responsible for many services closely affecting the citizens' welfare. So are the Local Authorities, especially in the nation-building sphere of education. Each layer of Government, jealous of its powers under the Constitution, has a job to do and some overlapping is unavoidable. In short, no complete and no logical solution of financial authority is possible.

The main lesson of this study can be briefly summed up as follows. There is, as we have seen, already in operation official and non-official bodies in existence studying at close quarters financial relations in the various Federations. These should be developed after a complete revolution has taken place in financial thought in regard to this all-important problem. The Committee on American Intergovernmental Fiscal Relations has summed up this view in regard to the United States thus: "The Federal Government has a vital interest in maintaining and strengthening both State and local governments. Much valuable energy has been wasted unnecessarily in quarrelling over the proper spheres of the Federal Government and the States, when the seeds of solid achievement lie in the scantily tilled field of intergovernmental co-operation and co-ordination. Progress in this field requires some willingness to compromise, to surrender vested interests, and to forget jealousies on the part of both the Federal Government and the States. A change in attitude of revolutionary proportions seems to be needed. The American governmental system has not been viewed as a unit by most public officials, with loyalties evoked and encouraged for the entire system." The Committee recommends the creation of a Federal-State authority.[1] Before this Report was received a permanent official commission was the chief solution which had been in view as a result of the detailed study of intergovernmental financial relations in Federations. Co-ordination is a continuous study and in the near future there will be more and greater demands on the Federal Governments for assistance in what has hitherto been State or Provincial and Local authority matters. The necessity, for example, of more and better education in Australia and in India will mean that the Federal Government will be asked for grants for this purpose. Social services and developmental services will necessitate greater co-operation between Federal, State and Local authorities. The main work of this official financial authority (the recommended Federal-State Authority) will be the continuous promotion of collaboration and study of the day-to-day co-ordination of revenues and expenditures with the many difficulties that crop up in the practical work of Government. The

[1] See Appendix II.

taxation of income by Federal and State authorities and even by Local authorities bristles with knotty points. The taxation of business, death taxation and sales taxation are similarly requiring study and co-operation in their administration. The proposed authority would be worth its cost many times over if it succeeded in settling between the Federal and State authorities many outstanding and recurring difficulties. Ultimately the authority might be able to administer some of the taxes through delegated powers and to introduce the beginnings of joint returns and joint audit. It would also increase inter-State co-operation, which is easier in some Federations where there are fewer States than in the United States where there are forty-eight. It would also strengthen the weakest link in the chain of Governments in Federations — Local Authorities which are often small and financially most weak. Such an authority would undertake (1) research on the collection, incidence and effects of taxes; (2) the education of public opinion by deft publicity. The authority would have to be official and staffed and paid for on an agreed basis by the Federal, State, and if possible also by Local Authorities. At the outset its cost may be defrayed by Federal and State authorities only. Its personnel need not be large. The recent American Committee suggested three members — one to be appointed by the President of the United States, one to be selected by a conference of delegates named by State governors, and one named by these two. All three members were to be suitably qualified in the field of intergovernmental financial relations. This body of experts was to be assisted by a Council affording "direct representation of Congressional committees and recognised organisations of State and Local and Federal officials. Further representation for municipalities might also be secured by a provision requiring that one of the three experts be especially informed on municipal affairs."

The substance of the whole matter shows the necessity of a complete change of outlook, a revolutionary change, in intergovernmental financial relations. In thirty years' service under the Crown in India, where the writer served under the Central Government — the Government of India — and under Provincial Governments — the Government of Bengal and the Government of Bombay — the urgent reform of a change of attitude was evident, especially since the granting of provincial self-government in 1921 consequent upon the Government of India Act, 1919. A colleague from the Home Civil Service who founded the Labour Office of the Government of Bombay with the writer in 1921 went to discuss matters with the Central Government and on his return to Bombay was asked by His Excellency the Governor why he had been so long away. "We know the Government of India." "Yes," said my colleague, "when I arrived in New Delhi I was told 'We know the Government of Bombay'." It is true that the Government of India, as already pointed out in Chapter VII, had the elastic revenues including income tax, whereas the Provinces had with comparatively inelastic revenues to finance the expanding nation-building services. As a result of the Niemeyer award they had access to income tax. Similarly in Canada and Australia the proceedings of Premiers' Conferences show the same rivalry. The same lack of seeing the other man's point of view is seen in the United States. "The American governmental system has not been viewed as a unit by most public officials, with loyalties evoked and encouraged for the entire system. If the mayor of a municipality believes that a change in the Federal income tax would embarrass his own Government, he is likely to feel no great concern as to whether the change is needed to strengthen and equalise the Federal system of personal taxation. Federal administrators show equally unfortunate blind spots. Very often they lose, in addition, a proper sense of proportion, and conclude that all wisdom and authority are concentrated in Washington. State officials who object to this frequently show the same attitude in dealing with municipalities. Some of this is but the inherent limitation of human beings. But much of it could be eliminated by more conscious effort." [1]

The great point in favour of a Federal-State Financial Authority is that it will meet the need of to-day — continuous and constant co-operation at a time when Federal and State relations demand a new outlook and when inter-State relations must be so close that inter-State rivalries and inter-State trade barriers require an antidote. Co-operation must not end with this institutional change. Non-official bodies of all kinds such as the Council of State Governments in the United States, and official bodies such as the meetings of State Premiers in Canada and Australia with the Federal Government, together with every possible step to create public interest and disseminate information, must continue in all directions.[2] The old Federalism in which the Federal Government and the States or Provinces each went their separate ways without much regard as to what the others were doing is giving place to the new Federalism, a co-operative Federalism. With the development of social security and of business of all kinds in the Federations in the last decade there must be this co-operation to carry out functions which neither the Centre nor the States can do alone. Uniform or at least integrated action on common problems is vital.

[1] Senate Document, No. 69, 78th Congress — Report of Committee on *Intergovernmental Fiscal Relations*, Washington, 1943, vol. i, chap. i.

[2] Cf. *Tax Yields*, Annual Tax Collection Statistics for the various Units of Government in the U.S.A.: Philadelphia, Tax Institute of the University of Pennsylvania. *Tax Systems of the World*, the annual publication of the Tax Research Foundation, prepared under the direction of the New York State Tax Commission. Chicago (Commerce Clearing House, Inc., of the Corporation Trust Co.).

CHAPTER IX

SPECIFIC PROBLEMS OF INTERGOVERNMENTAL FINANCIAL RELATIONS

I. The Difficulty of generalising on Specific Problems

Plato in the *Republic* reminds us that the philosopher is one who takes general views and Adam Smith in his *Essay on the History of Astronomy* always looks for " connecting principles ". These are difficult indeed when we deal with specific expenditures and specific taxes in intergovernmental relations. The reason is not far to seek. In the first place the Federations differ in a large degree historically, economically and financially. Their economies, too, are made up of a number of diverse and highly specialised areas. A very large proportion of the surplus income of the country is concentrated in a few areas and planning in terms of an integrated Federalism is most difficult. What applies to one country may be unsuitable for another. As a result of national policies and of the specialised nature of the resources or industries of the regions, the States or Provinces while dependent on each other are, at the same time, notably in the United States, Canada and Australia, widely different in economic strength and taxable capacity. It is, therefore, difficult for the Federal Government to insist on equal standards everywhere. The more prosperous States or Provinces in a Federation have to bear burdens heavier than those of the poorer, which sometimes are inclined to think that they are completely disregarded by their wealthier neighbours and that they must be content with inferior social and developmental services. To-day more than ever before there is in Federations a demand for the better distribution of governmental burdens in all layers of Government, for a fairer distribution of social benefits, for a more equitable tax system, and for a financial policy which will stimulate and not depress the national income. The war has quickened this demand. As Adam Smith reminds us in his *Wealth of Nations* (which " declined into the world " on 9th March 1776, a few weeks after Gibbon's first volume of his masterpiece was published), " The expense of government to the individuals of a great nation is like the expense of management to the joint tenants of a great estate, who are all obliged to contribute in proportion to their respective interests in the estate. In the observation or neglect of this maxim consists what is called the equality or inequality of taxation." [1]

These facts have to be remembered when the problem of intergovernmental financial relations as applied to specific expenditures and

[1] Book V, chap. ii, Part ii.

specific taxes is discussed. The student of Federal Finance requires in a high degree in this part of his subject what Cavour called " tact des choses possibles ". What is flawless in logic is not always practicable and we must know the illogicality of facts. We should have the instinct for what is possible. " Very pretty," as the late Lord Milner used to say, " but it won't work." It is not an easy matter to do what the lumberman does in a log-jam and pick out the key log which, once moved, sets the rest going. We have, for example, the highly centralised type of Federation in the U.S.S.R., the German Reich and the Union of South Africa. The U.S.S.R. has one Budget which consists of the Federal Budget and the budgets of the sixteen federated republics and their Provinces. The Government of the Union fixes the taxes of the whole Union and agrees to the levying of supplementary taxes to satisfy the requirements of the federated republics. The Budget is approved by the Central Executive Committee (ZIK–USSR). In addition to prescribed shares, the republics may retain surpluses of their own and levy special taxes.[1] In the United States of Venezuela State and municipal taxation is of little importance because the States and municipalities follow with very few exceptions the Federal jurisdiction under the Constitution " in all that is related to the legislation of the principal taxes ". The taxes are almost entirely indirect. In the United States of Mexico and in Switzerland, on the other hand, the States and municipalities have their own tax systems in addition to the Federal which relies on the taxation of land, corporations, incomes, stamps, films, and a tax on the exportation of capital or income, known as the absentee tax. The United States of Brazil, under its Constitution of 16th July 1934, has exclusive power to levy certain taxes, such as consumption taxes except on gasoline, and taxes on income and rents except on income from real property, but it has concurrent power to levy taxes except those reserved exclusively for the States. Some Federal Governments have far greater taxing powers in relation to functions requiring expenditure than the States, as in the Commonwealth of Australia, and devices referred to in Chapter V have been used to distribute Commonwealth or Federal revenue to the States. For the duration of war in Canada and Australia the Federal Governments have federalised part of the Provincial or State tax systems, but these, unlike the United States, have a highly developed system of grants from the Centre, and Provincial or State income tax rates were substantially higher than in the States of the American Union. State and Local autonomy in Canada and Australia is also less developed than in the United States.

[1] For a detailed analysis of the tax system in the U.S.S.R. see the tax chart in *Tax Systems of the World*, published by the Tax Research Foundation, Chicago (Corporation Trust Co., 205 W. Munroe Street).

II. Policy and Public Expenditures

Conflicts in intergovernmental financial relations arise from public expenditures as well as from taxes. In recent years expenditures on social and developmental services have increased at an extraordinary rate in several of the Federations studied, *e.g.* in the United States, Canada and Australia. " In the particular circumstances of a given age or nation," wrote John Stuart Mill in the last chapter of his *Principles*, " there is scarcely anything really important to the general interest which it may not be desirable or even necessary that the Government should take upon itself, not because private individuals cannot effectually perform it, but because they will not. . . . In many parts of the world the people can do nothing for themselves which requires large means and combined action. All such things are left undone, unless done by the State." This appeared in 1848, and about a century later, remembering the tremendous changes in educational and other expenditure on the social services, especially unemployment relief, we have seen increased expenditures on social and developmental services which would have been regarded even a decade or so ago as impossible. Education and welfare services on a national basis cannot be left to State or Provincial or to Local Authorities. New factors have been introduced into a more highly geared and vulnerable mechanism as a result of industrial and agricultural specialisation. Mass unemployment is a national business and not a local one and is concerned with more than providing subsistence for its victims. It is concerned with national financial policy—monetary and exchange policy, national taxation, deficit financing tariff policy and other weapons in the national armoury. States and Local Authorities are interested in the highest possible standards of living and national security, and many of the social services are best administered by co-operation between the layers of Government so that due heed is paid to local circumstances. The following two tables bring out the importance of social and developmental services and the differences existing between the Federal systems studied. They refer to the pre-war years. The table relating to the war years is given in Part III. The changes in the war years are striking, especially in the United States. In the year ending 30th June 1944 it is estimated that the aggregate expenditure of the Federal Government will be $106,000 millions, and taxation $38,000 millions, leaving a deficit of $68,000 millions. Thus 36 per cent of the total Government expenditure was met by taxation, as against 47 per cent in Canada and almost 52 per cent in Great Britain. The national income is estimated to reach a new high record of $150,000 millions. The Public Debt on 1st July 1944 is likely to be $206,000 millions. The classification of the expenditures has been explained in Chapter II.

TABLE I

COMPARATIVE TABLE OF EXPENDITURES FROM REVENUE IN RELATION TO THE NATIONAL INCOME, TOTAL FOR ALL GOVERNMENTS, 1937–38

	Per cent of the National Income				
	United States	Canada	Australia	South Africa	India
1. *Primary Functions :*					
Legislation, administration, justice, pensions, etc. .	4	5	3	3	3
Defence	1	1	1	*	3
Debt services . . .	2	6	7	3	1
Total, Primary Functions	7	12	11	6	7
2. *Secondary Functions :*					
(1) *Social Services :*					
Education . . .	3	3	2	3	1
Unemployment relief .	3	3	1	*	..
Other . . .	2	3	4	2	1
Sub-total, Social Services	8	9	7	5	2
(2) *Developmental :*					
Transportation . .	2	2	2	2	2
Other . . .	4	1	2	1	1
Sub-total, Developmental	6	3	4	3	3
(3) *Miscellaneous* . .	*	..	1	*	*
Total, Secondary Functions . . .	14	12	12	9	5
Less Duplications . .	..	..	..	..	..
NET TOTAL EXPENDITURE .	21	24	23	15	12
National Income (in millions) .	$69,400	$4300	£796	£370	Rs. 19,000

* Less than 0·5 per cent.

The characteristics of each Federation's public expenditures have been dealt with in the chapters in Part I. The following points in recent years are of special importance. In the first place there has been an element of flexibility in the interpretation of the Constitution, especially in the United States in regard to the New Deal. Direct Federal assistance has

TABLE II

Comparative Table of Expenditures from Revenue, All Governments, 1937–38

(Percentage distribution)

	United States [3]			Canada				Australia				South Africa				India			
	National 1937–38	State 1936–37	Local 1931–32	Dominion	Provincial	Municipal	Total	Common-wealth	State	Local	Total	Union	Provincial	Municipal	Total	Central	Provincial	Local	Total
1. *Primary Functions :*																			
Legislation, administration and justice [1]	6	9	16	11	13	28	15	5	10	9	9	17	2	12	14	10	44	†	†
Defence	13	..	..	7	..	..	3	8	..	..	4	5	..	..	3	43	..	..	22
Pensions	9	..	..	12 [6]	..	..	6	11	3	..	6	7	..	2	5	2	8	†	†
Debt services [2]	12	4	10	35	20	20	27	19	46	17	35	15	4	44	18	12	2	†	†
Miscellaneous	..	..	..	..	4	..	1	..	..	..	..	..	..	..	..	..	..	..	..
Total, Primary Functions	40	13	26	65	37	48	52	43	59	26	54	44	6	58	40	67	54	24	58
2. *Secondary Functions :*																			
(1) *Social Services :*																			
Education	..	24	28	..	12	27	10	..	14	..	7	4	55	..	20	1	14	26	9
Unemployment relief	29 [4]	..	..	14	16	5	13	..	7	..	4	1	..	..	1	..	..	..	..
Public health	..	6	5	9	17	9	13	1	5	10	5	12	8	10	12	..	6	25	6
Other welfare	12	18	5					23	6	..	13					..	..	..	..
Sub-total, Social Services	41	48	38	23	45	41	36	24	32	10	29	17	63	10	33	1	20	51	15
(2) *Developmental :*																			
Transportation	4	13	9	4	10	11	8	7	..	45	10	19	25	19	23	27 [8]	10 [8]	18 [8]	20 [8]
Other	15	23 [5]	25 [5]	4	8	..	4	8	6	15	9					1	13	2	5
Sub-total, Developmental	19	36	34	8	18	11	12	15	6	60	19	19	25	19	23	28	23	20	25
(3) *Miscellaneous*	..	3	2	..	..	..	..	2	3	4	2	2	6	13	5	1	3	5	3
Total, Secondary Functions	60	87	74	31	63	52	48	41	41	74	50	38	94	42	61	30	46	76	43
Grants, etc.	..	..	..	4	.. [7]	..	2	16	..	..	7	18	..	..	11	3	.. [9]	..	1
Grand Total	100	100	100	100	100	100	102	100	100	100	111	100	100	100	112	100	100	100	102
Less duplications	..	..	..	5	..	..	2	16	7	..	11	19	..	..	12	3	1	..	2
Net Total	100	100	100	95	100	100	100	84	93	100	100	81	100	100	100	97	99	100	100
Percentage share of each Government in Total Expenditures	*	*	*	46	26	28	100	37	48	15	100	52	30	18	100	51	35	14	100

* See Chapter III. [1] Includes protection to person and property. [2] Includes sinking fund and other payments in the cases of South Africa and Australia.
[3] No complete and comparable data are available for all Governments in 1937–38. Hence the latest available year has been given in each case, and the "Total" column omitted. State figures include 32 per cent of grants to Local Authorities.
[4] Expenditure on Recovery and Relief programmes. [5] Includes "outlays", *i.e.* capital expenditure from revenue. [6] Military pensions and after-care.
[7] Provincial subsidies to Municipalities have been deducted from offsetting expenditures in the Rowell-Sirois Report, from which the Canadian data are taken.
[8] Includes expenditure on buildings. [9] Not given separately in the Finance and Revenue Accounts. † Details not available.

been extended, and since the great depression grants-in-aid have been more common than was formerly the case. In Australia the system of grants-in-aid has been specially noticeable. Much still remains to be done to provide national minima without burdening Local Authorities. This is especially desirable in the sphere of education, above all of elementary education. The economic and cultural value of such a policy on the part of Federal Governments cannot be over-estimated. The Intergovernmental Fiscal Relations Committee of the American Treasury made a recommendation which has reference to Federations generally on the subject of Federal assistance: "Unemployment is a national problem, and important advantages would result from changes which would put the Federal Government in a position to develop its social security system as a whole. On the other side, the interests in experimentation, participation and adjustment of programmes to local diversities may be cited. A law suited for New York may be badly adapted to Nebraska. Were the programme to be inaugurated now, it is probable that a national system would have the preponderance of advantages. Since the States have been granted the leading role in the system, they should be given time and Federal assistance to demonstrate whether they can handle it successfully. Constant threats to federalise the function will only interfere with cordial Federal-State relations." [1] The Committee also holds that a very strong case for a functional transfer can be made to make it incumbent on Corporations doing an inter-State business to secure a Federal charter. This, however, is a point to which reference has been made in the previous chapter when dealing with the general problem. The Royal Commission on Dominion-Provincial Relations in Canada [2] would centralise to a degree which might interfere with the real democratic working of the lower layers of Government by its proposition to relieve the provinces and municipalities entirely of the burden of relief for the employable unemployed and their dependants and at the same time assume the whole of the provincial but not the municipal debts, except in Quebec where the provincial debt bears an unusually low proportion of combined provincial and municipal debt. The Dominion in the case of Quebec would assume 40 per cent of the net cost of the combined provincial and municipal debt service. The Dominion, as we have seen, was to ask the Provinces to withdraw from certain important tax fields and to surrender existing subsidies and give to certain Provinces a National Adjustment Grant. The Dominion Government accepted the Report, but owing to opposition from some Provinces decided to take over for the duration of the war

[1] Senate Document No. 69, 78th Congress — Report of Committee on *Intergovernmental Fiscal Relations*, vol. i, Major Conclusions and Recommendations, chap. vi (Washington Treasury Department, 1943).

[2] See Appendix I.

income taxation on payment of an agreed annual sum to the Provinces. It is questionable whether so great a change as the Royal Commission envisaged is in the long run in the interests of Federal expenditures, especially where State and Local autonomy is developed. Are not other co-ordination devices preferable ? In war-time we are apt to believe that Federal Governments are so predominant that the day for Provincial or State autonomy and for Local self-government has entirely gone. As stated in the previous chapter this is a fallacy, since these other layers of Government can spend, all things considered, wisely. There cannot be a completely clear-cut solution of Federal expenditure.

III. Policy and Specific Taxes

Emphasis has been laid in the previous section on the importance of public expenditures in intergovernmental financial relations because these functional expenditures play a great part in the relations between layers of Government in Federations. They are important for another reason. These expenditures must be examined before we come to definite conclusions on the burden of taxation. Those who are at the bottom of the income scale pay mostly in indirect taxation, in the form of taxes on consumption goods, but, on the other hand, they receive free educational benefits and other social services of value. It will be noticed in Table II above that the distribution varies not only between the different layers of Government but also between the different Federations. Some have, for example, high expenditures on the social services or on developmental services, while others have scarcely any or comparatively little. Some spend much on education, others on defence and so on. We are here dealing with specific taxes and intergovernmental relations in regard to those taxes which overlap and, because of their overlapping, bring about conflicts. Of these the most important are the progressive taxes — income and death or inheritance taxes ; taxes on property ; corporation or business taxes ; and mainly consumption taxes such as those on liquor, tobacco, gasoline and sales. Pay-roll taxes in the United States are also combined Federal and State taxes.

The following table shows at a glance the tax structures of the Federations studied with the distribution of the taxes among the various layers of Government—Federal, State and Local Authorities. When placed side by side, the differences between the structures are striking and the overlapping jurisdictions are evident. The basis of the classification has been described in Chapter II. The main idea is to show the degree of progression or regression of the taxes, as well as the spread of the taxes among the various layers. It is with this latter point we are now mainly concerned,

TABLE III

Comparative Table of Revenue Systems, All Governments, 1937–38

(Percentage distribution)

	United States [1]				Canada				Australia [5]				South Africa				India			
	National	State	Local	Total	Dominion	Provincial	Municipal	Total	Common-wealth	State	Local	Total	Union	Provincial	Municipal	Total	Central	Provincial	Local	Total
Group I. *Progressive Taxes :*																				
Taxes on individual income	24	7	..	11	11	5	1	6	8	28	..	18	9	7	..	7	7	1	..	4
Death taxes	8	5	..	5	..	15	..	4	2	5	..	3	2	..	..	2	..	..	..	..
Other	..	..	..	..	..	..	..	..	..	..	..	..	2	3	..	2	..	..	..	..
Total, Group I	32	12	..	16	11	20	1	10	10	33	..	21	13	10	..	11	7	1	..	4
Group II. *Taxes on Property :*																				
Taxes on private property	3	8	94	36	..	2	88	28	2	2	54	9	..	5	45	9	..	31	30	16
Government property	..	..	..	..	..	9	..	2	..	5	..	3	1	..	6	2	..	5	2	2
Total, Group II	3	8	94	36	..	11	88	30	2	7	54	12	1	5	51	11	..	36	32	18
Group III. *Taxes on Business :*																				
Corporation Income Taxes	25	6	..	12	15	6	..	9	5	..	..	2	} 37 [3]	9	..	27 [4] {	5	..	..	2
Other	1	7	..	2	..	11	3	4	..	3	1	2					..	..	1	..
Total, Group III	26	13	..	14	15	17	3	13	5	3	1	4	37	9	..	27	5	..	1	2
Group IV. *Mainly Consumption Taxes :*																				
Customs	7	..	..	3	25	..	..	13	44	..	..	19	27	..	..	18	35	3	..	19
Excise	} 32	67	..	29 {	11	..	..	4	20	..	..	9	7	..	..	5	6	17	..	9
Other taxes and licenses					33	41	1	26	11	10	..	10	..	19	..	5	8	16	14	12
Sub-total	39	67	..	32	69	41	1	43	75	10	..	38	34	19	..	28	49	36	14	40
Public utilities and services	..	..	..	..	3	..	2	1	4	20	16	14	4	..	28	7	28	14	21	23
Miscellaneous	..	..	6	2	2	3	5	3	4	16	3	11	11	5	21	12	10	9	28	12
Total, Group IV	39	67	6	34	74	44	8	47	83	46	19	63	49	24	49	47	87	59	63	75
Grants, etc.	..	..	..	..	..	8	.. [2]	2	..	11	26	10	..	52	..	15	1	4	4	2
Grand Total	100	100	100	100	100	100	100	102	100	100	100	110	100	100	100	111	100	100	100	101
Less duplications	..	..	..	..	5	..	..	2	13	7	..	10	17	..	..	11	3	2	..	1
Net Total	100	100	100	100	95	100	100	100	87	93	100	100	83	100	100	100	97	98	100	100
Percentage share of each Government in Total Revenues, excluding pay-roll taxes in the case of the U.S.A.	41	27	32	100	44	25	31	100	38	47	15	100	55	28	17	100	50	36	14	100

[1] Tax revenues only.
[2] Provincial subsidies to municipalities have been deducted from offsetting expenditures in the Rowell-Sirois Report, from which the Canadian data are taken.
[3] Of this, Mining Revenue 25 per cent of total Union revenues.
[4] Of this, Mining Revenue 17 per cent of total revenues.
[5] State income taxes are all given in Group I, as it has not been possible to separate out those on companies.

but we cannot be blind to the cumulative effect of the taxes in each layer of Government and in each group. As one's eye runs down the table, one is struck by the lack of progression in some Federations, as for example in Canada and India, and how much of the taxation is on costs rather than, as in the case of income taxation, on surplus or net incomes. Taxes on business based not on net income but on arbitrary capitalisation of income and taxes which increase the cost of living at the subsistence level and increase wage costs are taxes on costs. Efficiency in taxation is not merely efficiency in collection but efficiency in the sense of collecting it with the least burden on the national income. Lack of co-ordination and a high number of taxes affect the efficiency of a tax system positively through restriction on production, and therefore on employment and also on investment. It may also be said to affect it negatively by the fact that financial policy is not used to increase the national income. These facts have to be remembered in dealing with the problem of conflicts in regard to specific taxes in the four groups of taxes in the table — progressive taxes, taxes on property, taxes on business and consumption taxes.

The co-ordination of progressive taxes — personal income taxes and succession duties or death taxes — is the most important problem awaiting solution in Federal finance. It has to be considered from a pragmatic or realistic point of view, and this means that an analysis of each Federation must be undertaken separately. The science of Public Finance and especially the taxation part of it is not in the strict sense of the term an exact science.

Income Taxes

Take, for example, the taxation of income. In a Federal economy the difficulties of this, the most fair and most highly developed instrument of taxation, are serious tax injustice and friction among competing taxing authorities in an integrated and complementary economy. In the United States about two-thirds of the State Governments levy income taxes. In Canada all Provincial Governments except Quebec, Nova Scotia and New Brunswick have recourse to this form of taxation. All the six States of the Australian Commonwealth have income taxes which, especially in Queensland and New South Wales, were important. During the present war the Federal Governments in Canada and in Australia have taken this head of taxation to themselves and compensated the Provinces and States in order to get the greatest possible revenue collected with the maximum of efficiency. The variation in rates between the Federal tax and those of the States or Provinces and in some cases between Local Authorities and the division of jurisdiction have led, especially in the higher ranges of income, to great inequalities. Even before the war the Canadian Dominion tax was one of the highest in the world, for the largest incomes and the combined Dominion-Provincial tax in Manitoba, Saskatchewan, Alberta and British Columbia was, as shown in Chapter IV, the most burdensome in any Federation, varying from 33 per cent in Nova Scotia to 58 per cent in Saskatchewan. There were also great differences in exemptions. In Alberta and British Columbia no exemption of Dominion income tax paid was allowed, while exemption was permitted in Ontario. When the definition of income varies, tax-collecting offices, increased costs of audits, unnecessary costs and annoyance of tax-compliance to taxpayers result. Income taxation to-day is regarded as the equaliser of the whole tax system, but it cannot be so in the above circumstances nor when there are heavy tax burdens on business costs, marginal industry and on the lowest income groups in which the burden of consumption taxes is heavy. Those in favour of having this instrument of taxation under one authority emphasise the importance of the rate of progression which results.

No single method of co-ordination applicable to all Federations is possible. One method, however, is for the whole of income taxation to be collected by the Federal authority and for the States or Provinces, as in India, to get a share. As years go on, Federal Governments will have to assist the social services to a greater degree than obtains to-day and States themselves may wish to have more access to progressive taxes. It is, therefore, suggested that these units be permitted to add a percentage to the Federal tax, due care being taken to avoid differences among the units as regards rates and jurisdiction. A generally applied standard avoids jurisdictional conflicts. Where this is not the case, as in pre-war Canada and Australia, tax injustice is bound to arise. A second proposal to avoid conflicts is for the Federal Government alone to levy the tax. This is the recommendation of the Canadian Royal Commission on Dominion-Provincial Relations.[1] The Provinces are, it is proposed, to cease to use this form of taxation. An exception is made permitting them to levy a proportionate tax on wages and salaries to meet premiums for social insurance within provincial jurisdiction. The Commission bases this recommendation and indeed those regarding the withdrawal of the Provinces from the field of corporation taxes and inheritance taxes, on two grounds: (1) the withdrawal is part of its Financial Plan under which the Dominion will assume all deadweight provincial debt, responsibility for unemployed employables, and new National Adjustment Grants to certain Provinces; all Provinces, therefore, receive a *quid pro quo* for withdrawal from these fields: and (2) equity between different Provinces and the exploitation of the tax with the least harm to the national income will be achieved by a single jurisdiction administering the tax. It must be remembered that in Canada as in

[1] See Appendix I.

Australia there is a well-developed system of grants-in-aid from the Central Government to the Provinces or States, and the tradition of Provincial or State and indeed Local autonomy is not so deep-rooted as in the United States. There is another point to be considered with care. Should, from the point of view of self-government in the units, access to progressive taxation be withdrawn? The value of State or Provincial independence in financial affairs cannot lightly be set aside. The advantages of the Federal Government's assuming the role of sole authority in income taxation have to be set against the disadvantages of such a policy.

A third method is a method to continue but to improve greatly the collection of income tax by both Federal and State or Provincial authorities. In the United States, for example, the withdrawal of State authorities from the field of income taxation would be outside the realm of practical politics because of the importance of income taxation in State taxation, and also because of the large measure of financial independence on the part of the States, a growth of over a century and a half. In the United States, too, there has developed a system of co-ordination (*e.g.* in regard to income tax deductibility), although co-ordination in administration and in other directions is still far from what it might be. There is much room for the development of co-operation between the Federal Government and the States and between the States themselves. For example, the principle of deductibility could be extended. It should be the rule that in calculating taxable income not only should the Federal tax paid during the year be deducted from the income before arriving at the State taxable income, but the reverse process should be universally applied in all the thirty-five States where net income taxes prevail. The States themselves should see that this principle is enforced between one State and another. Here the Federal-State authority would be useful in avoiding problems such as conflicting jurisdictions, high compliance costs, and inter-State competition. An alternative would be to use the Federal tax as the basic one for all States and by a great improvement, much overdue, to make the State tax a supplement. The principle of deductibility has the additional advantage that it prevents the combined Federal and State rates becoming confiscatory. It is a curb to tax avoidance by migration and also reduces the amounts which the Federal Government collects from the taxpayers of income tax levying States than from those in non-levying income tax States with equal incomes before taxes are paid.[1] The most

[1] Cf. Senate Document No. 69, 78th Congress — Report on *Intergovernmental Fiscal Relations*, vol. i, chap. iv: "If each Government allows the deduction of taxes paid the other, the combined load of an 80 per cent Federal and a 15 per cent State rate is only 80·7 per cent (77·3 per cent Federal and 3·4 per cent State). . . . At the $5000 level, the differential in total income taxes between a New York and non-income tax State taxpayer (1942 rates) is 1·1 per cent of net income and 14·7 per cent of the total tax of the latter taxpayer."

desirable form of co-ordination, as will be clear from what has been said, is in administration. State supplements would hardly be possible without uniformity and a considerable improvement in administration. In this connexion the Committee on Intergovernmental Fiscal Relations stated, "A sound precedent for delegated administration has evolved in both Canada and Australia, and the development of joint administration has been suggested as an improvement upon these successful experiments. Utilisation by the States of Federal income tax information is already developed to some extent and some informal co-operation between administrative staffs now occurs. But the field has scarcely been scratched. Joint returns, joint audits, joint use of personnel and more uniform laws are a few of the possibilities," and on the subject of multiple taxation added, "Jurisdictional conflicts constitute a problem in which the Federal Government is most strategically situated to make decisions. The rules that should be applied and the means of promoting them must remain somewhat vague for the present. But the outlines of a desirable procedure are fairly clear. They call for (1) conference and consultation between Federal and State officials as to acceptable uniform jurisdictional rules; (2) joint promotion of the adoption of these rules; (3) acceptance of Federal arbitration in cases of dispute; and (4) Federal development of incentives for State compliance. The Federal Government should gradually develop techniques to purchase compliance with such rules regarding jurisdiction as it may establish, *in consultation with the States*." [1]

The position, in short, is that the income tax in some Federations is so important to the States that it cannot be a purely Federal head of revenue. Take, for example, the United States. The following table shows that income tax was the second most important tax in 1940 in the tax structure as a whole, and the fourth most important State tax.

It is being increasingly realised that too much time has been wasted in the past in conflicts on income tax by attempting a comprehensive single plan for immediate adoption so that one layer has the whole field of income taxation. In Federations a single uniform Federal tax is not always possible. Where it is, the States may be permitted to add a supplement under definite conditions. In the majority of Federations, however, the goal should be a uniform Federal and State income tax, and to achieve this continuous and exhaustive consultation *with the States* is desirable and a Federal-State authority would greatly advance this. The revolutionary change in attitude has been emphasised in the previous chapter.

[1] Report of Committee on *Intergovernmental Fiscal Relations* — Major Conclusions and Recommendations, vol. i, chap. iv.

TABLE IV

UNITED STATES TAXES IN ORDER OF IMPORTANCE IN 1940

($ millions)

Tax	Federal	State	Local Governments (Estimated)	Total	Percentage
Property	..	240	4445	4,685	36
Income	2130	369	20	2,519	20
Gasoline	257	853	5	1,115	9
Alcoholic beverages	624	244	4	872	7
Tobacco	608	98	..	706	5
Sales taxes	28	491	70	589	4
Motor vehicle	119	412	2	533	4
Inheritance, Estate and Gift	360	116	..	476	4
Customs	350	..	..	350	3
Other	384	444	200	1,028	8
TOTAL	4860	3267	4746	12,873	100
Percentage of total, excluding pay-roll taxes	38	25	37	100	..
Percentage of total, including pay-roll taxes	39	28	33	100	..

Source.—Tax Yields 1940.

Note.—Income tax includes personal and corporate income taxes based upon net income. Pay-roll taxes in 1940 were Federal $838 millions, State $851 millions, a total of $1689 millions (Old Age Benefits $605 millions, Unemployment $1084 millions).

Death Taxes

In the United States death taxes are levied by the Federal as well as by State authorities. The Federal Government levies an estate tax, a progressive tax, on the entire estate regardless of the division of the estate among successors, and it grants a credit for State death taxes to those States which levy a similar estate tax either as a substitute for an inheritance tax or as a supplement to it. The result has been that all States except one (Nevada) levy death taxes either in the form of estate or inheritance taxes, both being paid after death. The estate tax is levied on the whole estate, while the inheritance tax is graded according to the individual bequest and the relationship of the successor to the deceased. Death taxes are supplemented by gift taxes, as in the case of the Federal gift tax and some of the State taxes. In Canada inheritance taxes are a provincial head of revenue, although the Royal Commission on Dominion-Provincial Relations recommended, as we have seen, that it should be solely a Federal tax. The Constitutional limitation that the Provinces are restricted to "direct taxation within the Province" has been a fruitful subject of legal decisions as to the validity of provincial statutes in this regard. In the competition for revenues difficulties of double taxation, impediments to the free movement of capital and excessive costs of tax compliance and administration have arisen. Two estates of the same amount even in the same Province are differently taxed. If the deceased was domiciled in one Province and the beneficiaries are in that Province, the estate is taxed once. If in several Provinces the estate is taxed by each Province on the assets situated within it, and it will be taxed on the transmission of the property to the beneficiaries in the Province in which they reside. The application of rules ascribing an artificial *situs* to intangible personal property such as company shares and moneys payable under insurance policies, as well as the taxing of real property and tangible personal property, have given rise to conflicts. The absence of reciprocal agreements among Provinces and delays owing to administrative regulations have added to the difficulties already noted. In Australia there are Federal and State duties which were in the period 1926 to 1935 from 1·8 to 3·8 times as large *per capita* as in Canada. In South Africa the duties are Federal. In India this form of taxation is provincial, as in Switzerland, but it is as yet undeveloped, although the making of all successions liable to taxation as well as the imposition of an estate duty even on the joint Hindu family are feasible [1] and await the sickle of the tax-gatherer.

No clear-cut principle can be laid down as to the federalisation or the reverse of the tax. Much can be said for making the tax a Federal one whether it is levied on the corpus of the estate (an estate tax) or on the shares passing to beneficiaries (an inheritance tax, succession or legacy duty). It will do much to avoid conflict among State or Provincial Governments and unfairness and inequality. In addition to the criticisms already made in regard to the systems in Canada and Australia, there are those concerning (1) the inequality of the yield as between provinces; (2) the Federal Government in most Federations being responsible for a large part of the cost of social security; and (3) the detrimental effect of the present system on the national income. In regard to (1) nearly nine-tenths of succession duty collections between 1926 and 1939 were collected in Ontario and Quebec, while in the same period these Provinces produced 65 per cent of the national income. If the tax were made entirely Federal the variability would not unbalance Federal revenues as it does Provincial revenues, for Dominion revenues are so much larger and the base would be much larger, covering a wider population. In regard to (2), the nine Provincial Governments of Canada cannot meet the cost of the responsi-

[1] See G. Findlay Shirras, *Science of Public Finance*, vol. ii, chap. xxiii, p. 567 (1936, London, Macmillan & Co.).

bility of unemployéd employables, and already before the war the major share was being borne by the Dominion Government. Excessive rates of death taxation, as in the case of income taxation which makes the taxpayer refrain from earning additional income, may lead him to avoid accumulating wealth and instead to buy annuities. An alternative scheme would be for the Provinces or States in consultation with the Federal Government to come to an agreed policy of death taxation for all Provinces or States and for the Federal Government to collect the tax on its own behalf and on behalf of the Provinces or States. The American Committee in its Report realised the truth of this when it said, " on strictly logical grounds a very strong case could be made for separation of sources as a co-ordination device in the death tax field. If this were recommended, the Federal Government would be the choice as the taxing unit. The State tax is plagued by interstate competition and multiple taxation, and especially by the fact that estates are highly concentrated in a relatively few States, though the wealth represented may have been accumulated over a much wider area. On the other hand, the States, with one exception, have a proprietary interest in this field and any proposal for surrender would rouse intense antagonism. Moreover, any method of getting the States out of the field, short of a constitutional amendment, would involve a distribution of revenues not very different from the present." [1]

Death taxes are co-ordinated in some Federations by a system of credits. The deceased's estate tax is given a credit against the Federal tax to the extent of death duties paid to the States. This applies to the Federal Estate tax but not to the gift tax, although there is no reason why it should not be extended to the latter. A credit computed under the Federal estate tax is allowed up to 80 per cent. When a credit is in force, a Federal Government should, in consultation with the States or units, arrive at an agreed method of exemptions, common to both the Federal Government and the States, and the Federal Government should broaden it (1) to secure single administration and (2) to avoid multiple taxation. There is no reason why the Federal Government should be responsible for administration, but it should determine the taxpayer's liability to the States. Alternatively the Federal-State financial authority may be entrusted with the administration of the tax. A thorough overhauling of the system is overdue in most Federations. Its introduction in countries which are of industrial importance and in which death taxes have not yet taken their due share in the tax system should be seriously considered. India is a case in point.

[1] Senate Document No. 69, 78th Congress—Report of Committee on *Intergovernmental Fiscal Relations,* Major Conclusions and Recommendations, vol. i, chap. iv.

Business Taxes

The present position of business taxes from the viewpoint of intergovernmental financial relations is, to parody Pope, a mighty maze without a plan. In addition to Federal and State corporation income taxes there are taxes levied on capital, the number of branches, gross revenue, physical volume of output, mileage of track or wire, mileage worked, note circulation, volume of deposits, and insurance premiums. These taxes are levied on a plethora of concerns such as banks, insurance companies, transport, telegraph and telephone companies, gas and electric power companies, chain stores and miscellaneous companies. The basis of taxation varies and may be said to run counter to the canons of taxation. The Federal tax was in origin a part of personal income tax, but the two taxes are now independent, dividends being taxed under the personal income tax and the corporation tax being levied on corporations *qua* corporations, *i.e.* business is taxed as such. Provinces and States look on business as a goose which lays the golden eggs and do not care how much cackling takes place in plucking it. The result is not only complexity but black chaos in the competition for revenue. Federal-State co-ordination, in the absence of any strong policy from the Federal Government, is most difficult. It goes without saying that business is accepted as a subject suitable for taxation, and this is, without the present disadvantages, possible by direct taxation. Not only are investments in different Provinces taxed at different rates even in the same class of business, but different forms of business in the same Province are subject to different rates and businesses operating throughout the Federation are taxed twice and three times without relation to net income. In these circumstances tax compliance is high.

How is this inequity, divided jurisdiction, increased business costs and the eradication of the marginal firm to be overcome ? One solution is a uniform centralised system based on net income. Corporations, therefore, operating at a loss would not be taxed. A general business tax levied by the Federal Government and shared with States and Local Authorities is the ideal. The States and Local Authorities would vacate gross and net income taxes, capital stock taxes and other taxes on business. This does not mean that bona-fide Provincial or State and Local licence fees, real estate taxes and consumption taxes collected through corporations would be excluded. State or Provincial taxes on business are, as a rule, vexatious, detrimental to the expansion of the national income and are, as we have seen, a source of inter-State or inter-Provincial jealousy. They are often taxes on costs rather than on profits. Two recent authorities have emphasised the necessity for correlation of taxes on business. The

Canadian Royal Commission, as we have seen, recommended that the Provinces should withdraw completely from the taxation of corporations. Similarly the Intergovernmental Fiscal Relations Committee of the American Treasury reported that a Federally collected tax with distribution to lower layers of Government may be the solution but added that public opinion is not yet ready for such drastic action. Research would be needed, as the change " would involve heavy complications, including the separation of business taxes from property taxes, Federal apportionment, and the adaptation of the programme to the needs of the States. Against these must be balanced compliance costs resulting from diversities, injustices and losses of revenue owing to jurisdictional confusion, and the repressiveness of State forms of taxation. A quantitative appraisal of what these causes for action add up to is not possible without research that cannot be attempted in an emergency like the present. The results might support a recommendation for complete federalisation of business taxes by application of a Federal sharing programme." [1] Until this is done, the Committee suggests (1) better integration of the personal and corporate income tax at the Federal level ; (2) State use of a system similar to the Federal, with resulting possibilities of joint administration, mitigation of multiple taxation and State supplementation ; (3) research and education in this whole field ; and (4) Federal incorporation of corporations engaged in inter-State business.

Nothing has been said about the excess profits tax which may or may not be used beyond times of emergency. It has proved to be of great importance in war finance and has values other than as a revenue-producer, being an anti-inflation instrument. But it has been in recent years, where industry is of great importance, a first-rate revenue-producer. The tax captures, as its name implies, excess war profits as well as monopoly profits that have slipped through the net of other controls and " windfall " income. In war-time the principle is that no one should be allowed to make excessive profits out of war conditions. A normal or standard profit may be measured by reference to the profits over an average of years, on the supposition, of course, that the business was making normal profits in those years. In fixing normal profits a percentage on the capital employed may also be taken, but here discrimination between different classes of businesses has to be considered. Other problems, such as the rate of tax, the checking of wasteful expenditure, the items to be included in computing capital, allowances in respect of wasting assets, the treatment of new subsidiaries, are of great importance and have to be mentioned only to show how essential Federal direction is. Here again the Federal-State Authority, proposed in the previous chapter, will be invaluable.

[1] *Op. cit.* vol. i, chap. iv.

Taxes on Property

The high percentage which taxes on property play in Federal financial structures is well seen in Table III, *e.g.* under the United States. Changes have been developing in the present century in the oldest of the Federations studied so that the tax has become less and less a State tax and more and more a Local Government tax, the States depending on such taxes as the gasoline tax, the general sales tax, the income tax, the motor vehicle tax and the pay-roll tax, each of which, as Table IV shows, is more important than the property tax. In fact, the property tax since the beginning of the century has fallen from 50 to 5 per cent of the total of State revenues. It was in 1940 the largest single tax of any layer of Government. The general tax is levied on all forms of property — real and personal, tangible and intangible, but, as the experience of the great depression has shown, it is not a tax to depend on and it makes one agree with Seligman who held that it was " one of the worst taxes known in the civilised world ".[1] The method of levying the tax, the numerous exemptions, statutory limitations and so on,[2] coupled with the memories of New York City's great difficulties when the tax failed it just over a decade ago, are not peculiar to one of the Federations but in some degree are common to all. The problem of Local Government finance bristles with difficulties connected with this form of taxation, and in the enquiries made, especially in regard to Australia and India, statistical information has been sadly wanting. One of the first reforms in Federal finance after the war should be research on local finance with a view to improving the taxation available to Local Authorities, especially cities. This, too, raises the question of better representation of the Local Authorities in the State or Provincial legislatures which in the past have curbed the powers of Local Authorities in regard to expanding the possibilities of property taxation and to the greater diversification of revenues. Local Authorities should devise new sources of revenue which should cover the vast body of its population without conflicting with Federal and State taxes. They should also improve old sources, especially the property tax and its administration. With great advantage they might consider a retail sales tax, a tax on rentals of occupied premises, a development of special assessments, unearned increment taxation, and, as in South Africa, the taxation through public utilities by charging prices higher than are

[1] *Essays in Taxation* (9th ed., New York, 1921), p. 62.

[2] See the comprehensive charts on property taxes, especially those of Professor Mabel A. Magee, of Wells College, on Constitutional limitations on municipal taxes, Statutory limitations on property taxes of cities, towns, villages and townships of certain States and on local property tax exemptions. *Tax Systems of the World* (The Tax Research Foundation, 7th ed., Chicago, 205 W. Monroe Street), pp. 90-133.

required to cover costs including depreciation of all kinds. Federal and State Governments might also assist with grants-in-aid for unemployment relief and more and better education. The entire question of exemptions also requires careful examination. This does not refer to exemptions merely of individuals but also of Governments holding property other than commercial or industrial enterprises (which should be taxed as private property). Governments may make *ex gratia* payments based on the benefits from municipal services as well as on the nature of the property. It should not be difficult to lay down general principles on exemptions and on the methods governing the payments. A strict interpretation of property tax exemptions and a detailed examination of possible new sources of independent revenue are much overdue. Greater co-operation between Federal and State Governments with a view to grants-in-aid should also be worked out.

Consumption Taxes

One of the most arresting facts in the table of comparative tax structures (Table III above) is the overlapping jurisdiction in regard to consumption taxes (Group IV of the table). These consumption taxes in some of the Federations studied are an important part of the whole, and this is especially the case in India and Australia, although in the latter the States' share is small. These taxes are in general regressive, *i.e.* they take a larger percentage from low incomes than from high, although as we have seen if sales taxes are omitted from necessities such as food and if luxuries bear a high rate of tax, there is a degree of progression even in regard to taxes on commodities. The importance of this group of taxes in the present consideration is not whether they are regressive, as indeed they are, or whether they are on costs rather than on surplus, but is in regard to the conflicts caused by various layers of Government levying the same tax. The solution of conflicts in the taxation of selective sales taxes such as those on liquor, tobacco and gasoline, or of general sales taxes or turnover taxes, depends greatly on historical and geographical factors in each Federation. Federations often cover large areas which differ considerably. In the co-ordination of revenues this must never be lost sight of. As a general rule the wider the jurisdiction the more effective the administration of the tax. This does not mean that all taxes should be federalised as far as practicable, since what is aimed at in federal finance is an integrated system. It is worth repeating that in every Federation there are fundamental conflicts, and when conflicts are of this nature they do not admit of any single solution.

These general principles may be illustrated by several of the taxes in

Group IV, mainly consumption taxes, that are levied by Federal, State and Local Authorities. Where the Federal Government and State Governments tax liquor there are almost certainly differences of outlook in regard to the liquor question and this naturally causes differential taxes in the units. Not infrequently there are inter-State barriers to the trade. The history of the taxation of alcoholic liquor in the United States may be cited as an example. Under prohibition the attitude of the States was certainly not uniform, and in 1934 Federal collection and State sharing was definitely negatived. The best method is to have reciprocal legislation among the States and by conference and otherwise to understand the other State's point of view. One thing is very clear. There can be no question of one layer of Government, say the Federal or the State, taking to itself the field of liquor taxation. It is a suitable source of revenue for all three layers — Federal, State (or Province) and Local Authority. Similarly, tobacco has, in some Federations in recent years, been a popular source of revenue for both State and Local Authorities. Here, however, there is room for Federal collection and State sharing as (1) there is danger of evasion and (2) some units do not get what they should from the tax. Even in the United States to-day State tobacco administration is only between 70 and 80 per cent effective.[1] Each Federation should weigh up the disadvantage, the curtailment of State independence, with the advantages such as productivity and efficient administration, and see whether this would not result in far more grist being brought to the State mill and the mill of Local Authorities.

Another tax which overlaps is the stock transfer tax or stamp duty, levied by the Federal Government and State Governments. On balance, it might be said that the taxation of stock transfers may be left to both Federal and State authorities. In the United States, however, where the Federal Government and seven States occupy this field, it is held that the combined Federal and State taxes are levied without regard to each other and the combined tax is excessive. It has been suggested that a credit should be given for State taxes against the Federal tax. The Intergovernmental Fiscal Relations Committee think such a credit might give rise to the States exploiting this tax. It doubts if the burden of the combined taxes is excessive, and even if it were this could be solved by eliminating the crudities in the present laws. "The Stock transfer tax," it concludes, "because of its incidence, is best suited for national exploitation, and on this ground separation of sources, with the tax to be levied by the Federal Government, might be recommended. But New York has a strong proprietary interest in its stock transfer tax and is not likely to surrender it except under considerable pressure." The tax is of far

[1] Cf. Intergovernmental Fiscal Relations Committee's Report, vol. i, chap. iv.

greater importance to New York than to the Federal Government, and the Committee concludes that in the circumstances forbearance, with most of the restraint to be exercised by New York State, is recommended.

In recent years a tax suitable for States or Provinces has been the taxation of gasoline and motor vehicles. For the upkeep of roads and other purposes it could be further developed in some Federations. The growth of the gasoline tax in the United States has made it possible for the States to relinquish the field of property taxation in favour of Local Authorities, but it could be further developed. Some States have a tax of only 2 or 3 cents a gallon while others have 6 or 7 cents, the average being 3·85 cents a gallon.[1] The Federal Government as in other Federations is interested in the taxation of gasoline. It levies a motor vehicle use tax ostensibly to finance Federal highway aid. The State motor vehicle taxes are paid by users of the roads. The Federal Government should vacate the field of motor vehicle taxation and it might be possible for the States to be left with the entire taxation of gasoline, except perhaps with the exception of gasoline used in aviation as has been suggested.[2] The solution of the conflict will vary with each Federation, but gasoline is a specially suitable head of revenue for State or Provincial Governments, and indeed for Local Governments, such as cities, in search of funds.

The revenue possibilities of general sales or turnover taxes have proved to be very great and all Governments, Federal, State or Provinces and Local Authorities, have competed in this field. The Federal Governments in the Dominion of Canada and the Commonwealth Government of Australia have found the sales tax to be a good revenue-producer and easy to administer, although evasion has to be carefully guarded against. The Federal Government of the United States has not so far levied this tax notwithstanding the fact that twenty-three State Governments have adopted it, and it is not improbable that some of the twenty-five remaining States may find it a useful and much-needed source of revenue after the war. Similarly in Canada many Governments may be compelled to use it. The Province of Saskatchewan and the city of Montreal have already found that its virtues greatly outweigh its defects. The city of New York introduced a retail sales tax in 1934 and found its revenue possibilities very great. The experience of Federations in regard to sales taxation has been the same as Germany, the U.S.S.R. and other European countries which introduced a turnover tax since the war of 1914–18 when the tax was rediscovered. Sales taxation is one of the oldest of taxes and can be

[1] For State gasoline tax rates *vide* pp. 168 and 224, *Tax Systems of the World* (7th ed., Chicago, 205 W. Monroe Street).

[2] Cf. Report of Intergovernmental Fiscal Relations Committee, vol. i, chap. iv.

traced back to Athens, Egypt and Rome. It was introduced into Spain in 1342 and was called the Alcavala. Adam Smith, it will be remembered, criticised its costliness of collection and the inconvenience which it gave to the taxpayer, but had he been living to-day he would have been struck by the low rate of tax as compared with the rates that obtained at the time when he wrote. The 8 per cent sales tax in Canada in the lower ranges of incomes took in 1940 from 3½ to 5½ per cent of income, a higher percentage than in other countries, before the war, and a percentage not very different from the percentage taken by the pay-roll or similar tax to finance social expenditures elsewhere, and Canada has so far introduced no such tax to finance expenditures of this nature.[1] The turnover tax of the U.S.S.R., in the Soviet Union Budget of 1939 amounted to no less than R.92,500 millions out of a total tax revenue of R.98,500 millions or, including health and insurance contributions (R.7000 millions) and State industries (R.17,500 millions), R.123,000 millions. The tax, which was established by a law of 26th July 1921, is divided between the National and Local Governments and is collected under two main heads subdivided into three and four sub-groups respectively. The main heads are " Private business and industrial occupations " and " Enterprises of the socialised sector ". Under the former small artisans, small traders " with push-carts, stands, mats on the ground or floor, not using other help but members of their own families, or using not over 2-3 workers ", innkeepers in villages, petty brokers and agents, etc., are included, and under the latter State monopolies, State enterprises not members of the monopolies, mixed corporations (*i.e.* in which part of the capital belongs to the State and part to private interests) and co-operative members of the General Co-operative system are taxed. In the case of small artisans, etc., the tax is arbitrarily fixed for each group and each locality within limits prescribed by law, and in other cases on gross receipts. The rates vary according to groups and industries or commodities. Invalids are exempted, as are sales from one enterprise of the socialised sector to the others if for the purpose of sale. The assessment is made by the People's Commissariat of Finance of the U.S.S.R. or of separate republics respectively or Regional or District Officers of the corresponding Commissariats of Finance. The State Bank and local offices of the Commissariat of Finance are responsible for the collection of the tax, which is shared on

[1] Before the war Canada was the only self-governing Dominion without a compulsory contributory social insurance scheme of any sort, although there were provincial workmen's compensation schemes and non-contributory pensions for the aged at 70 and the blind at 40. In July 1941 a national unemployment insurance scheme, now covering over three million workers, came into operation. In March 1943 the Canadian House of Commons set up an all-party Special Committee to report on a national plan of social security.

a percentage basis. In 1937, the respective Budgets of the Federated Republics were given shares varying from 15·4 to 88·2 per cent, the balance going to the All-Union Budget.[1]

Federations in years to come are likely to extend the use of sales taxation such as a retail sales tax because they are productive of revenue and convenient. No objection as a rule is taken by the taxpayer, who regards them as part of the price of the product. As we have seen, they are regressive, those on the lowest incomes spending a greater proportion of their income on food, clothing and other necessaries than those on the higher incomes. For this reason, however, in times of depression, since the poor are not exempted, the taxes are productive. They are good from the administrative and from the tax compliance point of view. On the other hand, it is sometimes argued that the tax is not a good tax since the tax is pyramided. If it is collected from the manufacturer, each subsequent dealer in it calculates his profit on the price which he pays, and this price includes the tax, so that, if the tax takes a percentage of the manufacturer's price, the ultimate taxpayer pays approximately the same percentage of the retail price. With a general retail sales tax this is not a very serious criticism when revenue is required. The main point to emphasise is the necessity of getting a complete list of vendors, State and municipal, and of keeping this severely up to date as old businesses disappear and new businesses take their place. The co-ordination most suitable for sales taxes in a Federation is without doubt joint administration. This not only minimises evasion but makes it possible to have a single system of returns and of control. The Federal-State Authority would be an ideal body to carry this out.[2]

With the development of social security after the war and the provision of funds to implement this policy it is necessary to examine briefly the pay-roll taxes of the United States. Whether we agree or not with the explanation of the high sales tax in Canada, as suggested by the Royal Commission on Dominion-Provincial Relations, that it renders unnecessary a special levy on the part of the Dominion Government to meet the cost of social security services, it is advisable from the viewpoint of conflicts to examine the very productive pay-roll tax. The tax in 1940 was the most productive after the income tax of individuals and corporations in Federal revenues and in State taxes came second, being outstripped only by gasoline taxes. In 1940 the Federal Social Security (1935) Old-Age Benefits receipts amounted to $605 millions and Unemployment Compensation, etc., $233 millions. The State pay-roll (unemployment insurance) receipts

[1] See also Paul Haensel, "Recent Changes in the Soviet Tax System," *Taxes*, (Commerce Clearing House, Inc., Chicago), Nov. 1941.

[2] For further discussion, see chap. xxv (Sales or Turnover Taxes), vol. ii, *Science of Public Finance*, G. Findlay Shirras (London, Macmillan & Co.).

were $851 millions. Old-age benefits therefore brought in $605 millions and unemployment insurance $1084 millions — a total of $1689 millions.[1] In the same year the Federal old-age benefit was 2 per cent of the pay-roll, half paid by the employer and therefore added to his costs, and half deducted from the worker's wage. The unemployment benefit tax was 3 per cent of pay-rolls and is a combined Federal and State levy. In some States the tax is somewhat higher than 3 per cent. As in the estate tax the Federal Government grants a credit and all States take advantage of this pay-roll tax credit; even Nevada (which forgoes the Estate tax credit) has agreed to this scheme of achieving uniformity. The Government does not contribute to social security in order to lighten the burden on the pay-roll and therefore on the employer. If the Government were to do so, differential payments according to wages would have to end as such payments could hardly be paid from tax revenues.

The main lesson of pay-roll taxes apart from the crediting device is the great productivity of the tax. If this system of taxing for social security were to be introduced in other Federations the following points should be considered: (1) Should the tax be completely centralised so that administrative costs as well as the costs of compliance may be kept at a minimum? (2) If the tax is not centralised, how can the credit system be best introduced with a view to the co-ordination of unemployment compensation? Could not the Federal Government lay down minimum standards in regard to tax rates, benefits or reserves? In some States in the United States the threat of inter-State competition (to counteract which the crediting system was introduced) has reappeared in the form of merit rating schemes by which firms with good employment records obtain a pay-roll advantage. Unfair competition of this sort leads to the undermining of standards, as the Committee on Intergovernmental Fiscal Relations has emphasised. It has sometimes been suggested that the rates fixed should be increased beyond the cost for social security. This is indeed possible but it would change the whole object of the tax.

IV. Conclusions

1. The main conclusion of this Enquiry is that by an analysis of the tax structures of the Federal Governments of the United States, Canada, Australia, South Africa and India it has been possible to judge the extent to which taxes are progressive and which are on surplus rather than on costs. In many ways this has necessitated much careful investigation and analysis. The results, it must be admitted, have been worth while. The division of tax revenues among the main layers of government —

[1] For details see pp. 37 and 114, *Tax Yields* (Tax Institute, University of Pennsylvania, Philadelphia, 1941).

Federal, State or Provincial and Local Authorities — in the federations studied has shown (*a*) the wide differences that exist and (*b*) the need for reform of some taxes that are at present levied by the various Governments. Table III in Chapter IX on p. 250 shows at a glance the revenue systems of the United States, Canada, Australia, South Africa and India classified under the following heads — progressive taxes, taxes on property, taxes on business and other taxes, mainly consumption taxes. There are striking differences between Federations, some Federations having a greater degree of progression than others, whereas others such as India and, to a lesser degree, Australia favour taxes on consumption which are, therefore, in the main regressive and on costs.

2. The tax structures, however, must be studied in relation to expenditures and here again the differences between Federations are noteworthy. Since the great depression which set in after 1929 and continued well into the thirties there has been increased expenditures on the social services. Table II in Chapter IX on p. 247 summarises the direction of public expenditures classified under the primary functions of government, and the secondary functions which are subdivided again under (*a*) Social Services, (*b*) Developmental and (*c*) Miscellaneous Secondary Functions. Grants are also shown. It is therefore possible to form a judgment of the public expenditures as a whole for each Federation and at the same time of their distribution among the layers of Government. Data for war years are given as they are for revenues in Parts I and III.

3. The third most important set of conclusions is that dealing with the indebtedness of Governments. The burden of public debts has been examined in each Federation and it is clear that the burden in some Federations differs considerably. Thus, in the case of India, the debt is not only almost entirely internal — India since the war has turned from debtor to creditor status — but it is productive to a degree higher than that in any other country of the world. It is important, too, to note the distribution of the debt among the layers of Government. Many valuable lessons may be learnt from a comparison of the public debts and from their relative burden as expressed as a percentage of the national income. The effect of war on public debts is also of capital importance.

4. A major conclusion of this Enquiry is that no one plan of complete co-ordination for a Federal financial system is possible because of differences of economic conditions, historical development and so on, and because of the varying degree of opposition arising from a conflict of interests between the Centre and other units of Government. It is of interest to note that the Intergovernmental Fiscal Relations Committee of the American Treasury has made this a major recommendation in its Report.[1]

[1] See Appendix II.

5. Since Federal finance is in essence dynamic and not static, constant readjustment of Federal-State-Local financial relations is called for.

6. A Federal-State Authority should be set up in each Federation. This official body will be of vital assistance in furthering the revolutionary change of outlook so much overdue, a change of attitude in all layers of Government and among all officials and non-officials in Federal, State (or Provincial) and Local Authorities. The main functions of the Federal-State Authority include (*a*) the co-ordinating of financial relations between the layers of Government ; (*b*) advice of a continuous nature and control of the practical application of this new co-ordination and co-operation by (i) administering overlapping taxes, and (ii) encouraging inter-State (or inter-Provincial) co-operation and thereby eliminating competition among Federal, State (or Provincial) and Local Authorities ; conflicts from overlapping taxes and the multiplicity of taxing authorities competing for revenues are the greatest weaknesses of Federations to-day ; (*c*) research in regard to specific taxes and financial policy generally since more and better research is necessary to get at the factors, peculiar to each Federation, upon which co-ordination and co-operation are possible ; and (*d*) the possible ultimate administration by the Authority of some of the taxes through delegated powers and the introduction of joint returns and joint audits to reduce costs of collection and of tax compliance.

7. Federal finance is far too serious a matter to be left to the experts. A sound and modernised Federal finance requires a revolutionary change of attitude which must be shared not merely by all layers of Government and by officials but by non-officials and non-experts. Non-statutory bodies, such as the meetings of Provincial Premiers in Canada and of State Premiers in Australia with their respective Federal Governments, the Council of State Governments in the United States and the Tax Research bodies must continue their activities in every possible direction. Universities must also take a greater part in the teaching of and in research into the science of Public Finance.

8. The importance of studying taxes, public expenditures and public debt in relation to the national income, the trade or business cycles and the question of full employment has been and still needs to be stressed.

9. The necessity of more comprehensive and accurate statistics has showed itself in many ways from the beginning of this Enquiry. In some Federations more up-to-date statistics in regard to Local Authorities, especially in the Commonwealth of Australia and in India, and in regard to the separation of capital and revenue accounts on a scientific basis are much overdue.

The most important lesson perhaps of this long and difficult Enquiry is perhaps just this. No one plan of co-ordination is possible for all

Federations. On the contrary, in the struggle to get at hidden uniformities, to understand men's actions in Federal finance rather than to bewail or to denounce them, it is necessary to follow the patient and tedious method of research, an unspectacular method it is true, but the most profitable. This shows how impossible it is to offer any one solution of the Federal financial problem. The vitality of the great and friendly republic the United States, of Canada and of Australia, not to mention the Union of South Africa and to a less degree India, makes one optimistic of the future of these Federations in the sphere of their internal intergovernmental financial relations.

PART III

LIST OF UNITED STATES TABLES

Table 1 U.S.A., NATIONAL GOVERNMENT, ORDINARY RECEIPTS, 1937–38

	$ millions		Per cent
1. *Taxes on Income* (other than Social Security taxes):			
Income tax	2634·6		42·2
Unjust enrichment tax [1]	5·7		0·1
Total	2640·3		42·3
2. *Taxes under the Social Security Act and upon Carriers and their Employees* [2]	754·6	Internal Revenue 5674·4 90·9	12·1
3. *Other Taxes:* [3]			
Miscellaneous internal revenue	2279·5		36·5
Customs	359·2		5·8
Panama Canal tolls, etc.	25·1		0·4
Seigniorage	35·6		0·5
Total	2699·4		43·2
4. *Interest and Other Receipts from Securities*	65·6		1·1
5. *Miscellaneous Receipts*	81·9		1·3
TOTAL RECEIPTS, GENERAL AND SPECIAL ACCOUNTS [4]	6241·8		100·0

[1] See Chapter III, Table VII, note 4.
[2] Social insurance contributions of employers and employed.
[3] Excludes a few small items included under Miscellaneous Receipts.
[4] In order to obtain a figure more comparable to the total given in Chapter III, Table VII, p 42. ($5277 millions), add Internal Revenue other than Social Security taxes ($4920 millions) and Customs ($359 millions). The resulting total is $5279 millions, or 84·6 per cent of total receipts. If Social Security taxes are included, the figures become $6034 millions, or 96·7 per cent of total receipts.

Source.—Statistical Abstract of the United States, 1940.

Table 2 U.S.A., NATIONAL GOVERNMENT ORDINARY EXPENDITURES 1937–38

	$ millions	Per cent
1. *Primary Functions :*		
Legislation, administration and justice [1, 2]	500·1	6·6
Pensions [3, 4]	655·0	8·6
Debt services	926·3	12·1
Defence [2]	974·2	12·8
Total, Primary Functions	3055·6	40·1
2. *Secondary Functions :*		
(1) *Social services :* [5]		
Recovery and relief	2237·6	29·3
Social Security Act [6]	332·0	4·4
Old-age Reserve Account [4]	387·0	5·1
Railroad Retirement [4, 7]	145·0	1·9
Sub-total, Social Services	3101·6	40·7
(2) *Developmental :*		
Post Office [8]	47·2	0·6
Public buildings [2]	60·8	0·8
Public highways [2]	152·0	2·0
Shipping Board	3·0	..
River and harbour work and flood control [2]	165·0	2·2
Panama Canal	11·4	0·1
Tennessee Valley Authority	42·0	0·5
Rural electrification administration	10·6	0·1
Reclamation projects [2]	39·9	0·5
Civilian Conservation Corps [2]	325·0	4·3
Agriculture [2, 4, 9]	473·0	6·2
Public works, etc. [2, 4, 10]	133·7	1·8
Sub-total, developmental	1463·6	19·1
(3) *Miscellaneous :* District of Columbia (U.S. share)	5·0	0·1
Total, Secondary Functions	4570·2	59·9
GRAND TOTAL [11]	7625·8	100·0

[1] Departmental expenditure (excluding expenditure of the Post Office Department, the Department of Agriculture and the Shipping Board, but including non-military expenditure of the War Department) $441 millions, and refunds of receipts (other than to States of taxes collected under the Social Security Act) $59·1 millions. Departmental expenditure includes several small items which would have been classified under Secondary Functions, especially education, had comparable details been available.

[2] Additional expenditure included under Recovery and Relief.

[3] Veterans Administration ($582 millions) and Government employees retirement fund ($73 millions).

[4] Includes revolving funds and transfers to trust accounts.

[5] A few small items (*e.g.* education) are included under Legislation, Administration and Justice. (See footnote 1.)

[6] Administrative expenses and grants to States ($291 millions) and refunds to States of taxes collected under the Act ($41 millions).

[7] Part of the Social Security system, not pensions to Government employees.

[8] Departmental expenditure (Post Office Department) $3·2 millions and postal deficiency $44 millions.

[9]

Department of Agriculture	112·7	$ millions
Agricultural Adjustment Programme	361·6	,,
Farm Tenant Act	3·1	,,
Farm Credit Administration	8·2	,,
Total	485·6	,,
Less excess of credits on revolving funds :		
Farm Credit Administration	8·4	,,
Other	4·2	,,
Total	12·6	,,
Net Total, Agriculture	473·0	,,

[10] Loans and grants to States, municipalities, railways, etc., and U.S. Housing Authority ($165,000).

[11] Total, General and Special Amounts, less debt retirements.

Source.—Statistical Abstract of the United States, 1940.

Table 3

U.S.A., STATE REVENUES, 1937 [1]

	$ millions	Per cent
A. TAXES:		
GROUP I. *Progressive Taxes:*		
Individual income	164·2	4·0
Inheritance and estate	114·9	2·8
Total	279·1	6·8
GROUP II. *Taxes on Property:*		
General	206·4	5·0
Selective	47·9	1·2
Special	119·1	2·9
Total	373·4	9·1
GROUP III. *Taxes on Business:*		
Corporation income	81·0	2·0
Other business	304·9	7·4
Total	385·9	9·4
GROUP IV. *Mainly Consumption Taxes:*		
Motor fuel	649·3	15·9
General sales and use	431·0	10·5
All other sales	208·4	5·1
Severance	44·1	1·1
Motor vehicles	309·5	7·6
All other non-business licences and permits	17·4	0·4
Poll	4·7	0·1
Miscellaneous	55·9	1·4
Total	1720·3	42·1
Unemployment compensation	346·7	8·5
Total, Tax Revenues	3105·4	75·9
B. NON-TAXES:		
Special assessments and special charges	2·8	0·1
Charges for current services	179·1	4·4
Contributions from public service enterprises	50·8	1·2
Grants [2]	585·4	14·3
All other	169·7	4·1
Total, Non-Tax Revenues	987·8	24·1
GRAND TOTAL	4093·2	100·0

[1] Excluding public service enterprises.

[2] Made up as follows:

From minor civil divisions	$20,613,000
From Federal Government:	
Highways	$317,409,000
Education	24,844,000
Public health	12,933,000
Relief	155,061,000
Unemployment compensation administration	9,236,000
All other	45,323,000
Total	$564,806,000
Total	$585,419,000

Source.—Statistical Abstract of the United States, 1940.

Table 4 U.S.A., STATE EXPENDITURES FROM REVENUE, 1937 [1]

($ millions)

	Direct Expenditure	Grants to Minor Civil Divisions	Total
1. *Primary Functions :*			
General administration, legislation and justice	151·0	..	151·0
Protection to person and property	102·2	3·9	106·1
Correction	65·5	..	65·5
Debt services	122·0	..	122·0
Total	440·7	3·9	444·6
2. *Secondary Functions :*			
(1) *Social Services :*			
Education	193·7	636·3	830·0
Public health [2]	224·1	2·2	226·3
Relief ("charities")	391·2	220·4	611·6
Sub-total	809·0	858·9	1667·9
(2) *Developmental :*			
Highways	248·3	209·8	458·1
Development and conservation of natural resources	77·1	0·8	77·9
Contributions to public service enterprises	2·6	..	2·6
Sub-total	328·0	210·6	538·6
(3) *Outlays* [3]	711·9	..	711·9
(4) *Miscellaneous*	65·3	35·0	100·3
Total	1914·2	1104·5	3018·7
GRAND TOTAL	2354·9	1108·4	3463·3

[1] Excluding public service enterprises.
[2] Includes recreation.
[3] Expenditure of a capital nature out of revenue, *e.g.* for purchase and improvement of land, erection of new buildings, or purchases to increase the collection of libraries.

Source.—Statistical Abstract of the United States, 1940.

able 5 U.S.A., STATE EXPENDITURES FROM REVENUE, 1937 [1]

(Percentage distribution)

	Division into Direct Expenditure and Grants			Percentage Distribution of All Expenditures		
	Direct Expenditure	Grants to Minor Civil Divisions	Total	Direct Expenditure	Grants to Minor Civil Divisions	Total
1. *Primary Functions :*						
General administration, legislation and justice	100	..	100	6·4	..	4·3
Protection to person and property	96	4	100	4·3	0·3	3·1
Correction	100	..	100	2·8	..	1·9
Debt services	100	..	100	5·2	..	3·5
Total	99	1	100	18·7	0·3	12·8
2. *Secondary Functions :*						
(1) *Social Services :*						
Education	23	77	100	8·3	57·4	24·0
Public health	99	1	100	9·5	0·2	6·5
Relief (" charities ")	64	36	100	16·6	19·9	17·7
Sub-total	49	51	100	34·4	77·5	48·2
(2) *Developmental :*						
Highways	54	46	100	10·5	18·9	13·2
Development and conservation of natural resources	99	1	100	3·3	0·1	2·3
Contributions to public service enterprises	100	..	100	0·1	..	0·1
Sub-total	61	39	100	13·9	19·0	15·6
(3) *Outlays*	100	..	100	30·2	..	20·6
(4) *Miscellaneous*	65	35	100	2·8	3·2	2·8
Total	63	37	100	81·3	99·7	87·2
GRAND TOTAL	68	32	100	100·0	100·0	100·0

[1] Excluding public service enterprises. See also footnotes to Table 4.

Table 6 U.S.A., LOCAL GOVERNMENT REVENUES AND EXPENDITURES, 1932 [1]

($ millions)

	Counties	Cities, Towns, Villages, Boroughs	Other Local	Total
A. REVENUES:				
1. *Taxation:*				
General and selective property	877·1	2057·5	1426·7	4361·3
Inheritance	1·5	3·7	0·3	5·5
Income	1·6	49·6	2·7	53·9
All other special	3·2	19·3	2·6	25·1
Poll	5·3	4·6	3·2	13·1
Licences and permits	132·1	116·6	8·3	257·0
Total revenue from taxation	1020·8	2251·3	1443·8	4715·9 [2]
2. *Other Sources of Revenue:*				
Special assessments [3]	32·2	226·4	36·5	295·1
Fines, forfeits and escheats	10·3	19·4	0·8	30·5
Grants	139·1	137·8	341·7	618·6
Donations, gifts and pension assessments	2·5	33·3	2·9	38·7
Highway privileges, rents and interest	19·1	131·0	18·0	168·1
Charges for current services	89·0	87·4	80·9	257·3
Earnings of public service enterprises	0·8	487·0	32·0	519·8
Total Revenue from Other Sources	293·0	1122·3	512·8	1928·1
TOTAL, LOCAL GOVERNMENT REVENUES	1313·8	3373·6	1956·6	6644·0
B. EXPENDITURES:				
1. *Operation and Maintenance of General Government:*				
General administrative, legislative and judicial	251·2	..	..	..
Protection to person and property	44·2	..	..	..
Health and sanitation	32·8	..	..	..
Highways	236·4	..	..	..
Charities, Hospitals and corrections	182·1	..	..	..
Schools	178·4	..	..	..
Libraries	3·8	..	..	..
Recreation	7·6	..	..	..
Miscellaneous	44·7	..	..	..
Total Operation and Maintenance of General Government	981·2	2070·2 [4]	1496·3 [4]	4547·7 [4]
2. *Operation and Maintenance of Public Service Enterprises*	0·5	282·9	18·2	301·6
3. *Interest*	118·9	424·1	188·6	731·6
4. *Outlays* [5]	311·2	817·4	347·2	1475·8
TOTAL, LOCAL GOVERNMENT EXPENDITURES	1411·8	3594·6	2050·3	7056·7

[1] Fiscal year ending on a date between 1st July 1931 and 30th June 1932.
[2] Of this total, cities of 100,000 or more inhabitants account for $1841·7 millions, other local authorities for $2874·2 millions.
[3] Receipts from property owners to meet costs of cleaning streets, sidewalks, etc., and receipts from assessment certificates when issued against individual owners and not in the name of the civil division.
[4] Details not available.
[5] Expenditure of a capital nature out of revenue, *e.g.* for purchase and improvement of land, erection of new buildings, extension of water-supply systems, or purchases to increase the collection of libraries.

Source.—Financial Statistics of State and Local Governments, 1932.

Table 7 U.S.A., LOCAL GOVERNMENT REVENUES 1932 [1]

(Percentage distribution)

	Counties	Cities, etc.[2]	Other Local	Total
(*a*) As given in Table 6 :				
1. *Taxation :*				
General and selective property	66·8	61·0	72·9	65·6
Inheritance	0·1	0·1	..	0·1
Income	0·1	1·5	0·1	0·8
All other special	0·2	0·6	0·1	0·4
Poll	0·4	0·1	0·2	0·2
Licences and permits	10·1	3·4	0·5	3·9
Total Revenue from Taxation	77·7	66·7	73·8	71·0
2. *Other Sources of Revenue :*				
Special assessments	2·4	6·7	1·9	4·4
Fines, forfeits and escheats	0·8	0·6	..	0·5
Grants	10·6	4·1	17·5	9·3
Donations, gifts and pension assessments	0·2	1·0	0·1	0·6
Highway privileges, rents and interest	1·4	3·9	0·9	2·5
Charges for current services	6·8	2·6	4·2	3·9
Earnings of public service enterprises	0·1	14·4	1·6	7·8
Total Revenue from Other Sources	22·3	33·3	26·2	29·0
TOTAL, LOCAL GOVERNMENT REVENUES	100·0	100·0	100·0	100·0
(*b*) By groups :				
I. *Progressive Taxes :*				
Income	0·1	1·5	0·1	0·8
Inheritance	0·1	0·1	..	0·1
Total	0·2	1·6	0·1	0·9
II. *Taxes on Property :*				
General and selective	66·8	61·0	72·9	65·6
All other special	0·2	0·6	0·1	0·4
Total	67·0	61·6	73·0	66·0
III. and IV. *Taxes on Business, Consumption and Miscellaneous :*[2]				
Licences and permits	10·1	3·4	0·5	3·9
Poll	0·4	0·1	0·2	0·2
Total	10·5	3·5	0·7	4·1
TOTAL, TAX REVENUE	77·7	66·7	73·8	71·0
Non-Tax Revenue :[3]				
Grants	10·6	4·1	17·5	9·3
Public service enterprises	0·1	14·4	1·6	7·8
All other	11·6	14·8	7·1	11·9
TOTAL, NON-TAX REVENUE	22·3	33·3	26·2	29·0
GRAND TOTAL	100·0	100·0	100·0	100·0

[1] Fiscal year ending on a date between 1st July 1931 and 30th June 1932.
[2] Cities, towns, villages, boroughs.
[3] For comparison with other chapters, add Public Service Enterprises and All Other Non-tax Revenue to Groups III and IV.

Table 8 U.S.A., LOCAL GOVERNMENT EXPENDITURES, 1932[1]

(Percentage distribution)

	Counties	Cities, etc.[2]	Other Local	Total
1. *Operation and Maintenance of General Government:*				
General administrative, legislative and judicial	17·8	..	..	..
Protection to person and property	3·1	..	..	..
Health and sanitation	2·3	..	..	..
Highways	16·7	..	..	..
Charities, hospitals and corrections	12·9	..	..	..
Schools	12·7	..	..	..
Libraries	0·3	..	..	..
Recreation	0·5	..	..	..
Miscellaneous	3·2	..	..	..
Total, Operation and Maintenance of General Government	69·5	57·6[3]	73·0[3]	64·4[3]
2. *Operation and Maintenance of Public Service Enterprises*	..	7·9	0·9	4·3
3. *Interest*	8·4	11·8	9·2	10·4
4. *Outlays*	22·1	22·7	16·9	20·9
TOTAL, LOCAL GOVERNMENT EXPENDITURES	100·0	100·0	100·0	100·0
Percentage share in total expenditures of the various classes of local government	20·0	50·9	29·1	100·0

[1] Fiscal year ending on a date between 1st July 1931 and 30th June 1932.
[2] Cities, towns, villages, boroughs.
[3] Details not available.

Table 9 REVENUES AND COST PAYMENTS OF CITIES OF 100,000 OR MORE INHABITANTS, 1937 [1]

	$ millions	Per cent
A. REVENUES :		
1. *General Government :*		
General property taxes . .	1767·0	56·8
Other local taxes and licences .	172·6	5·5
Shared taxes	97·5	3·1
Grants	405·0	13·0
Service charges for current services.	84·0	2·7
Miscellaneous	182·2	5·9
Total	2708·3	87·0
2. *Public Service Enterprises* . .	403·6	13·0
GRAND TOTAL	3111·9	100·0
B. COST PAYMENTS :		
1. *Primary Functions :*		
General administration, legislation and justice . . .	159·6	5·2
Police	192·7	6·3
Fire	122·1	4·0
Interest (General Government) .	222·6	7·2
Total	697·0	22·7
2. *Secondary Functions :*		
(i) Social Services :		
Education . . .	596·1	19·4
Public health [2] . . .	256·1	8·3
Charities [3] . . .	332·1	10·8
Sub-total . . .	1184·3	38·5
(ii) Developmental :		
Highways . . .	106·3	3·4
Public service enterprises (including interest and outlays)	459·4	14·9
Sub-total . . .	565·7	18·3
(iii) Outlays [4] (General Government)	372·9	12·1
(iv) Miscellaneous . . .	260·1	8·4
Total . . .	2383·0	77·3
GRAND TOTAL	3080·0	100·0

[1] The figures cover the government of the city corporation proper and also independent school districts, sanitary districts and other independent districts practically co-extensive with the cities, and also include a percentage of the financial statistics of the county Governments in which there are cities having over 300,000 population.
[2] Includes recreation.
[3] Mainly poor relief.
[4] Expenditure of a capital nature and of revenue, *e.g.* for purchase and improvement of land, erection of new buildings, extension of water-supply systems, or purchases to increase the collection of libraries.

Source.—Statistical Abstract of the United States, 1940.

Table 10 U.S.A., GRANTS AND SHARED TAXES, 1936–37

	$ millions		Per cent
A. *State Revenues:*			
Taxes (including social insurance contributions)	3105·4		75·9
Grants [1]	585·4		14·3
Other non-tax revenue	402·3		9·8
Total, State Revenues	4093·1		100·0
B. *State Expenditures:*			
Other than grants	2354·8		68·0
Grants to minor civil divisions	1108·5		32·0
Total, State Expenditures	3463·3		100·0
	$ millions		
C. *State Aid to Minor Civil Divisions, by Purpose and Type of Aid:*	Grants	Shared Taxes (local shares)	Total
General purposes	35·0	145·0	180·0
Protection to person and property	3·9	..	3·9
Highways	209·8	92·2	302·0
Development and conservation of natural resources	0·9	..	0·9
Health and sanitation	2·2	..	2·2
Charities	220·4	0·1	220·5
Schools	636·3	6·3	642·6
Miscellaneous	..	2·6	2·6
Undistributed	..	13·8	13·8
Total	1108·5	260·0	1368·5
	Per cent		
General purposes	3·2	55·8	13·1
Protection to person and property	0·3	..	0·3
Highways	18·9	35·5	22·0
Development and conservation of natural resources	0·1	..	0·1
Health and sanitation	0·2	..	0·2
Charities	19·9	..	16·1
Schools	57·4	2·4	47·0
Miscellaneous	..	1·0	0·2
Undistributed	..	5·3	1·0
Total	100·0	100·0	100·0
Percentage distribution of total aid between grants and shared taxes	81·0	19·0	100·0

Table 10—(*continued*)

D. *Revenues of Cities of 100,000 or more Inhabitants* :	$ millions	Per cent
Local taxes	1939·6	71·6
Shared taxes	97·5	3·6
Grants	405·0	15·0
Other sources of revenue	266·2	9·8
Total revenues	2708·3	100·0

E. *Social Security and Public Assistance* :

Federal expenditure under this head, apart from such heads as N.R.A., A.A.A. or C.C.C., is mainly administered by grants to States.

During the *fiscal year 1939–40* the following advances were certified by the Social Security Board to the Secretary of the Treasury for Public Assistance and for Administration of the Unemployment Compensation Laws and State Employment Services :

($ millions)

	Public Assistance				Unemployment Compensation and State Employment Services			Total
	Old-age Assistance	Dependent Children	Aid to the Blind	Total	Social Security Act	Wagner-Peyser Act	Total	
States and District of Columbia	230·8	45·9	6·2	282·9	58·1	3·3	61·4	344·3
Territories	0·3	0·2	..	0·5	0·2	..	0·2	0·7
Total	231·1	46·1	6·2	283·4	58·3	3·3	61·6	345·0

[1] Made up as follows : From minor civil divisions $20,613,000

From Federal Government :	
Highways	$317,409,000
Education	24,844,000
Public health	12,933,000
Relief	155,061,000
Unemployment compensation administration	9,236,000
All other	45,323,000
Total from Federal Government	$564,806,000
Total State revenue from grants	$585,419,000

Source.—Statistical Abstract of the United States, 1940.

Table 11 U.S.A., REVENUES OF ALL GOVERNMENTS, BY REGIONS,[1] 1932 AND 1937

	$ millions		Percentage Increase
	1932	1937	
National Government	2,005·7	5,293·8	164
State Governments : [2]			
1. North-eastern States	759·8	1,424·5	87
2. South-eastern States	358·5	607·0	69
3. Middle States	558·1	1,110·9	99
4. Mountain and Great Plain States	155·5	224·6	44
5. South-western States	174·7	303·7	74
6. California	118·9	287·5	141
7. Pacific North-western States	82·4	135·0	64
Total, State Governments	2,207·9	4,093·2	85
Local Governments : [3]			
1. North-eastern States	2,611·3	..	..
2. South-eastern States	641·6	..	..
3. Middle States	2,022·2	..	..
4. Mountain and Great Plain States	360·3	..	..
5. South-western States	310·0	..	..
6. California	512·2	..	..
7. Pacific North-western States	186·5	..	..
Total, Local Governments	6,644·1	6,700·0 [3]	..
GRAND TOTAL [4]	10,857·7	16,087·0	48
Less duplication due to intergovernmental grants	867·9	1,693·8	95
NET TOTAL [4]	9,989·8	14,393·2	44

[1] The regions are as follows : (1) *North-eastern States* : Maine, New Hampshire, Vermont, Massachusetts, Rhode Island, Connecticut, New York, New Jersey, Pennsylvania, Delaware, Maryland, District of Columbia (under Local Governments), West Virginia. (2) *South-eastern States* : Virginia, North Carolina, South Carolina, Georgia, Florida, Kentucky, Tennessee, Alabama, Mississippi, Arkansas, Louisiana. (3) *Middle States* : Ohio, Indiana, Illinois, Michigan, Wisconsin, Minnesota, Iowa, Missouri. (4) *Mountain and Great Plain States* : North Dakota, South Dakota, Nebraska, Kansas, Montana, Wyoming, Colorado, Utah, Nevada. (5) *South-western States* : Oklahoma, Texas, New Mexico, Arizona. (6) *California*. (7) *Pacific North-western States* : Washington, Oregon, Idaho.

[2] 1937 figures exclude public service enterprises, as do the corresponding expenditure figures in Table 12. This should be borne in mind when comparing the figures, and especially the percentages in the two tables.

[3] No data are available for 1937. The figure of $6700 millions is a rough estimate. The change between 1932 and 1937 is likely to have been very much less than in the case of National and State figures.

[4] The definition of revenue is not quite the same for the National and for the other figures. The totals for all governments combined should therefore be used only with caution.

Source.—Statistical Abstract of the United States.

Table 12 U.S.A., PUBLIC EXPENDITURES FROM REVENUES, ALL GOVERNMENTS, BY REGIONS,[1] 1932 AND 1937

	$ millions		Per-centage Increase
	1932	1937	
National Government [2]	4,535·2	8,442·4	86
State Governments : [3]			
1. North-eastern States	905·4	1,133·6	25
2. South-eastern States	451·3	530·5	18
3. Middle States	599·1	947·4	58
4. Mountain and Great Plain States	159·0	227·3	43
5. South-western States	176·0	267·5	52
6. California	134·3	232·4	73
7. Pacific North-western States	80·7	124·6	54
Total, State Governments	2,505·8	3,463·3	38
Local Governments : [4]			
1. North-eastern States	2,958·1	..	..
2. South-eastern States	644·9	..	..
3. Middle States	2,032·6	..	..
4. Mountain and Great Plain States	355·2	..	..
5. South-western States	334·4	..	..
6. California	537·7	..	..
7. Pacific North-western States	193·9	..	..
Total, Local Governments	7,056·8	5,900·0 [5]	..
GRAND TOTAL [6]	14,097·8	17,805·7	26
Less duplication due to intergovernmental grants	867·9	1,693·8	95
NET TOTAL [6]	13,229·9	16,111·9	22

[1] See Table 11, footnote 1.
[2] Expenditure chargeable against ordinary receipts, other than debt retirements.
[3] Cost payments. Figures for 1932 include 1931 figures in the case of 18 States. 1937 figures are exclusive of public service enterprises.
[4] Cost payments. 1937 data are not available.
[5] Estimated.
[6] The definition of expenditure is not quite the same for the National and for the other figures. The totals for all Governments combined should therefore be used only with caution.

Source.—Statistical Abstract of the United States.

Table 13 NET DEBT OF STATE AND LOCAL GOVERNMENTS, BY REGIONS, 1932 AND 1937[1]

	$ millions		Percentage Change
	1932	1937	
State Governments :			
1. North-eastern States	662·0	965·9	+46
2. South-eastern States	693·1	744·7	+7
3. Middle States	411·0	439·0	+7
4. Mountain and Great Plains States	59·3	72·2	+22
5. South-western States	19·3	55·4	+188
6. California	142·4	106·3	−25
7. Pacific North-western States	42·5	41·1	−3
Total	2,029·6	2,424·6	+19
Local Governments :			
1. North-eastern States	6,271·3	6,548·1	+4
2. South-eastern States	2,190·6	1,948·7	−11
3. Middle States	3,758·0	3,255·2	−13
4. Mountain and Great Plain States	581·8	514·6	−11
5. South-western States	1,014·4	875·0	−14
6. California	953·7	1,250·3	+31
7. Pacific North-western States	446·1	432·2	−3
Total	15,215·9	14,824·1	−3

[1] Net debt is gross debt less sinking fund assets, including debt of public service enterprises, except in the case of State debt in 1937. State figures for this year represent funded or fixed debt less sinking fund assets, and exclude debt of public service enterprises. State figures for 1932 contain 1931 figures for 7 States. For regions see Table 11, footnote 1.

Source.—Statistical Abstract of the United States, 1940.

Table 14 U.S.A., PERCENTAGE DISTRIBUTION OF STATE TAX REVENUES, SELECTED STATES, 1937–38 [1]

Tax	All States	California	Delaware	Georgia	Illinois	Nevada	New Jersey	New York	North Dakota	Oklahoma	Vermont
Net income (personal and corporate)	12·8	17·9	14·2	14·0	..	..	..	39·7	3·5	14·0	7·8
Inheritance, estate and gift	4·6	4·4	4·9	0·3	4·5	..	7·7	7·7	0·6	0·6	4·2
Property (State tax only)	8·1	.. [2]	0·8	12·6	0·7	37·0	15·3	..	23·7	0·2	10·6
Franchise	3·4	..	34·2	1·0	1·6	1·4	3·6	7·0	.. [2]	1·1	0·9
Insurance company	2·7	2·8	2·3	3·5	4·7	2·1	2·3	0·4	2·2	1·8	3·8
Licence	0·4	..	2·3	1·9	..	..	..	0·1	..	..	..
Stock transfer and document registry	0·9	..	..	..	..	..	..	5·3	..	..	..
Liquor	7·0	6·4	6·5	5·2	5·9	6·1	7·3	9·8	8·1	1·7	9·9
Tobacco	1·8	..	..	6·5	..	..	..	..	3·7	3·6	3·6
Severance [3]	2·0	0·2	..	..	..	2·1	..	..	..	21·6	..
Gasoline, etc.	25·0	19·8	20·0	48·6	21·2	37·1	20·1	15·0	21·2	22·8	26·8
Motor vehicle	12·1	11·2	10·6	4·7	11·6	14·2	15·5	11·2	13·1	13·9	24·9
Racing	0·3	1·1	2·1	..	0·3	..	..	0·1	..	..	..
Utility	3·7	.. [2]	1·6	..	6·2	..	28·1	3·5	..	0·1	3·1
General sales	14·4	36·1	0·3	..	43·3	..	..	0·1	23·9	18·6	..
Other	0·6	0·1	0·2	1·7	..	..	0·1	0·1	.. [2]	..	4·4
TOTAL	100·0	100·0	100·0	100·0	100·0	100·0	100·0	100·0	100·0	100·0	100·0
TOTAL (in $ millions)	3139·7	240·4	10·3	41·2	187·2	3·3	119·2	444·0	12·2	61·0	9·7

[1] The selection of the States is designed to show differences in tax structure. [2] Less than 0·05.
[3] Taxes levied upon natural resources at the time of production, or severance from the earth. Examples are taxes on mineral resources, oil and gas, timber and sea products.

Source.—Tax Yields : 1940 (Tax Institute, University of Pennsylvania).

Table 15 U.S.A., EXPENDITURES AND INTEREST CHARGES OF STATES, 1937[1]

Region and State	Cost Payments, $ thousands	Interest Payments, $ thousands	Interest Payments as a Percentage of Cost Payments
1. *North-eastern States :*			
Maine	28,017	1,175	4·2
New Hampshire	16,909	513	3·0
Vermont	11,127	297	2·7
Massachusetts	98,617	737	0·7
Rhode Island	22,802	1,008	4·4
Connecticut	45,918	291	0·6
New York	429,734	23,126	5·4
New Jersey	107,496	7,655	7·1
Pennsylvania	273,682	5,427	2·0
Delaware	12,038	88	0·7
Maryland	37,565	1,912	5·1
West Virginia	49,661	3,681	7·4
Total, North-eastern States	1,133,566	45,910	4·1
2. *South-eastern States :*			
Virginia	55,990	955	1·7
North Carolina	74,709	7,044	9·4
South Carolina	32,857	1,722	5·2
Georgia	40,396	24	0·1
Florida	49,290	..	..
Kentucky	47,593	1,384	2·9
Tennessee	46,205	4,730	10·2
Alabama	49,391	3,223	6·5
Mississippi	40,159	2,317	5·8
Arkansas	26,633	5,017	18·8
Louisiana	67,248	6,032	9·0
Total, South-eastern States	530,471	32,448	6·1
3. *Middle States :*			
Ohio	192,501	483	0·3
Indiana	76,909	170	0·2
Illinois	175,820	8,654	4·9
Michigan	162,431	4,388	2·7
Wisconsin	79,484	83	0·1
Minnesota	102,711	4,311	4·2
Iowa	75,960	337	0·4
Missouri	81,605	4,856	6·0
Total, Middle States	947,421	23,282	2·5
4. *Mountain and Great Plain States :*			
North Dakota	20,520	1,305	6·4
South Dakota	20,419	2,155	10·6
Nebraska	32,105	17	0·1
Kansas	42,175	982	2·3
Montana	20,895	470	2·2
Wyoming	13,161	141	1·1
Colorado	49,155	347	0·7
Utah	21,216	469	2·2
Nevada	7,676	43	0·6
Total, Mountain and Great Plain States	227,322	5,929	2·6

Table 15—(*continued*)

Region and State	Cost Payments, $ thousands	Interest Payments, $ thousands	Interest Payments as a Percentage of Cost Payments
5. *South-western States :*			
Oklahoma	71,381	561	0·8
Texas	153,784	1,111	0·7
New Mexico	23,281	569	2·4
Arizona	19,101	111	0·6
Total, South-western States .	267,547	2,352	0·9
6. *California*	232,402	9,088	3·9
7. *Pacific North-western States :*			
Washington	71,033	679	1·0
Oregon	35,352	2,233	6·3
Idaho	18,210	107	0·6
Total, Pacific North-western States	124,595	3,019	2·4
GRAND TOTAL	3,463,324	122,028	3·5

[1] Exclusive of public service enterprises.

Source.—Statistical Abstract of the United States, 1940.

Table 16 PUBLIC EXPENDITURES FROM REVENUES, ALL GOVERNMENTS, 1932 [1]

($ millions)

	National	State	Local	Total
1. *Primary Functions :*				
General administration, legislation and justice	701·2 [2]	123·3	511·6 [10]	1,336·1
Protection to person and property	..	86·8	568·2 [10]	655·0
Pensions [3]	1023·4	..	..	1,023·4
Debt services	599·3	112·2	731·6	1,443·1
Defence	826·0	..	..	826·0
Total, Primary Functions	3149·9	322·3	1811·4 [10]	5,283·6
2. *Secondary Functions :*				
(1) *Social Services :* [4]				
Education	..	604·5	1964·8 [10]	2,569·2
Public health [5]	..	45·3	354·5 [10]	399·9
Charities,[6] hospitals and corrections	..	274·9	373·4 [10]	648·3
Government Life Insurance Fund	51·4	..	..	51·4
Sub-total	51·4	924·7	2692·7	3,668·8
(2) *Developmental :*				
Post Office [7]	203·0	..	..	203·0
Panama Canal	10·7	..	..	10·7
Shipping Board	51·5	..	..	51·5
Highways	..	235·7	597·9 [10]	833·6
Development and conservation of natural resources	..	73·0	12·1 [10]	85·1
Agriculture [8]	580·2	..	..	580·2
Reconstruction Finance Corporation	767·7	..	..	767·7
Public service enterprises	..	6·3	301·6	307·9
Sub-total	1613·1	315·0	911·6 [10]	2,839·7
(3) *Outlays* [9]	..	885·9	1,475·8	2,361·7
(4) *Miscellaneous*	47·3	57·9	165·3 [10]	270·5
Total, Secondary Functions	1711·8	2183·5	5245·4 [10]	9,140·7
GRAND TOTAL	4861·7	2505·8	7056·8	14,424·3
Less grants and subventions made by the Federal Government to the States, by the latter to Local Governments, and by Local Governments to States	238·1	618·6	11·2	867·9
NET TOTAL	4623·6	1887·2	7045·6	13,556·4

[1] National Government: fiscal year ended 30th June 1932. State and Local Governments: fiscal years ending on a date between 1st July 1931 and 30th June 1932. National Government figures include trust and related accounts totalling $326·5 millions.

[2] Departmental expenditure and refunds of receipts. The former contains a few small items which, if details were readily available on a comparable basis, would have been classified under Protection to person and property and under Secondary Functions such as Education. All War and Navy Department expenditure is given under Defence, and that of the Department of Agriculture under Agriculture.

[3] Separate figures for pensions are not available in the case of State and Local Governments.

[4] National Government figures not readily available on a comparable basis. The amounts would be small. See also footnote 2.

[5] Excludes hospitals but includes recreation.

[6] Mainly poor relief.

[7] Mainly postal deficiency.

[8] $319·0 millions Department of Agriculture, $136·2 millions Agricultural Marketing Fund and $125·0 subscription to stock of Federal land banks.

[9] Expenditures of a capital nature out of revenue, *e.g.* for purchase and improvement of land, erection of new buildings, extension of water-supply systems, or purchases to increase the collection of libraries.

[10] Estimate, subject to revision. Details are not available for all types of Local Government in all States.

Sources.—Statistical Abstract of the United States; Financial Statistics of State and Local Governments, 1932.

'able 17 PUBLIC EXPENDITURES FROM REVENUES, ALL GOVERNMENTS, 1932

(Percentage distribution)

	Percentage Share of each Government in Total Expenditures				Percentage Distribution of each Government's Expenditure			
	National	State	Local	Total	National	State	Local	Total
1. *Primary Functions :*								
General administration, legislation and justice	53	9	38	100	15	5	7	9
Protection to person and property	..	13	87	100	..	3	8	5
Pensions [1]	100	..	..	100	21	..	..	7
Debt services	41	8	51	100	12	5	11	10
Defence	100	..	..	100	17	..	..	6
Total, Primary Functions	60	6	34	100	65	13	26	37
2. *Secondary Functions :*								
(1) *Social Services :*								
Education	..	24	76	100	..	24	28	18
Public health	..	11	89	100	..	2	5	3
Charities, hospitals and corrections	..	42	58	100	..	11	5	4
Government Life Insurance Fund	100	..	..	100	1	..	..	..
Sub-total	1	25	74	100	1	37	38	25
(2) *Developmental :*								
Post Office	100	..	..	100	4	..	..	1
Panama Canal	100	..	..	100	..	..	..	..
Shipping Board	100	..	..	100	1	..	..	..
Highways	..	28	72	100	..	9	8	6
Development and conservation of natural resources	..	86	14	100	..	3	..	1
Agriculture	100	..	..	100	12	..	..	4
Reconstruction Finance Corporation	100	..	..	100	16	..	..	5
Public service enterprises	..	2	98	100	..	..	5	3
Sub-total	57	11	32	100	33	12	13	20
(3) *Outlays*	..	38	62	100	..	36	21	16
(4) *Miscellaneous*	18	21	61	100	1	2	2	2
Total, Secondary Functions	19	24	57	100	35	87	74	63
GRAND TOTAL	34	17	49	100	100	100	100	100
Less grants and subventions	28	71	1	100	5	25	..	6
NET TOTAL	34	14	52	100	..	..	..	..

[1] Separate figures for pensions are not available in the cases of State and Local Governments.

Table 18 U.S.A., NATIONAL OUTPUT BY INDUSTRIES[1]

($ billions)

	1929	1932	1935	1937	1939	1941
Agriculture	7·3	2·6	5·3	6·4	5·8	7·4
Mining	1·9	0·5	1·0	1·6	1·3	2·0
Manufacturing	20·4	6·1	12·5	17·5	16·4	27·6
Contract construction	3·5	0·8	0·9	1·8	2·1	3·7
Transportation	7·1	3·7	4·1	5·2	5·0	6·4
Power and gas	1·4	1·1	1·2	1·4	1·4	1·6
Communications	1·0	0·7	0·7	0·9	0·9	1·1
Trade	11·1	5·1	7·5	9·6	9·6	13·2
Finance	11·7	6·2	6·3	7·7	7·6	9·0
Government	5·6	5·9	7·1	8·1	8·9	10·7
Service	9·9	5·7	6·8	8·6	8·8	8·0
Miscellaneous	4·0	2·4	2·7	3·2	3·4	4·4
Corporation income and excess profits taxes	1·4	0·5	1·0	1·6	1·5	6·9
Capital outlays charged to current expense	0·8	0·4	0·6	0·8	0·8	1·8
Inventory revaluations	0·5	1·2	−0·6	−0·7	−0·3	−3·2
Less—						
Social security contributions of employers	..	..	..	−1·0	−1·3	−1·6
Revision and rounding-off errors	..	−0·1	−0·1	−0·1	0·1	0·1
NET NATIONAL OUTPUT AT FACTOR COST	87·6	42·8	57·0	72·6	72·0	99·1

[1] The definition of national income and output used here differs slightly from that of the U.S. Department of Commerce (see Table 19), in that Mr. Stone excludes from the total social security contributions of employers and Federal debt interest, but includes imputed rents on owner-occupied houses, corporation income and excess profits taxes, capital outlays charged to current expense and inventory revaluations.

Source.—Richard Stone, "The National Income, Output, and Expenditure of the United States", *Economic Journal*, June–Sept. 1942, Table I.

Table 19 U.S.A., NATIONAL INCOME, BY INDUSTRIES [1]

($ millions)

	1929	1932	1935	1937	1939
Agriculture	7,258	2,551	5,276	6,378	5,635
Mining	1,883	524	1,028	1,530	1,232
Electric light and power and gas	1,425	1,096	1,152	1,380	1,384
Manufacturing	20,308	6,009	12,402	16,994	15,425
Contract construction	3,670	906	964	1,902	2,148
Transportation	7,108	3,622	4,133	5,088	4,800
Communication	1,047	722	723	839	863
Trade	11,314	5,290	7,608	9,131	9,135
Finance	8,915	4,895	5,131	6,189	5,983
Government, excluding work-programme wages	6,330	6,355	6,584	7,370	8,015
Work-programme wages	..	132	1,339	1,783	1,869
Government, including work-programme wages	6,330	6,487	7,923	9,153	9,884
Service	9,615	5,579	6,828	8,477	8,374
Miscellaneous	4,012	2,393	2,695	3,161	3,319
Social security contributions of employers	..	..	7	950	1,196
NATIONAL INCOME	82,885	40,074	55,870	71,172	69,378

[1] These figures, taken from the Statistical Abstract of the United States, 1940, are based on a definition of national income differing slightly from that used by Mr. Richard Stone (see Tables 18—especially footnote—and 20 C, also Chapter III, Chart IV (p. 33) and Table VI (p. 38), and Richard Stone, *op. cit.*). Data on dividends, interest and corporate savings by industrial divisions from 1934 onwards are based on a different industrial classification than those for earlier years, though the changes are small for total income as distinct from specific items in particular industries.

Table 20 U.S.A., GOVERNMENT REVENUES AND EXPENDITURES AND THE NATIONAL INCOME

($ billions)

	1929	1930	1932	1935	1937	1938	1939	1940	1941
A. *Income, Deficit and Expenditure of Public Authorities*:									
Direct taxes, etc.:									
Federal corporate income and excess profits taxes	1·2	0·8	0·4	0·9	1·4	1·0	1·3	2·6	6·6
State corporate income taxes	0·2	0·1	0·1	0·1	0·2	0·2	0·2	0·2	0·3
Direct personal taxes	3·0	2·6	1·9	2·3	3·1	3·3	2·9	3·0	3·8
Social security contributions of employees	0·2	0·2	0·2	0·2	0·7	0·7	0·7	0·9	0·8
Sub-total	4·6	3·7	2·6	3·5	5·4	5·2	5·1	6·7	11·5
Indirect taxes, etc.:									
All other federal business taxes	1·2	1·0	1·0	2·1	2·4	2·1	2·3	3·1	4·2
All other state and local business taxes	4·4	4·9	4·6	5·0	5·0	5·0	5·8	5·9	6·5
Social security contributions of employers	..	..	..	..	1·0	1·2	1·3	1·3	1·6
	5·6	5·9	5·6	7·1	8·4	8·3	9·4	10·3	12·3
Total Income of Public Authorities	10·2	9·6	8·2	10·6	13·8	13·5	14·5	17·0	23·8
Deficit	1·5	2·3	3·3	3·1	1·5	3·3	3·1	2·0	3·2
Total Expenditure of Public Authorities	11·7	11·9	11·5	13·7	15·3	16·8	17·6	19·0	27·0
Transfer Payments:									
Federal debt interest	0·7	0·6	0·6	0·8	0·9	0·9	1·0	1·1	1·1
Other transfer payments	0·7	0·7	1·3	1·8	1·7	2·4	2·5	2·7	2·4
Sub-total	1·4	1·3	1·9	2·6	2·6	3·3	3·5	3·8	3·5
Government Expenditures for Goods & Services:									
National defence	} 2·0	1·8	1·8	3·1	5·2	5·9	{ 1·4	2·8	11·2
Federal non-defence							{ 4·4	4·1	4·1
State and local	8·3	8·8	7·8	8·0	7·5	7·6	8·3	8·3	8·2
Sub-total	10·3	10·6	9·6	11·1	12·7	13·5	14·1	15·2	23·5
Total Expenditure of Public Authorities	11·7	11·9	11·5	13·7	15·3	16·8	17·6	19·0	27·0

Table 20—(*continued*)

	1937	1938	1939	1940	1941
B. *Government Expenditure Compared with the National Income :*					
(1) Total Government expenditure at market prices	15·3	16·8	17·6	19·0	27·0
(2) *Less* transfer payments, including federal debt interest	−2·6	−3·3	−3·5	−3·8	−3·5
(3) Government expenditure on goods and services at market prices	12·7	13·5	14·1	15·2	23·5
(4) Personal expenditure on consumption at market prices	63·8	59·9	63·5	67·7	77·4
(5) *Less* all " other " business taxes	−7·4	−7·1	−8·1	−9·0	−10·7
(6) Adjusted personal expenditure on consumption	56·4	52·8	55·4	58·7	66·7
(7) Sum of (3)+(6)	69·1	66·3	69·5	73·9	90·2
(8) Item (3) as a percentage of item (7)	18	20	20	21	26
Comparable percentages for the United Kingdom	..	19	..	44	52
C. *Taxation Compared with the National Income :*					
(1) Net national income	72·6	66·1	72·0	79·8	99·1
(2) Direct taxes, etc.	5·4	5·2	5·1	6·7	11·5
(3) Indirect taxes, etc.	8·4	8·3	9·4	10·3	12·3
(4) Total tax payments, *i.e.* (2)+(3)	13·8	13·5	14·5	17·0	23·8
(5) Total tax payments as a percentage of net national income	19	20	20	21	24
Comparable percentages for the United Kingdom (based on the White Paper [1])	..	25	..	29	37

[1] Budget White Paper, Cmd. 6347, 1942, Section B.

Source.—Richard Stone, " The National Income, Output and Expenditure of the United States ", *Economic Journal*, June–Sept. 1942.

Table 21

U.S.A., THE CHANGE IN PUBLIC FINANCE RESULTING FROM THE NEW DEAL

($ millions)

	Fiscal Year ending 30th June					
	1929	1930	1932	1935	1938	1939
National Government						
A. REVENUES AND EXPENDITURES:						
I. Ordinary receipts	4,033[1]	4,178[1]	2,006[2]	3,800	6,242	5,668
II. Ordinary expenditures other than those listed under III.	..	..	..	2,775	3,746	3,920
III. Recovery and relief and other expenditure on agricultural aid, Civilian Conservation Corps, Tennessee Valley Authority, and similar projects, as well as social security payments	..	..	..	4,235	3,880	5,290
IV. Total ordinary expenditures[3]	3,299[1]	3,440[1]	4,535	7,010	7,626	9,210
V. Surplus (+) or Deficit (−)[3]	+734	+738	−2,529	−3,210	−1,384	−3,542
VI. Surplus (+) or Deficit (−) apart from III	..	..	..	+1,025	+2,496	+1,748
B. PUBLIC DEBT:						
Bonds[4]	12,125	12,111	14,250	14,936	23,602	27,572
Floating debt[4]	3,907	3,047	4,603	12,076	10,301	8,550
Special issues to Government agencies and trust funds	607	764	308	633	2,676	3,770
Total interest-bearing debt	16,639	15,922	19,161	27,645	36,579	39,892
Non-interest-bearing debt	292	263	326	1,056	588	553
TOTAL GROSS DEBT	16,931	16,185	19,487	28,701	37,167	40,445

[1] 1929 and 1930: these figures include trust and related accounts, which are excluded from the official figures for later years. The figures for these accounts are liable to vary considerably from year to year. In 1935 the receipts under this head were of the order of $400 millions.

[2] The discrepancy between this figure and that for 1930, although largely due to the depression, partly represents the exclusion of trust and related accounts. (See footnote 1.)

[3] Excluding public debt retirements.

[4] Other than special issues to Government agencies and trust funds.

Source.—U.S. Statistical Abstract, 1940.

LIST OF CANADIAN TABLES

Table 1 CANADA, THE REVENUE SYSTEM, ALL GOVERNMENTS, 1940 [1]

($ millions)

	Dominion	Provincial	Municipal	Total
GROUP I. *Progressive Taxes :*				
Personal income taxes . . .	76	14	3	93
National defence tax . . .	28	..	..	28
Succession duties . . .	..	25	..	25
Total, Group I . .	104	39	3	146
GROUP II. *Taxes on Property :*				
Property taxes on land . . .	..	4	136	140
Property taxes on buildings . .	..	2	108	110
Business property taxes . .	..	..	14	14
Public domain	2	21	..	23
Total, Group II . .	2	27	258	287
GROUP III. *Mainly Taxes on Business :*				
Corporation taxes . . .	145	57	..	202
Excess profits tax . . .	24	..	..	24
Company fees, licences, etc. . .	3	8	10	21
Total, Group III . . .	172	65	10	247
GROUP IV. *Mainly Consumption Taxes :*				
Customs (including liquor) . . .	131	..	..	131
War exchange tax . . .	61	..	..	61
Sub-total, Import Taxes . .	192	..	..	192
Excise (including liquor) . . .	88	..	..	88
Other, Similar Taxes and Licences :				
Manufacturer's taxes . . .	42	..	..	42
Sales taxes	179	13	5	197
Gasoline tax	..	53	..	53
Liquor control (other than customs and excise)	..	32	..	32
Automobile licences . . .	..	27	..	27
Amusement taxes . . .	..	3	..	3
Sub-total, Other Taxes and Licences	221	128	5	354
Surplus Utility Earnings . .	7	2	7	16
Miscellaneous (taxes and receipts) .	38	5	29	72
Total, Group IV . . .	546	135	41	722
Dominion subsidies to Provinces . .	..	19	..	19
GRAND TOTAL	824	285	312	1421
Less duplications	19	..	..	19
NET TOTAL	805	285	312	1402

[1] The figures are based on *Comparative Statistics of Public Finance*, 1936–1940 (Dominion-Provincial Conference, January 1941), but have been corrected for changes in actual results as compared with budget estimates.

able 2 CANADA, THE REVENUE SYSTEM, ALL GOVERNMENTS, 1940

(Percentage distribution)

	Percentage Share of each Government in Total Revenues				Percentage Distribution of each Government's Revenues			
	Dominion	Provincial	Municipal	Total	Dominion	Provincial	Municipal	Total
GROUP I. *Progressive Taxes :*								
Personal income taxes . . .	81	15	4	100	9	5	1	6
National defence tax . . .	100	..	..	100	3	..	..	2
Succession duties . . .	..	100	..	100	..	8	..	2
Total, Group I . . .	69	29	2	100	12	13	1	10
GROUP II. *Taxes on Property :*								
Property taxes on land . . .	..	3	97	100	..	1	44	10
Property taxes on buildings . .	..	2	98	100	..	1	35	8
Business property taxes . . .	..	..	100	100	..	..	4	1
Public domain	9	91	..	100	..	7	..	2
Total, Group II . . .	1	9	90	100	..	9	83	21
GROUP III. *Mainly Taxes on Business :*								
Corporation taxes . . .	72	28	..	100	16	20	..	14
Excess profits tax . . .	100	..	..	100	3	..	..	2
Company fees, licences, etc. . .	14	38	48	100	..	3	3	2
Total, Group III . . .	70	26	4	100	19	23	3	18
GROUP IV. *Mainly Consumption Taxes :*								
Customs (including liquor) . .	100	..	..	100	16	..	..	9
War exchange tax . . .	100	..	..	100	7	..	..	5
Sub-total, Import Taxes . .	100	..	..	100	23	..	..	14
Excise (including liquor) . . .	100	..	..	100	10	..	..	6
Other, Similar Taxes and Licences :								
Manufacturer's taxes . . .	100	..	..	100	5	..	..	3
Sales taxes	91	7	2	100	21	4	2	14
Gasoline tax	..	100	..	100	..	19	..	4
Liquor control (other than customs and excise)	..	100	..	100	..	11	..	2
Automobile licences . . .	..	100	..	100	..	10	..	2
Amusement taxes . . .	..	100	..	100	..	1	..	..
Sub-total, Other Taxes and Licences	63	36	1	100	26	45	2	25
Surplus Utility Earnings . .	44	12	44	100	1	1	2	1
Miscellaneous (taxes and receipts) .	54	7	39	100	9	2	9	5
Total, Group IV . . .	75	19	6	100	69	48	13	51
Dominion subsidies to Provinces . .	..	100	..	100	..	7	..	1
GRAND TOTAL	58	20	22	100	100	100	100	101
Less duplications	100	..	..	100	2	..	..	1
NET TOTAL	58	20	22	100	98	100	100	100

Table 3 CANADA, PUBLIC EXPENDITURES FROM REVENUE, ALL GOVERNMENTS, 1940

($ millions)

	Dominion	Provincial	Municipal	Total
1. *Primary Functions :*				
Legislation, administration and justice	57	41	73	171
National defence	852	..	..	852
Military pensions and after-care .	56	..	..	56
Debt charges	150	66	52	268
Total, Primary Functions . .	1115	107	125	1347
2. *Secondary Functions :*				
(1) *Social Services :*				
Education	..	36	81	117
Relief	31	23	6	60
Other public welfare . . .	36	55	37	128
Sub-total, Social Services .	67	114	124	305
(2) *Developmental :*				
Agriculture and public domain .	20	24	..	44
Transportation	17	31	32	80
Sub-total, Developmental .	37	55	32	124
Total, Secondary Functions .	104	169	156	429
Subsidies to Provinces	19	..	..	19
GRAND TOTAL	1240	276	279	1795
Less duplications	19	..	..	19
NET TOTAL	1221	276	279	1776

able 4 CANADA, PUBLIC EXPENDITURES FROM REVENUE, ALL GOVERNMENTS, 1940

(Percentage distribution)

	Percentage Share of each Government in Total Expenditures				Percentage Distribution of each Government's Expenditure			
	Dominion	Provincial	Municipal	Total	Dominion	Provincial	Municipal	Total
1. *Primary Functions :*								
Legislation, administration and justice	33	24	43	100	5	15	26	10
National defence	100	..	..	100	69	..	..	48
Military pensions and after-care .	100	..	..	100	4	..	..	3
Debt charges	56	24	20	100	12	24	19	15
Total, Primary Functions . .	83	8	9	100	90	39	45	76
2. *Secondary Functions :*								
(1) *Social Services :*								
Education	..	31	69	100	..	13	29	7
Relief (unemployment) . .	50	40	10	100	2	8	2	3
Other public welfare . . .	29	43	28	100	3	20	13	7
Sub-total, Social Services .	22	38	40	100	5	41	44	17
(2) *Developmental :*								
Agriculture and public domain .	46	54	..	100	2	9	..	2
Transportation	21	39	40	100	1	11	11	5
Sub-total, Developmental .	28	48	24	100	3	20	11	7
Total, Secondary Functions .	24	39	37	100	8	61	55	24
Subsidies to Provinces . . .	100	..	..	100	2	..	..	1
GRAND TOTAL	69	15	16	100	100	100	100	101
Less duplications	100	..	..	100	2	..	..	1
NET TOTAL	69	15	16	100	98	100	100	100

Table 5 CANADA, PERCENTAGE DISTRIBUTION OF PROVINCIAL AND MUNICIPAL REVENUES, 1937-38

	Prince Edward Island	Nova Scotia	New Brunswick	Quebec	Ontario	Manitoba	Saskatchewan	Alberta	British Columbia	All Provinces
GROUP I:										
Income taxes on persons .	2	..	1	1	3	8	1	2	4	2
Succession duties . .	2	3	3	8	10	1	1	3	3	6
GROUP II:										
Real property taxes .	20	37	31	43	51	48	43	45	38	45
Public domain . .	..	4	8	5	2	2	2	4	8	4
GROUP III:										
Corporation taxes . .	8	6	4	7	5	5	3	5	13	6
GROUP IV:										
Sales taxes . .	..	..	..	3	..	..	3	2	..	1
Gasoline taxes and motor vehicle licences . .	20	18	18	10	12	10	10	11	12	12
Liquor control . .	2	7	8	5	5	5	3	7	8	5
Miscellaneous taxes, licences, fees, etc. .	14	15	16	16	11	14	19	16	11	15
Total revenue from Provincial sources . .	68	90	89	98	99	93	85	95	97	96
Federal subsidies . .	32	10	11	2	1	7	15	5	3	4
TOTAL	100	100	100	100	100	100	100	100	100	100

Table 6 CANADA, PERCENTAGE DISTRIBUTION OF PROVINCIAL AND MUNICIPAL EXPENDITURES, 1937–38

	Prince Edward Island	Nova Scotia	New Brunswick	Quebec	Ontario	Manitoba	Saskatchewan	Alberta	British Columbia	All Provinces
1. *Primary Functions :*										
General Government and miscellaneous	15	17	14	22	21	20	17	17	24	20
Net debt charges	17	21	30	20	18	21	19	17	21	20
2. *Secondary Functions :*										
(1) *Social Services :*										
Education	28	23	21	15	23	20	18	27	18	20
Public welfare	..	..	..	..	..	..	..	..	..	..
Unemployment relief	4	3	2	14	8	14	23	8	9	11
Other	14	19	15	12	17	15	14	16	15	15
(2) *Developmental :*										
Agriculture and public domain	2	3	5	7	2	2	3	3	4	4
Transportation	20	14	13	10	11	8	6	12	9	10
TOTAL	100	100	100	100	100	100	100	100	100	100

Table 7 CANADA, DEBTS OUTSTANDING, ALL GOVERNMENTS, 1913–40

($ millions)

	1913	1921	1926	1930	1936	1937	1940
Dominion	521	3520	3570	3779	4800	4855	5879
Provinces	285	633	951	1246	1836	1960	2190
Municipalities	505	804	1038	1238	1279	1271	1143
Sub-total	1311	4957	5559	6263	7915	8086	9212
Less Intergovernmental debts :							
Dominion-Provincial	12	50	61	58	178	193	241
Provincial-Municipal	1	24	33	31	29	30	48
Net outstanding debt	1298	4883	5465	6174	7708	7863	8923

Table 8

CANADA, TOTAL RELIEF EXPENDITURES (INCLUDING RELIEF WORKS CHARGED TO CAPITAL ACCOUNT), 1930-37

($ millions)

	1930	1931	1932	1933	1934	1935	1936	1937
Through Provincial-Municipal agencies :								
1. Dominion share	3	34	34	28	43	41	52	55
2. Provincial share	9	42	37	39	74	70	59	79
3. Municipal share	5	16	21	23	24	23	23	18
Sub-total	17	92	92	90	141	134	134	152
Dominion expenditure through own agencies	1	5	3	8	17	39	26	13
GRAND TOTAL	18	97	95	98	158	173	160	165

Table 9 CANADA, RELIEF EXPENDITURES, ALL GOVERNMENTS, 1937–38

	$ thousands
TOTAL RELIEF EXPENDITURES (Dominion, Provincial and Municipal Shares combined):	
Prince Edward Island	577
Nova Scotia	2,560
New Brunswick	1,470
Quebec	30,823
Ontario	28,161
Manitoba	9,789
Saskatchewan	62,312
Alberta	7,649
British Columbia	9,013
TOTAL, COMBINED EXPENDITURE	152,354
Share of Each Government	
EXPENDITURE THROUGH PROVINCIAL-MUNICIPAL AGENCIES:	
Total Dominion share	54,547
Total Provincial share	79,466
Total Municipal share	18,341
TOTAL EXPENDITURE, through Provincial-Municipal Agencies	152,354
Add Dominion Expenditure, through own agencies	12,802
TOTAL, COMBINED EXPENDITURE	165,156

able 10 CANADA, COMPOSITION OF TOTAL DEBT, ALL GOVERNMENTS, 30TH NOVEMBER 1940

($ thousands)

	Total	Funded Debt, less Sinking Funds	Treasury Bills	Floating Debt	Guaranteed Bank Loans	Other Contingent Liabilities
All Governments	8,922,744	7,948,979	349,090	557,411	64,758	2506
Less Intergovernmental Debts:						
Dominion-Provincial	240,637	46,591	157,296	2,989	33,761	..
Provincial-Municipal	48,398	6,322	..	12,047	25,012	5017
Dominion and Canadian National Railways	5,878,567	5,199,931	230,325	363,245	85,066	..
Provinces	2,189,769	1,755,418	276,061	112,302	38,465	7523
Municipalities	1,143,443	1,046,543	..	96,900	..	..

Table 11

RELATION OF CANADIAN WAR EXPENDITURE TO NATIONAL INCOME AND PUBLIC FINANCE IN 1937–38, 1940–41 AND 1941–42

	1937–38	1940–41	1941–42
Net National Income ($ thousands):			
Tentative results entered for calendar years 1937, 1940, 1941	4,348,001	5,386,582	6,514,000
Government Revenue ($ thousands):			
National	516,693	872,170	1,488,536
Provincial	287,940	304,564	305,000 [1]
Municipal	309,067	314,500	312,700
Total	1,113,700	1,491,234	2,106,236
As percentage of national income	25·6	27·7	32·3
Government Expenditure ($ thousands):			
National	534,408	1,249,601	1,885,066
Provincial	274,100	273,503	274,000 [1]
Municipal	311,297	314,000	309,300
Total (including defence or war expenditure)	1,119,805	1,837,104	2,468,366
Defence or war expenditure	32,760 [2]	778,424 [3]	1,382,491 [3]
Total Government expenditure as percentage of national income	25·7	34·1	37·9
Defence or war expenditure as percentage of national income	0·7	14·5	21·2
Population (thousands)	11,120	11,385	11,507
Per Head ($):			
Income	391	473	566
Government revenue	100	131	183
Government expenditure	101	161	215
Government defence or war expenditure	3	68	120

[1] Estimated.
[2] Ordinary Expenditures of the National Defence Department.
[3] Including amounts charged to active assets.

Note.—Tentative approximate estimate of Net National Income in 1942 is $7500 millions. Expenditure for war in the fiscal year ended 31st March 1943 was tentatively given in the Budget speech of 2nd March 1943 as $3,802,765,000; this figure includes the $1000 millions gift to the United Kingdom. Total Dominion revenue for this fiscal year was $2,308,400,000; total expenditure $4,469,958,000 (preliminary figures).

Source.—Dominion Statistician, Ottawa. (See also Table II, Chapter IV.)

LIST OF AUSTRALIAN TABLES

Table 1 AUSTRALIA, COMMONWEALTH REVENUES, 1940–41 AND 1941–42[1]

	£ thousands		Percentage Distribution	
	1940–41	1941–42	1940–41	1941–42
GROUP I. *Progressive Taxes:*				
Income tax (individuals)[2]	18,872	24,265	14·1	16·0
Pay-roll tax	..	8,000	..	5·3
Estate duty	2,364	2,800	1·8	1·8
Total, Group I	21,236	35,065	15·9	23·1
GROUP II. *Taxes on Real Property:*				
Land tax	3,191	3,150	2·4	2·1
GROUP III. *Taxes on Business:*				
Income tax (companies)[2]	20,443	26,285	15·3	17·3
War-time (company) tax and super-tax	3,990	4,000	3·0	2·6
Gold tax	1,452	1,300	1·1	0·9
Non-tax revenue under Group III	311	299	0·2	0·2
Total, Group III	26,196	31,884	19·6	21·0
GROUP IV. *Mainly Consumption Taxes:*				
Customs	29,410	20,440	22·0	13·4
Excise:				
Liquor	13,597	14,960	10·2	9·8
Tobacco (including cigars and cigarettes)	7,805	9,130	5·8	6·0
Other	2,967	3,020	2·2	2·0
Sub-total, Excise	24,369	27,110	18·2	17·8
Other Similar Taxes:				
Sales tax	19,793	24,000	14·8	15·8
Flour tax	1,499	1,580	1·1	1·0
Sub-total, Other Taxes	21,292	25,580	15·9	16·8
Net Revenue from Business Undertakings:[3]				
Post Office	3,199	3,733	2·4	2·5
Miscellaneous:				
Territories[4]	507	497	0·4	0·3
Interest[5]	1,172	1,100[6]	0·9	0·7
Other	3,134	3,472	2·3	2·3
Sub-total, Miscellaneous	4,813	5,069	3·6	3·3
Total, Group IV	83,083	81,932	62·1	53·8
GRAND TOTAL	133,706	152,031	100·0	100·0

[1] 1940–41 figures are actual receipts; those for 1941–42 Budget estimates. The figures represent receipts of the Consolidated Revenue Fund, except that net revenues only of business undertakings are included.

[2] In the absence of separate data of individual and company income tax, the total income tax receipts have been split up in the ratio of assessments in 1939–40. In view of the repeated changes in the income tax law as more and more reliance has been placed on this source of revenue, there is a considerable margin of error in the figure given above.

[3] Net revenues of Post Office only. These were net expenditures on railways.

[4] Excluding business undertakings.

[5] Excluding balance of interest on States' debts payable by States.

[6] No details available. The figure of £1,100,000 is a rough estimate obtained by taking approximately the proportion of "Miscellaneous Receipts" (the head in the Budget accounts) represented by interest in 1940–41. In this way the Budget estimate of Miscellaneous Receipts for 1941–42 has been split up. The total of Miscellaneous Revenue in this table is not affected.

Source.—Commonwealth Budget Papers.

Table 2 AUSTRALIA, COMMONWEALTH EXPENDITURES FROM CONSOLIDATED REVENUE, 1940–41 AND 1941–42 [1]

	£ thousands		Percentage Distribution	
	1940–41	1941–42	1940–41	1941–42
1. *Primary Functions :*				
Legislation, administration and justice	4,072	4,176	3·0	2·8
Defence [2]	67,481	66,597	49·4	43·8
Pensions	8,252	8,223	6·0	5·4
Debt services [3]	13,603	14,914	10·0	9·8
Total, Primary Functions	93,408	93,910	68·4	61·8
2. *Secondary Functions :*				
(1) *Social Services :*				
Education [4]	111	125	0·1	0·1
Public health	271	291	0·2	0·2
Invalid and old-age pensions	17,366	18,750	12·7	12·3
Repatriation and War Service Homes Commission	791	945	0·6	0·6
Child endowment	..	13,000	..	8·6
Maternity allowances	408	425	0·3	0·3
Miscellaneous	168	368	0·1	0·2
Sub-total, Social Services	19,115	33,904	14·0	22·3
(2) *Developmental :*				
Railways (net)	608	628	0·4	0·4
Shipping and mail services	62	67	..	..
Federal Aid roads [5]	3,485	1,600	2·6	1·1
Civil aviation	382	474	0·3	0·3
Bounties	61	163	..	0·1
Research and publicity [6]	546	694	0·4	0·5
Relief to primary producers	3,023	3,776	2·2	2·5
New works	3,212	3,831	2·4	2·5
Miscellaneous	53	26	..	..
Sub-total, Developmental	11,432	11,259	8·3	7·4
(3) *Miscellaneous :*				
Territories	1,238	1,348	0·9	0·9
Total, Secondary Functions	31,785	46,511	23·2	30·6
Payments to or for States	11,441	11,610	8·4	7·6
GRAND TOTAL	136,634	152,031	100·0	100·0

[1] 1940–41 actual figures, 1941–42 Budget estimates. The grand totals differ from those in the official accounts in that net expenditure only on business undertakings is included, and in that expenditure from excess receipts (£2,928,375 on defence in 1940–41) has been added to ordinary expenditure.

[2] Expenditure of defence departments from revenue (other than on pensions and debt services), and miscellaneous expenditure on account of the war of 1914–18.

[3] Interest, sinking fund, exchange, and loan redemption and conversion expenses.

[4] Soldiers' children education scheme (expenditure on account of 1914–18 war) and National Library.

[5] Paid to States, but does not appear in State Consolidated Revenue accounts.

[6] Includes expenditure on scientific research and similar items which have been included under education in the State figures (Tables 5 and 6 and Chapter V Tables XI and XII), as well as in other chapters, but cannot be separated out in this case.

Source.—Commonwealth Budget Papers.

Table 3 AUSTRALIA, STATE REVENUES, BY STATES, 1937–38
(£ thousands)

	New South Wales	Victoria	Queensland	South Australia	Western Australia	Tasmania	Total
GROUP I. *Progressive Taxes :*							
Taxes on income [1]	11,649	4,980	3,251	1994	1655	743	24,272
Probate and succession duties	1,951	1,206	366	240	80	108	3,951
Total, Group I [1]	13,600	6,186	3,617	2234	1735	851	28,223
GROUP II. *Taxes on Real Property :*							
Land tax	2	420	233	319	98	84	1,156
Non-tax revenue from lands	1,872	434	1,543	217	375	66	4,507
Total, Group II	1,874	854	1,776	536	473	150	5,663
GROUP III. *Taxes on Business :* [2]							
Stamp duties	1,196	802	364	273	223	79	2,937
Licences and other taxes	63	100	76	37	34	22	332
Total, Group III	1,259	902	440	310	257	101	3,269
GROUP IV. *Mainly Consumption Taxes :*							
Taxes :							
Liquor	341	197	46	34	60	23	701
Motor vehicles	2,260	1,538	471	660	341	148	5,418
Entertainments	106	220	..	89	69	30	514
Racing	350	349	55	277	63	37	1,131
Lotteries	..	..	50	..	..	423 [3]	473
Sub-total, Taxes	3,057	2,304	622	1060	533	661	8,237
Revenue from Business Undertakings : [4]							
Railways, tramways and omnibuses	7,105	2,507	1,512	672 [5]	1048	..	12,844
Harbours, rivers and lights	841	8	..	550	249	..	1,648
Water supply, sewerage, irrigation and drainage	246	304	..	697	511	..	1,758
Other	..	785	..	11	128	13	937
Sub-total, Business Undertakings	8,192	3,604	1,512	1930	1936	13	17,187
Miscellaneous :							
Interest	653	2,255	1,299	914	449	351	5,921
Other	4,182	972	1,259	518	697	190	7,818
Sub-total, Miscellaneous	4,835	3,227	2,558	1432	1146	541	13,739
Total, Group IV	16,084	9,135	4,692	4422	3615	1215	39,163
Grants and other Commonwealth payments	3,008	2,127	1,097	1783 [6]	1051	841	9,907
GRAND TOTAL	35,825	19,204	11,622	9285	7131	3160	86,225

[1] Includes taxes on company income, which could not be separated out from those on individual income.
[2] Taxes on company income are included under Group I.
[3] Includes income tax on lotteries, £277,313 (8·8 per cent of Tasmanian revenues).
[4] Net revenue only. In calculating the total for all States, the losses of some have not been offset against the profits of others, but given separately in the expenditure tables (Nos. 5 and 6).
[5] Includes £120,000 (1·3 per cent of South Australian revenues), portion of Commonwealth Special Grant paid direct to railways.
[6] Excludes £120,000 (1·3 per cent of South Australian revenues), portion of Commonwealth Special Grant paid direct to railways.

Source.—Finance, 1927–28 to 1937–38, Commonwealth Bureau of Census and Statistics, Bulletin No. 29.

able 4 AUSTRALIA, STATE REVENUES, BY STATES, 1937–38
(Percentage distribution)

	New South Wales	Victoria	Queensland	South Australia	Western Australia	Tasmania	Total
GROUP I. *Progressive Taxes :*							
Taxes on income [1]	32·5	25·9	28·0	21·5	23·2	23·5	28·1
Probate and succession duties	5·5	6·3	3·1	2·6	1·1	3·4	4·6
Total, Group I [1]	38·0	32·2	31·1	24·1	24·3	26·9	32·7
GROUP II. *Taxes on Real Property :*							
Land Tax	..	2·1	2·0	3·4	1·3	2·7	1·4
Non-tax revenue from lands	5·2	2·3	13·3	2·3	5·3	2·1	5·2
Total, Group II	5·2	4·4	15·3	5·7	6·6	4·8	6·6
GROUP III. *Taxes on Business :* [2]							
Stamp duties	3·3	4·2	3·1	2·9	3·1	2·5	3·4
Licences and other taxes	0·2	0·5	0·7	0·4	0·5	0·7	0·4
Total, Group III	3·5	4·7	3·8	3·3	3·6	3·2	3·8
GROUP IV. *Mainly Consumption Taxes :*							
Taxes :							
Liquor	1·0	1·0	0·4	0·4	0·8	0·7	0·9
Motor vehicles	6·3	8·0	4·1	7·1	4·8	4·7	6·3
Entertainments	0·3	1·2	..	1·0	1·0	0·9	0·6
Racing	1·0	1·8	0·5	3·0	0·9	1·2	1·3
Lotteries	..	..	0·4	..	..	13·4 [3]	0·5
Sub-total, Taxes	8·6	12·0	5·4	11·5	7·5	20·9	9·6
Revenue from Business Undertakings : [4]							
Railways, tramways and omnibuses	19·8	13·1	13·0	7·3 [5]	14·7	..	14·9
Harbours, rivers and lights	2·3	..	..	5·9	3·5	..	1·9
Water supply, sewerage, irrigation and drainage	0·7	1·6	..	7·5	7·2	..	2·0
Other	..	4·1	..	0·1	1·8	0·5	1·1
Sub-total, Business Undertakings	22·8	18·8	13·0	20·8	27·2	0·5	19·9
Miscellaneous :							
Interest	1·8	11·7	11·2	9·9	6·3	11·1	6·8
Other	11·7	5·1	10·8	5·5	9·8	6·0	9·1
Sub-total, Miscellaneous	13·5	16·8	22·0	15·4	16·1	17·1	15·9
Total, Group IV	44·9	47·6	40·4	47·6	50·8	38·5	45·4
Grants and other Commonwealth payments	8·4	11·1	9·4	19·2 [6]	14·7	26·6	11·5
GRAND TOTAL	100·0	100·0	100·0	100·0	100·0	100·0	100·0

For footnotes see Table 3.

Table 5

AUSTRALIA, STATE EXPENDITURES, BY STATES, 1937–38

(£ thousands)

	New South Wales	Victoria	Queensland	South Australia	Western Australia	Tasmania	Total
1. *Primary Functions :*							
Legislation, administration, and justice	1,578	842	994	445	510	290	4,659
Public safety	2,141	1,013	650	348	298	158	4,608
Pensions	712	1,020	213	280	144	17	2,386
Debt services	14,242	8,114	6,566	5091	4245	1219	39,477
Total, Primary Function	18,673	10,989	8,423	6164	5197	1684	51,130
2. *Secondary Functions :*							
(1) *Social Services :*							
Education	5,123	3,093	1,712	1015	837	374	12,154
Public health (including hospitals)	2,174	1,247	508	448	190 [1]	168	4,735
Relief of aged, indigent, etc.	1,297 [2]	9 [3]	285	171	95	94	1,951
Unemployment relief	3,114	1,934	213	319	62	175	5,817
Child welfare	103	305	101	40	56	55	620
Family endowment [4]	1,470	..	..	..	..	..	1,470
Miscellaneous	348	54	1	40	111	8	562
Sub-total, Social Services	13,629	6,642	2,820	2033	1351	834	27,309
(2) *Developmental :*							
Railways	..	..	..	..	..	213 [5]	213
Miscellaneous business undertakings	..	..	2 [5]	..	..	..	2
Lands and survey	368	845	300	70	52	10	1,645
Agriculture	701	304	162	127	287	103	1,684
Forestry	77	171	40	..	83	35	406
Public works	688	79	84	576	8	134	1,569
Sub-total, Developmental	1,834	1,399	588	773	430	495	5,519
(3) *Miscellaneous*	1,635	143	20	188	164	140	2,290
Total, Secondary Functions	17,098	8,184	3,428	2994	1945	1469	35,118
GRAND TOTAL	35,771	19,173	11,851	9158	7142	3153	86,248

[1] Exclusive of £256,800 from Hospital Trust Account.
[2] Includes widows' pensions, and payments to deserted wives, widows and children.
[3] Portion only. Remainder included with hospitals in the official statistics, and hence under "Public Health" in this table.
[4] Up to July 1941 Government family endowment was confined to the State scheme in New South Wales. Since then there has been a more comprehensive Commonwealth system. (See Table 2.)
[5] Net loss.

Source.—*Finance, 1927–28 to 1937–38*, Commonwealth Bureau of Census and Statistics, Bulletin No.

Table 6

AUSTRALIA, STATE EXPENDITURES, BY STATES, 1937–38

(Percentage distribution)

	New South Wales	Victoria	Queensland	South Australia	Western Australia	Tasmania	Total
1. *Primary Functions :*							
Legislation, administration and justice	4·4	4·4	8·4	4·8	7·1	9·2	5·4
Public safety	6·0	5·3	5·5	3·8	4·2	5·0	5·3
Pensions	2·0	5·3	1·8	3·1	2·0	0·5	2·8
Debt services	39·8	42·3	55·4	55·6	59·5	38·7	45·8
Total, Primary Functions .	52·2	57·3	71·1	67·3	72·8	53·4	59·3
2. *Secondary Functions :*							
(1) *Social Services :*							
Education	14·3	16·1	14·4	11·1	11·7	11·9	14·1
Public health (including hospitals) .	6·1	6·5	4·3	4·9	2·7 [1]	5·3	5·5
Relief of aged, indigent, etc. .	3·6 [2]	* [3]	2·4	1·9	1·3	3·0	2·3
Unemployment relief . . .	8·7	10·1	1·8	3·5	0·9	5·6	6·7
Child welfare	0·3	1·6	0·9	0·4	0·8	0·5	0·7
Family endowment [4]	4·1	..	..	..	..	..	1·7
Miscellaneous	1·0	0·3	..	0·4	1·5	0·3	0·7
Sub-total, Social Services .	38·1	34·6	23·8	22·2	18·9	26·4	31·7
(2) *Developmental :*							
Railways	..	..	..	..	..	6·8 [5]	0·2
Miscellaneous business undertakings	..	..	* [5]	..	..	..	*
Lands and survey	1·0	4·4	2·5	0·7	0·7	0·3	1·9
Agriculture	2·0	1·6	1·4	1·4	4·0	3·3	2·0
Forestry	0·2	0·9	0·4	..	1·2	1·1	0·5
Public works	1·9	0·4	0·7	6·3	0·1	4·2	1·8
Sub-total, Developmental .	5·1	7·3	5·0	8·4	6·0	15·7	6·4
(3) *Miscellaneous*	4·6	0·8	0·1	2·1	2·3	4·5	2·6
Total, Secondary Functions .	47·8	42·7	28·9	32·7	27·2	46·6	40·7
GRAND TOTAL	100·0	100·0	100·0	100·0	100·0	100·0	100·0

For footnotes see Table 5.

* Less than 0·05 per cent.

Table 7

AUSTRALIA, LOCAL GOVERNMENT REVENUES, BY STATES, 1937–38

(£ thousands)

	New South Wales	Victoria	Queensland	South Australia	Western Australia	Tasmania	Total
GROUP II. *Taxes on Real Property:*							
Rates	5,304	3706	2266	871	673	333	13,295
Penalties [1]	106	33			1	2	
Total, Group II	5,410	3739	2266	871	674	335	13,295
GROUP III. *Taxes on Business:*							
Licences	73	88	33	30	20	9	253
GROUP IV. *Mainly Consumption Taxes:*							
Miscellaneous taxes	45	..	..	..	..	..	45
Public Works and Services:							
Sanitary and garbage services	456	155	382	14	71	11	1,089
Council properties	567	538	288	84	91	53	1,621
Street construction	340	163	18	66	8	1	596
Other	158	49	19	17	4	8	255
Sub-total, Public Works and Services	1,521	905	707	181	174	73	3,561
Profits from business undertakings	..	265	5	1	48	32	351
Miscellaneous	96	62	180	72	400 [2]	29	839
Total, Group IV	1,662	1232	892	254	622	134	4,796
Government Grants:							
Unemployment relief	1,834	789	729	13	127	26	5,692
Roads	1,380	84	385	312		13	
Other	298	139	214	30	2	4	687
Total, Grants	3,512	1012	1328	355	129	43	6,379
GRAND TOTAL	10,657	6071	4519	1510	1445	521	24,723

[1] In the case of Queensland and South Australia it has not been possible to separate penalties from rates.
[2] Includes £332,395 (23·0 per cent of the total for Western Australia) collected in connexion with vehicles registration.
Source.—Finance, 1939–40, Commonwealth Bureau of Census and Statistics, Bulletin No. 31.

Table 8

AUSTRALIA, LOCAL GOVERNMENT REVENUES, BY STATES, 1937–38
(Percentage distribution)

	New South Wales	Victoria	Queensland	South Australia	Western Australia	Tasmania	Total
GROUP II. *Taxes on Real Property :*							
Rates	49·8	61·0	50·2	57·7	46·5	63·9	53·8
Penalties [1]	1·0	0·5			0·1	0·3	
Total, Group II	50·8	61·5	50·2	57·7	46·6	64·2	53·8
GROUP III. *Taxes on Business :*							
Licences	0·7	1·4	0·7	2·0	1·4	1·9	1·0
GROUP IV. *Mainly Consumption Taxes :*							
Miscellaneous taxes	0·4	..	..	..	..	..	0·2
Public Works and Services :							
Sanitary and garbage services	4·3	2·6	8·5	0·9	4·9	2·2	4·4
Council properties	5·3	8·9	6·3	5·6	6·3	10·2	6·6
Street construction	3·2	2·7	0·4	4·4	0·6	0·2	2·4
Other	1·5	0·8	0·4	1·1	0·3	1·5	1·0
Sub-total, Public Works and Services	14·3	15·0	15·6	12·0	12·1	14·1	14·4
Profits from business undertakings	..	4·4	0·1	0·1	3·3	6·2	1·4
Miscellaneous	0·9	1·0	4·0	4·7	27·7 [2]	5·5	3·4
Total, Group IV	15·6	20·4	19·7	16·8	43·1	25·8	19·4
Government Grants :							
Unemployment relief	17·2	13·0	16·1	0·9	8·8	4·9	23·0
Roads	12·9	1·4	8·5	20·6		2·5	
Other	2·8	2·3	4·8	2·0	0·1	0·7	2·8
Total, Grants	32·9	16·7	29·4	23·5	8·9	8·1	25·8
GRAND TOTAL	100·0	100·0	100·0	100·0	100·0	100·0	100·0
Distribution of Total Revenues by States	43·1	24·6	18·3	6·1	5·8	2·1	100·0

For footnotes see Table 7.

Table 9

AUSTRALIA, LOCAL GOVERNMENT EXPENDITURES, BY STATES, 1937–38

(£ thousands)

	New South Wales	Victoria	Queensland	South Australia	Western Australia	Tasmania	Total
1. *Primary Functions :*							
General administration	678	614	293	137	126	58	1,906
Public safety [1]	101	73	25	[2]	23	4	226
Debt Services : [3]							
Interest	847	496	545	47	97	37	2,069
Redemption and other items	1,152	418	397	72	142	26	2,207
Sub-total, Debt Services	1,999	914	942	119	239	63	4,276
Total, Primary Functions	2,778	1601	1260	256	388	125	6,408
2. *Secondary Functions :*							
(1) *Social Services.:*							
Health administration	133	184	92	91	38	31	569
Sanitary and garbage services	630	261	564 [4]	56	92	22	1,625
Hospitals and ambulances	21	39	215	[2]	20	1	302
Other charities			1	3	1	1	
Sub-total, Social Services	784	484	872	150	151	55	2,496
(2) *Developmental :*							
Roads, streets and bridges	5,698 [5]	2121 [6]	1764	870	578	222	11,253
Street lighting	341	175	68	55	43	24	706
Council properties	1,092	793	251	122	237	58	2,553
Other public works and services	212	73	204	69	13	17	588
Sub-total, Developmental	7,343	3162	2287	1116	871	321	15,100
(3) *Miscellaneous*	– 115 [7]	895	106	2	43	27	958 [7]
Total, Secondary Functions	8,012	4541	3265	1268	1065	403	18,554
GRAND TOTAL	10,790	6142	4525	1524	1453	528	24,962

[1] Grants to fire brigades.
[2] Compulsory contributions included in the official statistics under public works and services, and hence in this table under Developmental Expenditure.
[3] Excludes business undertakings. [4] Includes £215,074 (4·8 per cent of the total for Queensland) for sewerage and drainage.
[5] Includes £199,315 (1·8 per cent of the total for New South Wales) of grants to Main Roads Department and Harbour Bridge Fund.
[6] Includes £164,836 (2·7 per cent of the total for Victoria) of grants to Country Roads Board.
[7] Includes deductions for duplications which cannot be allocated to the various heads, £230,035 (2·1 per cent of the total for New South Wales and 0·9 per cent of that for all States).

Source.—Finance, 1934–40, Commonwealth Bureau of Census and Statistics, Bulletin No. 31.

Table 10

AUSTRALIA, LOCAL GOVERNMENT EXPENDITURES, BY STATES, 1937–38

(Percentage distribution)

	New South Wales	Victoria	Queensland	South Australia	Western Australia	Tasmania	Total
1. *Primary Functions :*							
General administration	6·3	10·0	6·5	9·0	8·6	11·0	7·7
Public safety [1]	0·9	1·2	0·5	[2]	1·7	0·8	0·9
Debt Services : [3]							
Interest	7·8	8·1	12·0	3·1	6·7	7·0	8·3
Redemption and other items	10·7	6·8	8·8	4·7	9·8	4·9	8·8
Sub-total, Debt Services	18·5	14·9	20·8	7·8	16·5	11·9	17·1
Total, Primary Functions	25·7	26·1	27·8	16·8	26·8	23·7	25·7
2. *Secondary Functions :*							
(1) *Social Services :*							
Health administration	1·2	3·0	2·0	6·0	2·5	5·9	2·3
Sanitary and garbage services	5·9	4·2	12·5	3·7	6·3	4·0	6·5
Hospitals and ambulances	0·2 (incl. other charities)	0·6 (incl. other charities)	4·8	[2]	1·4	0·2	1·2 (incl. other charities)
Other charities			*	0·2	0·1	0·3	
Sub-total, Social Services	7·3	7·8	19·3	9·9	10·3	10·4	10·0
(2) *Developmental :*							
Roads, streets and bridges	52·8	34·5	39·0	57·1	39·8	42·1	45·1
Street lighting	3·2	2·9	1·5	3·6	3·0	4·6	2·8
Council properties	10·1	12·9	5·5	8·0	16·3	11·0	10·2
Other public works and services	2·0	1·2	4·5	4·5	0·9	3·1	2·4
Sub-total, Developmental	68·1	51·5	50·5	73·2	60·0	60·8	60·5
(3) *Miscellaneous*	– 1·1	14·6	2·4	0·1	2·9	5·1	3·8
Total, Secondary Functions	74·3	73·9	72·2	83·2	73·2	76·3	74·3
GRAND TOTAL	100·0	100·0	100·0	100·0	100·0	100·0	100·0
Distribution of Total Expenditures by States	43·2	24·6	18·2	6·1	5·8	2·1	100·0

For footnotes see Table 9.

* Less than 0·05 per cent.

Table 11 AUSTRALIA, COMMONWEALTH AND STATE DEBT, 30TH JUNE 1941

	Maturing in—			
	Australia, £000 (Austr.)	London, £000 (Stg.)	New York, £000 ($4·8665)	Total, £000 [1]
For Commonwealth Purposes				
(1) *War Debt* (1939–41):				
Stock and bonds [2]	84,178	5,775	..	89,953
Advance loan subscriptions [2]	872	..	..	872
Citizens' National Emergency Loans [2]	5,390	100	..	5,490
War savings certificates and stamps [2]	17,460	..	..	17,460
Public Treasury bills (short-term debt)	1,750	..	..	1,750
Indebtedness to United Kingdom Government	..	12,000	..	12,000
Sub-total, War Debt (1939–41)	109,650	17,875	..	127,525
(2) *War Debt* (1914–19):				
Stock and bonds [2]	171,073	11,020	..	182,093
Miscellaneous [2]	167	..	..	167
Indebtedness to United Kingdom Government	..	79,724	..	79,724
Sub-total, War Debt (1914–19)	171,240	90,744	..	261,984
(3) *Works and other Purposes*:				
Stock and bonds [3]	28,766	61,664	15,877	106,307
Treasury bills and debentures (short-term debt)	..	3,720	..	3,720
Internal Treasury bills [3]	10,692	..	..	10,692
Sub-total, Works and other Purposes	39,458	65,384	15,877	120,719
Total, Commonwealth Purposes	320,348	174,003	15,877	510,228
On Account of States				
Stock and bonds	459,072	206,381	15,584	681,037
Treasury bills and debentures (short-term debt)	45,423	23,155	..	68,578
Balance of debts of States taken over by Commonwealth and still represented by State securities	..	154,505	11,902	166,407
Total, on Account of States	504,495	384,041	27,486	916,022
GRAND TOTAL, COMMONWEALTH AND STATE PUBLIC DEBT	824,843	558,044	43,363	1,426,250

[1] Total "face" or "book" value of the debt without adjustment on account of relative currency changes since the loans were floated.

[2] Funded with the public.

[3] Funded debt.

Source.—Finance, 1940–41, Commonwealth Bureau of Census and Statistics, Bulletin No. 32.

Table 12

AUSTRALIA, STATE DEBT, BY STATES, 30TH JUNE 1938

	New South Wales	Victoria	Queensland	South Australia	Western Australia	Tasmania	Total
Maturing in Australia :							
£ thousands (Austr.) :							
Funded	150,931	106,636	53,469	58,405	41,670	12,033	423,144
Short-term	30,870	3,385	2,183	4,130	5,860	170	46,598
Total	181,801	110,021	55,652	62,535	47,530	12,203	469,742
Maturing in London, £ thousands (Stg.):							
Funded	149,481	56,805	63,012	39,358	41,160	12,918	362,734
Short-term	9,965	5,885	..	3,816	2,998	491	23,155
Total	159,446	62,690	63,012	43,174	44,158	13,409	385,889
Maturing in New York, £ thousands ($4·8665) :							
Funded	12,920	4,517	7,118	1,742	2,024	229	28,550
Total Debt, £ thousands : [1]							
Funded	313,332	167,958	123,599	99,505	84,854	25,180	814,428
Short-term	40,835	9,270	2,183	7,946	8,858	661	69,753
GRAND TOTAL	354,167	177,228	125,782	107,451	93,712	25,841	884,181

[1] Total " face " or " book " value of the debt without adjustment on account of relative currency changes since the loans were floated.

Source.—Finance, 1937–38, Commonwealth Bureau of Census and Statistics, Bulletin No. 29.

Table 13 AUSTRALIA, LOCAL GOVERNMENT DEBT, BY STATES, 1937–38

Debt of Local Authorities in—	Maturing in—				
	Australia £000 (Austr.)	London £000 (Stg.)	New York £000 ($4·8665)	New Zealand £000	Total £000
New South Wales :					
Due to Central Government	3,987	..	..	..	3,987
Due to banks (net overdraft)	250	..	..	..	250
Due to public creditor .	27,159	5,477	1913	..	34,549
Total . . .	31,396	5,477	1913	..	38,786
Victoria :					
Due to Central Government	664	..	..	..	664
Due to banks (net overdraft)	324	..	..	..	324
Due to public creditor .	12,075	..	..	31	12,106
Total . . .	13,063	..	..	31	13,094
Queensland :					
Due to Central Government	10,152	..	..	..	10,152
Due to banks (net overdraft)	708	..	..	..	708
Due to public creditor .	9,200	5,500	3588	..	18,288
Total . . .	20,060	5,500	3588	..	29,148
South Australia :					
Due to Central Government	394	..	..	..	394
Due to banks (net overdraft)	45	..	..	..	45
Due to public creditor .	846	..	..	..	846
Total . . .	1,285	..	..	..	1,285
Western Australia :					
Due to Central Government	43	..	..	..	43
Due to banks (net overdraft)	32	..	..	..	32
Due to public creditor .	2,589	552	..	..	3,141
Total . . .	2,664	552	..	..	3,216
Tasmania :					
Due to Central Government	362	..	..	..	362
Due to banks (net overdraft)	43	..	..	..	43
Due to public creditor .	1,658	1,194	..	..	2,852
Total . . .	2,063	1,194	..	..	3,257
All States :					
Due to Central Government	15,602	..	..	..	15,602
Due to banks (net overdraft)	1,402	..	..	..	1,402
Due to public creditor .	53,527	12,723	5501	31	71,782
GRAND TOTAL . . .	70,531	12,723	5501	31	88,786

Note.—The "Total" column shows the total "face" or "book" value of the debt without adjustment on account of relative currency changes since the loans were floated. Net overdrafts represent aggregate net overdrafts of all funds. The credit balances of other authorities which do not carry overdrafts have not been deducted.

Source.—Finance, 1938–39, Commonwealth Bureau of Census and Statistics, Bulletin No. 30.

Table 14 AUSTRALIA, DEBT OF SEMI-GOVERNMENTAL AND OTHER PUBLIC AUTHORITIES, 1937–38

Debt of Authorities in—	Maturing in—			
	Australia £000 (Austr.)	London £000 (Stg.)	New York £000 ($4·8665)	Total £000
New South Wales :				
Due to Central Government	22,387	..	..	22,387
Due to banks (net overdraft)	234	..	..	234
Due to public creditor .	42,886	3,989	1442	48,317
Total . . .	65,507	3,989	1442	70,938
Victoria :				
Due to Central Government	2,703	..	..	2,703
Due to banks (net overdraft)	166	..	..	166
Due to public creditor .	32,475	6,669	..	39,144
Total . . .	35,344	6,669	..	42,013
Queensland :				
Due to Central Government	8,301	..	..	8,301
Due to banks (net overdraft)	1,271	..	..	1,271
Due to public creditor .	2,605	..	..	2,605
Total . . .	12,177	..	..	12,177
South Australia :				
Due to Central Government	7,079	..	..	7,079
Due to banks (net overdraft)	26	..	..	26
Due to public creditor .	810	..	..	810
Total . . .	7,915	..	..	7,915
Western Australia :				
Due to Central Government	299	..	..	299
Due to banks (net overdraft)	4	..	..	4
Due to public creditor .	104	..	..	104
Total . . .	407	..	..	407
Tasmania :				
Due to Central Government	371	..	..	371
Due to public creditor .	487	..	..	487
Total . . .	858	..	..	858
All States :				
Due to Central Government	41,140	..	..	41,140
Due to banks (net overdraft)	1,701	..	..	1,701
Due to public creditor .	79,367	10,658	1442	91,467
GRAND TOTAL	122,208	10,658	1442	134,308

Note.—The " Total " column shows the total " face " or " book " value of the debt without adjustment on account of relative currency changes since the loans were floated. Net overdrafts represent aggregate net overdrafts of all funds. The credit balances of other authorities which do not carry overdrafts have not been deducted.

Source.—Finance, 1938–39, Commonwealth Bureau of Census and Statistics, Bulletin No. 30.

Table 15 AUSTRALIA, PUBLIC DEBT CHARGES AND NET LOSSES OF THE STATES, 1937–38 AND 1940–41

Year	New South Wales	Victoria	Queensland	South Australia	Western Australia	Tasmania	Total
	Interest, Sinking Fund and Exchange Charges						
	£ millions	£ millions	£ millions	£ millions	£ millions	£ millions	£ millions
1937–38 . .	16·2	8·1	6·5	5·1	4·2	1·2	41·3
1940–41 . .	16·9	8·6	6·9	5·3	4·5	1·3	43·5
	Per Head						
	£ s. d.	£ s. d.	£ s. d.	£ s. d.	£ s. d.	£ s. d.	£ s. d.
1937–38 . .	5 19 3	4 6 11	6 11 5	8 11 4	9 4 11	5 3 6	6 0 7
1940–41 . .	6 1 9	4 10 3	6 15 8	8 18 1	9 15 9	5 10 1	6 3 7
	Net Losses after Debiting these Charges and Crediting Earnings						
	£ millions	£ millions	£ millions	£ millions	£ millions	£ millions	£ millions
1937–38 . .	5·0	3·6	3·8	2·5	1·9	1·2	18·0
1940–41 . .	6·6	3·9	3·9	2·7	2·2	1·1	20·4
	Per Head						
	£ s. d.	£ s. d.	£ s. d.	£ s. d.	£ s. d.	£ s. d.	£ s. d.
1937–38 . .	1 17 2	1 18 9	3 15 5	4 4 8	4 2 1	5 1 3	2 12 5
1940–41 . .	2 7 2	2 0 8	3 17 1	4 9 11	4 14 2	4 15 6	2 17 9

Note.—The figures are not strictly comparable, because of differences in services controlled and in accounting practice.

Source.—Commonwealth Grants Commission, Eighth Report (1941), Appendix No. 21, p. 126, and Ninth Report (1942), Appendix No. 20, p. 98.

Table 16 AUSTRALIA, LOCAL GOVERNMENT AUTHORITIES, INTEREST PAYABLE, 1937–38

Interest on Debt of Local Authorities in—	Payable in—				
	Australia £000 (Austr.)	London £000 (Stg.)	New York £000 ($4·8665)	New Zealand £000	Total £000
New South Wales :					
To Central Government .	134	..	..	..	134
To banks (net overdraft) .	11	..	..	..	11
To public creditor . .	1175	284	105	..	1564
Total . . .	1320	284	105	..	1709
Victoria :					
To Central Government .	27	..	..	..	27
To banks (net overdraft) .	15	..	..	..	15
To public creditor . .	538	..	..	2	540
Total . . .	580	..	..	2	582
Queensland :					
To Central Government .	451	..	..	..	451
To banks (net overdraft) .	32	..	..	..	32
To public creditor . .	394	291	189	..	874
Total . . .	877	291	189	..	1357
South Australia :					
To Central Government .	20	..	..	..	20
To banks (net overdraft) .	2	..	..	..	2
To public creditor . .	37	..	..	..	37
Total . . .	59	..	..	..	59
Western Australia :					
To Central Government .	2	..	..	..	2
To banks (net overdraft) .	2	..	..	..	2
To public creditor . .	114	24	..	..	138
Total . . .	118	24	..	..	142
Tasmania :					
To Central Government .	15	..	..	..	15
To banks (net overdraft) .	2	..	..	..	2
To public creditor . .	70	57	..	..	127
Total . . .	87	57	..	..	144
All States :					
To Central Government .	649	..	..	..	649
To banks (net overdraft) .	64	..	..	..	64
To public creditor . .	2328	656	294	2	3280
GRAND TOTAL . . .	3041	656	294	2	3993

Note.—The "Total" column shows the nominal amount of interest payable, taking no account of exchange. Net overdrafts represent aggregate net overdrafts of all funds. The interest on the credit balances of other authorities which do not carry overdrafts has not been deducted.

Source.—Finance, 1938–39, Commonwealth Bureau of Census and Statistics, Bulletin No. 30.

Table 17 AUSTRALIA, SEMI-GOVERNMENTAL AND OTHER PUBLIC AUTHORITIES, INTEREST PAYABLE, 1937–38

Interest on Debt of Authorities in—	Payable in—			
	Australia £000 (Austr.)	London £000 (Stg.)	New York £000 ($4·8665)	Total £000 [1]
New South Wales:				
To Central Government	783	..	..	783
To banks (net overdraft)	11	..	..	11
To public creditor	1524	160	79	1763
Total	2318	160	79	2557
Victoria:				
To Central Government	107	..	..	107
To banks (net overdraft)	7	..	..	7
To public creditor	1448	311	..	1759
Total	1562	311	..	1873
Queensland:				
To Central Government	341	..	..	341
To banks (net overdraft)	23	..	..	23
To public creditor	103	..	..	103
Total	467	..	..	467
South Australia:				
To Central Government	280	..	..	280
To banks (net overdraft)	1	..	..	1
To public creditor	35	..	..	35
Total	316	..	..	316
Western Australia:				
To Central Government	13	..	..	13
To banks (net overdraft)	[2]	..	..	[2]
To public creditor	4	..	..	4
Total	17	..	..	17
Tasmania:				
To Central Government	16	..	..	16
To public creditor	20	..	..	20
Total	36	..	..	36
All States:				
To Central Government	1540	..	..	1540
To banks (net overdraft)	42	..	..	42
To public creditor	3134	471	79	3684
GRAND TOTAL	4716	471	79	5266

[1] Nominal interest payable, taking no account of exchange. [2] Less than £500.

Note.—Net overdrafts represent aggregate net overdrafts of all funds. The interest on the credit balances of other authorities which do not carry overdrafts has not been deducted.

Source.—Finance, 1938–39, Commonwealth Bureau of Census and Statistics, Bulletin No. 30.

Table 18 PAYMENTS BY THE COMMONWEALTH TO OR FOR THE STATES, SUMMARY, 1930–31 TO 1941–42 [1]

(£ thousands)

Year and Item	New South Wales	Victoria	Queensland	South Australia	Western Australia	Tasmania	Total
1930–31 :							
From Revenue	4290	3080	1826	2460	1330	695	13,681
From Loan Fund	..	..	..	..	..	..	..
Total	4290	3080	1826	2460	1330	695	13,681
1931–32 :							
From Revenue	3968	2757	1679	2262	1314	646	12,626
From Loan Fund	1075	785	65	833	690	2	3,450
Total	5043	3542	1744	3095	2004	648	16,076
1932–33 :							
From Revenue	4615	3254	1768	2805	2048	751	15,241
From Loan Fund	366	238	275	216	172	22	1,289
Total	4981	3492	2043	3021	2220	773	16,530
1933–34 :							
From Revenue	5025	3470	1866	3245	2288	911	16,805
From Loan Fund	23	230	29	9	[2]	9	300
Total	5048	3700	1895	3254	2288	920	17,105
1934–35 :							
From Revenue	6252	4413	2295	3910	2763	1029	20,662
From Loan Fund	20	221	70	31	85	46	473
Total	6272	4634	2365	3941	2848	1075	21,135
1935–36 :							
From Revenue	5207	3776	2087	3506	2529	1018	18,123
From Loan Fund	230	230	140	81	346	70	1,097
Total	5437	4006	2227	3587	2875	1088	19,220
1936–37 :							
From Revenue	4808	3440	2112	2947	1932	1192	16,431
From Loan Fund	626	572	95	279	320	46	1,938
Total	5434	4012	2207	3226	2252	1238	18,369
1937–38 :							
From Revenue	4956	3463	2314	2857	2132	1169	16,891
From Loan Fund	840	840	170	280	300	70	2,500
Total	5796	4303	2484	3137	2432	1239	19,391
1938–39 :							
From Revenue	5531	3709	2396	3080	2529	1021	18,266
From Loan Fund	465	550	300	300	300	85	2,000
Total	5996	4259	2696	3380	2829	1106	20,266
1939–40 :							
From Revenue	5842	3724	2390	3016	2621	1097	18,690
From Loan Fund	210	210	100	100	100	30	750
Total	6052	3934	2490	3116	2721	1127	19,440
1940–41 :							
From Revenue	5481	3728	2145	3023	2647	1237	18,261
From Loan Fund	725	395	115	215	315	5	1,770
Total	6206	4123	2260	3238	2962	1242	20,031
1941–42 : [3]							
From Revenue	4816	3638	1921	2918	2372	1745	17,410
From Loan Fund	185	308	140	190	277	..	1,100
Total	5001	3946	2061	3108	2649	1745	18,510

[1] The figures include all payments by the Commonwealth to or for the States, such as those under the Financial Agreement, the Federal Aid Roads Agreement, special grants, bounties and assistance to primary industries.

[2] Less than £100.

[3] Budget estimates.

Sources.—Commonwealth Grants Commission Reports and Commonwealth Budget Papers.

Table 19 AUSTRALIA, PAYMENTS BY THE COMMONWEALTH TO OR FOR THE STATES, DETAILS, 1937–38

(£ thousands)

	New South Wales	Victoria	Queensland	South Australia	Western Australia	Tasmania	Total
Payments from Revenue :							
Under Financial Agreement :							
Contribution towards interest on State debts	*2918*	*2127*	*1096*	*704*	*473*	*267*	*7,585*
Contribution towards sinking fund on State debts	*603*	*287*	*193*	*170*	*163*	*38*	*1,454*
Sub-total, Financial Agreement [1]	3521	2414	1289	874	636	305	9,039
Grant for Federal Aid Roads	1166	726	793	461	797	207	4,150
Special grants [1]	..	..	..	1200	575	575	2,350
Unemployment relief :							
Metalliferous mining	*14*	*19*	*24*	..	*10*	*3*	*70*
Forestry	*13*	*25*	*8*	*4*	*25*	*6*	*81*
Sub-total, unemployment relief [1]	27	44	32	4	35	9	151
Grants for youth employment [1]	79	55	25	19	14	8	200
Grants for local public works [1]	39	27	14	9	7	4	100
Contribution under Port Augusta–Port Pirie Railway Agreement	..	..	..	20	..	..	20
Medical research	5	4	2	2	1	1	15
Grants for other research	8	8	4	5	3	2	30
Grants for after-care treatment of infantile paralysis	..	10	..	5	..	4	19
Sub-total, payments from revenue other than relief of primary producers	4845	3288	2159	2599	2068	1115	16,074
Assistance for relief of primary producers :							
Bounties	42	68	95	208	9	39	461
Other	69	107	60	50	55	15	356
Sub-total, primary producers	111	175	155	258	64	54	817
Total Payments from Revenue	4956	3463	2314	2857	2132	1169	16,891
Payments from Loan Fund :							
Assistance for relief of primary producers :							
Farmers' debt adjustment	840	840	170	280	300	70	2,500
GRAND TOTAL	5796	4303	2484	3137	2432	1239	19,391
Per head (£)	2·1	2·3	2·5	5·3	5·3	5·3	2·8

[1] Included in the item "Grants and Similar Intergovernmental Payments" in Table XI on page 139 of Chapter V. (Other items are given under other heads.)

Sources.—Budget Papers, 1941–42, Table 21, p. 80 ; Commonwealth Grants Commission, Sixth Report (1939), Appendix No. 23, pp. 142-3.

Table 20 AUSTRALIA, SPECIAL GRANTS PAID BY THE COMMONWEALTH TO THE STATES, 1910–11 TO 1942–43

(£ thousands)

Year	South Australia	Western Australia	Tasmania	Total
1910–11	..	250	..	250
1911–12	..	240	..	240
1912–13	..	230	95	325
1913–14	..	220	90	310
1914–15	..	210	90	300
1915–16	..	200	90	290
1916–17	..	190	90	280
1917–18	..	180	90	270
1918–19	..	170	90	260
1919–20	..	160	90	250
1920–21	..	150	90	240
1921–22	..	140	85	225
1922–23	..	130	85	215
1923–24	..	120	85	205
1924–25	..	110	146	256
1925–26	..	450	68	518
1926–27	..	300	378	678
1927–28	..	300	378	678
1928–29	..	300	220	520
1929–30	360	300	250	910
1930–31	1170	300	250	1720
1931–32	1000	300	250	1550
1932–33	1000	500	330	1830
1933–34	1150	600	380	2130
1934–35 [1]	1400	600	400	2400
1935–36 [1]	1500	800	450	2750
1936–37 [1]	1330	500	600	2430
1937–38 [1]	1200	575	575	2350
1938–39 [1]	1040	570	410	2020
1939–40 [1]	995	595	430	2020
1940–41 [1]	1000	650	400	2050
1941–42 [1]	1150	630	520	2300
1942–43 [2]	550	800	575	1925

[1] Paid in accordance with the recommendations of the Commonwealth Grants Commission.
[2] Recommendations of the Commonwealth Grants Commission.

Source.—Commonwealth Grants Commission, Ninth Report (1942).

LIST OF SOUTH AFRICAN TABLES

Table 1

SOUTH AFRICA, REVENUES AND EXPENDITURES OF THE UNION AND PROVINCES[1]

Year	Revenue			Expenditure			Interest on Capital from Railways and Harbours
	Union	Provincial	Total	Union	Provincial	Total	
	£	£	£	£	£	£	£
1913–14	12,606,150	1,289,190	13,895,340	11,100,686	3,324,136	14,424,822	3,198,926
1928–29	30,501,650	5,186,622	35,688,272	23,180,076	10,886,812	34,066,888	5,917,421
1931–32	27,740,746	5,016,726	32,757,472	22,975,664	11,557,257	34,532,921	6,492,296
1938–39	44,075,726	8,456,721	52,532,447	35,094,971	19,039,989	54,134,960	5,813,051

[1] The figures include gross revenues and expenditures of public utilities. Figures of Provincial revenues and Union expenditures are exclusive of grants and subsidies.

Table 2

SOUTH AFRICA, DISTRIBUTION OF ORDINARY REVENUES UNDER MAIN GROUPS

(£ thousands)

Year	Union Government				Provincial Administration				Grand Total
	Taxation	Services	Public Estate	Miscellaneous	Taxation	Services	Public Estate	Miscellaneous	
1913–14	8,552	2041	1289	724	1175	91	8	15	13,895
1928–29	21,632	4570	1951	2349	4503	508	87	88	35,688
1931–32	18,890	4994	1138	2718	4389	424	114	90	32,757
1938–39	32,707	6669	1466	3342	7461	530	177	289	52,641

Table 3

SOUTH AFRICA, REVENUES FROM TAXATION

(£ thousands)

Year	Union Government	Provincial Administrations					Grand Total
		Cape of Good Hope	Natal	Transvaal	Orange Free State	Total, All Provinces	
1913–14	8,552	400	87	557	131	1175	9,727
1928–29	21,632	1401	628	1968	506	4503	26,135
1931–32	18,890	1461	643	1885	400	4389	23,279
1938–39	32,707	2502	857	3576	526	7461	40,168

Table 4

SOUTH AFRICA, REVENUES FROM TAXATION PER HEAD OF EUROPEAN POPULATION

Year	Union Government	Provincial Administrations					Grand Total
		Cape of Good Hope	Natal	Transvaal	Orange Free State	Total, All Provinces	
	£ s. d.	£ s. d.	£ s. d.	£ s. d.	£ s. d.	£ s. d.	£ s. d.
1913–14	6 8 7	0 13 5	0 16 5	1 4 10	0 14 0	0 17 8	7 6 3
1928–29	12 8 10	1 18 6	3 14 11	3 2 0	2 8 6	2 11 9	15 0 7
1931–32	10 6 6	1 19 0	3 12 5	2 14 1	1 18 1	2 8 0	12 14 6
1938–39	15 14 4	3 1 9	4 7 3	4 1 10	2 12 4	3 11 8	19 6 0

Table 5 SOUTH AFRICA, DETAILS OF REVENUES OF THE UNION GOVERNMENT, 1937–38 [1]

	£
Customs	10,677,913
Excise	2,911,558
State mining revenue	582,407
Licences	191,114
Stamp duties and fees	1,305,011
Income tax	16,286,332
Surtax on interest	42
Estate and succession duties	1,037,547
Native taxes	567,409
Pass fees	62,123
Quintrent and farm taxes	15,393
Forest revenue	141,936
Rents of Government property	177,469
Interest	2,458,844
Departmental receipts	788,074
Fines and forfeitures	328,078
Miscellaneous	539,237
Postal	2,406,781
Telegraph and telephone	3,133,473
Total	43,610,741

[1] Including gross revenues from public utilities.

Table 6 SOUTH AFRICA, MINING REVENUE, 1937–38

	£ thousands
Gold mines	13,592
Diamond	441
Coal	106
Other	441
Total	14,580
From taxation	9,845
Other	4,735
Credited to Revenue Account	10,190
To Loan Account	4,390

Table 7 SOUTH AFRICA, RAILWAYS, REVENUE AND EXPENDITURE, 1937–38

	£ thousands
Revenue :	
Gross traffic receipts	33,389
Miscellaneous	1,656
Total	35,045
Expenditure :	
Gross working expenditure	23,219
Interest	4,924
Miscellaneous expenditure	1,320
Total	29,463
Surplus	5,582

Table 8 SOUTH AFRICA, HARBOURS, REVENUE AND EXPENDITURE, 1937–38

	£ thousands
Revenue	2111
Expenditure :	
Gross working expenditure	826
Interest	566
Total	1392
Surplus	719

Table 9 SOUTH AFRICA, UNION EXPENDITURES, 1937–38 AND 1940–41 [1]

	1937–38	1940–41
	£	£
General Government	1,371,680	1,536,840
Law, order and protection	6,284,430	17,140,810
Higher education, science, etc.	1,165,049	1,355,198
Labour and social welfare	1,273,234	2,096,300
Public health	1,312,844	1,804,300
Commerce and industries	280,206	330,380
Mining	618,180	766,800
Native affairs	528,251	764,866
Land and agriculture	2,294,456	2,741,509
Assistance to farmers	1,609,619	2,222,900
Public works	1,313,337	1,696,933
Posts and telegraphs	3,985,214	4,398,830
Pensions	4,742,968	5,314,975
Public debt	5,348,434	5,889,975
Government printing works	351,144	410,413
Miscellaneous	149,898	75,100
Total	32,628,944	48,546,129
Provincial Subsidies, etc.[2]	6,654,761	7,193,253
GRAND TOTAL	39,283,705	55,739,382

[1] Including gross expenditure on public utilities.
[2] Includes a grant of £340,000 per annum in respect of native education, to the South African Native Trust.

Table 10 SOUTH AFRICA, TOTAL REVENUES OF PROVINCES

(1) *Subsidies of Union Government to Provinces*

Year	Cape of Good Hope	Natal	Transvaal	Orange Free State	Total
1911–12	1085	431	1367	419	3302
1926–27	2054	480	1901	736	5171
1931–32	2220	520	1947	738	5425
1937–38	2634	670	2081	934	6319
1938–39	2699	691	2157	942	6489

(2) *Revenue Collections of each Province*

Year	Cape of Good Hope	Natal	Transvaal	Orange Free State	Total
1911–12	..	..	..	..	..
1926–27	1580	616	1843	419	4458
1931–32	1850	769	1956	441	5016
1937–38	2702	1002	3906	623	8233
1938–39	3037	1049	3770	601	8457

Table 11

SOUTH AFRICA, REVENUE SYSTEM OF THE PROVINCES, 1937–38

Item	(1) £ Thousands					(2) Per Cent of Total Revenue					(3) Pounds per Head of European Population					(4) Pounds per Head of Total Population				
	Cape	Natal	Transvaal	O.F.S.	Total	Cape	Natal	Transvaal	O.F.S.	Total	Cape	Natal	Transvaal	O.F.S.	Total	Cape	Natal	Transvaal	O.F.S.	Total
GROUP I. *Mainly Progressive Taxes:*																				
Income taxes on individuals	308	131	626	116	1,181	5	6	9	6	7	0·38	0·68	0·74	0·58	0·58	0·09	0·07	0·18	0·15	0·12
Native pass fees	..	..	604	..	604	..	..	9	..	4	..	..	0·71	..	0·29	..	..	0·17	..	0·06
Total, Group I	308	131	1230	116	1,785	5	6	18	6	11	0·38	0·68	1·45	0·58	0·87	0·09	0·07	0·35	0·15	0·18
GROUP II. *Taxes on Property (incl. Transfer)*	315	98	451	72	936	5	5	7	4	5	0·39	0·50	0·53	0·36	0·45	0·09	0·05	0·13	0·09	0·09
GROUP III. *Taxes on Business:*																				
Companies tax	154	62	515	18	749	2	3	8	1	4	0·19	0·32	0·61	0·09	0·36	0·04	0·03	0·15	0·02	0·08
Other business taxes	277	95	280	43	695	4	5	4	2	4	0·35	0·49	0·33	0·22	0·34	0·08	0·05	0·08	0·06	0·07
Total, Group III	431	157	795	61	1,444	6	8	12	3	8	0·54	0·81	0·94	0·31	0·70	0·12	0·08	0·23	0·08	0·15
GROUP IV. *Mainly Consumption Taxes:*																				
Motor vehicle licences	848	256	829	203	2,136	13	12	13	11	13	1·06	1·32	0·98	1·02	1·04	0·24	0·13	0·24	0·26	0·22
Other licences	104	26	18	17	165	2	1	..	1	1	0·13	0·13	0·02	0·08	0·08	0·03	0·01	0·01	0·02	0·02
Entertainment and racing	211	148	363	19	741	3	7	5	1	4	0·26	0·76	0·43	0·09	0·36	0·06	0·07	0·10	0·03	0·07
Other taxes	7	5	43	62	117	..	..	1	3	1	0·01	0·03	0·05	0·31	0·06	..	..	0·01	0·08	0·01
Sub-total	1170	435	1253	301	3,159	18	20	19	16	19	1·46	2·24	1·48	1·50	1·54	0·33	0·21	0·36	0·39	0·32
Miscellaneous revenues	478	181	176	73	908	7	9	3	4	5	0·60	0·93	0·20	0·37	0·44	0·13	0·09	0·05	0·09	0·09
Total, Group IV	1648	616	1429	374	4,067	25	29	22	20	24	2·06	3·17	1·68	1·87	1·98	0·46	0·30	0·41	0·48	0·41
TOTAL COLLECTIONS	2702	1002	3905	623	8,232	41	48	59	33	48	3·37	5·16	4·60	3·12	4·00	0·76	0·50	1·12	0·80	0·83
Grants and subsidies	3876	1074	2766	1239	8,955	59	52	41	67	52	4·84	5·54	3·25	6·19	4·34	1·08	0·54	0·80	1·58	0·91
GRAND TOTAL	6578	2076	6671	1862	17,187	100	100	100	100	100	8·21	10·70	7·85	9·31	8·34	1·84	1·04	1·92	2·38	1·74

Table 12 SOUTH AFRICA, DETAILS OF ORDINARY PROVINCIAL REVENUES, 1937–38

Classification	Cape of Good Hope	Natal	Transvaal	Orange Free State	All Provinces
	£	£	£	£	£
Auction sales tax	..	..	43,095	15,710	58,805
Companies tax	153,726	61,613	515,165	18,502	749,006
Departmental receipts	146,766	105,086	151,864	48,590	452,306
Education receipts	321,064	72,839	13,066	22,568	429,537
Entertainments tax	145,511	60,999	117,507	16,272	340,289
Fines and forfeitures	10,224	3,657	10,312	2,293	26,486
Licences:					
Dog, fish and game	4,662	25,580	18,907	16,890	66,039
Importers	98,950	..	..	..	98,950
Liquor	86,869	21,313	61,275	9,352	178,809
Motor vehicles	848,471	255,598	829,314	203,447	2,136,830
Trades and professions	190,078	73,978	219,012	32,282	516,350
Native pass fees	..	..	604,007	..	604,007
Personal and income tax	307,720	131,062	625,764	115,545	1,180,091
Provincial property tax	13,947	..	..	..	13,947
Racing taxation	65,171	87,299	245,338	2,451	400,259
Transfer duty	301,568	98,024	451,103	71,573	922,268
Trankskeian roads tax	7,025	..	..	..	7,025
Wheel tax	..	5,206	..	46,408	51,614
Total Collections	2,701,752	1,002,254	3,905,729	622,883	8,232,618
Union Government subsidies	2,634,463	669,926	2,081,149	933,619	6,319,157
Grant:					
S.A. Native Trust	427,000	157,740	170,467	61,300	816,507
National Road Fund	814,763	241,557	508,659	243,827	1,808,806
Other	..	4,585	5,844	..	10,429
TOTAL REVENUE	6,577,978	2,076,062	6,671,848	1.861,629	17,187,517

Table 13 SOUTH AFRICA, ORDINARY EXPENDITURES OF THE PROVINCES

(£ thousands)

Period	Cape of Good Hope	Natal	Transvaal	Orange Free State	Total
1911–12	**931**	**376**	**1200**	**377**	**2,884**
1926–27	**3910**	**1090**	**3641**	**1207**	**9,948**
1931–32	**4751**	**1409**	**3974**	**1423**	**11,557**
1938–39	**7887**	**2474**	**6673**	**2005**	**19,039**

Table 14 SOUTH AFRICA, AVERAGE EXPENDITURE OF THE PROVINCES PER HEAD OF MEAN POPULATION

Period	Cape of Good Hope		Natal		Transvaal		Orange Free State		Total	
	Total Population	European	Total Population	European	Total Population	European	Total Population	European	Total Population	European
	s. d.	£ s. d.	s. d.	£ s. d.	s. d.	£ s. d.	s. d.	£ s. d.	s. d.	£ s. d.
1911–12	7 3	1 11 11	6 3	3 16 2	14 2	2 16 9	14 2	2 3 0	9 7	2 5 1
1926–27	26 5	5 10 8	13 11	6 17 2	32 4	6 2 10	34 8	5 18 11	26 5	5 18 7
1931–32	28 10	6 6 9	15 10	7 18 9	27 5	5 14 1	38 9	6 18 6	26 6	6 6 4
1938–39	43 5	9 14 8	24 6	12 11 8	37 9	7 12 9	50 9	9 18 8	38 2	9 2 11

Table 15 SOUTH AFRICA, ORDINARY EXPENDITURES, PROVINCES, 1937–38 AND 1939–40

1937–38	
	£
Administration	458,275
Education	9,610,821
Hospitals and charitable institutions	1,515,576
Roads, bridges and local works	4,384,857
Miscellaneous services	929,733
Interest and redemption charges	672,542
Total	17,571,804

1939–40	Cape of Good Hope	Natal	Transvaal	Orange Free State	All Provinces
	£	£	£	£	£
General administration	193,874	77,230	210,700	53,116	534,920
Education	4,322,374	1,068,943	3,972,748	1,031,234	10,395,299
Hospitals and charitable institutions	525,598	401,858	728,505	165,765	1,821,726
Roads, bridges and local works	2,509,319	767,922	2,035,070	686,694	5,999,005
Miscellaneous	55,136	27,979	7,230	19,724	110,069
Interest and redemption	325,624	136,907	303,572	90,840	856,943
Total	7,931,925	2,480,839	7,257,825	2,047,373	19,717,962

Table 16 SOUTH AFRICA, DETAILS OF REVENUES OF MUNICIPALITIES, 1937–38

	Cape of Good Hope	Natal	Transvaal	Orange Free State	Union
	£	£	£	£	£
Rates	2,170,567	619,605	1,705,210	232,401	4,727,783
Sanitary fees . . .	192,300	68,506[1]	1,037,383	73,581	1,371,770
Water	867,849	336,392	955,309	171,516	2,331,066
Licences . . .	55,489	109,626	403,205	16,853	585,173
Abattoirs . . .	88,572	41,499	171,969	15,584	317,624
Building plans, fees . .	7,230	6,996	46,846	1,781	62,853
Cemeteries . . .	8,577	7,686	36,241	2,279	54,783
Estate (incl. Town Hall) .	294,318	140,019	100,343	62,870	597,550
Fines	18,915	20,199	70,127	904	110,145
Fire brigades and ambulances	13,210	6,778	16,805	2,734	39,527
Locations . . .	138,354	136,540	281,711	77,360	633,965
Markets. . . .	71,212	73,765	77,548	16,968	239,493
Pounds	3,384	342	5,468	2,788	11,982
Forestry . . .	3,517	12,601	8,934	1,000	26,052
Parks, gardens, recreation grounds, swimming baths, bathing and wash-houses .	56,375	37,195	48,307	10,039	147,416
Interest on investments .	80,115	7,097	62,851	22,066	172,129
Electricity supply . .	1,967,459	831,370	1,941,566	254,150	4,994,545
Gas supply . . .	2,584	..	153,747	..	156,331
Tramways and bus services .	37,185	300,178	1,087,889	20,357	1,445,609
Native beer . . .	2,119	70,939	25,915	..	98,973
Other revenue . . .	610,984	175,293	141,937	53,547	981,761
Total . . .	6,690,315	3,002,626	8,374,811	1,038,778	19,106,530

[1] Including Public Health.

Table 17 SOUTH AFRICA, DETAILS OF EXPENDITURES OF MUNICIPALITIES, 1937–38

	Cape of Good Hope	Natal	Transvaal	Orange Free State	Union
	£	£	£	£	£
Administration	277,384	85,675	256,664	62,100	681,823
Sanitary	387,657	191,007	713,548	65,457	1,357,669
Public health	286,805	..	205,761	23,376	515,942
Streets and bridges	311,663	154,204	481,701	59,573	1,007,141
Street lighting	98,392	13,697	170,742	14,313	297,144
Water supply	304,391	97,697	525,213	81,568	1,008,869
Electricity supply	1,437,937	586,060	1,090,975	121,908	3,236,880
Gas supply	4,500	..	101,452	..	105,952
Tramways and bus service	31,419	279,563	1,056,711	21,069	1,388,762
Abattoirs	60,147	27,415	130,555	13,915	232,032
Cemeteries	16,275	9,878	51,129	2,319	79,601
Estate	93,677	23,203	42,324	24,822	184,026
Fire brigades and ambulances	70,103	32,034	100,235	6,058	208,430
Locations	111,124	75,145	225,259	66,285	477,813
Markets	50,835	56,814	67,027	14,982	189,658
Pounds	5,427	219	7,969	2,016	15,631
Forestry	11,318	14,719	10,629	1,797	38,463
Town halls, parks, gardens, recreation grounds, swimming baths, bathing and wash-houses	173,755	140,676	272,177	37,650	624,258
Mayoral allowances	8,301	3,350	17,457	4,525	33,633
Public entertainments	10,566	5,400	8,871	3,013	27,850
Grants to hospitals and other institutions	136,709	40,218	195,471	15,055	387,453
Elections	1,476	129	15,337	572	17,514
Valuation	5,981	8,760	14,911	1,524	31,176
Legal and audit	19,059	7,075	28,965	6,167	61,266
Insurance	17,763	4,429	52,939	3,884	79,015
Pensions and gratuities	107,674	34,383	79,163	4,985	226,205
Traffic control	38,463	25,559	102,160	1,417	167,599
Licensing	16,219	..	65,816	..	82,035
Police	..	..	..	..	..
Loan charges:					
Interest	1,240,271	592,661	956,622	147,376	2,936,930
Redemption	603,636	134,191	408,086	98,072	1,243,985
Other	300	4,015	255	2,463	7,033
Maintenance and depreciation	53,259	35,108	142,794	10,147	241,308
Native beer	2,502	21,321	18,073	..	41,896
Other expenditure	421,648	119,175	171,455	29,034	741,312
Total	6,416,636	2,823,780	7,788,446	947,442	17,976,304

Table 18

SOUTH AFRICA, GROWTH OF EDUCATION

	European				Native				Indian and Coloured			
	1910	1920	1930	1937	1910	1920	1930	1937	1910	1920	1930	1937
Number of pupils (in thousands)	165	314	370	398	80	185	287	399	..	55	99	148
Percentage of population	13	21	20	20	2	4	5	6	..	8	11	15
Percentage of pupils of all grades in primary schools	89	87	84	80	100	99	98	98	..	..	99	97
Percentage of pupils of all grades in post-primary classes	11	13	16	20	..	1	2	2	..	..	1	3
	100	100	100	100	100	100	100	100	..	..	100	100
State expenditure on education (in £ thousands)	1596	6323	8369	9820[1]	107	340	612	836	..	..	457	812
Cost per head of population (in £)	1·27	4·22	4·66	4·80	0·03	0·08	0·1	0·1	..	..	0·5	0·8
Cost per pupil (in £)	9·65	20·16	22·60	24·66	1·25	1·83	2·1	2·1	..	..	4·6	5·5

[1] This differs from the expenditure figure in Table IV in Chapter VI because the Union figure in the latter includes grants for scientific research, libraries, etc., which are not included in the above table.

Table 19

SOUTH AFRICA, GROSS AND NET PUBLIC DEBT ON 31st MARCH, from 1912 to 1940

(£ millions)

Year	Gross Debt	Sinking Funds	Net Debt	Gross Debt per Head: Total Population	Gross Debt per Head: European Population	Net Debt per Head: Total Population	Net Debt per Head: European Population
				£ s. d.	£ s. d.	£ s. d.	£ s. d.
1912	117	6	111	19 6 0	90 5 5	18 7 0	85 15 5
1927	231	15	216	30 6 7	135 18 1	28 7 1	127 1 1
1932	264	20	244	29 16 8	142 5 8	27 15 10	131 7 3
1939	279	8	271	27 11 5	132 6 5	26 15 10	128 11 7
1940	291	6	285	28 6 2	135 19 3	27 13 9	132 19 4

Table 20 SOUTH AFRICA, EXTERNAL AND INTERNAL DEBT, 1912–40

(£ millions)

Date	External Debt		Internal Debt		Total Debt
	Amount	Per Cent of Total Debt	Amount	Per Cent of Total Debt	
1912	103	88·10	14	11·90	117
1927	148	63·85	84	36·15	232
1932	160	60·50	104	39·50	264
1939	101	36·26	178	63·74	279
1940	106	36·41	185	63·59	291

Table 21

SOUTH AFRICA, CAPITAL EXPENDITURES OF PROVINCES, 1913–14 TO 1938–39, AND PROVINCIAL LOAN INDEBTEDNESS

(£ thousands)

	Cape of Good Hope	Natal	Transvaal	Orange Free State	Total
Capital expenditure .	7261	4910	9146	4146	25,463
Total loan indebtedness .	5595	2413	4844	1468	14,320

Table 22

SOUTH AFRICA, LOAN INDEBTEDNESS, SINKING FUNDS AND RATEABLE VALUATION OF PROPERTY OF MUNICIPALITIES, 1937

(£ thousands)

	Indebtedness	Sinking Funds	Rateable Valuation on Property
Cape of Good Hope . .	31,621	6,640	125,940
Natal	15,787	3,467	52,228
Transvaal	23,227	3,993	185,434
Orange Free State . . .	3,276	765	17,602
Total . . .	73,911	14,865	381,204

LIST OF INDIAN TABLES

Table 1 INDIA, THE REVENUE SYSTEM, CENTRAL GOVERNMENT [1]
(Rs. millions)

	1939–40	1940–41	1941–42	1942–43
GROUPS I AND III. *Taxes on Personal Income and on Business:* [2]				
Taxes on income other than Corporation Tax	142	176	247	336
Corporation Tax	24	41	113	220
Total, Groups I and III	166	217	360	556
GROUP II. *Taxes on Real Property:*				
Land revenue	2	2	2	2
Forests	1	2	2	2
Total, Group II	3	4	4	4
GROUP IV. *Chiefly Consumption Taxes:*				
Customs	459	373	360	354
Excise: Central	65	95	123	126
Provincial	3	3	3	3
Sub-total, Excise	68	98	126	129
Other, Similar Taxes and Licences:				
Salt	109	76	91	90
Opium	4	5	7	8
Stamps	4	4	4	4
Miscellaneous	1	1	1	1
Sub-total, Other Taxes and Licences	118	86	103	103
Revenue from Public Utilities:				
Railways (net)	341	478	555	570
Post and telegraphs (net)	16	19	39	49
Civil works (roads and bridges)	3	4	3	4
Sub-total, Revenue from Public Utilities	360	501	597	623
Defence Receipts	7	12	13	20
Miscellaneous	71	154	110	120
Total, Group IV	1083	1224	1309	1349
Contributions from States	6	6	6	6
GRAND TOTAL	1258	1451	1679	1915

[1] 1939–40 and 1940–41, actual figures; 1941–42, revised estimate; 1942–43, Budget estimate.
[2] Excess profits tax is counted partly under corporation tax, partly under income tax. E.P.T. receipts were Rs. 20 millions in 1940–41, Rs. 80 millions in 1941–42 (both figures revised estimates). and are estimated at Rs. 200 millions in the Budget for 1942–43.

Table 2 INDIA, PUBLIC EXPENDITURES FROM REVENUES, CENTRAL GOVERNMENT [1]

(Rs. millions)

	1939–40	1940–41	1941–42	1942–43
1. *Primary Functions :*				
Civil administration, legislation and justice	129	140	157	163
Pensions	28	21	21	21
Debt services	120	128	90	107
Defence	503	748	1038	1350
Total, Primary Functions	780	1037	1306	1641
2. *Secondary Functions :*				
(1) *Social Services :*				
Education	9	10	10	10
Public health	3	5	4	4
Sub-total, Social Services	12	15	14	14
(2) *Developmental :*				
Railways	297	356	363	369
Aviation	4	8	10	12
Posts and telegraphs	7	7	7	7
Broadcasting	3	3	5	6
Civil works	27	30	39	33
Agriculture and irrigation	6	6	10	28
Industries	1	1	2	2
Sub-total, Developmental	345	411	436	457
(3) *Miscellaneous*	90	23	66	125
Total, Secondary Functions	447	449	516	596
Contributions to Provinces and miscellaneous adjustments	31	31	30	28
GRAND TOTAL	1258	1517	1852	2265

[1] 1939–40 and 1940–41, actual figures ; 1941–42, revised estimate ; 1942–43, Budget estimate.

Table 3

THE REVENUE SYSTEM OF INDIA, PROVINCES, 1937–38
(Rs. millions)

	Coorg	Madras	Bombay	Bengal	United Provs.	Punjab	Bihar	C.P. and Berar	Assam	N.W.F.	Orissa	Sind	Total
I. PROGRESSIVE TAXES:													
Personal income taxes	..	1·9	2·5	2·5	1·9	1·0	1·3	0·6	0·3	0·1	0·2	0·3	12·6
II. TAXES ON REAL PROPERTY:													
Land revenue	0·4	49·6	32·0	35·3	58·7	28·8	13·7	23·1	12·1	2·1	4·8	3·3	263·9
Forests	0·4	5·0	4·3	2·2	5·0	2·4	0·7	5·1	1·8	0·5	0·4	0·8	28·6
Sale of land	..	..	..	0·1	..	3·1	..	..	..	..	..	8·2	11·4
Total, Group II	0·8	54·6	36·3	37·6	63·7	34·3	14·4	28·2	13·9	2·6	5·2	12·3	303·9
IV. CHIEFLY CONSUMPTION TAXES:													
Customs	..	..	..	23·8	..	..	1·4	..	1·1	..	0·2	..	26·5
Excise: Liquor	0·2	35·4	25·5	8·6	8·2	6·3	9·3	4·2	1·9	0·6	0·9	2·4	103·5
Opium	..	2·8	1·9	3·5	2·5	3·4	0·8	1·5	1·2	0·1	1·9	0·5	20·1
Other	..	2·1	4·8	3·4	3·9	1·0	2·1	1·1	0·5	0·1	0·5	0·8	20·3
Sub-total, Excise	0·2	40·3	32·2	15·5	14·6	10·7	12·2	6·8	3·6	0·8	3·3	3·7	143·9
Other, Similar Taxes and Licences:													
Salt	..	..	..	0·1	..	..	..	..	..	..	..	..	0·1
Tobacco duties	..	..	2·0	0·3	..	0·1	..	..	..	..	..	0·1	2·5
Entertainment and betting	..	0·2	2·2	1·7	0·2	0·2	..	..	..	..	..	0·1	4·6
Automobile licences	0·1	5·4	4·4	2·1	1·1	0·8	..	0·4	0·3	0·1	0·1	0·2	15·0
Stamps: Non-judicial	..	8·2	8·2	8·1	2·8	3·4	2·5	0·9	0·5	0·4	0·4	1·1	36·5
Judicial	..	11·1	7·2	20·7	11·0	5·6	7·7	3·2	1·3	0·5	1·4	0·7	70·4
Registration	..	3·3	1·5	2·3	0·9	1·0	1·3	0·6	0·2	0·1	0·2	0·2	11·6
Sub-total, Other Taxes	0·1	28·2	25·5	35·3	16·0	11·1	11·5	5·1	2·3	1·1	2·1	2·4	140·7
Revenue from Public Utilities:													
Railways (net)	..	..	..	..	0·2	..	..	..	..	..	..	..	0·2
Irrigation (net)	..	18·5	2·3	−0·2	14·1	47·4	1·9	0·4	..	1·5	0·2	7·1	93·2
Civil works	0·1	4·1	5·8	2·8	1·3	3·8	0·8	1·0	1·6	1·0	0·4	0·6	23·3
Electricity duties	..	..	1·2	1·8	..	..	..	..	..	..	..	0·1	3·1
Sub-total, Utilities	0·1	22·6	9·3	4·4	15·6	51·2	2·7	1·4	1·6	2·5	0·6	7·8	119·8
Miscellaneous [1]	0·1	12·5	18·6	11·0	9·1	11·2	6·8	3·3	1·6	1·1	2·1	1·7	79·1
Total, Group IV	0·5	103·6	85·6	90·0	55·3	84·2	34·6	16·6	10·2	5·5	8·3	15·6	510·0
Grants-in-aid and miscellaneous adjustments	0·2	..	..	..	2·5	0·3	..	..	3·0	10·0	4·7	11·0	31·7
GRAND TOTAL	1·5	160·1	124·4	130·1	123·4	119·8	50·3	45·4	27·4	18·2	18·4	39·2	858·2

[1] Miscellaneous Receipts are the revenue from Debt Services, Administration of Justice, Jails and Convict Settlements, Police, Ports and Pilotage, Education, Medical Services, Public Health, Agriculture, Veterinary Services, Co-operation, Industries, Broadcasting, Miscellaneous Departments, Transfers from Famine Relief Fund, Receipts in Aid of Superannuation, Stationery and Printing, Miscellaneous Items, and Extraordinary Receipts other than from sale of land.

Table 4

THE REVENUE SYSTEM OF INDIA, PROVINCES, 1937–38
(Percentage distribution)

	Coorg	Madras	Bombay	Bengal	United Provs.	Punjab	Bihar	C.P. and Berar	Assam	N.W.F.	Orissa	Sind	Total
I. PROGRESSIVE TAXES:													
Personal income taxes	..	1	2	2	2	1	2	1	1	1	1	1	2
II. TAXES ON REAL PROPERTY:													
Land revenue	24	31	26	27	48	24	27	51	44	11	26	8	31
Forests	26	3	3	2	4	2	2	11	7	3	2	2	3
Sale of land	..	..	..	..	..	3	..	..	..	..	..	21	1
Total, Group II	50	34	29	29	52	29	29	62	51	14	28	31	35
IV. CHIEFLY CONSUMPTION TAXES:													
Customs	..	..	..	18	..	..	3	..	4	..	1	..	3
Excise: Liquor	14	22	20	7	7	5	18	9	7	3	5	6	12
Opium	..	2	2	3	2	3	2	4	4	1	10	1	2
Other	1	1	4	3	3	1	4	2	2	1	3	2	3
Sub-total, Excise	15	25	26	13	12	9	24	15	13	5	18	9	17
Other, Similar Taxes and Licences:													
Salt	..	..	..	..	..	..	..	..	..	..	..	..	..
Tobacco duties	..	..	1	..	..	..	..	..	..	..	..	..	..
Entertainment and betting	..	..	2	1	..	..	..	..	..	..	..	..	1
Automobile licences	7	4	4	2	1	1	..	1	1	..	..	1	2
Stamps: Non-judicial	1	5	7	6	2	3	5	2	2	2	3	3	4
Judicial	3	7	6	16	9	4	15	7	4	3	7	2	8
Registration	..	2	1	2	1	1	3	1	1	..	1	1	1
Sub-total, Other Taxes	11	18	21	27	13	9	23	11	8	5	11	7	16
Revenue from Public Utilities:													
Railways (net)	..	..	..	..	..	..	..	..	..	..	..	..	..
Irrigation (net)	..	11	2	..	11	40	3	1	..	8	1	18	11
Civil works	5	3	4	2	1	3	2	2	6	6	2	2	3
Electricity duties	..	..	1	1	..	..	..	..	..	..	..	..	..
Sub-total, Utilities	5	14	7	3	14	43	5	3	6	14	3	20	14
Miscellaneous	4	8	15	8	7	9	14	8	6	6	12	4	9
Total, Group IV	35	65	69	69	44	70	69	37	37	30	45	40	59
Grants-in-aid and miscellaneous adjustments	15	..	..	..	2	..	..	..	11	55	26	28	4
GRAND TOTAL	100	100	100	100	100	100	100	100	100	100	100	100	100
Percentage share of the Provinces in the total	..	19	15	15	14	14	6	5	3	2	2	5	100

Table 5

INDIA, EXPENDITURES FROM REVENUES, PROVINCES, 1937–38

(Rs. millions)

	Coorg	Madras	Bombay	Bengal	United Provs.	Punjab	Bihar	C.P. and Berar	Assam	N.W.F.	Orissa	Sind	Total
1. *Primary Functions :*													
Civil administration, legislation and justice	0·7	75·5	49·1	62·4	55·7	40·3	24·0	23·6	11·7	8·3	7·8	10·8	369·9
Pensions	0·1	10·2	11·1	10·2	10·0	7·3	4·2	4·2	2·1	0·9	1·0	1·6	62·9
Debt services	..	−4·4	12·5	−0·7	6·0	−1·0	0·6	−0·6	0·3	0·1	0·1	0·5	13·4
Total, Primary Functions	0·8	81·3	72·7	71·9	71·7	46·6	28·8	27·2	14·1	9·3	8·9	12·9	446·2
2. *Secondary Functions :*													
(1) *Social Services :*													
Education	0·2	25·9	16·9	13·7	20·6	16·1	7·0	5·5	3·6	2·1	2·6	3·0	117·2
Public health	0·1	13·9	6·8	8·3	5·7	6·5	3·5	2·0	2·2	0·8	1·1	1·0	51·9
Sub-total, Social Services	0·3	39·8	23·7	22·0	26·3	22·6	10·5	7·5	5·8	2·9	3·7	4·0	169·1
(2) *Developmental :*													
Civil works	0·3	13·8	13·1	12·0	6·1	13·9	4·7	5·9	5·3	4·0	2·0	2·1	83·2
Agriculture and irrigation	..	16·6	7·2	5·0	14·5	19·1	2·8	4·1	0·8	0·8	1·6	15·7	88·2
Industries	..	2·5	0·8	1·6	1·4	1·9	1·0	0·3	0·3	..	0·2	0·1	10·1
Co-operation	..	1·3	0·6	1·2	0·6	1·4	0·4	0·3	0·1	0·1	0·1	0·1	6·2
Sub-total, Developmental	0·3	34·2	21·7	19·8	22·6	36·3	8·9	10·6	6·5	4·9	3·9	18·0	187·7
(3) *Miscellaneous*	..	3·0	3·4	4·6	2·8	9·2	1·3	1·3	1·4	0·8	1·1	0·6	29·5
Total, Secondary Functions	0·6	77·0	48·8	46·4	51·7	68·1	20·7	19·4	13·7	8·6	8·7	22·6	386·3
GRAND TOTAL	1·4	158·3	121·5	118·3	123·4	114·7	49·5	46·6	27·8	17·9	17·6	35·5	832·5
Surplus (+) or deficit (−)	+0·1	+1·8	+2·9	+11·8	..	+5·1	+0·8	−1·2	−0·4	+0·3	+0·8	+3·7	+25·7
Total Ordinary Revenue [1]	1·5	160·1	124·4	130·1	123·4	119·8	50·3	45·4	27·4	18·2	18·4	39·2	858·2

[1] See Table 3.

Table 6

INDIA, EXPENDITURES FROM REVENUES, PROVINCES, 1937–38

(Percentage distribution)

	Coorg	Madras	Bombay	Bengal	United Provs.	Punjab	Bihar	C.P. and Berar	Assam	N.W.F.	Orissa	Sind	Total
1. *Primary Functions :*													
Civil administration, legislation and justice	47	48	40	53	45	35	49	50	42	47	45	30	44
Pensions	7	6	9	9	8	6	8	9	8	5	5	5	8
Debt services	1	−3	10	−1	5	−1	1	−1	1	1	1	1	2
Total, Primary Functions	55	51	59	61	58	40	58	58	51	53	51	36	54
2. *Secondary Functions :*													
(1) *Social Services :*													
Education	13	16	14	12	17	14	14	12	13	12	15	8	14
Public health	8	9	6	7	5	6	7	4	8	5	6	3	6
Sub-total, Social Services	21	25	20	19	22	20	21	16	21	17	21	11	20
(2) *Developmental :*													
Civil works	17	9	10	10	5	12	9	12	19	22	11	6	10
Agriculture and irrigation	3	10	6	4	12	17	6	9	3	4	9	45	11
Industries	..	2	1	1	1	2	2	1	1	..	1	..	1
Co-operation	1	1	1	1	..	1	1	1	..	1	1	..	1
Sub-total, Developmental	21	22	18	16	18	32	18	23	23	27	22	51	23
(3) *Miscellaneous*	3	2	3	4	2	8	3	3	5	3	6	2	3
Total, Secondary Functions	45	49	41	39	42	60	42	42	49	47	49	64	46
GRAND TOTAL	100	100	100	100	100	100	100	100	100	100	100	100	100
Percentage share of the Provinces in the total	..	19	15	15	14	14	6	5	3	2	2	5	100

Table 7 INDIA, DETAILS OF MUNICIPAL REVENUES, 1937–38

	Rs. millions	Per cent[1]
GROUP I. *Progressive Taxes*	..	..
GROUP II. *Taxes on Real Property :*		
Tax on houses and lands	50·1	28
Rents of lands, houses, etc.	5·0	3
Sale proceeds of land and produce of land, etc.	2·7	1
Total, Group II	57·8	32
GROUP III. *Taxes on Business :*		
Tax on professions and trades	3·4	2
GROUP IV. *Chiefly Consumption Taxes :*		
Various Taxes and Licences :		
Octroi	14·6	8
Tax on animals and vehicles	4·8	3
From pounds, hackney carriages, licences for the sale of spirits and drugs, etc.	1·5	1
Other taxes	19·6	11
Other fees, etc.	8·0	4
Total, Various Taxes and Licences	48·5	27
Revenue from Public Utilities :		
Tolls on roads and ferries	2·9	1
Lighting rate	4·0	2
Water rate	21·8	12
Conservancy rates and receipts (charges for the removal of night soil)	10·6	6
Receipts from markets and slaughter-houses	6·6	4
Fees from educational institutions	1·8	1
Total, Revenue from Public Utilities	47·7	26
Miscellaneous :		
Fines	1·1	1
Miscellaneous	9·1	5
Total, Miscellaneous	10·2	6
Total, Group IV	106·4	59
GROUP V. *Grants and Contributions :*		
Grants from Government	11·1	6
Grants from local funds	0·8	} 1
Other grants and contributions	0·5	
Total, Grants and Contributions	12·4	7
TOTAL, ORDINARY REVENUE	180·0	100
GROUP VI. *Extraordinary and Debt :*		
Sale proceeds of securities, etc.	55·7	..
Loans from Government	2·5	..
Loans raised from private individuals	11·0	..
Realisations of sinking fund	8·6	..
Advances	15·4	..
Deposits	115·4	..
Total, Extraordinary and Debt	208·6	..
GRAND TOTAL, GROSS RECEIPTS	388·6	..

[1] Per cent of Ordinary Revenue.

Table 8 INDIA, DETAILS OF MUNICIPAL EXPENDITURES, 1937–38

	Rs. millions	Per Cent[1]
1. *Primary Functions :*		
(1) *Civil Administration :*		
General administration	16·9	9
Public safety	15·6	9
Total, Civil Administration	32·5	18
(2) *Debt Services*	14·4	8
Total, Primary Functions	46·9	26
2. *Secondary Functions :*		
(1) *Social Services :*		
Education	23·5	13
Public health (including water supply, drainage and conservancy)	62·4	35
Other (*e.g.* public gardens)	1·6	1
Total, Social Services	87·5	49
(2) *Developmental :*		
Civil works (roads and buildings)	18·6	10
Other	7·3	4
Total, Developmental	25·9	14
(3) *Miscellaneous*	19·8	11
Total, Secondary Functions	133·2	74
TOTAL, EXPENDITURE FROM REVENUE	180·1	100
3. *Extraordinary and Debt :*		
Investments	56·1	..
Payments to sinking funds	6·0	..
Repayment of loans	11·7	..
Advances	21·2	..
Deposits	111·8	..
Total, Extraordinary and Debt	206·8	..
GRAND TOTAL, GROSS EXPENDITURE	386·9	..

[1] Per cent of Expenditure from Revenue.

Table 9 INDIA, INCOME OF DISTRICT AND LOCAL BOARDS, BY PROVINCES, 1937–38

(Rs. thousands)

Province	Provincial Rates	Civil Works	Other Sources	Total	Incidence per Head
					Rs. A. P.
Madras	11,053	11,133	25,110	47,296	0 14 10
Bombay	3,508	2,357	14,470	20,335	1 3 2
Bengal	9,305	2,615	5,748	17,668	0 5 7
United Provinces	7,987	1,446	10,422	19,855	0 6 11
Punjab	6,622	1,421	12,843	20,886	1 0 6
Bihar	7,029	3,986	5,121	16,136	0 8 0
Central Provinces and Berar	2,592	267	4,417	7,276	0 8 0
Assam	1,283	798	1,585	3,666	0 7 4
North-West Frontier Province	273	80	1,164	1,517	0 10 6
Orissa	782	232	1,730	2,744	0 5 9
Sind	1,274	342	2,931	4,547	1 4 4
Coorg	62	40	54	156	0 15 4
Ajmer-Merwara	29	50	53	132	0 3 9
Delhi	45	12	204	261	1 6 9
TOTAL	51,844	24,779	85,852	162,475	0 9 11
Percentage distribution	32	15	53	100	..

Source.—Statistical Abstract for British India, 1929–30—1938–39.

Table 10 INDIA, EXPENDITURE OF DISTRICT AND LOCAL BOARDS, BY PROVINCES, 1937–38

(Rs. thousands)

Province	Education	Civil Works	Sanitation, Hospital, etc.	Debt and Miscellaneous	Total
Madras	13,743	14,584	4,051	15,099	47,477
Bombay	11,276	3,609	997	4,555	20,437
Bengal	3,039	7,241	4,379	3,335	17,994
United Provinces	11,310	3,469	4,724	322	19,825
Punjab	11,233	3,234	2,916	3,561	20,944
Bihar	4,603	5,801	2,272	2,237	14,913
Central Provinces and Berar	3,010	813	381	3,131	7,335
Assam	1,479	1,092	600	544	3,715
North-West Frontier Province	996	157	120	285	1,558
Orissa	1,187	595	509	464	2,755
Sind	2,050	937	469	392	3,848
Coorg	79	12	36	28	155
Ajmer-Merwara	17	60	8	32	117
Delhi	160	31	54	24	269
TOTAL	64,182	41,635	21,516	34,009	161,342
Percentage distribution	40	26	13	21	100

Source.—Statistical Abstract for British India, 1929–30—1938–39.

Table 11

INDIA, RAILWAY FINANCES

(Rs. millions)

	1937–38	1939–40	1940–41
Capital outlay to end of year . . .	7538·0	7586·2	7609·3
Net revenue receipts	319·5	327·2	462·3
Percentage of net revenue receipts on capital outlay	4·24	4·31	6·08
Payments on account of share of surplus profits and of net revenue receipts . .	5·3	3·5	5·0
Interest on capital outlay	292·6	291·1	286·8
Total expenditure	297·9	294·6	291·7
Gain	21·6	32·6	170·6

Source.—Combined Finance and Revenue Accounts of the Central and Provincial Governments in India for the years 1937–38, 1939–40 and 1940–41.

Table 12 INDIA, CAPITAL AND OTHER EXPENDITURES (APART FROM REVENUE ACCOUNT) OF THE CENTRAL AND PROVINCIAL GOVERNMENTS TO THE END OF 1937–38

(Rs. millions)

Capital and Other Expenditure outside the Revenue A/c	Central Govt.	Coorg	Madras	Bombay	Bengal	United Provs.	Punjab	Bihar	C.P. and Berar	Assam	N.W.F.	Orissa	Sind	Total
1. *Capital Expenditure:*														
Commercial Departments:														
Railways	7,538·0	..	..	..	..	0·1	..	..	..	..	..	..	..	7,538·1
Posts and telegraphs	170·7	..	..	..	..	..	..	..	..	..	..	..	..	170·7
Irrigation	17·8	..	199·1	103·7	52·0	282·7	349·7	34·4	65·7	..	31·2	31·9	293·9	1,462·1
Electric schemes	..	..	37·4	..	..	..	64·8	..	..	..	4·3	..	..	106·5
Other commercial departments	59·0	..	1·6	..	..	..	0·9	..	..	..	..	..	..	61·5
Total, Commercial Departments	7,785·5	..	238·1	103·7	52·0	282·8	415·4	34·4	65·7	..	35·5	31·9	293·9	9,338·9
Other Departments:														
New capital at Delhi	156·0	..	..	..	..	..	..	..	..	..	..	..	..	156·0
Bombay development scheme	..	..	..	93·5	..	..	..	..	..	..	..	..	..	93·5
Other accounts	144·6	..	8·6	57·7	13·7	49·4	33·5	6·8	15·6	8·6	0·2	..	10·7	349·4
Total, Other Departments	300·6	..	8·6	151·2	13·7	49·4	33·5	6·8	15·6	8·6	0·2	..	10·7	598·9
Total, Capital Expenditure	8,086·1	..	246·7	254·9	65·7	332·2	448·9	41·2	81·3	8·6	35·7	31·9	304·6	9,937·8
2. *India's Financial Contribution to the War of 1914–18*	1,500·0	..	..	..	..	..	..	..	..	..	..	..	..	1,500·0
3. *Loans and Advances:*														
To Provinces	1,246·6	..	..	..	..	..	..	..	..	..	..	..	..	1,246·6
To Coorg	0·5	..	..	..	..	..	..	..	..	..	..	..	..	0·5
To Indian States	128·8	..	..	..	..	..	..	..	..	..	..	..	..	128·8
To Local Funds, etc.	85·1	0·5	45·2	156·8	8·1	23·5	7·8	15·6	10·1	0·6	2·7	0·7	5·3	362·0
To Government servants	4·2	..	0·2	0·3	0·3	0·9	0·5	0·3	0·2	0·5	0·1	0·0	0·1	7·6
Total, Loans and Advances	1,465·2	0·5	45·4	157·1	8·4	24·4	8·3	15·9	10·3	1·1	2·8	0·7	5·4	1,745·5
TOTAL, CAPITAL AND OTHER EXPENDITURE TO END OF 1937–38	11,051·3	0·5	292·1	412·0	74·1	356·6	457·2	57·1	91·6	9·7	38·5	32·6	310·0	13,183·3
4. *Deduct—Contribution from Revenue for Capital Expenditure to end of 1937–38*	185·8	..	27·6	14·9	19·8	9·5	54·3	0·2	4·1	0·5	..	1·5	12·0	330·2
NET CAPITAL AND OTHER EXPENDITURE OUTSIDE THE REVENUE ACCOUNT TO END OF 1937–38	10,865·5	0·5	264·5	397·1	54·3	347·1	402·9	56·9	87·5	9·2	38·5	31·1	298·0	12,853·1

Source.—Combined Finance and Revenue Accounts of the Central and Provincial Governments in India for the year 1937–38.

Note.—The amounts entered include all capital outlay provided from Government sources, whether financed out of Government loans or out of Revenue (but see item 4), Surplus Cash Balances, etc., and do not, therefore, entirely agree with the Statement of Public Debt. (See Chapter VII, Table XI, page 212.)

Table 13 INDIA, EXPENDITURE ON EDUCATION, BY PROVINCES, 1937–38
(Rs. millions)

	Coorg	Madras	Bombay	Bengal	United Provs.	Punjab	Bihar	C.P. and Berar	Assam	N.W.F.	Orissa	Sind	Other Areas	Total
Source of Funds:														
Government	0·2	23·5	15·9	14·7	21·2	16·5	4·5	5·1	3·2	2·0	2·0	2·9	2·4	114·1
District and local boards and municipalities	0·1	9·9	7·2	3·8	5·4	4·5	4·9	3·0	0·7	0·4	0·9	1·3	0·7	42·8
Fees	0·0	10·2	10·1	21·5	8·6	8·3	4·3	2·3	1·2	0·4	0·7	1·4	1·8	70·8
Other sources	0·0	12·8	5·4	7·3	5·6	3·5	2·6	1·0	0·8	0·3	0·5	0·8	1·4	42·0
Total	0·3	56·4	38·6	47·3	40·8	32·8	16·3	11·4	5·9	3·1	4·1	6·4	6·3	269·7
Population (millions)	0·2	46·7	18·0	50·1	48·4	23·6	25·7	15·5	8·6	2·4	5·3	3·9	2·0[1]	250·2
Per Capita Expenditure (in rupees)	1·7	1·2	2·1	0·9	0·8	1·4	0·6	0·7	0·7	1·3	0·8	1·6	3·2[1]	1·1
Allocation of Funds (Rs. millions):														
University and professional	..	6·1	5·2	8·9	10·0	5·5	1·9	1·1	0·5	0·3	0·4	0·5	0·9	41·3
Secondary	0·1	11·0	8·6	18·0	11·1	15·6	4·7	3·7	2·2	1·5	1·1	1·7	2·7	82·0
Primary	0·1	24·4	18·2	8·6	9·7	5·4	4·9	3·9	1·5	0·6	1·5	3·2	1·2	83·2
Other[2]	0·1	14·9	6·6	11·8	10·0	6·3	4·8	2·7	1·7	0·7	1·1	1·0	1·5	63·2
Total	0·3	56·4	38·6	47·3	40·8	32·8	16·3	11·4	5·9	3·1	4·1	6·4	6·3	269·7
Number of Scholars (thousands)	12	3187	1403	3381	1693	1302	1076	514	494	102	337	201	130	13,832
Expenditure per Scholar (in rupees)	22·9	17·7	27·5	14·0	24·1	25·2	15·1	22·2	11·8	30·4	12·1	31·9	48·8	19·5

[1] Estimated. [2] Special Instruction; Direction; Inspection; Buildings, Furniture and Apparatus; Miscellaneous.

APPENDIX I

Abstract of the Leading Recommendations of the Royal Commission on Dominion-Provincial Relations[1]

THE Report which the Commission has prepared is the outcome of two and a half years of carefully planned study. In the present summary the aim is to set out the principal recommendations embodied in the Report and to indicate briefly the reasons for them. At the heart of the problem lie the needs of Canadian citizens. The basic problem before the Commission lies, therefore, in finding a way in which the financial position of the Provinces could be improved and assured, without disastrous financial consequences to the Federal Government on whose efficient functioning all Provinces are dependent. National unity must be based on Provincial autonomy, and Provincial autonomy cannot be assured unless a strong feeling of national unity exists throughout Canada.

The Commission did find one onerous function of government which cannot, under modern conditions, be equitably or efficiently performed on a regional or Provincial basis. This function is the maintenance of those unemployed who are employable and of their dependants. In reaching this conclusion (which is amply supported by the Evidence and the research studies) the Commission merely confirmed conclusions which had been reached by earlier Commissions. So firmly is the Commission convinced of the validity of this conclusion that, even when it comes to consider the situation which will arise if its main recommendations are not implemented, it proceeds on the assumption that the relief of the unemployed who are able and willing to work will become a Federal function.

Another function closely analogous to that of relief for employables is that of assistance to a primary industry (*e.g.* agriculture) in the form of operating cost advances. When relief is on a small scale the responsibility can be borne without difficulty by the Province. But in the event of widespread disaster with which a Province is unable to cope without assistance from the Dominion, or in the event that the Dominion by such means as an exclusive marketing organisation has already established effective control of the industry concerned, the Commission recommends that the Dominion should assume direct administrative and financial responsibility rather than render indirect assistance by way of advances to the Provinces affected.

The Commission's treatment of these expensive functions of government may be contrasted with its treatment of another expensive function, namely the payment of non-contributory old-age pensions. As the Federal Government is already paying as high a proportion of their cost as it can reasonably pay without assuming control of the administration of the pensions, and as the Commission was convinced that it is more satisfactory that the Provinces

[1] *Vide* Report of the Royal Commission on Dominion-Provincial Relations, Book II, Section G. The Appendix above is a summary of the abstract in the Report.

should continue to administer non-contributory old-age pensions, it could not recommend any further financial help to the Provinces in this connexion. But the Commission is of the opinion that if non-contributory old-age pensions were to be superseded or supplemented by a contributory system the latter should, for various reasons, be under the control of the Dominion.

There is, however, an important financial burden of which Provincial Governments can be relieved without any sacrifice of autonomy. This is the deadweight cost of their debt service. The burden taken up by the Dominion, if it were to assume this deadweight cost, would be less than the burden of which the Provinces were relieved because, as maturities occurred, the debts could be refunded more advantageously by the Dominion than by the Provinces. To this extent a saving would accrue to Canadian taxpayers. The Commission has, therefore, recommended that the Dominion should assume all Provincial debts (both direct debts and debts guaranteed by the Provinces) and that each Province should pay over to the Dominion an annual sum equal to the interest which it now receives from its investments. The reason for this proviso is that it would not be expedient that the Dominion should take over liability for a debt which represented a self-liquidating investment retained by a Province. Conditions governing future Provincial borrowing are outlined in detail in the Report.

In the case of one Province this recommendation as to debt requires an important modification. The Provincial debt of the Province of Quebec is low in comparison with the *per capita* debt of other provinces, and is an unusually low fraction of the combined municipal and Provincial debt of the Province. To meet this situation, which has arisen through the policy of this Province in imposing on municipalities onerous functions which are performed elsewhere by Provincial Governments, the Commission has recommended that the Dominion should take over 40 per cent of the combined Provincial and municipal net debt service in Quebec.

If the Provinces are relieved, in accordance with this recommendation, of the deadweight burden of their debt, it is not unreasonable that they should surrender to the Dominion the subsidies, whatever their character, which they now receive. Prince Edward Island alone would give up subsidies more than equivalent to the deadweight cost of its debt, and, as will be seen, this apparent loss will be more than made up in other ways. The abolition of the Provincial subsidies will be in itself no inconsiderable reform, for their history is long and tortuous. The subsidies have been based on no clear principles and it has been impossible to say whether or not different Provinces have received equal treatment.

The Commission had also to consider how to provide the Dominion with sources of revenue which would enable it to carry its new burdens. This enquiry (as will be seen) was combined with the consideration of efficiency and equity in taxation specifically entrusted to the Commission. There could be no question of increasing the legal taxing powers of the Dominion since these are already unlimited. But the Provinces, in return for the benefits which they would receive, and for further payments which the Commission finds it necessary to recommend, should be prepared to renounce some of the taxes which they employ (or are entitled to employ) at present.

The Dominion, for its part, should be able and willing to refrain from competing with the Provinces in respect of sources of revenue left to them and should leave the Provinces free to collect these revenues in whatever way appears to them most efficient even if the method of indirect taxation should be involved.

Just as the assumption of Provincial debts by the Dominion will lead to savings in interest from which taxpayers will benefit, so there are several taxes from which, if they are under unified control, as great a revenue can be obtained as at present with less hardship to the taxpayer. What is more important, a reorganisation of these taxes, of a character which is possible only if they are under unified control, can remove many hindrances which in the recent past have been detrimental to the expansion of the national income (*i.e.* to the sum-total of the incomes of all citizens of Canada). As this income expands, as the result of what may be fairly termed greater efficiency in taxation, the same revenue as at present can be obtained by taxes imposed at lower rates than those of to-day.

The first of the taxes which the Commission recommends that the Provinces should renounce is the tax on personal incomes. Not all Provinces impose this tax. Those which get most revenue from it are often taxing incomes which other Provinces think that they should have a share in taxing, because they are in part at least earned in them although they are received in those Provinces in which investors live, or in which large corporations have their head offices. Nor is this all. The general equity of the whole Canadian tax system — and the Commission has been instructed to concern itself with equity as well as with efficiency in taxation — requires that the tax on personal incomes, which is one of the very few taxes capable of any desired graduation, should be used to supplement other taxes and should be uniform throughout Canada.

The second form of taxation which the Commission recommends that the Provinces should forgo includes those taxes imposed on corporations which individuals or partnerships, carrying on the same business as the corporation, would not be required to pay, and taxes on those businesses which only corporations engage in. They include, therefore, the tax on the net income of corporations and a multitude of taxes devised to raise revenue from particular classes of corporations which a Province cannot conveniently subject to a tax on net income. They do not include *bona fide* licence fees, the power to impose which would remain with the Province. These Provincial corporation taxes are peculiarly vexatious to those who pay them and particularly detrimental to the expansion of the national income. The cost of tax compliance is high. The tax is often payable by a corporation which has no net income. The tax is very likely to be a tax on costs rather than on profits. These taxes are also a frequent source of interprovincial jealousy. Great benefits may be expected if they are swept away and the equivalent revenue raised by Federal taxes chiefly on corporate net income.

To ask the Provinces to give up the entire revenue which they now derive from taxing corporations would, however, intensify a grievance of which the Commission received complaint in more than one Province; for the Dominion would receive a tax on income which was in part derived from the depletion of irreplaceable natural wealth. It is clearly desirable that revenue of this character should be used for developmental work which will compensate for the damage which has been done to the resources of a Province. The Commission has, therefore, recommended that the Dominion should pay over to the Province concerned 10 per cent of the corporate income derived from the exploitation of the mineral wealth of the Province. When what is required is the conservation of natural resources by maintaining their productivity, rather than compensation for depletion by new investment, the Provinces are in a position to use their own taxing power.

The third tax which the Commission recommends that the Provinces should forgo consists of various forms of succession duty. These differ from the income taxes in that they have not hitherto been used by the Dominion: but they are taxes to which the Dominion might at any time be compelled to resort. The use made of them by the Provinces has given rise to bitter complaint because the Provinces have not made equitable arrangements with one another so as to tax each item in an estate in one Province only. The differences in rates between Provinces, and the dangers of double taxation, seriously distort investment in Canada.

At this point there must be a refinement in the calculations. What is significant for the purposes of the Commission is the size of the surplus or deficit which would exist in a Province if it were to provide the normal Canadian standard of services and impose taxation of normal severity. It is not the services which each Province is at present providing, but the average Canadian standard of services, that a Province must be put in a position to finance. It is not the revenue which its taxes yield at their present level which matters, but the revenue which it would derive from them if its people were as heavily taxed as Canadians in general. Just as in the case of debt it is necessary to take account of the fact that some Provinces are more accustomed than others to provide services for their people through municipalities or other agencies instead of directly. The Commission has, therefore, attempted to compute, Province by Province, what the cost would be if the Province and its municipalities taken together were to provide services on the Canadian standard. Adjustments have been made for the cost of the developmental services appropriate to the Province, and for the weight of taxation in the Province. The result has been that the Commission has been able to make a recommendation as to the amount, if any, which each individual Province should receive from the Dominion annually to enable it to provide normal Canadian services with no more than normal Canadian taxation. The Commission recommends that each Province found to be in need of such a payment should receive it by way of an annual National Adjustment Grant from the Dominion. This grant as originally fixed would be irreducible. The Commission recommends, however, that National Adjustment Grants should be re-appraised every five years. For special emergencies, which might arise in respect of any Province (and which exist in one Province to-day), special provision should be made, as it would be undesirable either to fix an annual grant in perpetuity on the basis of conditions that are transitory, or to fail to provide for serious emergencies.

The Commission also recommends the establishment of a small permanent commission (which may be called the Finance Commission), assisted by an adequate technical staff, to advise upon all requests for new or increased grants, and to re-appraise the system of grants every five years.

The recommendations which have been described would, if implemented, safeguard the autonomy of every Province by ensuring to it the revenue necessary to provide services in accordance with the Canadian standard. Every Provincial Government (including those whose position will be so good as to make adjustment grants unnecessary) would be placed in a better financial position than it is in to-day. And the financial position of every Province would be immeasurably more secure than it is to-day. The Commission looks on this as its primary achievement. It is convinced that this fundamental problem must be faced and it has not been able to discover any alternative way in which it could be solved.

The recommendations which the Commission has made must be judged as a whole. They cannot with fairness either to the Provinces or to the Dominion be considered in isolation for any one of them taken alone might produce grotesque results.

At what cost, it may be asked, will the Provinces have secured these advantages? There will be a certain cost to the Dominion and, therefore, to the Dominion's taxpayers. The taxes forgone by the Provinces, if replaced by Dominion taxes of equal yield, would not provide all the money which the Dominion will probably be called on to pay under the Plan. It is necessary to say "probably" because the Dominion, unlike the Provinces, will be left with highly variable expenditures (*e.g.* those on unemployment relief) and variable revenues. The long-run effects of the proposed arrangements should, as has been explained, be to increase employment and to increase the national income and, therefore, the national revenue. But the expectation of the Commission is that the Dominion, in the first instance, will have to increase taxes somewhat. Even without increasing tax rates it will obviously increase the taxes payable by citizens of those Provinces which have no personal income tax to-day. It is hardly necessary to add that, in view of the end to be attained, the price seems low.

There will, of course, be adjustments. At every stage of the Commission's enquiry it has endeavoured to frame recommendations which, if implemented, will avoid the minor hardships or inequities that might result if the measures which have, perforce, been somewhat crudely described in this summary, were crudely applied. One or two examples will be given here. Others will be found in the Report itself. But the whole spirit of the Report would suggest that analogous adjustments should be made, even if the Commission has not thought of them and, therefore, has not mentioned them.

If the administration of a service or the collection of a tax is transferred from one Government to another it is desirable that those who have administered the service or collected the tax in the past should continue to do so in the future and that their skill and experience should not be lost to the nation nor their personal expectation of continuous employment disappointed. The Commission has, therefore, recommended that the Dominion, if it takes over a Provincial function, should continue the employment of those previously employed by the Provincial Government concerned. This recommendation is particularly important when questions of language are involved.

If a tax now levied by one Government is to be replaced by a tax levied by another the new tax should be adjusted to the circumstances of the people on whom it is to be imposed, and advantage should be taken of the opportunity to design the new tax as equitably as possible. Thus, if the Dominion collects succession duties, it is important that the administration for their collection should be decentralised and that small estates should be rapidly cleared without correspondence having to go through Ottawa. And the taxation scales should be arranged so as to tax an estate more lightly when it is divided among many children.

If legislative powers (*e.g.* in relation to unemployment insurance) are to be conferred on the Dominion in addition to those which it now enjoys, it is important that they should be strictly defined so as to avoid the danger of their being extended by interpretation in unexpected ways which might interfere with the civil code in Quebec, or with the corresponding interests of other Provinces.

This brief summary would lose its way among details were it to attempt to enumerate the recommendations — some of them important recommendations — which the Commission has felt bound to make in its Report. What has been said should indicate the structure of the Dominion-Provincial financial relations which would, in the opinion of the Commission, characterise a healthy Federal system in Canada. Before passing on to mention a few of the subsidiary recommendations, it may be worth while to point out that the Commission's financial proposals are, in terms of the economic life of 1939, very similar to what the provisions of the British North America Act were in terms of the economic life of 1867.

As far as the municipalities were concerned, they are the creatures of the Provinces in which they are situated and their financial powers and duties are such as the Province chooses to confer on them. The financial plan which has been described has taken account of municipal expenditures and taxation as part of the Provincial picture and it will, if it is implemented, have very important indirect effects on municipal finance. It will relieve the municipalities of their share in providing relief for employables and their dependants. It will put every Provincial Government in a better position than it is in to-day for extending such aid as it may think fit to its municipalities, whether by relieving them of the cost of services which they now perform, or by contributing financially to the cost of these services.

In respect to marketing legislation great difficulty has been experienced in framing Dominion and Provincial legislation which will cover the whole field, even when the wishes of Dominion and Provinces are identical. The Commission has sought to remedy this situation by recommending that the Dominion and the Provinces should have concurrent legislative powers to deal with the marketing of a named list of natural products to which additions may be made from time to time by common consent.

Nor is this the only instance in which it has seemed appropriate that a power of delegation should form part of Canadian Federal relations. The Commission has recommended that this power should be quite general and that the Dominion should be able to delegate any of its legislative powers to a Province, and that a Province should be able to delegate any of its legislative powers to the Dominion. Delegation should provide a convenient means of dealing with specific questions as they may arise from time to time without limiting in advance the power of either the Dominion or the Provinces. In some instances one or more of the Provinces might be prepared to delegate powers to the Dominion while other Provinces were unwilling, and in such cases the advantages of a power of delegation over constitutional amendment would lie in flexibility.

The Commission has come to consider the transportation problem of Canada one of the problems which cannot be solved without close collaboration between the Dominion and the Provinces. It realises, however, that its own technical competence is slight in this field and has, therefore, confined itself to discussing the issues which will have to be faced, in the hope of doing something to clarify the problem of jurisdiction. It points out, however, the great advantage which might be derived from a Transport Planning Commission which would be concerned both with planning transportation developments in a broad way, and with facilitating the co-operation between the Dominion and the Provinces in transportation matters which is necessary for the taxpayer.

Co-operation between the autonomous Governments of the Federal system has to-day become imperative. The Commission recommends as the principal means to this end that Dominion-Provincial Conferences, which have hitherto met at infrequent intervals, should now be regularised, and provision made for frequent meetings, say every year. It urges further that the Conference should be provided with an adequate and permanent secretariat for the purpose of serving the Conference directly, and of facilitating co-operation between the Dominion and the Provinces in general.

In conclusion of this summary it remains to add that the decisions underlying the recommendations contained in the Report were reached before the outbreak of war. The Commission decided, after deliberation, to complete the Report exactly as it would have been completed had war not been declared. The basic recommendations of the Commission concerning the re-allocation of the functions of Government and the financial relations of the Dominion and the Provinces were framed with the possibility of emergencies in mind and are, it is hoped, sufficiently flexible to be adjusted to any situation which the war may produce.

Of the subsidiary recommendations many are concerned with matters not in the least likely to be affected by the strains and stresses of war, while some may require modification in the light of events. The need for some action designed to enable the people of Canada to throw their whole weight into any great national effort, such as the struggle to which they have committed themselves, and at the same time to ensure the smooth working of the social and educational services on which the welfare of the mass of the people depends, is far greater and far more urgent in time of war and of post-war reorganisation than it is in time of peace. And it is precisely to these two main objectives that the chief recommendations of the Commission have been directed.

The financial proposals have been designed to enable every Province of

Canada to rely on having sufficient revenue at its command in war-time as in peace-time, in years of adversity as in years of prosperity, to carry out the important functions entrusted to it. They are also designed to produce this result while leaving the fiscal powers of the Dominion as wide in fact as they have always been in law, so that it may direct the wealth of the nation as the national interest may require. If some such adjustment of Canadian economic life appeared sufficiently urgent to lead to the appointment of the Commission in time of peace, how much more urgent is it in time of war? How much more urgent will it be in the critical transition from war to peace again? The Commission does not consider that its proposals are either centralising or decentralising in their combined effect but believes that they will conduce to the sane balance between these two tendencies which is the essence of a genuine Federal system and, therefore, the basis on which Canadian national unity can most securely rest.

JOS. SIROIS, *Chairman*
JOHN W. DAFOE
R. A. MACKAY
H. F. ANGUS

ALEX. SKELTON, *Secretary*
ADJUTOR SAVARD, *French Secretary*

APPENDIX II

Summary of Recommendations, made in the Report by the American Committee on Intergovernmental Fiscal Relations (Dr. Luther Gulick, Dr. Harold M. Groves and Dr. Mabel Newcomer), in Terms of an Action Programme for each Level of Government

I. Federal Government

A. *For Immediate Action*

1. Negotiate with State representatives and pass legislation to create a Federal-State Fiscal Authority.
2. Amend the income tax law to make State income taxes deductible on an accrual basis even though other expenses are reported on a cash basis.
3. Revise, modernise and broaden the death tax credit.
4. Give the Federal estate tax a thorough overhauling, integrating death and gift taxes, substantially reducing exemptions and co-ordinating the Federal and State taxes.
5. Eliminate tax-exempt securities in a manner to secure States and municipalities against loss arising from the taxability of their securities.
6. Defeat discrimination resulting from State community-property laws by providing that they shall not apply in the operation of Federal tax laws.
7. Provide a clearing-house and " board of appeals " (Federal-State Fiscal Authority) for more careful and consistent treatment of payments in lieu of property taxes on Federally owned property. Such payments should be generous, especially during the war.
8. Provide a special joint committee of Congress to consider legislative proposals for payments in lieu of taxes ; provide facilities for maintaining a permanent inventory of Government property.
9. Allow State sales tax application to contractors working on Government orders.
10. Modify and improve the co-ordination and efficiency in unemployment compensation by increasing the Federal credit from 90 to 100 per cent and requiring the States to furnish part of the cost of administration.
11. Disallow sales taxes as a deduction in Federal income tax practice ; if the deduction is retained, make it general and not conditioned upon certain technicalities in the tax law.
12. Pay more heed to cost of compliance in framing tax laws.
13. Extend the Civil Service coverage to include all personnel engaged in Federal tax administration.
14. Consider the provision of a suitable bond instrumentality for the investment of State and Local surplus funds during the war. This might take

the form of a non-negotiable bond redeemable after the emergency or upon a showing of war-created need, and to be matched by the Federal Government if used for approved public works.[1]

15. Continue and enhance co-operative efforts to improve State and Local accounting and reporting ; provide annual compilation of cost of government and total taxes.
16. Expend more effort on Federal-State collaboration in the administration of overlapping taxes.
17. Repeal the automobile use tax, or, if it is retained, require receipt as a condition for obtaining a State licence.
18. Further promote better uniform governmental accounting and reporting.
19. Assume the responsibility of annual calculation and publication of the over-all cost of government and other fundamental fiscal data.
20. Cultivate an attitude which regards States and Localities as partners in a joint enterprise.

B. *For Immediate or Future Action*

21. Develop in consultation with the States, standard rules for income and death tax jurisdiction ; develop suitable rewards for State compliance with these rules and other suitable procedures so that the Federal Government may serve as an umpire in multiple taxation disputes.
22. Develop in consultation with the States rules of uniform income tax procedure ; promote the adoption of such rules looking toward single administration of a relatively uniform State and Federal income tax.
23. Adopt a Federal-Collection-State-Sharing programme for the tobacco tax.
24. Enact legislation providing for Federal incorporation of corporations doing an inter-State business.
25. Provide distribution of welfare grants to the States through a graduated bracket system as suggested in the Connally amendment.

C. *For Future Action*

26. Abandon motor vehicle taxes to the States reserving the right to tax motor fuel used in aviation.
27. Inaugurate a thorough study of the cost of tax compliance and the burden of multiple taxation on inter-State companies ; reserve action on centralisation of business taxes until this evidence is available.
28. Use a public investment technique (if necessary) to cope with post-war deflation and unemployment ; dual Budget ; creative public works (health, housing, nutrition and regional development) ; full liquidation of outlays.
29. Reduce repressiveness of the tax system by de-emphasising business taxes and by equalising burden upon equity-financed companies compared with those financed by means of indebtedness (through a partial credit to the corporation for dividends paid out).
30. Broaden Federal aid to include relief and elementary education.
31. Broaden the Social Security programme to include uncovered groups under

[1] Written before recent developments which cover, to some extent, the needs of the States.

old-age insurance and unemployment compensation. This would not only provide more equitable coverage but would also make possible some simplification of pay-roll taxes.

32. Recognise a national minimum status for elementary education by provision of a differential (equalisation) grant.
33. Provide controls which will ensure improvement in the division of educational revenues, local districting, and the quality of the educational product, at the same time ensuring against coercive interference with Local autonomy and minority views concerning education.
34. Provide for Federal scholarships to ensure the adequate development of talent through higher education.
35. In the interest of simplification, repeal Federal liquor licence fees retaining licences where needed for administration.

D. *Contingent Action*

36. If a Federal retail sales tax is enacted, provide legislative implementation and administrative action to ensure the fullest co-operative use of State personnel and machinery.

II. State Governments

1. Negotiate with Federal representatives and collaborate in the development of a Federal-State Fiscal Authority.
2. Negotiate with Federal officials and Congress to inaugurate a programme for the elimination of tax-exempt securities in such manner as not to embarrass States and municipalities fiscally.
3. Tighten property exemption provisions; relax ceiling and uniformity requirements as to Local property tax levies; develop more adequate supervision of property tax administration.
4. In collaboration with municipalities, refrain from demanding unreasonable war-time aid from the Federal Government, thus recognising the importance of Local independence.
5. Apply surplus revenues, where possible, to the elimination of debt and the development of a reserve against war-time loss of revenue and post-war need for public works.
6. When revenues will permit, allow Federal income taxes as a deduction in calculating State income taxes.
7. Redouble attack on trade barriers, multiple taxation, and special inducements for the location of industry; use of education, reciprocal agreements and inter-State compacts toward these ends; pass legislation allowing credit to new residents for automobile licence taxes paid in the same year to other States.
8. Collaborate with the Federal Government looking toward Federal arbitration of jurisdictional disputes and joint determination and promotion of uniform practices in income and business taxation especially with regard to questions of jurisdiction.
9. Further collaborate with the Federal Government in the joint administration of overlapping taxes.

10. Adopt legislation on their own initiative that would make payment of Federal automobile use tax a condition for the receipt of a State licence.
11. Mitigate the rotten borough system by providing more adequate representation for cities in State legislatures.
12. Give more consideration to cities in the distribution of shared taxes, particularly motor vehicle taxes.
13. Adopt enabling legislation that would permit cities to supplement the general property tax with a rental tax on occupiers.
14. Adopt enabling legislation that would facilitate surplus financing during war-time.
15. Adopt legislation requiring more adequate and more uniform governmental accounting and reporting.
16. Cultivate an attitude that regards all Governments as partners in a joint enterprise.
17. Collaborate with the Federal Government on a broader and more generous programme of Federal aids, accepting controls, but insisting that they be co-operatively applied rather than dictated.

III. Municipal Governments

1. Negotiate with Federal representatives and collaborate in the development of a Federal-State Fiscal Authority.
2. Negotiate with Federal officials and Congress to inaugurate a programme for the elimination of tax-exempt securities that will not fiscally embarrass States and municipalities.
3. In collaboration with States, refrain from demanding unreasonable war-time aid from the Federal Government, thus recognising the importance of Local independence.
4. Apply surplus revenues, where possible, to the elimination of debt and the development of a reserve against war-time loss of revenue and post-war need for public works.
5. Broaden the property tax programme by supplementing the property tax with a rental tax on occupiers.
6. Strictly interpret property tax exemptions.
7. Inaugurate a thoroughgoing study of possible new sources of independent Local revenue.
8. Study successful procedures for safeguarding reserve funds, and enact legislation needed for this purpose.
9. Develop more metropolitan co-operation and the use of large metropolitan districts for financing functions of common interest.
10. Emphasise raw-material-producing districts' claim upon aids and shared taxes because their tax base does not represent their contribution to the national product.
11. Demand more equitable representation in State legislatures.
12. Demand more equitable distribution of shared revenues, particularly motor vehicle taxes.
13. Provide for more adequate governmental accounting and reporting.

14. Cultivate an attitude which regards all Governments as partners in a joint enterprise.
15. Prepare for collaboration with the Federal Government in a post-war public investment programme.
16. Collaborate with the Federal Government on a broader and more generous programme of Federal aids, accepting controls, but insisting that they be co-operatively applied rather than dictated.

INDEX

THE END

Printed in Great Britain by R. & R. CLARK, LIMITED, *Edinburgh.*